Junctions at Banbury:
a town and its railways since 1850

Other books written or edited by Barrie Trinder:

A Victorian MP and his Constituents: the correspondence of H.W. Tancred 1841-1859 (1969).
Drink and Sobriety in an early Victorian Country Town (with Sir Brian Harrison, 1969).
The Pergamon General Historical Atlas (with A.C. Cave, 1970).
The Industrial Revolution in Shropshire (1973, 1981, 2000, 2016).
The Darbys of Coalbrookdale (1974, 1978, 1981, 1992).
The Most Extraordinary District in the World: Ironbridge and Coalbrookdale (1977, 1988, 2005, 2017).
The Iron Bridge: Symbol of the Industrial Revolution (with Sir Neil Cossons, 1979, 2002).
Yeomen and Colliers in Telford: the probate inventories of Dawley, Lilleshall, Wellington and Wrockwardine (with Jeff Cox, 1980).
Victorian Banbury (1982, 2005).
The Making of the Industrial Landscape (1982, 1986, 1997).
A History of Shropshire (1983, 1998, 2017).
Victorian Shrewsbury (1984).
Industrial Heritage of Britain (1988).
The Blackwell Encyclopedia of Industrial Archaeology (1992).
The Industrial Archaeology of Shropshire (1996, 2016).
The English Heritage Book of Industrial England (with Michael Stratton, 1997).
Miners & Mariners of the Severn Gorge: the probate inventories of Benthall, Broseley, Little Wenlock & Madeley (with Nancy Cox, 2000).
Twentieth Century Industrial Archaeology (with Michael Stratton, 2000).
The Market Town Lodging House in Victorian England (2001).
Thomas Telford's Holyhead Road: the A5 in North Wales (with Jamie Quartermaine & Rick Turner, 2003).
Barges & Bargemen: A social history of the Upper Severn Navigation 1660-1900 (2005, 2011, 2017).
English Market Towns and their Suburbs in recent centuries (2005).
Beyond the Bridges: the Suburbs of Shrewsbury 1760-1960 (2006).
Britain's Industrial Revolution: the Making of a Manufacturing People (2013).
Victorian Banburyshire: Three Memoirs: Sarah Rusher, Thomas Ward Boss, Thomas Butler Gunn (2013).
European Industrial Heritage: the International Story (2016).

The Banbury Historical Society
General Editor: J.S.W. Gibson

Junctions at Banbury:
a town and its railways since 1850
Barrie Trinder

Volume 35

2017

FOR MY GRANDSON MARCUS

Published 2017 by
The Banbury Historical Society
c/o Banbury Museum, Spiceball Park Road, Banbury OX16 2PQ.
in association with Lamplight Publications,
260 Colwell Drive, Witney, Oxfordshire, OX28 5LW.

© The Banbury Historical Society, 2017
on behalf of Barrie Trinder
subject to copyright in some illustrations as acknowledged on p viii.

ISBN 978 0 900129 34 6 (BHS)
ISBN 978 1 899246 61 8 (Lamplight Publications)

This volume has been produced with the aid of a substantial grant from
the Greening Lamborn Trust which is acknowledge with gratitude.

The Greening Lamborn Trust's objective is to promote public interest in the history, architecture,
old photographs and heraldry of Oxford and its neighbourhood by supporting publications and
other media that create access to them.

Printed by in the United Kingdom by Henry Ling Limited at the Dorset Press, Dorset DT1 1HD
from computer-generated text prepared by Barrie Trinder and Jeremy Gibson.

Contents

Conventions: Place names; Dimensions; Census returns	vi
Abbreviations	vii
Acknowledgements for illustrations	viii
Acknowledgements	ix

1. Converging lines	1
2. The Setting	7
3. Narrowing Horizons	16
4. The Buckinghamshire Railway 1846-1914	25
5. East to West	32
6. The economic & social impact 1850-1914	43
7. The Great Western northern line 1861-1914	62
8. Ambition: the Great Central London Extension	74
9. The Great War and after 1914-23	90
10. Four great companies	98
11. The Second World War	123
12. Nationalisation and after 1948-60	138
12a. To and from the seaside	171
13. Shrinking: the 1960s	177
14. Mines of Precious Stone: Iron Ore in Banburyshire	197
15. Out of the Depths: 1948-94	213
16. Privatisation	227
Bibliography	241
Index	249

Maps:

1. Eight lines converging	x
2. The northern line of the Great Western Railway	21
3. Great Central connections	83
4. Routes to the South Coast	171

Conventions

Place names

The Buckinghamshire Railway/LNWR/LMSR terminus in Banbury is referred to as 'Merton Street station', although it was not always so called, and the eponymous street had not been laid out when it opened.

Similarly Banbury's station on the line from Birmingham to Oxford is called the 'GWR station' or the 'Western Region (or WR station)', although at different periods it was known as Banbury Bridge Street or Banbury General.

The station at the junction of the Oxford, Worcester & Wolverhampton Railway and the Chipping Norton Railway is usually called Kingham, the name by which it was known from 1909. Previously it was called Chipping Norton Junction.

Wolvercote, site of the junction north of Oxford, is spelt with an 'e' according to current Ordnance Survey usage, although in some railway contexts it appears without.

Stations in Wales are referred to by the current versions of their names used by National Rail, which may be in the Welsh language, although English versions may have been in current use at the times to which the text refers.

Dimensions

In this study it seems logical to use the Imperial measurements, current during most of the period covered in the text.

To avoid confusion, the twenty-four hour clock refers to train times throughout the book although it was not in general use for most of the period covered.

Census returns

Analysis of census returns is a feature of parts of this study. Most enumerators in all six censuses (1851-1901) seem punctiliously to have distinguished railway workers. Some points of ambiguity remain but they are unlikely to invalidate the main statistical conclusions. The term 'railway labourer' usually refers to a man concerned with the construction of railways, who on rare occasions may be called a 'navvy' or an excavator. On the LNWR local managers are usually called 'railway agents' in 1851, but are subsequently classified as stationmasters. Policemen over decades evolve into signalmen and pointsmen become shunters. The only women working on the railway in the census were sub-contracting carrying agents or keepers of refreshment rooms. The census of 1901 is the first to list retired railwaymen.

Abbreviations

ABR: Aylesbury & Buckingham Railway
ASLEF: Associated Society of Locomotive Engineers & Fireman
BA: *Banbury Advertiser*
BCDR: Banbury & Cheltenham Direct Railway
BG: *Banbury Guardian*
BGR: Birmingham & Gloucester Railway
BH: *Banbury Herald*
BHS: Banbury Historical Society
BLR. British Locomotive Record
BPP: British Parliamentary Papers
BRI: British Railways Illustrated
BRJ: British Railways Journal
BT: Back Track
C&CH: Cake & Cockhorse
CNR: Chipping Norton Railway
DNSR: Didcot, Newbury & Southampton Railway
DVT: Driving Van Trailer
ECJS: East Coast Joint Stock
EWJR: East & West Junction Railway
EHLR: Edge Hill Light Railway
FD: Flying Dutchman
GCR: Great Central Railway
GKN: Guest, Keen & Nettlefold
GNR: Great Northern Railway
GUV: General Utility Vehicle
GWE: Great Western Echo
GWR: Great Western Railway
GWRJ: Great Western Railway Journal
HST: High Speed Train
IAR: Industrial Archaeology Review
IRB: The Iron Road (Birmingham)
JTH: Journal of Transport History
LBR: London & Birmingham Railway
LBSCR: London, Brighton & South Coast Railway
LE: The Locomotive Enthusiast.
LMSR: London, Midland & Scottish Railway
LNER: London & North Eastern Railway
LNWR: London & North Western Railway
LPG: Liquified Petroleum Gas
LSWR: London & South Western Railway
lwb: long wheelbase
LYR: Lancashire & Yorkshire Railway
MDR: Modern Railways
mgr: Merry-go-round
MR: Midland Railway
MSLR: Manchester, Sheffield & Lincolnshire Railway.
MSWJR: Midland & South Western Junction Railway
NBJR: Northampton & Banbury Junction Railway
NER: North Eastern Railway
NUR: National Union of Railwaymen
OFCRR: Oxford, Fenny Compton & Rugby Railway
OWWR: Oxford, Worcester & Wolverhampton Railway
pb: paperback
RES: Rail Express Systems
RL: Railway Locomotives
RM: Railway Magazine
RO: Railway Observer
RR: Railway Record
RW: Railway World
SBR: Shrewsbury & Birmingham Railway
SCR: Shrewsbury & Chester Railway
SD: Steam Days
SMJR: Stratford & Midland Junction Railway
SER: South Eastern Railway
STR: Steam Railway.
SVRN: Severn Valley Railway Newsletter
RW: Railway World
TI: Trains Illustrated
TNA: The National Archive
WCJS: West Coast Joint Stock
WMR: West Midland Railway
WRL: West Riding Limited.

Acknowledgements for illustrations

Banbury Historical Society: page 203.
J D Edwards: page 30.
Great Western Trust Collection, Didcot: pages 20, 23, 67, 70, 94, 111, 126, 128, 136, 141.
Historic England, Swindon:
  Bedford Lemere Collection: pages 206, 207;
  Rokeby Collection: page 31.
Stephen Jakeman, page 26.
Ironbridge Gorge Museum Trust: pages 13, 101.
Record Office for Leicestershire, Leicester and Rutland, S W A Newton collection:
    pages 3, 45, 60, 61, 76, 77, 78, 79, 81, 88.
The late Russell Mulford: page 115.
John Powell: pages 214, 218, 219, 223, 225.
Ian Stratford: pages 4, 34, 35, 65, 96, 103, 110, 140, 148, 149, 154, 156, 161, 164, 172, 173, 176, 230.

The remainder are by the author, the negatives for which are now deposited with the Great Western Trust Collection at Didcot.

Acknowledgements

This book is a work of synthesis, drawing on many published sources and my first debt is to the authors of articles and books, some on very obscure aspects of railway history, on which I have been able to draw. My students in many places over many years have provided much information and many ideas, and I am especially grateful to the late Dr D F Harris for his 'discovery' of the life story of Peter Mottershead and to Stephen Duckworth for bringing articles to my attention. Tony Foster of Olney kindly allowed me to use a collection of journals of the 1940s which is in his possession, and Dr Jeff Cox provided helpful comments on his native Woodford. I was privileged to know the late Eric Tonks, and owe much to his encyclopaedic works on ironstone railways. I have been fortunate to be able to draw in the last two chapters on Hugh Jones's excellent account of the development of Chiltern Railways. I must also record my thanks to the individuals and institutions listed opposite who have made available illustrations. Once again, I am grateful to Geoff Gwatkin for his excellent maps. Some ideas discussed in the book are drawn from the works of the railway historians Simon Bradley, Michael Robbins and Jack Simmons.

The book originated with a 20-minute survey of the history of the railway through the Cherwell Valley that I gave to the Banbury Historical Society's village meeting at Somerton in the spring of 2014. It aroused such interest that it seemed worthwhile to put into book form an accumulation of data made over many decades. I am grateful that it has been accepted for publication in the Banbury Historical Society's Record Series and am delighted that Jeremy Gibson, having produced 34 volumes for the Banbury Historical Society during his 58 years as records editor, has set the pages for volume 35.

The text has been read wholly or in part by Dr Chris Day, Stephen Duckworth, John Powell, Ian Stratford and Laurence Waters, to all of whom I am grateful for helpful comments and observations. Any errors that remain are entirely my responsibility.

Finally I must thank my wife for her patience over many years with the often unreasonable demands of an author.

Barrie Trinder
Olney, March 2017

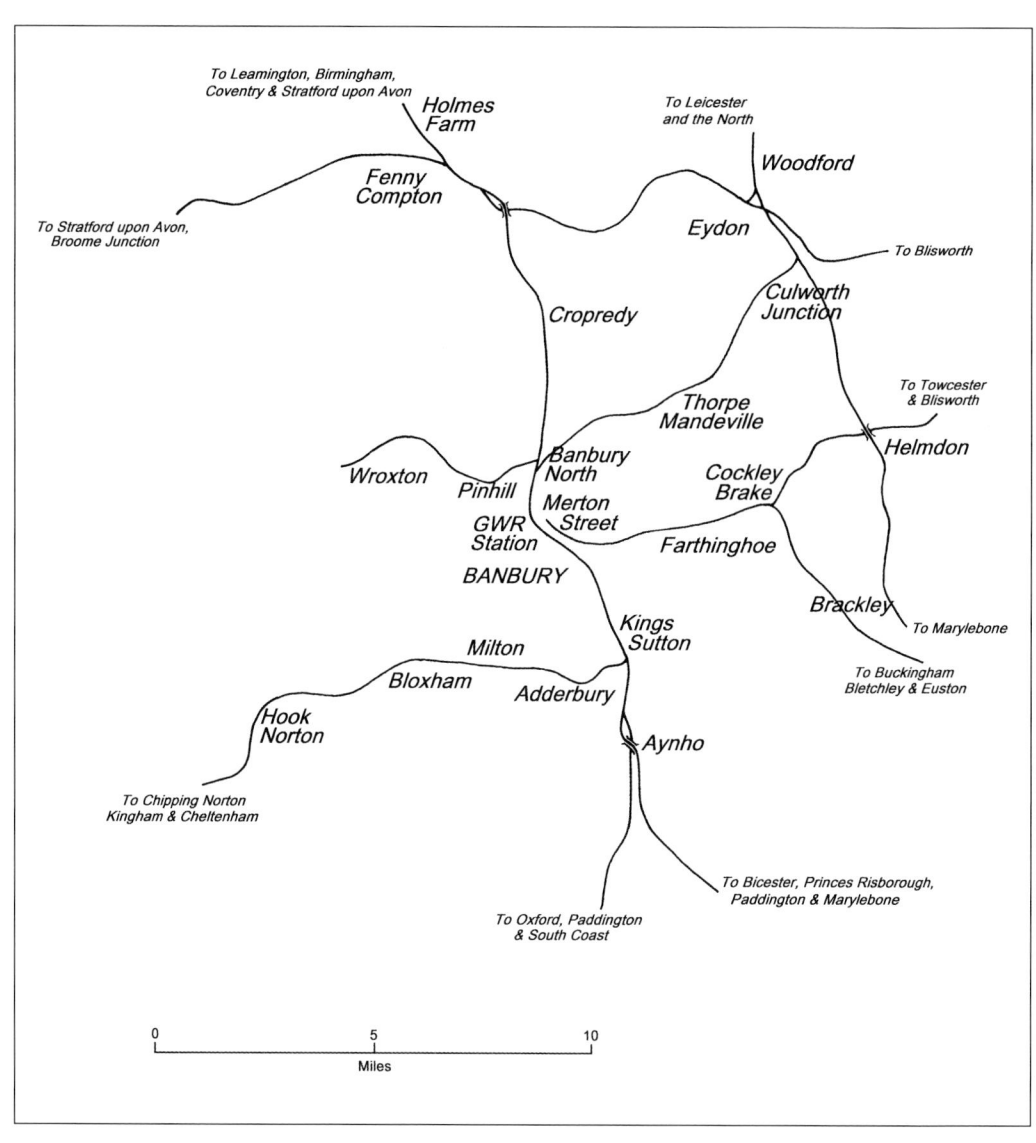

Eight lines converging.

1. Converging Lines

If we consider the steam engine outside its social context it becomes a very dry barren pursuit.
A E (Sam) Grigg.[1]

Banbury in north Oxfordshire was the meeting point of eight railways. This study analyses the role of those railways in shaping the economic and social history of a typical market town. It addresses the challenge issued to railway historians in 1993 by Sir Neil Cossons to communicate effectively with wider audiences, and that made in 1986 by Professor Jack Simmons, to explain the railways' contributions to towns of various kinds. Simmons acknowledged the sparsity of company records relating to traffic from particular places, and this study utilises many other sources, census, newspapers, railway periodicals, timetables and images. It is easy to assert that railways influenced urban development in the nineteenth and early twentieth centuries, delivering stock to retailers, carrying away the products of manufacturers, and increasing the possibilities for individual and group travel. Virtually every town of consequence was affected in these ways and no town in England larger than Banbury lacked railways. By 1900 towns gaining their first railways were much smaller, Padstow in 1899, Tenterden in 1903 and Thaxted in 1913. The presence of railways did not guarantee that a town would see economic growth. Macclesfield's population declined after 1851, due to circumstances in the silk trade – and Banbury stagnated after 1870.[2]

Published railway histories tend to concentrate on companies, particularly the smaller ones. This study owes much to the histories of the Banbury & Cheltenham Railway by Russell and by Hemmings and partners, those of the Stratford & Midland Junction Railway by Dunn and by Riley and Simpson, and Simpson's accounts of the Buckinghamshire Railway.[3]

Many books describe particular classes of locomotive, and an extensive literature is devoted to carriages and wagons. The study of Great Western coaching stock by the Banburian Jim Russell, and the account of Siphon vans

---

[1] A E Grigg, *Country Railwaymen* (Buckingham: Calypso, 1982), 17.
[2] S Bradley, *The Railways: Nation, Network and People* (London: Profile, 2015), 544; J Simmons, *The Railway in Town and Country 1830-1914* (Newton Abbot: David & Charles, 1986), 24-25, 280, 289, 291-92, 334; M Stratton & B Trinder, *Twentieth Century Industrial Archaeology* (London: Spon, 2000), 159-60; B Trinder, *Victorian Banbury* (Phillimore, 1982), 159.
[3] J M Dunn, *The Stratford-upon-Avon & Midland Junction Railway* (Lingfield: Oakwood, 1952); W. Hemmings, *The Banbury & Cheltenham Railway*, vol 1 (Didcot: Wild Swan, 2004); W Hemmings, P Karau & C Turner, *The Banbury & Cheltenham Railway*, vol 2 (Didcot: Wild Swan, 2004); R C Riley & B Simpson, *A History of the Stratford-upon-Avon & Midland Junction Railway* (Witney: Lamplight Publications, 1999).

by Slinn and Clarke have proved valuable.[4] Images are an important source for all aspects of industrial archaeology, and collections of railway photographs, particularly those that show trains rather than locomotives, have proved illuminating. There is a long tradition of amateur observation and recording of happenings on Britain's railways, preserved chiefly in the *Railway Magazine* which began publication in 1897 and the *Railway Observer* whose first issue appeared in 1929. There was also a remarkable rise in interest in railways in the closing years of the Second World War, marked by the publication of the first *ABC* locomotive listings by Ian Allan, but also by a proliferation of cyclostyled leaflets by groups of young railway enthusiasts.[5] Other publications record the recollections of railway workers amongst which those of John Drayton and Sam Grigg have proved particularly enlightening.[6]

The regal way to the capital: 'King' class 4-6-0 No 6010 'King Charles I' heads south from Banbury with the 14 coaches of the 11.45 Birkenhead–Paddington in the summer of 1961.

---

[4] J H Russell, *The Banbury and Cheltenham Railway 1887-1962* (Oxford: Oxford Publishing Co, 1977); J H Russell, *A Pictorial Record of Great Western Coaches 1903-1948* (Sparkford: Haynes, 1990); B Simpson, *The Banbury to Verney Junction Branch* (Oxford: Oxford Publishing Co, 1978); J N Slinn & B K Clarke, *GW Siphons* (Penryn: Atlantic, 1986).

[5] Obituary of Ian Allan (1922-1915), *The Guardian*, 6 July 2015; B Brooksbank, *Train Watchers No 1* (Burton-on-Trent, Pearson, 1982); see also Bibliography, p 241.

[6] J Drayton, *On the Footplate* (Truro: Bradford Barton, 1976); A E Grigg, *Country Railwaymen: A notebook of Engine Drivers' Tales* (Buckingham: Calypus, 1982); Stratton & Trinder, *Twentieth Century Industrial Archaeology* 118; A Vaughan, *The Great Western at Work 1921-1939* (Sparkford: Patrick Stephens, 1993); A Vaughan, *The Heart of the Great Western* (Wadenhoe, Silver Link, 1994).

The first impact of a railway on a town was on its topography.[7] The landscape of Banbury was not radically changed when the railways arrived, but the establishment of the stations led to some reorientation of the town centre. Railways certainly gave better opportunities for travellers to nearby market towns of the same order of size, and to London, while excursions provided prospects for visiting places previously accessible only to the wealthy.

Railways brought coal to Banbury from collieries that were not served by the canal system, and delivered it more conveniently to most country stations. Railways supplied Banbury's shops with goods from 1850s into the 1950s when a trailer stacked high with parcels would be delivered every weekday morning to the High Street premises of F W Woolworth. Manufactured goods sent to distant destinations in small consignments, in this case baskets of Banbury Cakes, also travelled by rail, as did larger manufactures, which at Banbury were agricultural machines carried on flat wagons. Railways also served primary industries, particularly the Oxfordshire quarries that produced ironstone for a century from the 1860s, but also the cement works at Harbury and Shipton-on-Cherwell.

Great Central: the shed master at Woodford with some of his staff and locomotive No 867, one of the 33 class 11A 4-4-0s (LNER class D6) designed by Harry Pollitt and built, specifically for the London Extension, in 1897-99.

Record Office for Leicestershire, Leicester and Rutland

---

[7] J R Kellett, *The Impact of Railways on Victorian Cities* (London: Routledge & Kegan Paul, 1969); Simmons, *Railway in Town and Country*, 297.

Railway were significant employers within local communities. The navvies who constructed the lines can be analysed in detail only if they were present in one of the census years, as they were north of Banbury in 1851, and on two constituent parts of the Stratford & Midland Junction Railway in 1871. Many of those who subsequently worked on the railways came from distant parts of England, and the census provides snapshots of the railway labour force at ten-yearly intervals. Banbury cannot be considered a railway town, in the sense that its dominant industry was the construction of railway vehicles, as at Crewe, Swindon and Ashford, although there was a prospect in 1865 that part of the Swindon works would be re-located there.[8] Nevertheless in the first thirty years of the twentieth century railwaymen were the largest occupational group in Banbury, and they probably comprised the second largest group after the opening of the aluminium factory in 1931 until the painful contractions of the 1960s.

The Buckinghamshire Railway: Banbury's Merton Street station before the introduction of the diesel car service in 1956. Standard 4MT class 2-6-4T No 80039 has arrived with the afternoon train from Bletchley from which the station staff are unloading parcels. The other platform is occupied by cattle trucks. Ian Stratford

---

[8] *BG* 30 March, 15 July 1865; L Woolley, 'How the Railway changed Oxford', *Oxfordshire Local History*, vol 9 (2013-14), 18-43.

The activities of Banbury's railwaymen had consequences beyond the town's boundaries. They drove, fired, signalled or shunted passing trains which had few direct consequences for local people. They enabled West Midlanders to participate in King George V's Silver Jubilee celebrations in 1935 and supporters of Newcastle United FC to see their team play at Fratton Park in 1952. Railways made possible the growth of the family seaside holiday from the 1930s, and its particular popularity between 1946 and 1964.

Carrying freight: trains taking fruit from the Channel Islands to the Midlands and the North passed through Banbury on most weekday summer evenings in the 1950s and early 60s. No 5963 'Wimpole Hall' approaches the station in 1961 with a train from Weymouth to Crewe.

The freight carried by the railways, coal, shop goods, raw materials for foundries, obviously helped to shape Banbury's economy, but some traffics which made only a marginal local impact were of consequence in a national setting. In the context of the food industry, Banbury railwaymen were involved for many decades in distributing fish from Grimsby and Hull, bananas from Avonmouth, tea and individual pork and fruit pies from J Lyons at Cadby Hall, Guinness from Park Royal, biscuits from Reading, Channel Islands fruit from Weymouth and Southampton and broccoli from Cornwall. They sustained the nation's need for energy by carrying coal and oil, and by moving parts between automotive plants in Oxford and the West Midlands. Railways were the principal means of inland transport in the world wars of the twentieth century. Official records are sparse, and censorship inhibited photography and the collection of data by individuals but it is possible to describe some aspects of operation. The junctions at Banbury lay at the heart of wartime railway activity.

This is a work of synthesis that draws heavily on the labours of others. It is written in the knowledge that it is not possible to trace every decision made about railways in the past. The principal sources noted above indicate that it is an observer's not a participant's book of railways. Hugh Jones's excellent book on Chiltern Railways shows the complexity of events between 1996 and 2010, making effective use of the memories of those involved.[9] While political and economic circumstances were different in earlier periods, commitments were probably undertaken in similar ways, but it is not possible to examine them in detail in this study.

Banbury's railways have undergone profound changes in the recent decades, and their future can be regarded with more optimism than in the past, although it must be acknowledged that local prosperity has come in the context of an expanding national railway network. The year 2017 will see the opening of a new depot by Chiltern Railways, some 51 years after the opening of the GWR's engine shed, which itself functioned only for 58 years. This study ends at an appropriate milepost.

---

[9] H Jones, *The Chiltern Railways Story* (Stroud: The History Press, 2010).

2. The Setting

Banbury...is famous for its malt liquor, its cheese, and the cakes that are called by its name ... its fairs and large weekly markets attract a considerable amount of trade, owing to its position, having within a circuit of ten miles, not less than 160 villages dependent upon it ... Banbury is as famous for its production of agricultural implements as for its cross and its cakes.

George Measom (1861).[1]

Communications 1800-1850

Banbury in the early nineteenth century was an influential market town, whose population grew from just over 4,000 in 1801 to nearly 9,000 in 1851. Between 1744 and 1802 it became the nodal point of seven turnpike roads but it lay at some distance from the nation's principal arteries of communication. None of the roads that converged on Banbury was as busy as Watling Street passing through Stony Stratford and Towcester about twenty miles east, which, as Thomas Telford's Holyhead Road, became one of Europe's best highways. Oxford, twenty miles south, served by roads from London via High Wycombe and Henley, was the focus for stage coach routes that radiated through most of Wales and the Marches. Only six of more than a hundred weekly coach departures from Birmingham to London in the mid-1830s travelled through Banbury, more than eighty taking the Holyhead Road and about twenty the route through Stratford and Oxford. Nevertheless Banbury's turnpikes provided easy communications with the nearest significant towns, Oxford, Chipping Norton, Leamington, Warwick, Coventry, Daventry, Towcester, Northampton, Brackley, Buckingham, Stony Stratford and Bicester. Arthur Young commended Oxfordshire's turnpikes in 1813, observing that all the towns in the county were linked by good roads.[2]

The most significant consequence of the improvement of the roads into Banbury was the growth from the 1790s of one of England's busiest networks of carriers' carts. By 1821 133 carriers were making 227 weekly journeys into the town from villages up to 20 miles away, and by 1851 189 were making 427 journeys. Only Leicester and Nottingham were visited by more carriers. Banbury was celebrated as the 'metropolis of the carriers' carts' and in consequence was an attractive location for business. Samuel Sidney observed in

---

[1] G Measom, *The Official Illustrated Guide to the Great Western Railway* (London: Measom, 1861), 195.
[2] A Rosevear, *Turnpike Roads to Banbury* (BHS 31, 2010), *passim*; K Tiller & G Darkes, eds, *An Historical Atlas of Oxfordshire* (Oxfordshire Record Society, 2010), 102-03; A Young, *General View of the Agriculture of Oxfordshire* (London: Sherwood, Neely & Jones, 1813), 324.

1851 that 'commercial travellers consider it one of the best towns in England, as it is a sort of metropolis to a great number of thriving villages'.[3]

Dorian Gerhold has shown that scheduled coaches and waggons ran between London and Banbury before 1700, and in the next hundred years such services proliferated. In 1830 sixteen coaches departed each week from Banbury to London, thirteen to Birmingham, six to Leicester and Oxford and three to Northampton and Kidderminster. Most operated from the *Flying Horse*, then kept by John Drinkwater who had interests in the Birmingham–Oxford *Regulator* service, which moved with him to the *White Lion* in the early 1830s. Rusher's *List* for 1836, the last year in which services were unaffected by railways, shows 22 weekly services to London, 19 to Birmingham and 12 to Oxford. Ponderous stage waggons and sprightlier carts, departing five times a week to London and four times to Birmingham carried away agricultural produce and brought in shop goods.[4]

The Banbury region notoriously lacked fuel in the eighteenth century and Banburians were influential in promoting the Oxford Canal which linked the town with the Warwickshire Coalfield. The section from its junction with the Coventry Canal at Hawkesbury to Banbury was opened in 1778, and its continuation to Oxford was completed in 1790. For about fifteen years, until the opening in 1805 of Blisworth Tunnel on the Grand Junction Canal, the canal through Banbury formed part of the waterways route between London and the Midlands. Once the Grand Junction route was completed it was still necessary for London-bound boats to use the Oxford Canal between Napton and Braunston, and the resulting tolls made the Oxford company exceedingly prosperous. The southern section remained busy. In 1842 9,900 boats passed over Claydon summit north of Banbury, an average of 190 a week, and while canal traffic subsequently declined, some established movements, of coal from the Black Country, Warwickshire and Leicestershire to the southern counties, of horse fodder northwards, and the southward carriage of road stone from Nuneaton and Hartshill, continued for many decades. There was a boat-building yard in Banbury from the 1790s, and several local coal merchants operated narrow boats, as did families at other places along the waterway.[5]

---

[3] B Trinder, 'Banbury: Metropolis of Carriers' Carts', *C&CH* vol 18 (2011), 210-43; S Sidney, *Rides on Railways* (London: Orr, 1851, ed B Trinder, Chichester: Phillimore, 1973), 32-33.

[4] D Gerhold, *Carriers & Coachmasters* (Chichester: Phillimore, 2005), 94-95, 142, 199-200, 213-14; J Drinkwater, *Inheritance* (London: Benn, 1931), 94-116.

[5] H Compton, *The Oxford Canal* (Newton Abbot: David & Charles, 1976), 25-26, 32-50, 106; C Hadfield, *The Canals of the East Midlands* (Newton Abbot: David & Charles, 1966), 17, 21, 25, 157; M Prior, *Fisher Row:* (Oxford: Clarendon Press, 1982), 180-229; B Trinder, *Victorian Banbury* (Chichester: Phillimore, 1982), 25-26; J S W Gibson, *Banbury and the Origins of the Coventry to Oxford Canal 1768-1778* (Banbury Historical Society, 2015), *passim*.

Banbury's role in the national pattern of transport before 1840 was therefore modest. As a market centre, the town generated inward and outward traffic on the canal. It was remarkable as a point of distribution for the surrounding *pays*, sometimes called 'Banburyshire', and it had coaching connections with surrounding towns. It was not regarded in the eighteenth century as a town 'of great thoroughfare', such as Stamford or Towcester.

The weaving of plush, Banbury's principal manufacture in the eighteenth century, was already declining when the railways opened. The making of agricultural implements, an industry that prospered in many market towns, was established in Banbury from 1839 when James Gardner opened a workshop to produce the turnip cutter which he patented five years earlier. He must have relied on the canal to deliver coke, limestone and pig iron for his cupola furnace. After his death in 1846 his foundry passed to Bernhard Samuelson under whom the making of agricultural machines became Banbury's principal manufacturing industry. Manufacturers of Banbury Cakes distributed their products nationally in baskets. One baker alone made 139,500 cakes in 1839.[6]

The first main line railways

The Liverpool & Manchester Railway opened in 1830 and immediately became a focus of public interest. Within the next decade the Lancashire cities were linked with the south by the Grand Junction and London & Birmingham railways which opened in 1837 and 1838. Main line railways impacted rapidly on coaching throughout England and stations on the LBR became magnets for Banbury's coach operators. The LBR opened from London to Tring in 1837 and almost immediately coaches were taking passengers to Aylesbury to connect with omnibuses to Tring station. The LBR was extended northwards from 9 April 1838 to Denbigh Hall near Bletchley which became the terminus of a coach called the *Railway* from the *Red Lion* in Banbury. Once the LBR was opened throughout, Wolverton became the railhead for Banbury. From October 1838 the town's mail was carried by a coach from Wolverton station, and the London–Banbury–Birmingham Royal Mail service was discontinued. Banburians travelling to London in 1838 had the choice between thirteen weekly coach departures that connected with trains at Wolverton and fifteen that still ran direct to the capital. The LBR branch from Cheddington to Aylesbury opened on 10 June 1839 and from April 1840 a coach connected with trains at Aylesbury which gave a journey time of six and a quarter hours to London that was reduced to six hours by 1845. The *Novelty* coach which ran three days a week from Cheltenham through Banbury to Northampton called at Wolverton, providing connections for London as well as for the north. By 1843 the *Regulator* coach

---

[6] Trinder, *Victorian Banbury*, 32-35; A Beesley, *The History of Banbury* (London: Nichols, 1841), 508-09.

from Oxford ran through Banbury to the station at Rugby where connections were offered via the LBR to Birmingham, and by the Midland Counties Railway, which opened in 1840, to Leeds and York. Milverton station at Warwick, on a branch from the LBR at Coventry, opened in 1844, and for eight years was the railhead for passengers from Banbury travelling to Birmingham.[7]

On 1 June 1840 the Great Western Railway was opened between London and Steventon, ten miles south of Oxford for which, for four years, it was the railhead. An omnibus from Banbury connected with another at Oxford to provide a connection with trains at Steventon. The Great Western's branch from Didcot to Oxford opened on 12 June 1844, and in the following year three coaches competed to take passengers from Banbury to Oxford for trains to London. By 1848 the fastest service to London was five hours by the Royal Mail coach to Wolverton and forward by the LBR, compared with 5 hours 25 minutes by the *Rival* coach to Oxford and the GWR. The *Sovereign* coach from Leamington, the last to run through from Banbury to London, began to call at Oxford station from 1845 and terminated there from 1846. By 1848 all the stage coaches from Banbury ran to the stations at Oxford, Aylesbury, Wolverton, Weedon, Rugby and Warwick, and while ten stage waggons made weekly journeys to London by road throughout, two travelled only as far as Weedon station and two to Wolverton.[8]

The Gauge Question

The alternatives offered to travellers from Banbury to London in the mid-1840s, whether to take an LBR train from Aylesbury or Wolverton or a Great Western train from Oxford, epitomised the choice that parliament was making on behalf of the nation, between broad gauge and narrow gauge systems. That Banburians had choices indicated the town's strategic position in what came to be called the 'battle' between the two systems.

The railways that had been laid in British coalfields from the seventeenth century proliferated in the eighteenth and by the early nineteenth century some lines, chiefly in the Welsh Borderland, were more than twenty miles long. Iron rails of various patterns came into use, steam power supplemented that of horses, and some lines required authorisation by Acts of Parliament. The Liverpool & Manchester Railway was the first to fulfil the five conditions that Michael Robbins regarded as the characteristics of a main line railway; its lines were segregated from public roads, it accommodated public traffic and carried passengers, its trains were hauled throughout by mechanical traction, and its activities were controlled by Acts of Parliament. The LMR made a striking public impact, and proved profitable.[9]

---

[7] Trinder, *Victorian Banbury*, 23-25.
[8] Trinder, *Victorian Banbury*, 77-79.
[9] B Trinder, *Britain's Industrial Revolution* (Lancaster: Carnegie, 2003), 181-85; M Robbins, *The Railway Age* (Harmondsworth: Penguin, 1965), 11-17.

George Stephenson, engineer of the Liverpool & Manchester Railway, used technologies that had evolved in North East England, notably the wrought-iron T-section Birkinshaw rail that originated at the Bedlington Ironworks and the steam locomotive with whose development at Tyneside collieries he had been involved for two decades. Railways proliferated in Lancashire and in 1833 Acts of Parliament were passed enabling the building of the Grand Junction and the London & Birmingham railways linking Liverpool and Manchester with London. There was a frenzy of railway speculation in the mid-1830s. Developments in the East Midlands culminated in 1844 in the formation of the Midland Railway which brought together the Midland Counties Railway running from Nottingham and Derby through Leicester to a junction with the LBR at Rugby, the North Midland from Derby to York, and later the Birmingham & Derby and the Birmingham & Gloucester. In 1846 the Liverpool & Manchester, Grand Junction and London & Birmingham companies amalgamated to form the London & North Western Railway. All these lines used the gauge of 4ft 8½ in that George Stephenson brought from the North East.[10]

For some years each individual railway was considered in isolation and there was no real concept in the 1830s of a national network, demonstrated by the consideration given in Banbury in 1838 to the construction of a horse tramway to Blisworth on the LBR. Insularity led to the adoption of varied gauges. The line from London to Colchester was initially built with a gauge of 5 ft, while main line railways in Ireland adopted a standard gauge of 5ft 3 in. The Great Western Railway from Bristol to London, authorised by an Act of Parliament in 1835, which did not specify a gauge, adopted, on the recommendation of its engineer I K Brunel, a wider gauge of 7ft 0¼in. The railway from Bristol to London was duly built and the broad gauge network was extended by subsidiary companies towards the West Country and South Wales.[11]

During the economic recession of the early 1840s the pace of railway speculation slackened; no new companies were established in England and Wales in 1840 or 1841, only five in 1842-43, and only thirteen in the six years from 1838 to 1843. By 1843 the economy was recovering and some established companies were distributing generous dividends – the London & Birmingham paid 10 per cent for example. Early in 1844 W E Gladstone, as President of the Board of Trade, halved the 10 per cent deposit that railway promoters had to make when bringing forward parliamentary bills. In July the House of Commons resolved that future railway bills should be examined by a five-member scrutinising committee of the Board of Trade. The following year saw the beginning of the epidemic of speculation that

---

[10] J Simmons, *The Railway in England and Wales 1830-1914: Vol I* (Newton Abbot: David & Charles, 1978), 25-26.
[11] Simmons, *The Railway in England and Wales, Vol 1*, 26-28.

gained the name of the 'Railway Mania'. The House of Commons committee looked at 217 bills in 1845, 435 in 1846 and 257 in 1847, and some 330 railway Acts were passed in the three parliamentary sessions of 1844-47.[12]

The Board of Trade wished to avoid the expenditure of public money that would result from imposing the compulsory conversion of gauges on lines that had already been built. The narrow gauge was declared to be the future standard, but the Great Western and its associated companies were allowed to continue to extend the broad gauge. It was hoped that the lines running northwards into the industrial Midlands would achieve a workable mixture of the two gauges.[13]

The Great Western Railway's branch from Didcot to Oxford opened in 1844 was perceived as a threat to the narrow gauge in the Midlands and the North. The bills promoted during the 'Railway Mania' included proposals to extend the broad gauge from Oxford to Birmingham and Rugby as well as schemes to take the narrow gauge across the Cherwell Valley to Worcestershire and beyond. The Acts for the mixed gauge Oxford, Fenny Compton & Rugby and Oxford, Worcester & Wolverhampton railways both passed on 4 August 1845, and that for the broad gauge Birmingham & Oxford Railway on 3 August 1846. The proposals for these lines offered the prospects of a broad gauge route from London to Birmingham rivalling the LBR. They were challenged by the authorisation in 1847 of the Buckinghamshire Railway, a narrow gauge line from the LBR at Bletchley to Oxford and Banbury, with ambitions for an extension to Worcester, and ultimately to Porth Dinlleyn, the chimeric packet port at the far extremity of Gwynedd. These issues were examined by a parliamentary commission which provided a wide-ranging overview of the economy of the region from Oxford and Banbury to the western fringes of the Black Country.[14] The Oxford & Rugby line was to follow the Cherwell valley to Banbury then to proceed through Fenny Compton to Rugby where it was to join the Midland Counties Railway line to Leicester and Derby and the LNWR which, in 1847, had opened its Trent Valley line from Rugby to Stafford providing a direct route to the north. The OFCRR formally amalgamated with the GWR on 14 May 1846. Construction between Oxford and Fenny Compton ceased between the summer of 1847 and the spring of 1848 after the failure of a contractor, and in August 1849, after further problems with the new contractors, the company agreed not to build the 15½ miles of track from its projected junction with the Birmingham & Oxford line to Rugby.[15]

---

[12] J Gibson, 'Railway Mania', *C&CH*.13 (1995), 129-33, reprints *BG*'s 23 May 1844 names of Banbury area signatories to a petition in favour of the narrow gauge.
[13] Simmons, *The Railway in England and Wales, Vol 1*, 47.
[14] BPP 1845, XI. *Reports from Commissioners, Railways, Gauges, Oxford, Worcester & Wolverhampton and Oxford & Rugby Railway Bills*.
[15] E T MacDermot, *History of the Great Western Railway* (1927, rev edn, ed C R Clinker, London: Ian Allan, 1964), vol 1, 294-95.

The Oxford & Rugby opened a single track broad gauge line from Oxford to Banbury on 2 September 1850. Trains reversed out of the original terminus near Folly Bridge, on the site of the present junction of Whitehouse Road with Marlborough Road, as far as Millstream Junction, starting point of the line to the north. During the next two years a through station was constructed north of the Botley Road, and on 30 September 1852 a double track mixed gauge line was opened through Banbury to Birmingham. The official train hauled by *Lord of the Isles*, the locomotive that the Great Western displayed at the Great Exhibition, was derailed at Aynho when it collided with carriages of a mixed train from Didcot which was carrying out shunting operations. *Lord of the Isles* was damaged, but none of the party on the footplate was injured. The journey to Birmingham was curtailed, and the locomotive from the mixed train took the special as far as Leamington where the completion of the line was celebrated with the customary feast.[16]

The 4-2-2 locomotive 'Lord of the Isles', designed by Sir Daniel Gooch, completed in 1851, and displayed at the Great Exhibition in Crystal Palace. It was withdrawn in 1884, but preserved and displayed, as here, at the World Columbian Exposition, held in Chicago between May and October 1893. It was scrapped in 1906. IGMT

---

[16] C R Potts, *An Historical Survey of Selected Great Western Stations, vol. 4* (Poole: Oxford Publishing Co, 1985), 12; MacDermot, *History*, vol 1, 168-69.

Aynho station opened to passengers with the line from Oxford to Banbury in 1850. On 30 September 1852 it was the scene of the crash involving the locomotive 'Lord of the Isles' hauling the inaugural train on Great Western's line to Birmingham.

The Buckinghamshire Railway opened its line into Banbury on 1 May 1850 and its route into Rewley Road terminus at Oxford on 20 May 1851. The difference of gauges precluded the making of connections with the Great Western.

The GWR station at Banbury in its early years.
Walford. *Stranger's Guide to Banbury, circa* 1860.

Meanwhile a further railway battle developed north-west of Wolverhampton. The Shropshire Union Railway & Canal Company was incorporated into the London & North Western company in June 1847, and opened its line from Shrewsbury to Stafford in 1849, sharing the track between Wellington and Shrewsbury with the Shrewsbury & Birmingham Railway whose trains ran into Wolverhampton, and connected at its opposite end with the Shrewsbury & Chester Railway, opened in 1848. The LNWR obstructed the SBR's approach to Birmingham, slashed fares and packed SBR shareholders' meetings in an attempt to force amalgamation. The smaller company, with its ally the SCR, sought allies elsewhere and in 1851 came to an agreement with the GWR which took over both the Shrewsbury companies in 1854, the year in which the GWR extended the broad gauge from Birmingham to Wolverhampton.[17]

The Oxford, Worcester & Wolverhampton Railway joined the Oxford & Rugby at Wolvercote Junction north of Oxford and proceeded up the Evenlode valley and along the western fringe of Banbury's hinterland through Charlbury, Moreton-in-Marsh and Chipping Camden, passing through the Camden (or Mickleton) Tunnel into the valley of the Warwickshire Avon, then through Evesham to Worcester, and subsequently through Droitwich, Kidderminster, Stourbridge and Dudley to Wolverhampton. Isambard Kingdom Brunel was the line's engineer but its construction was troubled, most notably in July 1851 when Robert Marchant, contractor for the Mickleton Tunnel, had not been paid and urged his men to down tools. Brunel assembled a force of navvies from other projects and ensured that Marchant lost his contract. Nevertheless Brunel resigned from his post on the OWWR in March 1852. Even before the Battle of Mickleton Tunnel the OWWR, originally an ally of the GWR, made an agreement on 21 February 1851 to co-operate with the LNWR and Midland Railways. The line was opened on 4 June 1853. It was theoretically of mixed gauge and officials inspected the line in a broad gauge inspection train, but most of the points were for narrow gauge only, and the railway became a protagonist on the narrow gauge side in the Battle of the Gauges.[18]

---

[17] MacDermot, *History*, vol 1, 177-204; B Trinder, *The Industrial Revolution in Shropshire* (Chichester: Phillimore, 2000), 130.
[18] F Booker, *The Great Western Railway: A New History* (Newton Abbot: David & Charles, 1977), 56-57.

3. Narrowing Horizons

'I am absolutely indifferent upon the subject of broad gauge or narrow, & am only sorry that I cannot vote for both'.

Henry William Tancred, MP, 23 July 1844.[1]

The Battle of the Gauges shaped railways in the south Midlands for a decade after the first lines reached Banbury in 1850 and its implications continued to be influential in the decades after the declaration of peace in 1860. The route mileage of the national railway network increased from 6,266 in 1851 to 9,446 in 1861 and it became evident that effective operation depended on uniformity of gauges. In October 1852 the fastest Great Western trains reached Birmingham from Paddington in 2 hours 45 minutes, stopping only at Oxford and Leamington, although the service was soon decelerated, initially on account of flooding in the Oxford area. By December 1852 the fastest train did the journey in 3 hours 5 minutes, and most services took at least 15 minutes more.[2]

The westward expansion of the narrow gauge was ultimately halted at Banbury. The terminus of the Buckinghamshire Railway was designed as a through station and it was not until 1877 that it was accepted that the line would progress no further. The expansion of the broad gauge was similarly frustrated. Abandoned earthworks near Holmes Farm, Knightcote, provide evidence of the failure of the Oxford, Fenny Compton & Rugby Railway to reach its northern objective, while the blue brick Duddeston Viaduct, striding across the inner suburbs of Birmingham from a junction near Bordesley station, never made contact with the lines to the north. The Birmingham, Wolverhampton & Dudley Railway, a Great Western subsidiary, extended the broad gauge to Wolverhampton in 1854 but it progressed no further.[3]

Gloucester, where from 1844 the standard gauge Birmingham & Gloucester Railway joined the broad gauge Bristol & Gloucester, was the most notoriously chaotic meeting point of the two gauges. Another was at Wolvercote where the Oxford, Worcester and Wolverhampton Railway joined the Great Western line from Banbury. When the OWWR opened in 1853 it was effectively a narrow gauge line, allied with the LNWR. From April 1854 a loop line from Yarnton linked the OWWR with the Buckinghamshire Railway, and the line was used until 1861 by trains from the Worcester direction travelling to and from Euston.[4]

---

[1] B Trinder, ed, *A Victorian MP and his Constituents* (BHS, 1969), 15.
[2] E T MacDermot, *History of the Great Western Railway* (1927, rev edn, ed C R Clinker, London: Ian Allan, 1964), vol 1, 648.
[3] MacDermot, *History*, vol 1, 226; G P Neel, *Railway Reminiscences* (London: McCorquedale, 1904; rep Wakefield: EP Publishing, 1974), 26.
[4] MacDermot, *History*, vol 1, 266-67; 288-89.

The main line from Banbury to Leamington north of Fenny Compton near Holmes Farm, Knightcote. The scrub to the left covers the earthworks of the junction of the line to Rugby that was never completed.

Duddeston Viaduct which strides across the inner suburbs of Birmingham south of the city centre. It was built to enable trains from Banbury and the south to reach the LNWR and MR lines to the north, but never carried trains.

Wolvercote Junction, meeting point of the Oxford, Fenny Compton & Rugby and the Oxford, Worcester & Wolverhampton railways, seen here in 1962 with 2-6-2T No 6144 passing with a stopping train from Banbury to Oxford.

Every extension raised questions about gauge. The branch to Stratford-upon-Avon from the Great Western main line at Hatton was opened as a mixed gauge single line on 10 October 1860, and linked from 24 July 1861 with the narrow gauge OWWR branch from Honeybourne to Stratford, which itself had opened on 11 July 1859. The broad gauge Wycombe Railway from Maidenhead on the Great Western main line to High Wycombe was opened on 1 August 1854, and extended through Princes Risborough to Thame on 1 August 1862. The completion of a line from Thame to the Great Western at Kennington Junction south of Oxford opened on 24 April 1864, created an alternative route from Oxford (or Banbury) to Paddington. Broad gauge branches were built from the Great Western main line to Abingdon in 1856, Henley in 1857 and Wallingford in 1866, while the OWWR constructed narrow gauge lines to Chipping Norton in 1855 and to Witney in 1861.[5]

Southbound broad gauge trains from the Banbury direction could join the Great Western main line to Bristol and the West of England at Foxcote Junction, Didcot, opened on 22 December 1856. The broad gauge Great Western branch from Reading to Basingstoke was opened on 1 November 1848. This was one of the first places where the Great Western acknowledged that ultimately the two gauges could not peacefully co-exist, and that the future lay with the narrow gauge. In 1856 the mixed gauge on the Birmingham & Oxford line was extended from Oxford round a new curve to Reading West and on to Basingstoke.

---

[5] MacDermot, *History*, vol 1, 173, 229, 455-57, 461-6; vol 2, 23, 307-08.

Operational confusion remained in 1857 when excursionists from Banbury bound in broad gauge carriages for Portsmouth found that the London & South Western Railway had failed to provide narrow gauge vehicles to take them forward from Basingstoke, but on the same working in 1858 the excursionists travelled all the way to the coast in narrow gauge carriages.[6]

The outbreak of peace

By 1860 the railway 'wars' were ending. Hostilities diminished first in the north-west. After some years of competition the Great Western and London & North Western companies came to an agreement in 1860-62 on the joint working of lines focussed on Shrewsbury and Chester. A GWR/LNWR Joint Committee had its headquarters at Shrewsbury station and managed two sections of the GWR's route to Merseyside, the line from Shrewsbury to Wellington, used from 1849 by the Shrewsbury & Birmingham and Shropshire Union railways, and the Birkenhead Railway, the first part of which had opened in 1840. The Joint Committee was also responsible for the branch to Welshpool opened in 1862 and the Shrewsbury & Hereford Railway opened throughout in 1853. The Joint Committee continued beyond the Grouping of 1923 until 1932.[7]

From 1858 the Great Western ceased to assert that its broad gauge trains should be able to follow the route from Wolvercote Junction to Worcester and beyond which eased its relationship with the Oxford, Worcester & Wolverhampton Railway. Two years later the OWWR changed its name to the West Midland Railway, and absorbed two other companies, the Worcester & Hereford and the Newport, Abergavenny & Hereford. On 30 April 1861 the merger of the Great Western and West Midland companies was formally announced, with its full effect taking place in 1863. The GWR took over some 280 miles of narrow gauge railway bringing its total route mileage to 1,104, of which 369 were narrow gauge and 189 mixed. There were breaks of gauge at more than 20 places on the system. From 30 September 1861 trains from the Worcester direction ceased to travel to Euston along the Yarnton loop and the Bletchley south curve, but went through Oxford station to Paddington.[8]

The Great Western's line to Merseyside became a narrow gauge route during the 1860s. From 1 October 1861 mixed gauge tracks were in operation from Reading West Junction to Paddington, and the first narrow gauge train from

---

[6] A Vaughan, A, *The Heart of the Great Western* (Wadenhoe, Silver Link, 1994), 121; McDermot, *History*, vol 1, 152, 453, 455; *BA* 16 Sep 1858.

[7] F Booker, *The Great Western Railway: A New History* (Newton Abbot: David & Charles, 1977), 50-55); G P Neel, *Railway Reminiscences*, 28. MacDermot, *History*, vol 1, 181-204, 207; vol 2, 339; B Trinder, *The Industrial Archaeology of Shropshire* (2nd edn, Logaston: Logaston Press, 2016), 202-03.

[8] Booker, *Great Western*, 56-57; B Simpson, *Oxford to Cambridge Railway, vol 1* (Oxford: Oxford Publishing Co, 1981), 14-15.

Paddington to Birmingham ran that day. Laying mixed gauge tracks through Reading station enabled the creation of a junction with the South Eastern Railway's line to Guildford and Redhill and the LSWR route to Staines and Waterloo. Local services between Birmingham and Wolverhampton were worked by narrow gauge trains from 1 November 1868, and in the timetable that began that day only one return service between Wolverhampton and Paddington ran over broad gauge tracks. The broad gauge was officially abolished from Wolverhampton through Birmingham and Banbury to Oxford from 1 April 1869, and from Oxford to Didcot North Junction from 26 November 1872. The original Oxford station near Folly Bridge, used for broad gauge freight after 1852, was closed at the same time. A Banbury newspaper observed in July 1869 that broad gauge rails were being taken up, but that it would make little difference to services since for some time almost every train had used the narrow gauge.[9]

The transit shed at Didcot where goods from Banbury and the north bound for Bristol and the south-west were moved from narrow to broad gauge wagons. The building has been moved from its original location to the Great Western Society's Didcot Railway Centre. Great Western Trust Collection

The legacy of the broad gauge persisted. Goods from Banbury and the north bound for Bristol and the south-west were manhandled from narrow to broad gauge wagons in the transit shed built at Didcot in 1869, now preserved by the Great Western Society. In 1877 armies of labourers installed cross sleepers on the

---

[9] *RM* vol 9 (1901), 555; P Collins, *Rail Centres: Wolverhampton* (Shepperton: Ian Allan, 1990), 56; *BA* 1 July 1869; Vaughan, *Heart of the Great Western*, 17-18.

line between Oxford and Leamington, replacing the longitudinal baulks favoured by Brunel for the broad gauge. Some baulks remained near Fenny Compton and Harbury into the 1890s. Nevertheless the broad gauge route from Paddington to Merseyside was dead by the spring of 1869, only 15 years after it had reached its northern extremity at Wolverhampton.[10]

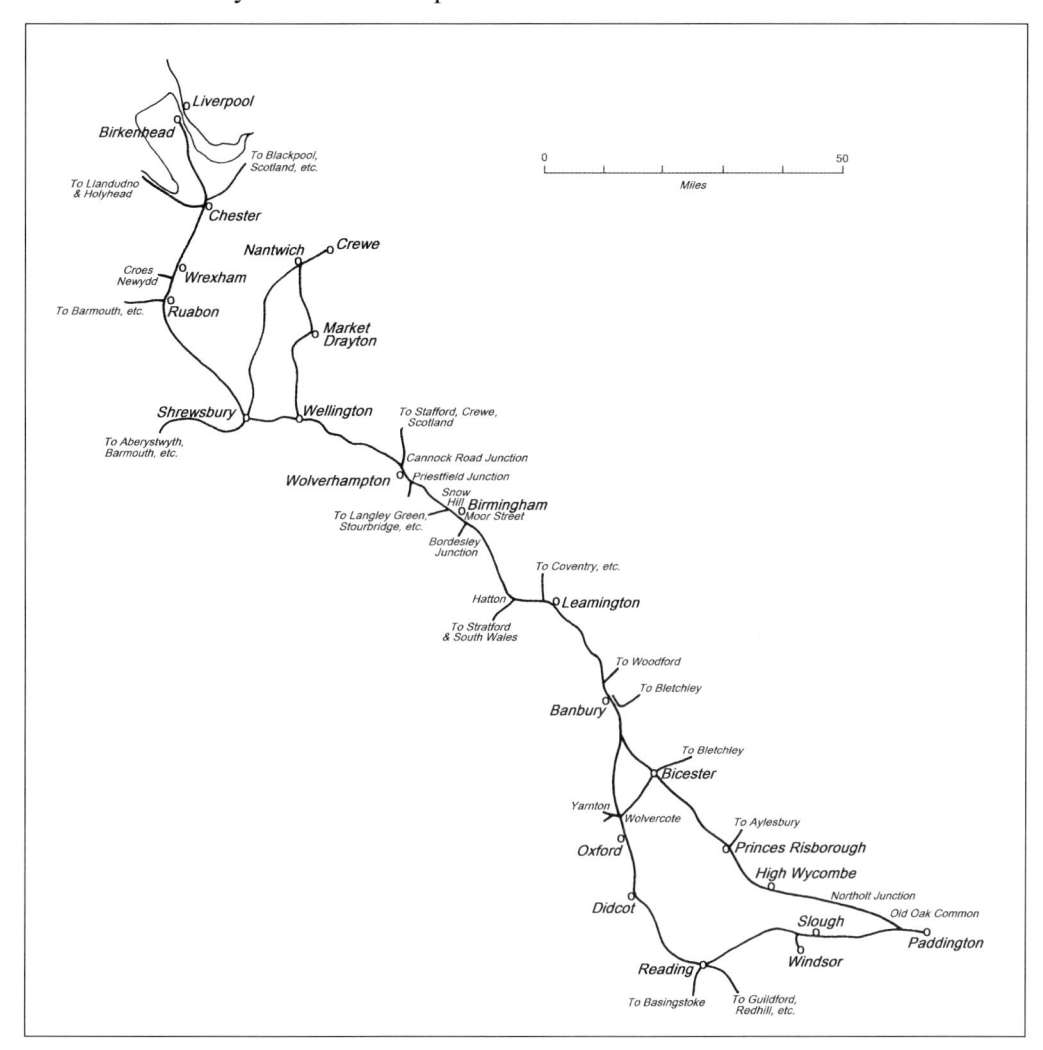

Map 2: The northern line of the Great Western Railway.

The Great Western's northern line became its frontier with the LNWR, with which there were links at every major town north of Oxford. The Yarnton loop provided the initial connection at Oxford. At Banbury a siding from the GWR ran

---

[10] *BG* 4 Jan 1877; *RM* vol 38 (1916), 263-64; L A Summers, ed, *The Didcot Guide* (Didcot: Great Western Society, 2016), 14.

WR 9400 class 0-6-0PT No 8407 shunting in the yard at Merton Street in 1954, while LMR 4F class 0-6-0 No 44447 waits to leave with freight for Swanbourne Sidings. The former has crossed to the ex-Buckingham Railway yard by the siding installed in 1863.

into the freight yard at Merton Street from 1863. In the same year a connection was made with the LNWR at Leamington which linked Banbury directly with the Warwickshire Coalfield, although it was not until after Nationalisation that the route was used by block coal trains, and only in the 1970s was it traversed by through passenger services. At Bordesley, on the southern edge of Birmingham, a junction was made in 1861 with the Midland Railway's Camp Hill route, the original main line of the BGR. At Priestfield Junction south of Wolverhampton the Great Western joined the OWWR and shared its tracks into what became Low Level station. The northern extremities of the broad gauge proved to be the lines laid in 1854 into the Victoria Basin freight depot (later re-named Herbert Street), that was opened by the Shrewsbury & Birmingham Railway in 1849, and Cannock Road Junction, where the OWWR bifurcated into a link with the Shrewsbury & Birmingham at Stafford Road Junction at the south end of Oxley Viaduct, and a line that joined the GJR at Bushbury where the LNWR and the GWR exchanged royal trains travelling to and from Balmoral.[11]

---

[11] Collins, *Wolverhampton*, 40-41; 56; 59, 107; MacDermot, *History*, vol 1, 455, 457; Neel, *Reminiscences*, 138.

Another link was the line from Wellington through Market Drayton to Nantwich on the LNWR route from Shrewsbury to Crewe, opened from 16 October 1867 (The section between Nantwich and Market Drayton had opened on 20 October 1863). This line carried long-distance freight trains, at some stages as many as twenty a day, as well as some passenger workings to and from Manchester. The LNWR route from Shrewsbury to Crewe was not a significant point of interchange for traffic from the Banbury direction, but the connection at Chester, where trains from the Shrewsbury direction could run through the station to Warrington and Manchester, was important, particularly for specials originating on the GWR for Blackpool and destinations in Scotland.[12]

Peter Mottershead drove the 4-2-2 single 'Alma' designed by Sir Daniel Gooch and completed in 1854, on some of the last Broad Gauge trains to pass through Banbury in the late 1850s. Great Western Trust Collection

Early workings

The changes of the 1850s and 60s were chronicled by an archetypal early railwayman. Peter Mottershead was born at Burnage, Manchester, on 6 January 1835. After leaving school at the age of 11 and experiencing unsatisfying jobs at a brickyard and a shop in central Manchester, he developed 'an inclination for railroading'. In 1853, at the age of 18, he obtained a job as a cleaner on the Shrewsbury & Chester Railway. He became a fireman in 1854, working for a

---

[12] MacDermot, *History*, vol 2, 307-8.

time with a driver who had been employed on the Stockton & Darlington Railway. In 1857, when he was 22, he was promoted to driver, based at Wolverhampton, from where, in 1860, he drove the daily freight train through Banbury to Basingstoke. The following year after the completion of mixed gauge from Reading the working was changed to terminate at Paddington. In 1865 he transferred to Birkenhead, but soon returned to Wolverhampton, and in 1867 to Birmingham. With the 4-2-2 *Alma* he worked some of the last broad gauge trains through Banbury, sometimes travelling the 42½ miles between Oxford and Leamington in 35 minutes. As an experienced driver, although only in his early thirties, he was receiving a wage of 7s.6d. per day, far above the average for workers in the Banbury area. When broad gauge working ended in 1869 he returned to Wolverhampton. In 1873 he and his family emigrated to Hamilton, Ontario, then to the United States, where, in 1908, at the age of 73, he was driving compound locomotives in Iowa.[13]

The infrequent service between Banbury and Oxford in 1850-52 was worked by two 2-2-2 locomotives of the 'Sun' class, *Gazelle* and *Meridian*, driven by George Thompson, who had been born in Co Durham in 1816, and lived with his wife, three children and his sister in Lower Cherwell Street. The engines were accommodated in a temporary shed that was closed when the line to Birmingham opened. By 1854 the Great Western provided seven daily services between Paddington and Banbury, the fastest in 2 hours 45 minutes, ten minutes slower than the fastest service from Euston via Bletchley. In December 1858 one of the first slip coaches was detached at Banbury from the 09.30 Paddington–Birmingham train, an innovation that was significant in the town's services for nearly eighty years. There were extensive changes to Great Western services after the completion of the mixed gauge into Paddington in 1861. In 1865 five trains from Paddington stopped at Banbury and another two dropped slip coaches. The fastest service now took only one hour 55 minutes.[14]

The broad gauge route from Paddington to Wolverhampton lasted only fifteen years. Brunel's system could not in the long term be accommodated within a national network which employed another technology. R B Dockray, engineer of the Buckinghamshire Railway, commented on 12 October 1860 when he heard that the Great Western was to lay mixed gauge tracks into London, that 'At last Robert Stephenson's long-sighted view has come about – that if you commence mixing the gauge it must go over the whole broad gauge system … unfortunately Parliament would not believe him'.[15]

---

[13] *Locomotive Engineers' Journal*, May 1908, 408. The late Dr D F Harris kindly provided this reference.
[14] *RM* vol 88 (1942), 57; *BA* 2 Dec 1858; *BH* 10 Oct 1861; *BG* 8 June 1865; *RM* April 2014 27-31.
[15] M Robbins, 'From R B Dockray's Diary', *JTH*, vol 7 (1965-66), 110.

4. The Buckinghamshire Railway 1846-1914

Now to describe the great Bucks line,
I think I'll have a try,
And tell you how the work went on,
Through hills both hard and high.

Charles Whitehall, *The Buckinghamshire Railway*.[1]

The Buckinghamshire Railway was a creation of the Gauge Wars, a consolidation in 1847 of proposals for narrow gauge lines heading north-west from the London & Birmingham Railway towards Worcester and the western parts of the Black Country. It evolved into a route from Bletchley through Winslow and Bicester to Oxford, from which diverged, two miles west of Winslow (later the site of Verney Junction station), a line extending 21 miles to the station at Banbury that was later called Merton Street. It was intended to progress towards Worcester. The Buckinghamshire company was effectively controlled by the London & North Western Railway, with which it was formally amalgamated in 1878. The Banbury banker Timothy Rhodes Cobb was a member of its management committee, and Edward Watkin, the company secretary said that the completion of the line owed more to Cobb than to any man living. Banbury's other bank, the Tory-inclined Gillett, Tawney & Gillett, also supported the line, as did most of the Liberals who controlled the borough corporation.[2]

The ambitions of the Buckinghamshire Railway to reach the Severn Valley ended at Merton Street station but in the nineteenth century the line to Banbury was more than a rural byway. Its infrastructure reflected the ambitions of its promoters. Although it was a single-line railway, its earthworks and bridges were constructed to carry two tracks, and its yard at Banbury was spacious. The company's ambitions were indicated by its three-track engine shed, capable of accommodating eight locomotives. The depot remained open, formally a sub-shed of Bletchley, until 1932. A connection with the Great Western at Banbury was impracticable while the broad gauge persisted, but a siding crossing the road to the gasworks was installed in 1863. Its alignment did not enable trains from the Buckinghamshire line to run into the GWR station. From 1 June 1872 the trains of the once ambitious Northampton & Banbury Junction Railway joined the Buckinghamshire line at Cockley Brake Junction between Farthinghoe and Brackley, and shared the facilities at Merton Street. Locomotives of passenger trains had to be detached and to run round before coaches could gain access to the platforms.

---

[1] C Whitehall, *The Buckinghamshire Railway* (1849, rep Charleston, North Carolina: Nabu, 2011).
[2] B Trinder, *Victorian Banbury* (Chichester: Phillimore, 1982), 77-80.

Edward Jakeman, station master for the LNWR at Banbury from the opening of the Buckinghamshire Railway in 1850 until 1875. His home was Laurel Cottage, No 91 Middleton Road, probably the first house erected on the Freehold Land Company's Grimsbury estate. The daguerreotype dates from 1855.

Stephen Jakeman

The decision in 1877 to lengthen the platforms, obviating the need for this manoeuvre, was an acknowledgement that Merton Street would remain a terminus, and that the Buckinghamshire Railway's ambition to penetrate the hills west of the Cherwell would not be fulfilled.[3]

The first public passenger train from Bletchley to Merton Street ran on May Day 1850. Initially the company offered four passenger trains a day. Freight services began a fortnight later. R B Dockray, the line's engineer, was concerned that the incomplete sidings would be insufficient to handle the hundred loaded coal wagons waiting to be hauled on to the branch. After the opening in 1847 of the LNWR Trent Valley route, from Rugby through Nuneaton and Atherstone to Stafford, the branch was well-situated to supply Banbury with coal from Warwickshire. The LNWR's affairs in Banbury were managed from the line's opening until his retirement in 1875 by Edward Jakeman, a native of Drayton Bassett, Staffordshire.[4]

---

[3] Trinder, *Victorian Banbury*, 77-79; B Simpson, *The Banbury to Verney Junction Branch* (Oxford: Oxford Publishing Co, 1978), 16, 39, 43; C Turner, 'Banbury Merton Street', *BRJ*, 70 (2001), 178-79; R Griffiths & P Smith, P, *The Directory of British Engine Sheds, vol 1* (Shepperton: Oxford Publishing Co, 1999), 108; G P Neel, *Railway Reminiscences* (London: McCorquedale, 1904; rep Wakefield: EP, 1974), 138; *BA* 6 June 1872; *BG* 13 Sep 1877.

[4] M Robbins, 'From R B Dockray's Diary', *JTH*, vol 7 (1965-66), 8.

The Oxford line of the Buckinghamshire Railway opened in 1851, and from 1854 carried trains from the Worcester direction to Euston across the loop line to Yarnton north of Oxford, although that service ceased in September 1861 when the OWWR, by then the West Midland Railway, became part of the Great Western. By 1902 ten daily freight trains left Bletchley heading for Oxford, some of them taking the route from Yarnton towards South Wales. Trains in the opposite direction carried Welsh coal to Dunstable and Tring. In March 1910 it was estimated that 7,500 coal wagons a month passed over the Yarnton loop. In March 1905 the LNWR introduced three daily through trains between Oxford and Cambridge, and the following October began a railmotor services between Oxford and Bicester calling at newly-opened halts.[5]

Competing for London traffic

For more than half a century the Buckinghamshire Railway competed with the Great Western for passengers between London and Banbury. Its route of 77½ miles to Euston was 8¾ miles shorter than the 'great way round' to Paddington through Oxford and Reading. In 1855 there were eight services between Paddington and Banbury, the fastest taking 2 hours 45 minutes and the slowest 6½ hours, while there were four from Merton Street to Euston, two of them with through coaches, the fastest taking 2 hours 35 minutes. From 1851 it was customary for trains leaving Bletchley for Oxford to carry coaches for Banbury which were detached at Winslow from where there were two separate single lines to Oxford and Banbury. In 1868 the Aylesbury & Buckingham Railway from Quainton Road joined the Buckinghamshire line at the point where its two branches diverged. A new station was opened, named Verney Junction after the landowning family from Claydon House, but the section from Winslow to the junction was not converted to double track operation until 1 December 1875. Subsequently coaches for Banbury were detached from Oxford trains at Verney Junction, but those on up workings continued to be attached at Winslow. In 1863 the illustrator and journalist Thomas Butler Gunn was living in London but preparing to marry his fiancée from Chacombe, and travelled frequently between the capital and Banbury. He always chose the route from Euston, and on 23 November 1863 the LNWR conveyed his dead father's coffin from London to Banbury in a bullion van. In the mid-1860s the number of daily passenger trains between Banbury and Bletchley increased from four to five. In 1901 the LNWR began to detach a slip coach for Banbury at Bletchley from the 16.00 Euston–Manchester express, a practice which continued until the Great War.

---

[5] B Simpson, *Oxford to Cambridge Railway, vol 1* (Oxford: Oxford Publishing, 1981), 41; *RM* vol 27 (1910), 27; *RM* vol 16 (1905), 261; vol 33 (1913), 376; vol 70 (1932), 63; L Waters, *Oxfordshire Railways in Old Photographs* (Gloucester: Sutton, 1989), 65; W Hemmings, *The Banbury & Cheltenham Railway, vol 1* (Didcot: Wild Swan, 2004), 20-21.

The LNWR service from Banbury via Bletchley to the north and east was competitive with that of the GWR. The timetable published in 1888 by Cheney & Son showed connections from the 09.50 Banbury–Bletchley reaching Liverpool at 15.00, Manchester at 14.40, Glasgow (Central) at 22.15 and Norwich at 15.53, while passengers off the 10.00 ex Glasgow (Central) could catch the 21.10 from Bletchley, reaching Merton Street at 22.25.[6]

An alternative route to London, only 71¾ miles from Banbury to Baker Street, became possible in 1868 with the completion of the Aylesbury & Buckingham Railway and the opening of Verney Junction station. In 1891 the A&BR was taken over by the Metropolitan Railway which from 1 June 1910 operated the Pullman buffet cars *Mayflower* and *Galatea* between Verney Junction and Liverpool Street. Nevertheless Banburians wishing to travel in luxury to or from the City would have endured lengthy waits for connections.[7]

Freight

The Buckinghamshire Railway's freight yard at Banbury included a timber goods shed, sidings for unloading coal wagons, cattle docks and a connection to the gasworks. A joint stock company to provide gas for Banbury had been established in 1833, and commenced operations in 1834 from a works on the canal bank, accessed from Bridge Street. The opening of the railway stations increased demand and in 1854 the gas company built a new works south of the town between the two railways, with sidings running through the premises, linked to the GWR on the western side and to the Buckinghamshire Railway to the east.[8]

The Bletchley–Banbury line served three intermediate market towns, Brackley with a population at mid-century of just over 2,000, Buckingham with just over 4,000 and Winslow with rather less than 2,000. From all of them the Buckinghamshire Railway offered the best passenger service to London, as well as providing convenient links to the market at Banbury. The railway installations at all three included goods sheds for general cargo, sidings for unloading coal, connections to gasworks, and docks for cattle. At Brackley the 'barrel line', a short, steeply graded siding worked by horses, gave access to the brewery of Hopcraft & Norris, which employed about fifty men by 1871. The principal customer for goods services became the factory established opposite the station at Buckingham by the Anglo-Swiss Condensed Milk Co, which received

---

[6] *RM* vol 106 (1960), 16, 126-27; *RD* 1855; *BG* 5 Jan 1854, 8 June 1865; Simpson, *Banbury to Verney Junction*, 34-36, 45, 60-63; B. Trinder, *Victorian Banburyshire: Three Memoirs* (BHS, 2013), 11-12, 265-66.

[7] R Davies & M D Grant, *Forgotten Railways: Chilterns and Cotswolds* (Newton Abbot: David & Charles, 1975), 90; *RM* vol 27 (1910), 9-11; C H Ellis, *The Engines that Passed* (London: George Allen & Unwin, 1968), 25-27.

[8] S Townsend & J Gibson, *Banbury Past through Artists' Eyes* (BHS, 2007), 93.

The factory of the Anglo-Swiss Condensed Milk Co opposite the station entrance at Buckingham, which received coal and milk, and sent out its products by rail. The building now houses the library of the University of Buckingham.

coal by rail, took in milk in churns from stations along the line, and despatched products to distant customers. At Winslow a brickworks north of the line was rail-connected and doubtless took in coal as well as sending out bricks. The lesser stations, Farthinghoe, opened by 1851, Fulwell & Westbury opened in 1879 and Padbury opened in 1878, and the isolated siding at Bacon's House (SP 645343) on the road from Finmere to Water Stratford, principally handled coal, cattle, and pink quartzite road stone from Hartshill near Nuneaton. For most of the 64 years between the line's opening and the First World War one or two daily trains in each direction handled freight traffic, with the addition on Thursdays of cattle workings serving Banbury market.[9]

Milk was an increasingly important traffic. It was conveyed in churns, and might be taken from intermediate stations for sale in the market towns, to the factory at Buckingham, or to Bletchley for loading on to trains for London. The folk lore concerning the village stations includes stories of farmers with carts hastening to load churns on to trains, and at Farthinghoe there were indentations in the fence and the timber platform caused by the regular handling of milk churns. An image of an LNWR 2-4-0 locomotive at Merton Street shows ranks of churns on the eastern side of the train shed, with a six-wheel brake van ready to receive them.[10]

---

[9] A E Grigg, *Town of Trains* (Buckingham: Barracuda, 1980), 79-87.
[10] Historic England, National Monuments Record, Swindon, Rokeby Collection, RO/07286/10.

The extensive yard at Merton Street station in the late 1950s. The buildings on the extreme right are part of the Midland Marts market complex, alongside which are three sidings filled with cattle wagons. The sidings approaching the goods sheds are overgrown. A coal lorry is loading on the extreme left.   J.D. Edwards

For most of its first half-century the northern half of the Buckinghamshire system was a self-contained operation, worked between Winslow and Merton Street by the enginemen and locomotives based in the sub-shed at Banbury. Most trains consisted of six-wheeled coaches hauled by locomotives with single driving wheels of the 'Small Bloomer' and 'Lady of the Lake' (or 'Problem') classes. Subsequently the predominant classes on the line were the elegant 2-4-2T tank engines introduced in 1890, which worked passenger trains, and the 'Cauliflower' 0-6-0s introduced in 1887, which handled freight and passenger workings. Both were designed by the formidable Francis William Webb, chief mechanical engineer of the LNWR.[11]

---

[11]   Simpson, *Banbury to Verney Junction*, 42-43.

Merton Street station at a time when it was exceptionally well-kept, probably in the 1920s. A 'Jumbo' class 2-4-0 waits to leave with a passenger train while ranks of milk churns await loading into a six-wheel brake van (see detail below). Historic England

The opening of the Great Western's 'Bicester cut-off' in 1910 reduced the appeal of the Buckinghamshire Railway for Banburians wishing to travel to London, just as the Great Central Railway's London Extension from 1899 provided competition for London-bound passengers from Brackley and Buckingham (from Finmere station). By 1914 the Banbury line had lost its usefulness for long-distance passengers, although it was still important for people going to Banbury market, for deliveries of coal, and for the movement of milk and cattle.

Ranks of milk churns await loading (detail of Merton Street station above).

5. East to West

'We want as many railways as we can get'.
Councillor Richard Edmunds (1865).[1]

The railways between south and north opened in 1850-52 quickly benefitted Banbury's economy, but even before they were completed the *Banbury Guardian* referred to an 'increasing desire to have a branch extended to the west' and in April 1851 promoters met to support the building of a Banbury, Moreton & Shipston Railway. Arguments were sharpened by the completion in the summer of 1853 of the Oxford, Worcester & Wolverhampton Railway which along its route across the Cotswolds passed through Evesham, Chipping Campden, Blockley and Moreton-in-Marsh on the fringes of Banbury's hinterland.[2]

Two strategic arguments were put forward for east-west railways through Banbury. First, it was hoped that such lines might carry the cattle which traditionally travelled with drovers from Wales and the Borders to graziers in Northamptonshire and Buckinghamshire. A Herefordshire dealer said in 1864 that, while he would welcome a new line, he was already sending lean cattle to Banbury market by rail through Gloucester and Swindon. There were fears that this trade might be lost to Moreton-in-Marsh.[3]

Iron ore was a more immediate consideration. Specimens of Northamptonshire ore were displayed at the Great Exhibition in 1851, and over the next decade quarrying for ironstone spread across the county. Most ore went by rail and canal to the Black Country, but some was smelted locally and some despatched to more distant ironworks. As early as 1853 Bernhard Samuelson urged the construction of a railway that could carry ore from Northamptonshire and Oxfordshire to the furnaces of South Wales.[4]

Three decades elapsed before it was possible to travel from Northamptonshire to the Severn Valley through Banbury. The first element of the route from Banbury to the west was the Chipping Norton Railway, opened in the summer of 1855, extending 4½ miles from the eponymous town to a station on the OWWR then called Chipping Norton Junction but renamed Kingham in 1909. The CNR was taken over by the OWWR in 1859.

---

[1] *NH* 24 June 1865.
[2] *BG* 2 Jan 1851; 24 Apl 1851; B Trinder, *Victorian Banbury* (Chichester: Phillimore, 1982), 80-81.
[3] *BG* 2 June, 17 Nov 1853; 10 Mar 1864; *NH* 24 June 1865.
[4] S Griffiths, *Griffiths' Guide to the Iron Trade of Great Britain* (1873, ed W K V Gale, Newton Abbot: David & Charles, 1967), 128-29, 181.

Northampton and Banbury

An Act was passed in 1847 for a line from Northampton to Banbury that, with further legislation, was envisaged as part of a 96-mile route to South Wales, the 'Midland Counties and South Wales Railway'. The company, re-named the Northampton & Banbury Junction Railway, and with reduced ambitions, opened a line from Blisworth to Towcester on 1 May 1866. By the autumn of 1870 an extension towards Banbury was 'being vigorously proceeded with'. The line was opened from Towcester to Helmdon on 31 July 1871, and after a junction had been made at Cockley Brake, with the Buckinghamshire Railway, NBJR trains began to run into Merton Street station in June 1872.[5]

The single track of the NBJR wound around sharp curves, climbed at 1 in 65 west of Helmdon as it approached the watershed between the valleys of the Tove and the Cherwell, and descended at 1 in 72 to Cockley Brake beyond the summit. The track was lightly laid and the bridges were incapable of carrying heavy locomotives. The company was burdened with debts, and operated its first trains with hired power. It could not pay for locomotives ordered from Neilson of Glasgow which were purchased by the Caledonian Railway. From 1876 trains were worked with locomotives and carriages from the LNWR. The annual receipts in the 1880s amounted to only about £7,500 pa, insufficient to pay the interest on capital expenditure which up to June 1897 amounted to £620,199.

The fortunes of the NBJR were intertwined with those of the East and West Junction Railway, whose route it shared from Towcester to Green's Norton. The company was authorised by an Act of Parliament of 1864 to build a 34-mile line from Towcester to Stratford-upon-Avon. The project was launched by Lady Palmerston on 3 August 1864 but shortage of capital caused delays and it was not until July 1869 that sufficient was raised for the completion of the route. The 6¼ mile line from Fenny Compton to Kineton was opened on 1 June 1871. Further funds had to be raised before the sections from Fenny Compton to Green's Norton and from Kineton to Stratford were opened on 1 July 1873. The EWJR went into receivership in 1875, and passenger services were suspended between 1877 and 1885.

By 1891 extensions at either end of its route enabled the EWJR to link two of the main lines of the Midland Railway. The Evesham, Redditch & Stratford-upon-Avon Junction Railway, formed in 1873, and opened in 1879, connected the EWJR at Stratford with Broom Junction, which enabled trains to proceed north to Redditch and Birmingham, or (initially with a reversal) south to

---

[5] B Trinder, *Victorian Banburyshire: Three Memoirs* (BHS, 2013), 43; J M Dunn, *The Stratford-upon-Avon & Midland Junction Railway* (Lingfield: Oakwood, 1952), 7-9; R C Riley & B Simpson, *A History of the Stratford-upon-Avon & Midland Junction Railway* (Witney: Lamplight Publications, 1999), 9; S C Jenkins, *The Northampton & Banbury Junction Railway* (Oxford: Oakwood, 1990), 18, 28-31; *BG* 20 Oct 1870; 27 Jly 1871.

Ashchurch on the main line from Birmingham to Bristol. In the east iron ore workings at Easton Neston were linked by rail to the EWJR at Towcester from the early 1870s; in 1879 an Act of Parliament was obtained for a company originally called the Easton Neston Mineral & Towcester, Roade & Olney Junction Railway. This built a 10½-mile line to Ravenstone Wood near Olney on the Midland Railway's route from Northampton to Bedford, opened in 1862, which joined the main line to St Pancras at Oakley Junction. The company changed its name in 1882 to the Stratford-upon-Avon, Towcester & Midland Junction Railway, and opened the route from Towcester to Olney to goods on 13 April 1891, and to passenger trains on 1 December 1891. Passenger demand was minimal and trains were withdrawn at the end of March 1893, one of the shortest-lived services in British railway history.[6]

A notice published by the SMJR warning against trespassing.   Ian Stratford

East-West services

The early services on the Northampton & Banbury and the East & West lines were meagre, the three daily return services on the former were matched by only four on the latter, although on both there were additional trains on market days and Saturdays. In 1888 the EWJR advertised reduced fares for passengers from Kineton and Byfield wishing to attend Banbury market. The EWJR had access east of Towcester to ironstone quarries, but it did not carry their products very far. Several factors combined to improve the company's performance in the

---

[6] *BG* 25 Sep 1873; Dunn, *Stratford & Midland Junction*, 4, 13; Riley & Simpson, *History of the Stratford & Midland Junction*, 13, 18, 82-88.

closing years of the century. A junction was made at Woodford with the Great Central Railway's London Extension which enabled through passenger workings from Marylebone or northern England to Stratford-upon-Avon, which began in 1908. In the early 1890s the Midland Railway moved cautiously towards working freight trains between Broom Junction and Olney, following a working agreement made in 1889, while in March 1887 the LNWR began to move freight between Blisworth and Broom Junction. After an attempt to sell the company to the MR, the LNWR or the GCR, the EWJR passed under new management. In 1910 it was formally merged with the Northampton & Banbury Junction Railway to form the Stratford & Midland Junction Railway.

A typical freight train of the 1950s on the SMJR approaches Mor(e)ton Pinkney behind class 4F 0-6-0 No 44524 on 28 April 1956. Ian Stratford

For a few years the new regime demonstrated, as did Chiltern Railways a century later, the benefits that a railway can gain by paying attention to the needs of its customers, by cherishing the morale of its employees and by imaginative marketing. For four years from 1908 the SMJR had Harry Willmott as its chairman and his son Russell Willmott as its traffic manager. Harry Willmott had worked for the Great Eastern Railway, then progressed via the Lancashire, Derbyshire & East Coast to the Great Central. A second track was laid between Towcester and Green's Norton, and thereafter one line carried trains to and from Stratford, the other the Banbury services. The Midland Railway ran banana trains from Avonmouth to London via Broom, Towcester and Olney. The railway made the most of its connections with Shakespeare's birthplace, with Harvard House in

Stratford, and with the ancestral home of the Washington family at Sulgrave Manor. Excursions were promoted from the LNWR, the MR and the GCR, as well as short trips for visitors to Stratford who could take a train to Bidford-on-Avon, enjoy afternoon tea, and return by river steamer. The Willmotts' concern for their employees was reflected by a Sunday picnic for the company's staff at Compton Verney in 1911. When the younger Willmott left to manage the Isle of Wight Central Railway in 1912 it was remarked that he and his father had raised the SMJR from a poverty-stricken company to one with a 2½ per cent dividend and that 'no day was too long for him'. The withdrawal of the MR's long distance freight services in 1913 may have been a cause for concern, but by the outbreak of the First World War the SMJR had been transformed, and was paying a modest dividend to its shareholders.[7]

The Willmotts did relatively little to enliven the Northampton & Banbury line – indeed some of its better track was removed to the EWJR 'main line'. While the NBJR station at Helmdon station lay only two miles from Sulgrave Manor, it was Moreton Pinkney on the EWJR, three miles distant that was promoted as the railhead for the ancestral home of the Washingtons.

5100 class 2-6-2T No 4124 leaves Chipping Norton with a local freight train, 27 April 1961.

---

[7] Dunn, *Stratford & Midland Junction*, 9-10; Riley & Simpson, *History of the Stratford & Midland Junction*, 27-30, 42-43.

Westward

Banbury's railway from the east opened in 1872 but the components of a westward route fell into place slowly. The Chipping Norton Railway opened in 1855. It was joined at Kingham in 1862 by the 11-mile Bourton-on-the-Water Railway, absorbed by the GWR from 1 February 1874. Through the 1850s and '60s schemes for a line west of Banbury were put forward, some of them involving an extension of the NBJR. One of the issues was whether such a line should pass through Chipping Norton. It could be argued that Chipping Norton was part of Banbury's hinterland, and that there were good reasons for connecting the two towns. A contrary case could be made that the best route to South Wales would be by means of a junction with the OWWR at Blockley ten miles north of Kingham, providing a connection through Worcester and Hereford.

The Banbury & Cheltenham Direct Railway Company was constituted in 1872 and received its Act of Parliament the following year. From the beginning it was envisaged that the company would co-operate with the Great Western. The prospects of ironstone traffic were cited as the principal reason for building the line. The company proposed to construct five railways. Three were short spurs, but Railway No 1 was to extend 15¾ miles from a junction with the Oxford line at King's Sutton to Chipping Norton, while No 4 was to be a 16¾ mile line from Bourton-on-the-Water to Cheltenham. The contracts for building the BCDR between King's Sutton and Chipping Norton were let in November 1874, and the first sod cut with due ceremony at Adderbury on 9 February 1875. Early in October the works of the BCDR near Adderbury were inundated, and navvies' wheelbarrows floated on the flood. William Hemmings has meticulously chronicled the twelve years that passed before the line opened from Banbury, beset with storms, disputes with landowners, failing contractors, the need for minor deviations, the necessity for further legislation, and disputes over access to Cheltenham. The principal difficulties related to the line through Hook Norton to Chipping Norton that included a high embankment, two viaducts and two tunnels. There were 23 cuttings between Chipping Norton and King's Sutton.[8]

By October 1876 the chairman reported that track had been laid from the junction with the Oxford line at King's Sutton as far as Adderbury, and two thousand men, 120 horses and seven locomotives were constructing the embankments, tunnel and viaducts at Hook Norton. This was a false picture for during the autumn of that year excavation of the Chipping Norton tunnel was suspended, not to be resumed for seven years, and most other work came to a standstill.[9]

---

[8] *BA* 5 Nov 1874; *BG* 9 Feb, 14 Oct 1875; W. Hemmings, *The Banbury & Cheltenham Railway, vol 1* (Didcot: Wild Swan, 2004), 51-99.
[9] *BG* 7 Sept, 5 Oct 1876; Hemmings, *Banbury & Cheltenham Railway*, 65.

In November 1876 the contractor, W F Lawrence, stood down in acrimonious circumstances and on contested terms, to be replaced by his manager, Alfred Terry. Once work resumed Terry faced difficulties in paying his employees, and on 3 November 1877 his contract was terminated, ending work between King's Sutton and Hook Norton. A further Act of Parliament, which received the royal assent on 23 July 1877, permitted a diversion at Dowdeswell near Cheltenham, together with variations at Adderbury and Hook Norton, and the lengthening of the Chipping Norton tunnel. On 16 November 1877 another contractor, Henry Lovatt, was appointed to complete the railway from Bourton-on-the-Water to Cheltenham, but work was effectively suspended in November 1878, and Lovatt cancelled the contract on 21 February 1879. Nevertheless he resumed working with a new contract made in August 1879. A prediction that the line would be ready for traffic in November 1880 proved over-optimistic but on 1 June 1881 the 16¾ mile line connecting Bourton-on-the-Water with Lansdown Junction, Cheltenham was opened, with trains worked by the Great Western. Two travellers on the first train of that day, the 06.30 from Cheltenham St James, hoped to reach Epsom in time to see the Derby. Shortly afterwards, in conformity with the demands of a Board of Trade inspector, a small engine shed was built at Kingham.[10]

More than a year passed before the company contracted with Charles Eckersley Daniel to complete the line between King's Sutton and Chipping Norton. Work resumed in February 1883, and the scale of the difficulties that Daniel faced was indicated by his decision to use bricks intended for lining the tunnel to build three houses for his key workers at Chipping Norton (Nos 38/40/42 West End). With much difficulty heavy equipment was hauled through narrow lanes from the railhead at Chipping Norton to the workings around Hook Norton. The line from King's Sutton as far as Hook Norton was tested by the passage of Great Western locomotives. A Board of Trade inspector on 25 August 1884 found its condition satisfactory, subject to minor alterations in signalling and the installation of station clocks and lamps. Progress on the Hook Norton viaducts continued to be slow, and in March 1885 C E Daniel terminated his contact. Nine locomotives and other equipment were put on sale from 9 April. Agreements in July and August 1885 provided for the completion of the line by Henry Lovatt, by this time a director and the largest stockholder in the company. Several fatal accidents occurred during construction: on 3 December 1885 a gantry on top of one of the stone piers of the Hook Norton viaduct collapsed, resulting in deaths of two more men. The line was inspected in September 1886, and was judged ready to open on 18 October 1886. Further problems delayed the event until 6 April 1887, when there were neither public demonstrations nor ceremonies, and, due to minimal notice, few passengers.[11]

---

[10]   *BA* 5 Nov 1874; *BG* 5 Oct 1876, 9 Feb 1875; Hemmings, *Banbury & Cheltenham Railway*, 51.
[11]   Hemmings, *Banbury & Cheltenham Railway*, 63.

One of the two viaducts at Hook Norton.

There were discussions in 1882 whether the line should be worked from an extended King's Sutton station, as the Blenheim & Woodstock branch was worked from Kidlington, or from Banbury. In the event it was initially worked from Leamington where the Great Western then had a small engine shed west of the station – the shed on the Banbury side opened in 1906. Freight, including woollen cloth from the mill of Messrs Bliss at Chipping Norton, was also consigned initially to Leamington.[12] The passenger service to and from Kingham consisted at first of four trains a day in each direction. In 1887 the first left Leamington at 06.15, called at Banbury at 06.58, King's Sutton at 07.07, Chipping Norton at 07.50, and reached Kingham at 08.02. The last service left Kingham at 20.11, called at Banbury at 21.15, and reached Leamington at 21.55. The opening of the BCDR was probably the reason why the Great Western built a small engine shed at the south end of Banbury station in 1889. From the early years of the twentieth century up to six daily services were worked from Banbury by auto-trains. With effect from 1 July 1897 the BCDR was sold to the Great Western at a price of £450,000, no more than a quarter of the issued capital.

Traffic was sufficient at either end of the line for the Great Western to find it worthwhile to double the sections from Andoversford to Cheltenham, completed in 1903, which was also used by trains of the Midland & South Western Junction Railway, and between the junction at King's Sutton and Adderbury, completed in 1906. A new turntable, capable of accommodating a class 2301 'Dean Goods' 0-6-0 was installed at Kingham in 1904 and halts were opened between July 1906 and January 1908 at Sarsden, Rollright and Milton. The villages of Wigginton and Milcombe, both close to the line, remained without stations.[13]

The Great Western erected a board at Banbury station which proclaimed 'Change here for the Banbury and Cheltenham Line', but is not clear for whom this advice was intended. Passengers from Oxford could more easily access Chipping Norton or the western portion of the BCDR by travelling to Kingham on the OWWR, while those from Didcot or places further south could reach Cheltenham through Swindon and Gloucester. From Birmingham, and probably from Sheffield, Nottingham and Leicester, the Midland Railway offered a superior route to the spa town, and it was possible to get there from Leamington via Stratford and Worcester.

---

[12] Hemmings, *Banbury & Cheltenham Railway*, 85, 96, 99; R Griffiths & P Smith, *The Directory of British Engine Sheds, vol 1, Southern England, the Midlands, East Anglia and Wales* (Shepperton: Oxford Publishing Co, 1999), 154.

[13] Hemmings, *Banbury & Cheltenham Railway*, 119-21, 125 138-39.

Between East and West

This chapter has examined the concept of an east-west railway through Banbury and it is pertinent to examine the utility to passengers of the lines concerned. Connections between LNWR (and later LMSR) branch trains from Northampton to Blisworth and SMJR trains to Banbury were good. In 1922 a passenger catching the 08.50 from Northampton could transfer to the 09.18 from Blisworth, arriving at Banbury at 10.08. A brisk walk to the GWR station would enable him to catch the 10.37 to Kingham, arriving at 11.39, but he would have endured a long wait before the 13.14 departure for Cheltenham St James, which reached its destination at 14.16. Had the passenger departed Northampton five minutes earlier at 08.45 a slow train would have delivered him to Birmingham New Street at 10.50, with ample time to catch the Midland Railway's Bristol express at 12.02 arriving at Cheltenham at 13.04. A departure at 08.45, to Euston, would have afforded sufficient time to catch the 10.45 from Paddington reaching Cheltenham via Swindon only four minutes after the service via Banbury.

The benefits gained from the local services on the BCDR were limited. Doubtless the delivery of coal and cattle feed to goods yards closer to many customers than those in Banbury was a useful service, and it would certainly have been easier to take beasts bound for Banbury market to the cattle docks at Hook Norton, Bloxham and Adderbury than to drive them on the hoof. The passenger stations at Bloxham and Adderbury were on the edges of the villages, and journeys to Banbury were circuitous, 5¼ miles from Adderbury, taking 15 minutes, compared with 3 miles by road. The distance from Bloxham was 8¼ miles which took 28 minutes by train. The centre of Banbury was only 3½ miles away by road, and a traveller from the eastern edge of the village would probably have found it quicker to do the entire journey on foot rather than walk to the station and take the train.

The BCDR was an asset to the operators of iron ore quarries along its route (see chapter 14) but there is no evidence that the line carried significant quantities of Northamptonshire iron ore to South Wales. The most extensive workings, at Hook Norton, were operated by the ironworks company at Brymbo in North Wales, to which the obvious route was via Banbury and the Great Western main line.

The Banbury & Cheltenham line was no more fitted to be a strategic route between eastern England and Wales and the south west than the Northampton & Banbury. It was a single line railway, with few passing places. It was steeply graded with a long climb at 1 in 100 westbound from Bloxham, and a formidable ascent for eastbound trains from Kingham with sections as steep as 1 in 80 and 1 in 95. The tunnels and viaducts between Hook Norton and Chipping Norton were expensive to maintain. Most of the Great Western's express passenger and freight engines in the 1890s could use the line, but it was unable to carry the two-cylinder and four-cylinder 4-6-0s introduced after 1900.

The route of an express

Discussions with the Great Central, the North Eastern and the Barry railways led the Great Western to use the BCDR for an express service between northern England and South Wales. In consequence two spurs, envisaged in earlier plans for the BCDR, were constructed in 1906, a loop at Kingham connecting the lines from Banbury and Cheltenham and crossing the OWWR, and a spur at Hatherley that enabled trains to head south towards Gloucester. May Day 1906 saw the passage of the first *Ports-to-Ports Express* from Barry to Newcastle-upon-Tyne. (see Chapter 7). There may have been good reasons for running the 'express' by this route, but serving Gloucester and the station at Leckhampton (optimistically re-named Cheltenham South), can scarcely have compensated for the loss of potential traffic from Swindon and Oxford, and timings between Banbury and Newport would have been similar had the trains travelled via the north curve at Didcot, the Badminton route (opened in 1903) and the Severn Tunnel.

The concept of a main line from east to west through Banbury put forward in the 1850s was never realised. The NBJR carried at most three passenger trains a day, and insignificant amounts of freight. The passage of the northbound and southbound *Ports-to-Ports Expresses* gave the BCDR, twice daily, the appearance of a significant through route, although no other express services travelled that way, except when diverted. There was ironstone traffic from quarries along the line in 1914, and prospects of more, but no through traffic from Northamptonshire. A line whose passenger service consisted of no more than six daily return auto-train workings was unlikely to be profitable. The route from King's Sutton evolved into the Banbury and Chipping Norton rather than the Banbury and Cheltenham railway, and its subsequent history justified the warning issued in 1874 by Seymour Clarke, vice-chairman of the company: 'Sometimes a new Line is made to give access to a town locally important only, which being accessible through an unproductive country, can barely yield traffic enough to pay working expenses'.[14]

The sign from the East Ground Frame at Rollright on the BCDR, exhibited in the railway museum at Kidderminster.

---

[14] Hemming, *Banbury & Cheltenham Railway*, 55.

6. The economic and social impact 1850-1914

(The railway) will 'make quite a social revolution in the district which until the opening of this line may be said to have been almost cut off from the outside world'.

R B Dockray, 1 May 1850.[1]

Edward Cobb, banker and solicitor, and one of the wisest of Victorian Banburians, observed in 1852 that 'The Oxford Road is no longer the chief entrance into Banbury. Now it is from the bridge….' Others argued that Banbury could not 'swallow day after day the heaps and heaps of goods that both railways pour into the town'. The sense that the railways had re-oriented the town was reflected by the positioning of the new town hall, opened on 24 October 1854, whose frontage greeted visitors progressing into the town from the station.[2]

Topography

The Great Western's route through Banbury passed through the meadows alongside the Cherwell and the Buckinghamshire Railway terminus lay nearby. Neither made a direct impact on Banbury's urban fabric comparable to those inflicted on Shifnal or Knaresborough by the intrusion of viaducts, or on Belper or Wellington by deep cuttings. The passage of the Great Western through the meadows dictated the cessation of the Banbury Races after the meeting of 1846 and also brought about the demolition of Waterloo, an accumulation of about fifteen houses at the Northamptonshire end of the bridge over the River Cherwell, regarded as 'a lot of disreputable inhabitants, lodging houses and otherwise of the lowest character'. To Northamptonshire gentry Waterloo was 'a great public nuisance', since it lay outside the remit of the Banbury Borough police. It included several lodging houses accustomed to accommodating criminals, notably that of Thomas and Bridget Ward, natives of County Mayo, who settled in Banbury about 1836 and on census night in 1841 sheltered 21 lodgers, eight of Irish and eight of foreign birth. The Wards subsequently moved to Rag Row on Warwick Road.[3]

---

[1] M Robbins, 'From R B Dockray's Diary', *JTH*, vol 7 (1965-66), 8.
[2] *BG* 15 Jan 1852; B Trinder, ed, *A Victorian MP and his Constituents* (Banbury Historical Society 8, 1969), 86-87; B Trinder, *Victorian Banbury* (Chichester: Phillimore, 1982), 103.
[3] Trinder, *Victorian Banbury*, 10; B Trinder, 'Banbury's Victorian Lodging Houses', *C&CH* vol 16 (2004), 143-45; *BG* 21 May, 4 June 1846; G Herbert, *Shoemaker's Window* (3rd edn, Banbury: Gulliver Press, 1979), 80; B Little, *The Changing Faces of Grimsbury* (Witney: Boyd, 1999), 19.

Railway builders: the Great Western

The first impact of railways on Banbury came from the navvies who built them. The Great Western line through Banbury was constructed slowly. The first sections were staked out in September 1845, but work had not started by the following March, and Charles Saunders, secretary of the GWR, found it expedient to offer a public explanation for the delays. Work eventually began in May 1846, at Spital Farm and Twyford to the south, and at Cropredy and Hardwick to the north, and on three further sites in the following month. Navvies rioted at Harbury in the summer of 1847, apparently because they had not been paid. Activity had re-commenced by May 1849 when the tranquillity of the Cherwell Valley was disturbed by thunderous explosions of gunpowder as navvies excavated the cutting north of Cropredy.[4]

'King' class 4-6-0 No 6001 'King Edward VII' climbs Cropredy Bank, scene of momentous explosions in May 1849, with the 16.10 Paddington–Birkenhead on a summer evening in 1961.

The railway from Oxford to Banbury was opened in September 1850, and census returns suggest that most of the line to Leamington had been completed by the spring of 1851. Just over forty navvies remained resident in Banbury on

---

[4] *BG* 15 May 1846; 4 June 1846; 19 Aug, 2 Sep 1847; 10 May, 28 June 1849; B Trinder, 'Navvies in Banburyshire', *C&CH*, vol 19 (2013), 34-52.

30 March of that year, possibly engaged in doubling the track from Oxford. Only 192 were recorded along the route in the parishes of Bourton, Cropredy, Farnborough, Mollington, Claydon, Fenny Compton, Burton Dassett (Knighton township), Southam, Bishop's Itchington and Harbury suggesting that activity was winding down.[5] By comparison, 898 navvies were working on 30 March 1851 on the Great Northern Railway in the five Lincolnshire parishes north of Peterborough.

Huts were a feature of every railway construction project. This example, at Helmdon on the Great Central London Extension, was used by a branch of the Railway Mission.
Record Office for Leicestershire, Leicester and Rutland

The contractors or perhaps the railway company provided traditional shanties or huts at Fenny Compton. Seventy-six navvies remained in the parish on 30 March 1851. Eleven huts, alongside others that were no longer occupied, provided accommodation near the cutting alongside the canal tunnel for 68 people, 31 navvies, two blacksmiths, an engine driver and 34 dependents. Some had been recruited locally, but others came from Avebury, Bath, Bristol, Chelmsford, Norwich, Plymouth, Wells-next-the-Sea and Whitstable. Six more households

---

[5] Census evidence from TNA HO 107, 1734, 2077.

located 'Near the Tunnel' probably occupied similar huts. Two navvies, one of their wives and a contractor's agent were accommodated at the *Victoria* beer house near the tunnel. Sixteen navvies were staying with local people, and four, three locally-born and one from Somerset, appear to have rented houses in the village where they accommodated their families with some fellow workers. The contractor's timekeeper had a house on Wharf Road where he ran a butchery business alongside his official duties.

Abandoned navvies' shanties were also a feature of the landscape of Harbury in March 1851. The census enumerator recorded 36 unoccupied 'railway houses' or 'railway cottages', noting that 'Most of the uninhabited houses in this district are houses belonging to the Birmingham & Oxford Railway Company'. Forty-five construction workers were living in Harbury with 108 dependents. Thirty navvies with 54 dependents were living in Cropredy, and 19 men with 39 dependents at Claydon, but the census does not mention huts in either parish.

Most of the railway from Banbury to Leamington was clearly completed by March 1851. The men who used gunpowder to create the cutting north of Cropredy in 1849 were probably engaging two years later in similar pyrotechnics elsewhere. By 1851 the area around the railway appears to have been a slowly depopulating landscape, with scattered huts, most of them unoccupied, and a litter of life-expired tools and discarded domestic furnishings.

Table 6:1: Construction workers on the Banbury-Leamington line 1851

Parish	Number of navvies & associated workers	Dependents	Total
Cropredy + Mollington & Bourton	30	54	84
Farnborough	11	8	19
Claydon	19	39	58
Fenny Compton	76	86	162
Burton Dassett (Knightcote)	8	1	9
Harbury + Bishop's Itchington	45	108	153
Southam	3	19	22
Total	192	315	507

The specialist staff on the project included a civil engineer, two contractors, two agents, two timekeepers, six blacksmiths, two bricklayers, a cashier and an engine driver, but the majority were simply recorded as 'railway labourers'. Navvying was necessarily an occupation for young men, and the median age of those recorded on this line was just over 30. Some were seasoned railway builders.

Thomas Simpers, living in a hut at Harbury, came from Lincolnshire but had children born at Chippenham and in Kent. James Lewis, a Gloucestershire-born railway bricklayer, also living at Harbury, had children born along the line of the Birmingham & Gloucester Railway, at Chester, and at three different places in Kent. Railway construction offered opportunities to strong and ambitious country boys. The youngest employed on this line were two twelve-year-olds living in Fenny Compton. The oldest were William Arkell, a Warwickshire-born navvy staying at Claydon, who was 70, and 71-year-old John Fitzgerald, from County Limerick, who lived in one of the huts at Fenny Compton. The contractors had followed customary practice by recruiting men from the counties through which their line passed. Ninety, almost half of those recorded, were born in Oxfordshire, Warwickshire and Northamptonshire. Of the remainder, 84 were natives of 22 English counties, of whom 19 came from Buckinghamshire, the majority from the south of the county alongside the Great Western main line. Eleven were from Essex and nine from Somerset. The 192 included four Scots and a Welshman but only three Irishmen.

The contractor for the Birmingham & Oxford line was John Mitchell, an Irishman and a bachelor, who in 1851 was living in Farnborough, cared for by his mother and two domestic servants. He employed his brother-in-law, Thomas Flynn, as a clerk. He was probably related to David Mitchell, an agent on the line, who was living at Bourton Mill. After the line was completed John Mitchell spent several years at Bourton, but he had moved away by 1861, and died in 1873 in the Australian gold-mining town of Maldon, Victoria.[6]

Railway builders: East and West

The census of 1871 records the men who built the NBJR and the EWJR.[7] The line from Towcester to Cockley Brake was constructed by Aird & Son, the company established in 1848 by John Aird, superintendent of the Phoenix Gas Co works at Greenwich. He diversified from the construction of gas works into general civil engineering, and from 1851 his son, the subsequently distinguished Sir John Aird, was a member of the firm. His works included the removal of the Crystal Palace from Hyde Park to Sydenham, the Royal Albert Hall, the Covent Garden Opera House and the Aswan Dam.

In 1871 some 128 of Aird's men with more than 200 dependents were living along the lineside, 70 of them in Wappenham, more than a dozen each in Greatworth, Helmdon and Marston St Lawrence, and the remainder scattered through Abthorpe, Bradden, Green's Norton, Slapton, Sulgrave and Weedon Lois. No navvies were living in Towcester, although Joseph Crabtree, traffic manager of the NBJR, and an engine driver were resident there. The influx raised

---

[6] *BG* 6 May 1873.
[7] Census evidence from TNA RG 10, 1469, 1470, 1471, 1473, 3217, 3218.

the population of Wappenham from 567 in 1861 to 627 in 1871, but it slumped to 484 by 1881. A dozen railway builders from as far away as Suffolk, Devon and London were householders in Wappenham, as were two locally-born men, a 24-year-old navvy from Syresham, and the husband of the mistress of one of the village's two lace schools who had found work with the contractor. Other navvies lodged in 21 households in Wappenham, four with shoemakers, five with farm labourers, with the village's two publicans, and with Edward Bodley, shopkeeper and country carrier. The population of Helmdon rose from 602 in 1861 to 656 in 1871, declining to 529 ten years later.

Earthworks of the former NBJR west of Helmdon station constructed by the navvies described in this chapter.

Five navvies became householders, accommodating four fellow workers, while the remaining seven lodged with farm labourers. Of twelve railway builders in Marston St Lawrence, eight were natives of the parish. Greatworth's population increased from 180 to 243 between 1861 and 1871, and fell away to 207 by 1881. Five navvies became householders while the others were in lodgings. One John Turner who lived in Helmdon Road followed a career characteristic of navvying. Born at Twyford, Bucks, he married a wife from nearby Poundon and was living there in 1848-49 when he may have worked on the Buckinghamshire Railway's line to Oxford. He appears to have spent the next ten years building railways in London before joining Aird's labour force in Northamptonshire.

Of the 128 men working on the line in 1871, 60 were married, four widowed and 64 unmarried. The pattern of recruitment followed that observed on other lines. A substantial proportion of the men were recruited locally, some 33 from Northamptonshire parishes along the route. The remainder included men from 25 English counties, and one Scot, but, contrary to received wisdom, no Irishmen. The labour force was predominantly young, with a median age of 33.

The construction of the Kineton-Fenny Compton line was directed by another distinguished engineer, Thomas Russell Crampton. Born in Broadstairs, he worked as a young man on the GWR, and in 1843 patented what came to be called the Crampton locomotive, whose characteristics were a low boiler and large driving wheels on an axle behind the firebox. Its success was perhaps due more to its wide steam passages, generous bearing surfaces and large heating surfaces rather than to its unorthodox configuration. Some 320 were built, only 45 of them for railways in the United Kingdom. None is preserved in Britain, but a French example is one of the treasures of the railway museum at Mulhouse. From 1848 Crampton practised as a civil engineer, building railways in the Ottoman Empire and a waterworks in Berlin, and laying the submarine telegraph under the Straits of Dover. He constructed the waterworks in his native Broadstairs, now a museum, where he is commemorated by the Crampton Tower. Much of the work for which he was responsible on the EWJR was probably undertaken by his sons, Thomas Hellas Crampton, who lodged in Bridge Street, Kineton, and John George Crampton, who had accommodation on the Warwick Road in that village. The contractor was William Death, a Suffolk man. According to the census he employed 130 men which accords closely with the 136 identified in the area in enumerators' returns. In 1881 his son, William Price Death, was station master at Fenny Compton. Work on the two sections of the EWJR completed in 1873 was directed by a Scots civil engineer, James B Burke who lodged at Butlers Marston.[8]

Some 136 navvies were living in the parishes between Fenny Compton and Stratford-upon-Avon on census day in 1871, of whom five were in Stratford, 76 in Kineton and Butlers Marston, three at Gaydon, eight at Burton Dasset, and 25 at Fenny Compton, together with 15 at Harbury and four at Claydon and Cropredy who probably walked to their work. Living with the navvies were 175 dependents. The contractor erected a shed at Kineton which was manned overnight by 16-year-old John Plester from Deddington. One of the engine drivers, John Elliott, living in Kineton, was, like many locomotive men, a native of Co Durham, from Felling. The locomotive that Plester maintained and Elliott drove was probably the 0-6-0 saddle tank built by Manning Wardle of which a photograph appeared in the *Railway Magazine* in 1910.[9]

---

[8] Trinder, 'Navvies', 46-47.
[9] *RM* vol 26 (1910), 265-76; J M Dunn, *The Stratford-upon-Avon & Midland Junction Railway* (Lingfield: Oakwood, 1952), 20.

The labour force was similar in many respects to that building the Northampton and Banbury line. Of 136 men, 61 (45%) were married, five (4%) were widowed, and 70 (51%) unmarried. Navvies were accommodated by twenty householders in Kineton, of whom eleven were farm labourers, and two slept at one of the village pubs. The workers on both projects had a median age of about 33, and the proportion of men recruited from local parishes was 26 per cent in each case. On the EWJR there were men from 24 English countries other than Warwickshire, and just one Irishmen. Amongst those resident in the Market Place in Kineton was John Fisher, aged 42, a native of Witney who had married a wife from Fenny Compton. The birthplaces of their children, Reading, Salisbury, Canterbury and Aylesbury reflect the navvy's itinerant life.[10]

Railwaymen in Banbury

From the 1850s railwaymen comprised a significant proportion of the workforce in Banbury. The census of 1851 recorded 86 railway workers but at least 40 of them appear to have been navvies involved in doubling the track from Oxford or putting the last touches to the line to Leamington. Fifteen were living in lodging houses and beer houses and another seven were accommodated by James Walker, an Islip-born navvy with a house in Upper Cherwell Street. The census listed 13 enginemen, all of whom probably worked for the LNWR. They included an engine fitter, a 40-year old native of Newcastle-upon-Tyne who had previously been employed at Wolverton, and two footplate men from Co Durham. Another driver was a 34-year-old Kentishman, who had lived in south Lancashire, and, for several years, at Camden Town. The birthplaces of the children of an inspector, Burnham (Bucks), Reading, Wootton Bassett, Bristol, Ealing and Basingstoke, suggest an itinerant career on the Great Western. Several railway 'policemen', who carried out signalling duties, were recruited locally, while a 55-year-old Polish migrant who lived with his family in Cross Cherwell Street served as a railway night watchman.

Table 6: 2: Railway employees living in Banbury (including Neithrop, Grimsbury, Warkworth). Source 1851 census: HO 107; RG 9; RG 10; RG 11; RG12; RG13

	1851	1861	1871	1881	1891	1901
Construction	44	20	11	2	1	4
Permanent Way	4	1	5	14	12	28
Operations	25	29	30	37	62	99
Locomotive men	13	4	7	12	16	35
Sub-contractors	-	-	2	2	1	4
Others	-	-	2	7	1	5
Totals	86	54	57	74	93	175

---

[10] Trinder, 'Navvies', 47-48.

For the next twenty years the number of railwaymen in Banbury varied between fifty and sixty. There were 57 in 1861 of whom twenty railway labourers, distinguished by the enumerators from platelayers, appear to have been navvies. Eleven of the twenty were staying at the *Old George*, the *Jolly Waterman* and the *Britannia*, which suggests that they were passing through. The GWR station master was William Lucy, a 38-year-old native of Wotton-under-Edge whose family shared Cherwell House with a railway policeman. The census recorded only four footplate men, and no shunters or pointsmen. The situation in 1871 was similar. There were 57 railwaymen, eleven of whom, staying in beer houses or lodging houses, appear to have been navvies. The GWR station master, George Harris, then 39 years old, was a native of Brentford, but his wife was from Wrexham and his children were born in Southall, Bilston and Wednesbury, suggesting an itinerant Great Western career. He shared Cherwell House with a Gloucestershire-born inspector of railway works. Just one man was employed as a shunter, suggesting that little marshalling of trains took place at Banbury.

During the 1870s there was an increase in the railway labour force, which by 1881 numbered 74, of whom only two appear to have been navvies. Pointsmen were now called railway signalmen, of whom the census recorded five, and the presence of two wagon repairers reveals a new activity. The 1891 census recorded 93 railwaymen, none of them navvies apart from a pauper in the workhouse. There was a small increase in the number of locomen from 12 to 16, probably reflecting the opening of the GWR engine shed in 1889. There were now six signalmen, four shunters and a pointsman, 16 porters, 12 clerks, seven draymen and carmen, and five wagon examiners or greasers. The presence of a GWR bus conductor shows that the company was concerned to link the station with the town centre. A railway bookstall was managed by Henry Reynolds who lived in Merton Street.

The opening of the branch from Woodford stimulated further growth in the railway workforce which increased by 85 per cent to 175 in 1901. None are likely to have been Great Central employees since the branch was worked from Woodford. The number of locomen increased from 16 to 35, and there were 16 shunters and 26 porters, the first recorded ticket collector, and a railway cattle porter. There was still a railway omnibus driver, the manageress of a new railway refreshment room was lodging in West Street, and there were five railway pensioners. There had been an influx of engine drivers and firemen from other parts of the Great Western system including Reading, Bristol, Wiltshire, Somerset, Gloucestershire, Aberdare, Lye in the Black Country and St Blazey in Cornwall.

Table 6:3: Birthplaces of Banbury railwaymen

	1851	1861	1871	1881	1891	1901
Banbury/Neithrop	1	3	3	7	14	20
Grimsbury	-	1	-	4	6	20
Hinterland	10	15	14	13	14	27
Surrounding counties	29	13	21	28	39	58
London and SE	10	5	4	3	4	10
East Anglia	1	3	1	3	-	1
S and SW England	12	7	9	9	9	18
East Midlands	-	1	1	1	-	1
West Midlands	2	1	2	-	4	11
Northern England	6	4	2	2	1	4
Wales	4	-	1	3	1	3
Scotland	6	1	-	-	-	-
Ireland	-	-	-	-	-	1
Overseas	1	-	-	-	-	-
Not known	4	-	-	1	1	1
Totals	86	54	57	74	93	175

The railways drew many migrants to Banbury. The 86 railwaymen in 1851 included six Scots, four Welshman, a Pole and men born in 20 English counties extending from Devon to Northumberland. Only eleven, 13 per cent, were locally-born. The proportion of men born in Banbury or its hinterland subsequently increased, reaching 38 per cent, or 67 individuals, in 1901, but the majority of railwaymen, 108 or 62 per cent, were still incomers. A consistent feature of Banbury's nineteenth-century railwaymen was their youth. Their median age was 30 in 1851, rose to 32 in 1861 and to 34 in 1871, but in the following three censuses it was 31, 33 and 32, the 1901 figure excluding five pensioners.

Terraced houses were being built in 1850 immediately west of the newly-opened railways. Construction of houses in Upper and Lower Cherwell streets, linking Bridge Street with Fish Street, had begun by August 1843, 32 craftsmen and small shopkeepers living in the area were listed in the directory for 1848, and by 1851 the development was extending into Windsor Street. Unsurprisingly the area proved attractive to railwaymen, 35 of whom, 41 per cent of those in the town, were living there in 1851, but in that year Banbury Liberals sponsored the establishment of a Freehold Land Society to develop a 13-acre site in Grimsbury, north of the turnpike road to Middleton Cheney. The roads and drains were completed by 1853 when the first plots were allocated to shareholders by ballot. Development was slow, and many houses were constructed by speculators rather than by owner occupiers. The estate stimulated the building of other housing in Grimsbury, ribbon development on the road to Middleton Cheney and along the

Causeway to Warkworth and the laying-out of Duke Street, Merton Street and Gibbs Road. Grimsbury became the residential area of choice for Banbury's railwaymen, half of whom were living there in 1861. By 1871 the proportion had increased to 70 per cent, by 1881 to 77 per cent, by 1891 to 84 per cent, reaching 85 per cent (149 individuals) in 1901. Meanwhile no more than four railway families were recorded in the Cherwell Street area in any census after 1851.[11]

The growth in activity following the opening of the Great Central branch from Woodford in 1900 meant that for three decades railwaymen comprised the largest occupational group in Banbury. After the opening of the aluminium factory in 1931 they probably remained the second largest group until the contractions of the 1960s. Their presence could be seen on the streets, as drivers and fireman made their way to the engine sheds, on foot or on bicycles, usually carrying metal boxes containing meals to be eaten on duty. Railwaymen were prominent in trades unions, the Railway Mission and the St John Ambulance Brigade. Locomen took responsibility for their own training through mutual improvement classes. The Banbury branch of the Amalgamated Society of Railway Servants (from 1913 the National Union of Railwaymen, subsequently RMT) held its first meeting at the *Bell Inn*, Middleton Road in the late 1890s, and had 38 members by 1903. The local branch of the Amalgamated Society of Locomotive Engineers and Fireman (ASLEF) was formed at about the same time and met at the *Elephant and Castle* on the approach to Merton Street station. It had between 50 and 60 members by 1913. Several railwaymen were amongst the founders of the Banbury Local Labour Party in 1921.[12]

Railway business

Railways enhanced regional links, and it was possible by 1900 easily to travel from Banbury to the surrounding market towns of the same order of size, to Brackley, Buckingham, Towcester, Chipping Norton, Bicester, Stratford-upon-Avon and Rugby, as well as to the county towns of Oxford, Northampton and Warwick. The ability to reach London easily was obviously important, although evidence of how London services were used is largely anecdotal. The railways enabled country people to travel to Banbury's Michaelmas Fair, and took many Banburians to St Giles's Fair at Oxford. The initial effect of railways on Banbury's country carrying trade was a decline in the number of visiting carriers, principally of those travelling from places directly served by railway. The number of weekly visits from Brackley carriers fell from eleven to four, of Buckingham

---

[11] Trinder, *Victorian Banbury*, 98-100; S Gosling, '57-239 Causeway, Banbury', in Paine, C, *et al*, 'Working Class Housing in Oxfordshire', *Oxoniensia*, vol 43 (1978), 201-04.

[12] J Drayton, *On the Footplate* (Truro: Bradford Barton, 1976), 50; W Potts, *Banbury through One Hundred Years* (Banbury Guardian, 1942), 108-10; J Hodgkins, *Over the Hills to Glory* (Southend: Clifton Press, 1978), 136-46, 177-92.

carriers from six to two, and of those from Cropredy from thirteen to six. At the same time the market's success drew in carriers from villages on the periphery of the hinterland, from Ladbrook, Ardley, Cherrington and Napton, and during the 1860s while the number of carriers visiting Banbury remained more or less stable, the number of weekly journeys increased, and was widely quoted at around four hundred by 1870.[13]

Few records remain of the business conducted at individual railway stations, and only occasional items in the press illuminate the ways in which the companies in Banbury generated revenue. In 1866 Banbury's GWR station master, H R Brown, absconded towards Australia with some of the takings from the station. He was apprehended at Deal with money from the three largest freight accounts, those of the Britannia Works, Hunt Edmunds's brewery and the builders J and T Davies. At a meeting in 1869 Bernhard Samuelson stated that the Great Western's annual revenue at Banbury was £29,000, of which £13,000 came from passenger traffic. His own company, the Britannia Works had trebled the amount of traffic it provided since 1864. The scale of that traffic was reflected by the construction from 1870 of a tramway, linking the two parts of the works with a railside despatch depot south of the station. The importance of the passenger service to London was shown in 1869 when Banbury businessmen protested when the GWR decided to cease stopping the 08.40 train to Paddington in order to meet competition from the LNWR for traffic between Birmingham and London.[14]

The work of distributing from the goods depot consignments for Banbury shopkeepers and craftsmen, and collecting goods originating in Banbury for distant destinations, was done by agents. The decision of Messrs Pickfords to transfer their sundries business from canal to rail in 1847 is reckoned to have been the key element in the development of railway traffic in small consignments. Thomas Golby of 24 Bridge Street was agent both for Pickfords and the LNWR, and in 1861 employed seven men and a boy. In 1856 parcels for the LNWR were also handled at the *Red Lion* in High Street, while the agent for the GWR was John Drinkwater of the *White Lion*. Similar arrangements, with minor changes of personnel, continued for the rest of the century. In 1906 Cave & Son handled Great Western business from 8 Bridge Street. The LNWR operated their own delivery service, picking up goods consignments but not parcels from No 24 Bridge Street, while other business was transacted on behalf of a firm called Foster's Express from No 24 High Street.[15]

---

[13] B Trinder, 'Banbury: Metropolis of Carriers' Carts', *C&CH* vol 18 (2011), 210-43.
[14] *BG* 11 Feb 1866; *BA* 6 May 1869, 24 Feb 1870.
[15] Evidence from Rusher's *Banbury Lists and Directories*, and from census returns.

Coal

Samuel Sidney recorded in 1851 that the Buckinghamshire Railway had reduced the price of the 150,000 tons of coal per annum used by the inhabitants of Banbury from 22s to 15s per ton. Nevertheless for the remainder of the nineteenth century the railways competed with canal boats to supply coal to Banbury. Canal boats could readily bring coal from traditional suppliers alongside the Coventry Canal, and from the Moira Colliery in north Leicestershire. Table 6.4 shows that throughout the nineteenth century the number of coal dealers based alongside the canal exceeded, if only slightly, the number at railway wharfs. More coal was unloaded in the extensive yard of the LNWR station than in the GWR sidings, although some of it was probably brought to Banbury by the GWR. There are some indications of the origins of the coal. From 1900 a firm called the Staffordshire Coal Co was based in the LNWR yard, and in 1860 Richard Brazier was selling coal from Bennerley in Nottinghamshire from his yard in Cherwell Street. Collieries supplying coal at King's Sutton, Hook Norton and Chipping Norton included Littleton on Cannock Chase, opened in 1877, Baddesley (Ensor) west of Atherstone, where three shafts were sunk in the 1850s, and Binley near Coventry, opened in 1911.[16]

Table 6:4: Coal Merchants in Banbury 1853-1906
Source: *Rusher's Banbury Directories*.

Year	At canal wharfs	At railway yards	Elsewhere	Total
1853	7	5	12	24
1860	9	4	19	32
1870	8	5	14	27
1880	10	6	19	35
1890	9	6	18	33
1900	9	7	13	29
1906	8	7	8	23

---

[16] W Hemmings, P Karau & C Turner, *The Banbury & Cheltenham Railway, vol 2* (Didcot: Wild Swan, 2004), 337; S Sidney, *Rides on Railways* (London: Orr, 1851, ed B Trinder, Chichester: Phillimore, 1973), 32-33.

Excursions

One of the most significant contributions of the railways to popular culture came through excursion trains. The Buckinghamshire Railway opened at a time particularly opportune for the promotion of excursions, and more than 2,600 tickets were issued at Merton Street station to people travelling to London for the Great Exhibition between 5 May and 3 August 1851.[17]

Soon afterwards an acrimonious debate about excursion trains attracted national attention. Sabbatarian feelings ran high amongst some Banburians, who objected in 1849 that Post Office employees worked on Sundays, and supported a petition early in 1856 against the opening on Sundays of the Crystal Palace at Sydenham. The controversy began with the publication of a pamphlet in the autumn of 1855 by the minister of the Independent (Congregationalist) chapel, Joseph Parker, a 25-year-old sparsely-educated Northumbrian, who spent five years at Banbury and secured the construction of a prestigious chapel in South Bar. His fellow ministers regarded him as eccentric. Parker wrote in his pamphlet that 'If we thoroughly knew the history of the Sunday excursionists, we should find amongst them the dirtiest, silliest, laziest and poorest of the working population'. He repeated his claims in a sermon and found the town adorned with hostile posters. Subsequently he described women who travelled on Sunday excursions: 'with very few exceptions they are accustomed to licentiousness, robbery and drunkenness. Do they not know that Sunday excursionists are likely to serve their demoralising designs? Of course they do!' Parker was satirised at a mock trial held at the *Wheatsheaf* on 18/19 April 1856, at which his opponents included secularists, such as the radical newsagent William Bunton, and a group of Unitarians who had espoused the teachings of the American theologian Theodore Parker.[18]

Railway excursions were organised in several ways in the 1850s and 60s. An excursion could be an offer of cheap seats on timetabled trains. It could be a special train put on by a railway company. It might be sponsored by an agent such as Henry Marcus or John Houlston, or it could be chartered by a local organisation, which in Banbury might be the Britannia Ironworks, the Mechanics' Institute, the Temperance Society, the Conservative Club, the Co-operative Society, the Oddfellows or the Ancient Order of Foresters. Excursionists travelling outwards by special trains were sometimes given tickets which enabled them to stay for several days at their destinations and return on service trains. Some well-supported excursions travelled short distances. Within

---

[17] *NH* 18 Aug 1851. For the development of excursion traffic in a national context, see S Major, *Early Victorian Railway Excursions* (Barnsley: Pen & Sword, 2015); A & E Jordan, *Away for the Day* (Kettering: Silver Link, 1991).

[18] B Trinder, 'Joseph Parker, Sabbatarianism and the Parson's Street Infidels', *C&CH*, vol 1 (1960), 25-30; Trinder, *Victorian Banbury*, 111-13.

three months of the opening of the Buckinghamshire Railway in 1850 crowds of Banburians took the train to see the flower show at Buckingham. In September 1856 700 people waited at the station to join 800 others on an excursion to St Giles's Fair, Oxford which originated at Wolverhampton. In 1870 the Royal Show was held in Oxford, and was visited by 600 from the Britannia Works, 200 from the foundry of Barrows & Stewart, and by parties from three breweries and the gasworks. Excursion trains sometimes ran on the humble Northampton & Banbury Junction Railway, which in 1876 took 70 members of the Banbury Sunday School Union to see Nicholas Hawksmoor's great house at Easton Neston near Towcester, and in 1888 carried members of the Conservative Club bound for Llandudno by an unlikely route through Helmdon, Towcester and Blisworth.[19]

By 1854 the Great Western was offering excursions to Portsmouth and the Isle of Wight, which involved changing trains at Basingstoke where there was a break of gauge, as did visits to Brighton and Dover, advertised in the following year. In 1857 Banburians were offered the opportunity to stay in Calais or Boulogne. A newspaper commented in May that 'it is seldom that this town and neighbourhood have as many opportunities afforded them of making cheap excursions in almost every direction'. Tickets were available to travel to Weymouth and Dorchester, to Shrewsbury, Chester and Liverpool, and to an art exhibition in London. At the end of June the Mechanics' Institute organised an excursion to Warwick Castle and the newspaper observed 'In the good old times and even within a few years boys and girls were shut up in the little towns and villages in which they were born till they were close upon 20 years of age, but now excursion trips are announced and we see them preparing for jaunts to London, Portsmouth, Manchester or Warwick without timidity or unnecessary excitement'.[20]

Excursions took Banburians to national events, to the Royal Show at Canterbury in 1860, to a performance of Haydn's *The Creation* at the Crystal Palace in 1861; to Epsom for the Derby in 1864, and in most years through the 1870s to the Oxford & Cambridge Boat Race. The choice of destinations was to some extent constrained by the networks of the GWR and LNWR, and the relationships they enjoyed with other companies. The Great Western had no difficulty in running excursions through to the south coast, but Blackpool, the most significant destination for excursions from many parts of the north and midlands, seems never to have featured in advertising for excursions at Banbury.[21]

---

[19] Trinder, *Victorian Banbury*, 137; *BG* 29 June 1876; *BA* 28 June 1888.
[20] *BG* 1 Jly 1854; 28 May 1857; 25 June 1857; *BA* 13 Sep 1855, 9 Jly 1857.
[21] *BA* 5 Jly 1860; *BH* 25 Apl 1861; *BG* 19 May 1864, 18 Mar 1875, 22 Mar 1877.

Long distance trips attracted plentiful custom – 109 Banburians went on a Great Western trip to Liverpool in September 1857, for example, 250 went to Birmingham to witness a royal visit in June 1858, and 130 travelled on Good Friday 1860 'to eat their Hot Cross Buns in Cockneydom'. Short journeys continued to be popular. The number travelling to St Giles's Fair in 1858 was less than in the previous year, but still totalled 560, and 1,200 went to Oxford in 1863 to see a review of Volunteer soldiers. The excursions organised for the Britannia Works in the 1870s were ambitious. Portsmouth was the destination in 1877 for 700 foundrymen and their families, some of whom had never previously seen the sea. The following year the special train left Banbury at 06.40 with 800 excursionists and by noon they were viewing The Needles from steamers. In 1880 1,200 people were conveyed to Weymouth where they inspected Bernhard Samuelson's yacht, after cheering while passing through the station at Frome, the constituency for which his son Henry Bernhard Samuelson was MP.[22]

Some members of the Mechanics' Institute made studious preparations for their trips, reading and compiling notes about their destinations, which included Malvern in 1865, Windsor in 1862 and 1870, and Ashridge Park in 1866. In 1861 working men proposing to travel to Paris to see the International Exhibition were taking lessons from a Frenchman resident in Banbury to enable them to converse with French working men whom they might meet.[23]

Most of the agencies that sponsored excursions also arranged public lectures, and the railways enabled lecturers with national reputations, such as George Dawson, Albert Smith and Henry Vincent, to visit Banbury, in the 1850s and '60s when the popularity of the public lecture was at its height. A newspaper commented in 1859 that 'the working classes now enjoy opportunities of hearing lectures, amusing or instructive as the case may be, of which their fathers never dreamed'[24].

Stations in Banburyshire

The inhabitants of King's Sutton in 1851, when the village lacked a station, included a railway agent, the wives of a railway contractor and a railway inspector, and five navvies, who were probably engaged in doubling the track. There were no railwaymen in the parish in 1861, but six locally-born platelayers were recorded ten years later. The station opened in 1872, and by 1881 Bloxham-born Edward Hermon, then aged 31, was stationmaster, supervising eight platelayers and a signalman. There were 16 railway employees in King's Sutton in 1891, and 19 in 1901, when Hermon was still stationmaster, doubtless with responsibilities for the ironstone traffic from nearby sidings.[25]

---

[22] *BG* 1 Oct 1857, 17 June, 9 Sep 1858, 12 Apl 1860, 26 June 1863; Trinder, *Victorian Banbury*, 137.
[23] *BG* 28 Mar 1861, 17 Jly 1862, 22 June 1865, 19 Jly 1866; *BA* 21 Jly 1870.
[24] Trinder, *Victorian Banbury*, 139-42; *BA* 11 Oct 1959.
[25] R Humm, 'King's Sutton Station', *C&CH*, vol 5 (1973), 96. See also chapter 14.

In Aynho, where the GWR acquired land from the Cartwright family of Aynhoe Park, construction of the railway began in 1846. The following year William Cartwright was fearful that the navvies might take game and in 1849 one of them was charged at Northampton Assize with stealing a sheep. Sir Thomas Cartwright was annoyed that the railway purchased the *Alfred's Head* pub from the Oxford Canal Company and was expecting him to buy it since 'public convenience requires that a small Inn or Public House should be established there with sufficient stabling to enable travellers to put up their horses & vehicles, and the innkeeper to keep a fly or two or a gig and a fly'. He told his agent that the railway company could not be trusted.

The passenger station at Aynho opened in 1850, and the goods depot two years later. The Revd William Cotton Risley of Deddington reveals in his diary that he soon began to use the station, two miles down the hill, for journeys to Oxford and London - it was later re-named *Aynho for Deddington*. A community of traders grew up around the station and the adjacent canal wharf. The railway staff in 1861 comprised two porters and a policeman (or signalman). Henry Wrighton, then aged 20, had set up a brickworks nearby, which impressed the word 'AYNHO' on its products. By 1871 the *King Alfred's Head* had been renamed the *Great Western Arms*, and its landlord, Richard Howe, traded as a coal merchant. The railway staff comprised two policeman and a porter. In 1881 Joseph Souter, from Eltham, Kent, was stationmaster, managing three platelayers, two porters, and a signalman. In 1891 Henry Wrighton was living at Brickyard Cottage, and Richard Howe still kept the *Great Western Arms*. In 1901 there were four railwaymen at the station, one of whom, a porter, was a son of Henry Wrighton, and the 80-year-old Richard Howe was still landlord of the *Great Western Arms*, assisted in his coal business by two sons. In 1867 the Cartwrights leased a field near the station to Paxton & Clark, auctioneers, for use as cattle market which flourished and held its 450th sale in 1904, when a slip carriage attached to a fast down train brought buyers to Aynho station. The market was still being held in the 1920s.[26]

Richard Longhurst, a railway contractor, was living in Somerton in 1851, together with five navvies. The station opened in 1855, with a siding serving a goods yard and cattle dock. Within the next five years a nearby farmhouse was adapted as a public house, the *Railway Tavern*, by a locally-born farmer, John Collingridge, who also traded as a coal merchant. By 1871 the pub and the coal agency had been taken over by Frederick Walton whose family were still running the businesses in 1901.

---

[26] N Cooper, *Aynho: A Northamptonshire Village* (BHS 29, 1984), 227, 234, 237, 263; G Smedley-Stevenson, ed, *Mid-Victorian Squarson: the diaries of William Cotton Risley 1849-69* (BHS 32, 2012), *passim*.

The station at Cropredy lay south of the village and most of those employed there lived in the township of Great Bourton. In 1861 a Devonian stationmaster supervised four GWR policeman, a 17-year-old porter and a labourer. In 1871 the stationmaster was 31-year-old, Culworth-born William Ward whose staff included five platelayers and a ganger, two policeman, a 16-year-old porter, and a gateman controlling the Mill Lane level crossing. The level crossing at Claydon was supervised by William Thompson, then aged 54, a native of Co Durham who had been paralysed for seven years, probably as a result of an industrial accident. He remained at Claydon ten years later. Ward was still in charge of Cropredy station in 1901, by which time his workforce comprised 14 platelayers, two signalmen and a lad porter.

The opening of the BCDR in 1887 stimulated employment at Adderbury, where the stationmaster, Henry Brown, a native of Stoke Poges, had in his charge five platelayers and two porters in 1891. At Bloxham there were six platelayers and a porter as well as the stationmaster in 1901. The workforce at Hook Norton then comprised the station master John Morris, from Hartlebury, Worcestershire, a signalman, two porters and eight platelayers.

The only station on the Buckinghamshire Railway in the immediate vicinity of Banbury was called Farthinghoe, although it was situated in the parish of Middleton Cheney. In 1851 five permanent way men lived nearby and similar numbers were recorded in subsequent censuses. A stationmaster's house alongside the station buildings was the home in 1851 of John Horn, railway agent, the term the LNWR then used for its stationmasters. Edward Wallis in 1861 was designated stationmaster, as, in 1871, was John Simkiss, a Leicestershire man who had been a railway policeman in Banbury ten years earlier. William Tustain in 1891 was recorded as a railway clerk, but ten years later he was called the stationmaster, although subsequently operations were supervised by a reclusive porter.[27]

Cockley Brake (SP 546414), 5¼ miles from Merton Street station, where the NBJR joined the Buckinghamshire Railway, was, in the context of the English Midlands, an unusually isolated railway outpost, approachable only across fields. The LNWR installed a standard signal box there when the NBJR was opened in 1872. There was a short loop where passing trains could be held, which also enabled a locomotive assisting the train engine of a heavy up freight train to be released and return to Banbury. Single line staffs continued to be exchanged there after the closure of the NBJR in 1951 until its tracks were lifted in 1955. The tedium of life in an isolated signal box was relieved by linnet-keeping and the cultivation of gooseberries.[28]

---

[27] A E Grigg, *Town of Trains* (Buckingham: Barracuda, 1980), 69.

[28] B Simpson, *The Banbury to Verney Junction Branch* (Oxford: Oxford Publishing, 1978), 79-83; R C Riley & B Simpson, *A History of the Stratford-upon-Avon & Midland Junction Railway* (Witney: Lamplight, 1999), 115.

Conclusions

Every aspect of economic, social and cultural life in Banbury and its hinterland in the half-century after 1850 was affected by the railways. Most goods sold in the town shops and not made locally were delivered by train, as was much of the town's coal supply. Manufacturers despatched agricultural machines, beer, textiles and cakes, while builders brought in timber, glass and, for prestigious projects, stone. Links with neighbouring towns were strengthened, and excursion trains offered opportunities for self-improvement and self-indulgence. All these features applied to almost every market town in England of similar size to Banbury, which in the 1890s could scarcely be described as a 'railway town'. This changed after 1900 when the role of the town's railwaymen in handling long-distance traffic increased, and Banbury became one of the key points in the national network.

Evening excursion ticket to Oxford.

7. The Great Western northern line 1861-1914

'It is humiliating ... that ... for over 60 years there has not been a really efficient train service between London and Birmingham'.[1]

The Great Western context

The Great Western's northern line was inaugurated on 1 October 1861, when the first through train to Merseyside left Paddington on the standard gauge rails of newly-laid mixed tracks. By 1872 broad gauge operations north of Didcot had ceased. Nevertheless the end of the broad gauge in the Midlands began a period of stagnation. The speediest broad gauge train reached Birmingham from Paddington in 2 hours 50 minutes, but by the 1870s the fastest service on the narrow gauge took 30 minutes more. The railway historian T R Perkins commented in 1902 that 'Until a comparatively recent date none but the older classes of locomotives were ever seen on the northern section of the Great Western system'.[2]

Failings in management were revealed by a tragic accident. On Christmas Eve 1874, an extremely cold day, the 10.00 from Paddington to Birkenhead, consisted of 14 overcrowded coaches, to which another, a four-wheeler built in 1855 by Wright & Sons of Saltley for the Newport, Abergavenny & Hereford Railway, was added at the front when engines were changed at Oxford. Two 7 ft singles double-headed the train northwards. At Shipton, about four hundred yards south of the bridge over the River Cherwell, a piece of the wrought-iron tyre on the right hand leading wheel of the old coach broke off. The wheel disintegrated derailing the coach. As the locomotive crews applied the brakes, the four-wheeler was crushed between the engines and the remainder of the train. Nine of the following coaches crashed over the canal bridge and three were derailed but stayed upright. Prompt implementation of rule book procedures prevented other trains from hitting the wreckage but 34 passengers were killed and 65 severely injured. Enquiries revealed that the wheels of the four-wheeler had been re-tyred in 1868 by a method that the Great Western had discontinued on safety grounds in 1855. The cord communication between driver and train failed because it was not tested after being connected at Oxford. The train was adjudged deficient in braking power, and was marshalled contrary to the rule book. The company was criticised for failing to provide instruction to drivers in how to deal with this kind of emergency, and the rule book was afterwards appropriately modified.[3]

---

[1] *RM* vol 3 (1898), 115.
[2] *RM* vol 11 (1902), 399; S C Jenkins, *The Great Western & Great Central Joint Railway* (Tarrant Hinton, Oakwood, 1978), 7.
[3] L T C Rolt, *Red for Danger: A History of Railway Accidents and Railway Safety Precautions* (London: John Lane, 1955), 77-80; *BA* 31 Dec 1874.

The Great Western context

The exterior of Banbury GWR station in 1900. The vehicles in the siding are horse boxes.
Record Office for Leicestershire, Leicester and Rutland

In 1880 Banbury was scarcely more than a wayside station on the Great Western, with two through tracks, a loop east of the passenger platforms for up freight trains, and a yard west of the main line with a goods shed and cattle docks. It would have been necessary to have motive power to move slip coaches, and to shunt the goods yard and the link to the LNWR, but a turntable installed in 1871 near the gas works was one of the few facilities for servicing locomotives. In 1883-84 new brick buildings were added on the up side of the station and an up loop line for freight trains was installed, alongside which, north of the road bridge, were five sidings for sorting freight wagons, the nucleus of a marshalling yard. Additions were made to the goods shed and the cattle docks were moved east of the main line. The up platform was extended in 1903, and further up loop lines were added to accommodate freight traffic from the Great Central. Subsequently a stationmaster's office, a parcels depot, and a newspaper kiosk, were built on the down side. A refreshment room replaced a stall that sold Banbury Cakes. A small shed at the south end of the up side of the station was opened in 1889 accommodating engines used on the BCDR. The opening of the branch from Woodford necessitated more substantial facilities, and a contract for erecting a locomotive depot on the west side of the line south of the goods yard was awarded on 23 June 1907. The four-road shed, 210 ft long, was handed to the locomotive department on 6 September 1908. Banbury North signal box was opened in 1901, and the boxes at Astrop and Banbury South in 1908.

In November 1912 the Great Western authorised the extension of the down marshalling yard at Banbury North.[4]

Services through Banbury benefitted from improvements on distant parts of the Great Western. The main line from Paddington was quadrupled, as far as Taplow between 1874 and 1882, and from Taplow to Didcot between 1890 and 1896. The company rebuilt Snow Hill station in Birmingham in 1906-12, and opened new engine sheds at Old Oak Common outside Paddington on 17 March 1906, at Oxley north of Wolverhampton in 1907, and at Tyseley (Birmingham) in the following year.[5]

The interior of Banbury GWR station in 1900, looking south. By this time passengers were changing at Banbury, necessitating the finger post on the up platform identifying trains.
Record Office for Leicestershire, Leicester and Rutland.

---

[4] J Copsey, 'Banbury GWR: Pt 1: The Background', *BRJ* 15 (1987), 223-25; J Copsey, & M Clifton, 'Banbury – The Shed, the Engines and the Men', *GWRJ* No 3 (1992), 91, 93, 97; J Copsey, 'Goods Operations at Banbury', *GWRJ* No 92 (2014), 185; C R Potts, *An Historical Survey of Selected Great Western Stations, vol. 4* (Poole: Oxford Publishing Co, 1985), 12.

[5] A Williams, A, *Brunel and After* (London: Great Western Railway, 1925), 94-95; *RM* vol 30 (1912), 113-21, vol 19 (1906), 375; R Griffiths & P Smith, *The Directory of British Engine Sheds, vol 1, Southern England, the Midlands, East Anglia and Wales* (Shepperton: Oxford Publishing Co, 1999), 90, 162, 165.

Star' class 4-6-0 No 4061 'Glastonbury Abbey' acting as Banbury's station pilot on 18 April 1956. In the background is the small engine shed of 1889. The Great Western-style number on the front buffer beam was painted when the engine hauled an enthusiasts' special. The vehicle behind No 4061 is an auto-coach that was used, hauled by a 4-6-0, only on the 08.00 Banbury–Leamington and the 10.00 return. Ian Stratford

Long non-stop runs on the GWR were inhibited by the rights of the refreshment room proprietors at Swindon to stop all trains on the main line for sufficient time for passengers to take food and drink. The GWR bought out the rights in 1895 and subsequently installed water troughs enabling non-stop running between Paddington and Bristol. The first, at Goring (or Basildon) between Didcot and Reading, operated from 1 October 1895, and made possible the acceleration of trains to Oxford and the north. There were also troughs at Aynho, at Rowington (or Kingswood) near Knowle and at Denham (Ruislip). Troughs at Charwelton on the GC London Extension were completed in 1903.[6]

Several of the distant 'cut-off' routes built by the Great Western to reduce mileages between the principal cities affected trains passing Banbury. The Didcot, Newbury & Southampton Railway opened from Didcot to Newbury on 12 April 1882 and from Newbury to a junction with the LSWR at Winchester

---

[6] *RM* vol 20 (1907), 83; J H Russell, *The Banbury and Cheltenham Railway 1887-1962* (Oxford: Oxford Publishing Co, 1977), 17; G Dow, *Great Central, vol 3* (2nd edn., Shepperton: Ian Allan, 1971), 31; F Booker, *The Great Western Railway: A New History* (Newton Abbot: David & Charles, 1977), 107.

in 1885, provided an alternative route to the south coast avoiding Reading and Basingstoke. The Severn Tunnel opened during 1886, and the completion of the Badminton route from Wootton Bassett to Patchway in 1903, made South Wales more accessible for trains approaching from Didcot. A new line from Cheltenham to Honeybourne opened in 1906. Two years afterwards the track of the OWWR branch from Honeybourne to Stratford was doubled. This, with the building of the North Warwickshire Railway, created a new route from Birmingham to Bristol, which could be accessed at Stratford by freight trains from Banbury bound for South Wales. The end of the broad gauge on the main line to the West in 1892 brought benefits to the whole Great Western system, not least an enthusiasm for innovation in steam locomotives and in the quality of rolling stock.

The corridor train designed by William Dean which from 1892 was used on a daily service between Paddington and Birkenhead.

The fastest of the six principal down services from Paddington to Banbury in 1887 covered the 86¼ miles in 134 minutes, while the main morning up service did the journey in 116 minutes. Substantial changes to services on the northern line followed in the 1890s. From 7 March 1892, a new set of carriages was provided for the 13.30 Paddington–Birkenhead service. This was the first corridor train to be heated by steam and to provide access to lavatories for all three classes. Neither corridor coaches nor restaurant cars ran on the broad gauge. From 1896 an express from Paddington to the North was timetabled to pass non-stop through Oxford, leaving behind a slip coach, and in the same year the GWR began to convey through carriages for the resorts on the Welsh coast on trains from Paddington.[7]

---

[7] Booker, *Great Western*, 102-03; P Collins, *Rail Centres: Wolverhampton* (Shepperton: Ian Allan, 1990), 60; C W Judge, *Thro' the Lens* (Poole: Railprint, 1985), plate 152; *GWE* 117 (1992), 6-8.

The Bicester cut-off

The first decade of the twentieth century saw the completion of two more of the eight lines that radiated from Banbury. The branch from Woodford opened in 1900, is discussed below (Chapter 8). The complex route from London, commonly called the 'Bicester cut-off', was completed in 1910 and reduced the distance between Banbury and Paddington from 84¼ to 67½ miles. The route was an outcome of the work of a joint committee of the Great Western and Great Central Railways established in 1899. The first section of three miles from Paddington formed part of the Great Western main line from Bristol. From a junction at Old Oak Common, a line owned by the Great Western extended to Northolt Junction, where it was joined by a Great Central link from Neasden on its line into Marylebone. Jointly-owned tracks continued to High Wycombe. There they made a junction with the branch of the Great Western opened in 1864 that left the old main line at Maidenhead, and ran through Bourne End, High Wycombe and Princes Risborough to Thame and Oxford. The branch was upgraded and became part of the new main line between High Wycombe and Princes Risborough whence a joint line extended through Haddenham to join the London Extension at Grendon Underwood.

A train consisting of a Great Western auto-coach and 0-6-0PT No 5407 calls at Haddenham in August 1947. The upper quadrant signal shows that this is part of the Great Western & Great Central Joint line. Great Western Trust Collection

This provided the GCR with an alternative route to and from Marylebone to the line through Aylesbury which the GCR shared acrimoniously with the Metropolitan Railway. The line opened for freight traffic in 1905 and for passenger trains on 2 April 1906. The Great Western made a junction on this route at Ashendon. From there a new line extended through Ardley Tunnel and Bicester, and over viaducts at Souldern to Aynho, where it joined the company's original route to the north. The new line, built by Scott, Middleton & Co, was opened to freight traffic on 4 April 1910 and for passenger trains on 1 July of that year.[8]

Services on the new line were powered by 'Saint' and 'Star' class 4-6-0s, the Great Western's most modern locomotives, and soon proved popular. Initially four down-expresses reached Birmingham in two hours from Paddington and before the end of 1910 the company was adding extra vehicles to trains to accommodate surging demand. Most expresses travelled beyond Wolverhampton to Shrewsbury, Chester and Birkenhead, and one or two a day carried through coaches for Aberystwyth and Pwllheli. Most down-trains served Banbury by slip coaches, which were dropped in 1914 from the 09.10, 14.35 and 18.05 departures from Paddington. The opening of the Bicester cut-off and consequent competition with the LNWR stimulated the development of services between London and Birmingham, described by Professor Jack Simmons as 'the most lavish provision of express trains between two great cities in Europe over a distance of more than a hundred miles'. The timetable for July 1914 lists 38 trains between the two cities, 17 provided by the GWR at an average speed of 54.1 mph and 21 by the LNWR which averaged 53.4 mph, and, unlike the comparable services between Paris and Lille or Berlin and Hamburg, the trains of both companies were open for passengers of all classes.[9]

Cross-country

By 1914 Banbury was a staging point on several long-distance cross-country services. Those of the Great Central, considered below, gained the most publicity, but trains from the West Midlands and Merseyside were of equal importance.

The Great Western, with its southern neighbours, gradually developed a service which connected Merseyside and the West Midlands with the coastal resorts of Kent and Sussex. In 1863, after the installation of mixed gauge tracks at Reading, a train from Birkenhead with portions for Dover and Hastings (via Tonbridge and Battle) was shunted over contorted connections at Reading to gain access to the South Eastern Railway's line to Redhill, but this service was short-lived.

---

[8] B Trinder, 'Centenary Reflections on the Bicester Cut-Off', *C&CH* vol 18 (2010), 103-05; E T MacDermot, *History of the Great Western Railway* (1927, rev edn, ed C R Clinker, London: Ian Allan, 1964), vol 2, 235.

[9] J Simmons, *The Express Train* (Nairn: David St John Thomas, 1994), 188-89.

In 1897-98 a fast service from Tonbridge to Reading conveyed a coach from Folkestone to Liverpool which was attached to a northbound train at Reading. However, this too had a short life, and no through trains to the SER via Reading were listed in the GWR timetable of 1902. The following year the 09.25 from Birkenhead to Paddington carried a portion detached at Reading that went forward to Dover (Harbour) where it reversed and continued to Deal. There were variations in the years that followed. In 1905 a coach on the 07.00 from Birkenhead was detached at Southall and worked to Kensington Olympia (then Addison Road), whence it was conveyed to Dover on a train which also included through coaches from the LNWR. The basic pattern of through services from Birkenhead along the main line to Reading, then by the SER to Redhill, Dover, Deal and the Thanet resorts was established by 1914, and remained until the service was withdrawn due to wartime exigencies in 1916. From 1904 the service faced competition from trains under the brand name the 'Sunny South Express', which by 1914 linked Manchester, Liverpool and Birmingham on the LNWR, with Brighton, Eastbourne, Folkestone, Dover and Deal.

In 1896 the London & South Western Railway completed a new station at Basingstoke that facilitated the running of through trains from the Great Western's branch from Reading to Bournemouth and Portsmouth. In the summer of 1902 the 09.30 express from Birkenhead, which called at Banbury at 13.25, was divided at Oxford into portions for Paddington and Bournemouth which was reached, without a stop at Reading, at 17.47. In the winter the Bournemouth service consisted of a single carriage worked on a branch train to Basingstoke then shunted from the GWR station on to the rear of an LSWR Bournemouth express. On 1 July 1906 the GWR opened a new station at Reading West at which through trains to and from the north could call without reversing in the main station. By 1907 the summer service from Birkenhead also carried through coaches for Portsmouth. From 1910 a new train was inaugurated, worked by the LNWR from Manchester to Crewe, then by a GWR locomotive that took it through Market Drayton and Wellington to Wolverhampton. There the coaches from Birkenhead were added, and then to Oxford, where the train was handed over to an LSWR locomotive which worked it non-stop to Eastleigh. From October 1910 the trains from the North to Bournemouth faced competition from a service instigated by the LNWR. The train, later named the *Pines Express*, ran from Manchester to Birmingham, and then on the Midland Railway to Bath and over the Somerset & Dorset Joint Railway to Bournemouth.[10]

---

[10] *RM* vol 16 (1905), 322-27, vol 26 (1910), 70-71, 167.

In 1905 the Great Western began a service from Wolverhampton to Weymouth via Banbury, the Didcot north curve, Swindon, Westbury and Yeovil that competed with through coaches from the LNWR and GNR that the LSWR worked forward from Bournemouth.[11]

A 'Star' class 4-6-0 with an up express at King's Sutton   Great Western Trust Collection

Local trains

By 1880 there were nine village wayside stations along the GWR main line in Banburyshire, Kidlington (opened in 1852 and called Woodstock Road until 1890), Bletchington (opened in 1850 and known as Woodstock Road until 1855, and as Kirtlington until 1890), Heyford, opened in 1850, Somerton, opened in 1855 and called Fritwell & Somerton from 1907, Aynho, opened in 1850, King's Sutton, opened in 1872, Cropredy, opened in 1853, Fenny Compton, opened in 1852 and Southam Road & Harbury opened in 1852. They were served by four stopping trains in each direction, all running between Leamington and Oxford, and some originating at or travelling to more distant stations. They called at Banbury at 08.47, 13.06, 16.03 and 19.16 in the down direction, and at 07.38, 10.38, 14.48 and 19.51 southbound, and there was an additional up service on Thursdays which went only from Banbury to Heyford. The service offered in 1902 was similar except that there were five up trains. Northbound locals called at Banbury at 0.50, 13.05, 16.29 and 19.25, and up services at 07.39, 10.55, 15.00,

---

[11] *RM* vol 17 (1905), 22.

17.50 and 20.04. There were Thursday trains for Banbury market at 09.30 from Oxford calling at all stations to Banbury, and at 17.25 from Banbury to Leamington. Most local workings to and from Princes Risborough via the Bicester cut-off were worked by auto-trains calling at the pre-existing stations at King's Sutton, Haddenham and Brill & Ludgershall, and new ones at Blackthorn, Bicester (North), Ardley and Aynho Park Halt.

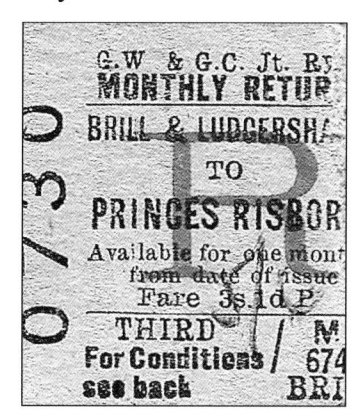

A Great Western & Great Central Joint Railway ticket from Brill & Ludgershall to Princes Risborough issued in 1962, nearly 40 years after the joint railway ceased to exist, hence the hand-written alteration of the fare.

Freight

A siding from which wagons could be exchanged with the Buckinghamshire Railway was installed in 1863, and one serving the gas works in 1867. Another, west of the main line, serving the despatch depot of the Britannia Works, was completed in 1873, three years after approval was given for the construction of a 2 ft. gauge tramway from the two parts of the works in George (then Fish) Street and Upper Windsor Street. After 1900 customers for freight services included Robinson Bros, tar distillers, whose works (known as Midland Tar Distillers from 1925) was served by a private siding west of the goods yard opened in 1912. Sidings were also installed near the station for the principal oil companies.[12]

Freight traffic in 1876 was carried by sixteen trains in each direction. Express goods trains linked London with Manchester, Birmingham and Wolverhampton, and Wolverhampton and Basingstoke. Nine of the southbound services carried coal and there were eight northbound trains of coal empties. Traffic for Banbury and village stations was handled on daily local goods trains between Oxford and Wolverhampton.[13]

---

[12] Copsey, 'Goods Operations', 184, 189; B Trinder, *Victorian Banbury* (Chichester: Phillimore, 1982), 84.
[13] Copsey, 'Goods Operations', 184.

The provision of new sidings in 1884 matched an increase in freight traffic. In 1887 33 up and 29 down trains called or passed through Banbury and the sidings increasingly served as a marshalling point for southbound traffic for the lines radiating from Oxford and Didcot, and for the LSWR beyond Basingstoke.[14] The opening of the Great Central line in 1900 further increased traffic, and in the autumn of 1901 the working timetable provided paths for 46 down and 46 up trains. They included conditional workings for trains carrying Channel Islands produce from Weymouth as far as Crewe, express meat trains from Merseyside to London and Bristol, five down services carrying iron ore, as well as the established coal trains and returning empties, and local trains taking cattle to and from Banbury market. There were ten transfer trips from Woodford in 1901. Two years later the frequency of goods traffic necessitated the regular employment of four shunting locomotives. In the summer of 1914 immediately before the outbreak of war there were 40 down and 43 up movements, five of which in each direction used the Bicester cut-off, and a fifth shunting locomotive roster had been added to handle increased traffic.[15]

Railwaymen

The consequence of developments between 1890 and 1910 was a substantial increase in the number of railway employees living in Banbury. The engine shed had an allocation of 13 locomotives in 1910, which increased to more than 20 by 1914, suggesting that at least a hundred men were employed there. Increasing freight traffic from the Great Central dictated the employment of more shunters and goods guards. Many of the new railwaymen were existing employees of the GWR who moved to Banbury from elsewhere.

One consequence of the growth in numbers of railwaymen was the establishment of the branch of the Railway Mission. The Mission was formally established on 14 November 1881, bringing together existing groups of Christian railwaymen. It organised services for men kept by their duties from Sunday worship, and also published a monthly journal, *The Railway Signal*. The mission also stressed temperance issues, and organised convalescent homes for its members. It had 270 branches by 1914, most of which had their own premises. The Banbury branch was established in a 'tin tabernacle' close to Merton Street station around 1905-06. After the First World War the branch continued although the building was used from time to time by other religious groups including the Salvation Army. The premises were taken over by the Elim Church in 1942.[16]

---

[14] Copsey, 'Goods Operations', 185.
[15] Copsey, 'Goods Operations', 188-92.
[16] *Victoria History of the County of Oxford, vol X, Banbury Hundred* (Oxford University Press, 1972), 120; D Clark, 'The Railway Mission', *RM*, June 2013, 35-39; A E Grigg, *Town of Trains* (Buckingham: Barracuda, 1980), 69.

The opening of the Railway Mission was, as much as the completion of the engine shed, an acknowledgement that Banbury had developed from a place with a wayside station and a branch terminus into a 'railway town' – where large numbers of men were employed to drive and service locomotives, to shunt wagons, to handle consignments of goods, to signal train movements and to attend to the needs of passengers. Seven lines met in the vicinity of Banbury, and there was shortly to be an eighth. Banbury may not have rivalled York or Swindon in the hierarchy of railway towns but the railways as employers had become a significant part of the local economy; the town's fame was spread by the 'Via Banbury' stickers found in parcels offices all over England.

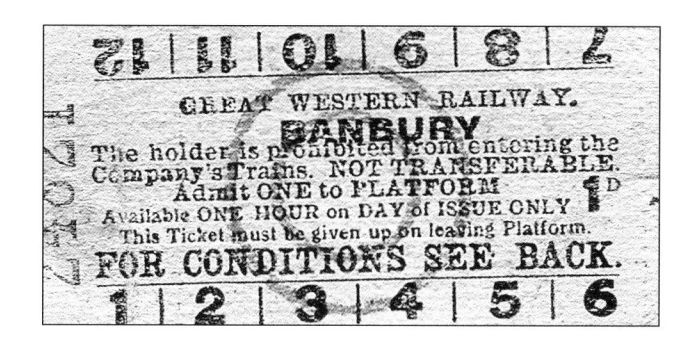

8. Ambition: the Great Central London Extension

'In those days Banbury station had its original wobbly wooden buildings which shook every time an express went through at the restricted speed. It was a great disappointment, for every large station had its "via Banbury" sticky label for handling traffic over to the LNER line, and it seemed in imagination of much more importance'.

George Behrend (December 1945).[1]

The expression 'Via Banbury' originated with the branch railway that extended 8¼ miles from Culworth Junction south of Woodford on the London Extension of the Great Central Railway, through the parishes of Eydon, Culworth, Thorpe Mandeville and Chacombe, to join the Great Western main line a mile north of Banbury station. The London Extension was a fruit of the ambition of Sir Edward Watkin, chairman from 1864 until 1894 of the Manchester, Sheffield & Lincolnshire Railway and a director until the end of 1900, chairman of the Metropolitan and South Eastern railways and the principal advocate for a Channel Tunnel. He was well-acquainted with the Banbury region, having been secretary of the Buckinghamshire Railway at the time of its construction and opening.

The MSLR was a provincial concern, with sources of revenue in Lancashire and Yorkshire, particularly from carrying coal westbound under the Pennines through the Woodhead Tunnel. It was intricately involved with the railway politics of the expanding coalfields of Nottinghamshire and south Yorkshire, and in 1893 opened a line from Beighton near Sheffield to a junction with the Leen Valley line of the Great Northern Railway at Annesley north of Nottingham. In the same year sanction was obtained for building the line subsequently known as the London Extension from Annesley through the centres of Nottingham and Leicester; thence south through Rugby, Lutterworth and Brackley to a junction at Quainton Road north of Aylesbury with the Metropolitan Railway, whose tracks it used into London, where it built its own terminus at Marylebone. The MSLR re-named itself the Great Central Railway with effect from 1 August 1897.

While Sir Edward Watkin conceived the idea of the London Extension it was left to others to finance and construct it. The company failed to negotiate with the Metropolitan Railway an effective means of accessing the South Eastern Railway in London, which would have enabled trains from the North to reach the Channel ports. In 1895 William Pollitt, the company's general manager, concluded that a link from the London Extension near Woodford to the Great Western at Banbury would provide a superior route, as well as being a better location than Aylesbury

---

[1] G Behrend, *Gone with Regret* (Sidcup: Lambarde Press, 1964), 114.

for the exchange of freight traffic with the GWR. The construction of the line was sanctioned by the MSLR Act, which received royal assent in August 1896. The MSLR lacked the £300,000 capital needed to build the branch but under the terms of an agreement made in July 1897 the money was provided by the Great Western at 3½ per cent interest. Later that month Walter Scott & Co contracted to complete the line within 22 months, using 175 navvies, three steam excavators, a locomotive and 11 horses.[2]

The Extension

The construction of the London Extension was recorded by the Leicester photographer S W A Newton. His images, of steam excavators, saddle tank locomotives hauling wagons of spoil along temporary tracks, and of navvies, some of them mere boys, and their living quarters, together with ritualistic ensembles of groups of station staff and of the first passengers provide compelling insights into social history as well as civil engineering practice.[3]

The building of the railway through Eydon was witnessed by the late Sydney Tyrrell. This section was built by Walter Scott & Co of Newcastle-upon-Tyne, one of the six companies awarded contracts for the line. Work began early in 1895 during a spell of hard weather. Parts for steam excavators, coal, rails for temporary tracks and blue engineering bricks were delivered by the East & West Junction Railway to Woodford and by the Northampton & Banbury Junction Railway to Helmdon. Accommodation for navvies was provided in huts at Woodford and Helmdon, to which were appended workshops for blacksmiths and carpenters and stables for horses. Groups of navvies took over empty cottages while others found accommodation with the families of farm labourers. In the summer months some slept in the open. The work was attractive to local men since the average wage for a farm labourer was 12s a week, while Scotts paid most of their navvies 3s 4d per day. The first workers to appear in Eydon cut gaps in the hedges, laid a temporary light railway along the route and built culverts to accommodate streams. Fencing was installed by two sub-contracting brothers from Market Harborough who dug every post hole by hand. Bricklayers constructed the bridges, before a steam excavator and locomotives with trains of tipper wagons began to create cuttings and embankments, working through the night to the light of acetylene flares.[4]

---

[2] D Hodgkins, *The Second Railway King* (Cardiff: Merton Priory Press, 2002), 650, 656; G Dow, *Great Central* (London: Locomotive Publishing Co, 1962), vol 2, 288-89, 302; E T MacDermot, *History of the Great Western Railway* (1927, rev edn ed C R Clinker, 3 vols, London: Ian Allan, 1964), 217.
[3] R D Abbott, ed, *The Last Main Line* (Leicester Museum and Art Gallery, 1961); L T C Rolt, *The Making of a Railway* (London: Hugh Evelyn, 1971).
[4] S J Tyrrell, *A Countryman's Tale* (London: Constable, 1973), 106-19.

The construction of the Great Central London Extension. The 0-6-0 saddle tank named 'Brackley', built by Hunslet in 1876 (works No 164), was employed on the contract for the Woodford–Brackley section between 1894 and 1898. Note the fencing that was remembered by Sidney Tyrrell.

Record Office for Leicestershire, Leicester and Rutland

The first coal trains from Annesley to London passed over the London Extension in July 1898, and public passenger services from Marylebone commenced on 15 March 1899. Trains to and from Leicester, Nottingham, Sheffield, Bradford and Manchester faced competition from other companies, and the GCR challenged its rivals by offering superior rolling stock and fast timings, encapsulated in the slogan 'Rapid Travel in Luxury'. Timings improved as the track was bedded in. It was anticipated that a substantial source of revenue would be the carriage to London of Yorkshire and Nottinghamshire coal, and a staging post for coal trains, with an engine shed and a marshalling yard, built on an embankment made up of spoil from Catesby Tunnel, was established at Woodford Halse, nine miles north-east of Banbury.[5]

Woodford and the adjoining townships of Hinton and Farndon lay on the fringe of Banbury's hinterland. They were already linked with Banbury by carriers' carts

---

[5] G Dow, *Great Central,* vol 3, 321.

The Extension 77

and the local Methodist societies belonged to the Banbury Wesleyan Circuit. Sydney Tyrell from neighbouring Eydon wrote that for the people of that village Banbury was 'our town'.[6]

A footbridge over the cutting on the GCR Woodford–Banbury branch near Thorpe Mandeville. The line remains incomplete with contractor's tipping wagons on the temporary track.

Record Office for Leicestershire, Leicester and Rutland

The first sod of the earthworks for the branch was cut on 6 October 1897 by Edward Chapman, the eminent scientist, who was the Great Central's deputy chairman. The line, built by Walter Scott & Co, included a long northbound climb at 1 in 132 through the deep cuttings that remain a feature of the landscape near Thorpe Mandeville. The earthworks and bridges were almost completed before the end of 1899 and the line opened for freight traffic on 1 June 1900.

A new GWR signal box, Banbury Junction, west of the main line to Leamington, controlled operations. Three daily trains from Woodford to Banbury conveyed wagons brought south by the Great Central that were previously handed over to the Great Western at Aylesbury. On 13 August 1900 the Great Western began passenger services over the branch with two daily return workings between Oxford and Leicester which initially did not stop at Banbury, although they did so before the end of the year.[7]

---

[6] *C&CH*, vol 3 (1966), 51.
[7] W J Scott, 'The New Competitor', *RM* vol 7 (1900), 305.

Culworth Junction on 14 April 1900, with the Banbury branch, which remains unballasted, to the right.

Record Office for Leicestershire, Leicester and Rutland

Soon afterwards the Great Central began a local service of three return trains daily between Banbury and Woodford. A photograph of 1906 shows three non-corridor coaches in the down bay at Banbury headed by a 2-4-0 designed by C R Sacré. During that year the company provided 12-wheel auto-coaches which were pushed-and-pulled by 2-4-0T tank locomotives, also designed by Sacré. Similar trains were employed between Verney Junction and Quainton Road. This rolling stock gave to the service the name 'Banbury Motor' (sometimes 'Little Banbury') by which it was known throughout its history. Simple two-platform halts were opened at Chacombe on 17 April 1911 and at Eydon Road on 1 October 1913.[8]

A railway village

The depot at Woodford originally accommodated 35 locomotives. Wagon repair shops were constructed together with shops for repairing tarpaulin wagon sheets and the GCR also acquired land for a carriage works that was eventually built at Dukinfield, Manchester. The company commissioned

---

[8] *RM* vol 1 (1897), 471, vol 5 (1899), 188, vol 7 (1900), 571, Vol 27 (1915) 218; Dow, *Great Central*, vol 3, 24, 141, 186, 250; R Partridge, 'Woodford Halse', N Harris, ed, *Railway World Annual 1987* (Shepperton: Ian Allan, 1986), 7-8; Tyrrell, *Countryman's Tale*, 114; R Robotham, *Great Central Railway's London Extension* (Shepperton: Ian Allan, 1999), 64; C R Potts, *An Historical Survey of Selected Great Western Stations, vol. 4* (Poole: Oxford Publishing Co, *1985*), 12.

The motive power depot at Woodford (to the right) circa 1900, with the carriage and wagon repair shop to the left.

Record Office for Leicestershire, Leicester and Rutland

the builders Melcombe Brothers of Bedford, to erect 136 houses within easy distance of the shed and the station. The streets, built with bricks made at Bethel's yard at Charwelton, were named Sidney Road and Percy Road after members of the Melcombe family, and Castle Road after their office in Bedford. The Great Central leased 136 houses from the builders for seven years from the beginning of 1900. When the lease expired the houses were sold to a property company and ultimately passed into private ownership. In 1907 four houses on Sidney Road were adapted as overnight accommodation for train crews operating on lodging turns. The census taken on Sunday 31 March 1901 recorded 226 railwaymen (but no railway women) at Woodford. Fifty houses were complete in Percy Road, of which two were unoccupied. On Sidney Street, the 35 houses on the odd-numbered side were occupied but only 12 of the 37 on the even side were tenanted, the rest apparently being incomplete. Only one of the 23 houses recorded in Castle Road was empty. The population had expanded from 526 in 1891 to 1,220 in 1901.[9]

Woodford was famously a place where everyone came from somewhere else. Census returns show that movement to the railway village was far from a

---

[9] *RM* vol 10, (1902), 296.

straightforward migration from the heartlands of the MSLR to rural Northamptonshire. The outstanding characteristic of Woodford's railwaymen some two years after the opening of the London Extension was their youth – the median age of the 226 railway employees was 28, and the stationmaster, Joseph Murfitt, from Tankersley near Barnsley who had spent several years working at Ulceby near Grimsby, was only 27. Only three railwaymen were aged more than 50.

All the 24 drivers were natives of Cheshire, Lancashire, Yorkshire, Lincolnshire, Nottinghamshire or Derbyshire. Their median age was 32, the youngest driver was 24 and the oldest 44. The pattern for the 21 firemen whose median age was 24 was similar. Eighteen came from the above six counties, one from Leicestershire, one from Hook Norton and one from nearby Byfield. The 19 fitters and others involved with the maintenance of locomotives were recruited from a wide area, one from Dorset, one from Limehouse, one from Reedham in Norfolk, one from Peterborough, one from Boston, two from the Wolverton area, perhaps poached from the LNWR, two from nearby Rugby, and only one from Manchester. Their median age was 28 and the oldest man was 44.

Of the 23 guards, 15 came from the five MSLR counties, one was locally recruited, and the remainder included a man from Plymouth. Their median age was 29. It is perhaps surprising that of the 13 signalmen recorded in the census seven came from nearby Northamptonshire parishes, one from Bodicote south of Banbury. Again they were predominantly young men, with a median age of 28, and the oldest man was 42. Twelve of the 15 platelayers were locally-born, but the foreman was from Worksop. Two of the four clerical workers and both porters were local men. Eight of the 20 men employed in the wagon works were locally-recruited, and four from the MSLR counties, while the remainder came from as far afield as Scotland, Cambridgeshire and Penzance. Fifteen men worked in the sheet repair shops, of whom three were locally-recruited, five came from Manchester, six from various places in the Midlands and one was born in Montreal.

In 1928 20 per cent of the men living in Eydon were employed by the LNER, but in 1901 only five railwaymen, a signalman, two platelayers and two labourers, were resident in the parish. Richard Hardy, who managed the shed in 1949-50, remarked of Woodford, 'the railway was the cornerstone of the lives of the great majority of the inhabitants, and a remarkable loyalty and feeling for the work and for the railway was still maintained and had become a tradition'. Social institutions in Woodford, particularly the Wesleyan and Moravian chapels, were strong, and the village band proudly provided music at an LNER exhibition at Leicester in 1930.[10]

---

[10] R Irons and S C Jenkins, *Woodford Halse* (Usk: Oakwood, 1999), 20, 49; Partridge, *Railway World Annual 1987*, 6-8; R H N Hardy, *Steam in the Blood* (London: Ian Allan, pb edn, 1975), 107; Tyrrell, *Countryman's Tale*, 119; *RM* vol 67 (1930), 80.

Members of the station staff at Woodford circa 1901, in front of posters for the resorts of Cleethorpes and Margate.

Record Office for Leicestershire, Leicester and Rutland

The Great Central Railway expanded ambitiously between 1900 and 1914, although its finances were notoriously precarious. It took over the Wrexham, Mold & Connah's Quay Railway and the travel agents Dean & Dawson in 1904, and the Lancashire, Derbyshire & East Coast Railway, with its 58¼ mile line from Chesterfield to Lincoln, in 1906. The company opened one of the country's largest marshalling yards, at Wath in South Yorkshire, in 1907. John George Robinson, its chief mechanical engineer, designed locomotives and rolling stock that were the equal of any in Britain. The company's general manager from 1902 was the flamboyant Sam Fay, who, from humble origins in Hampshire, joined the London & South Western Railway, and rose through its ranks. From 1892 to 1899 he managed the Midland & South Western Junction Railway at Cirencester before returning to the LSWR as superintendent of the line. His greatest achievement was the building of the port of Immingham, begun in 1906 and inaugurated with due ceremony on 22 July 1912 by King George V, who knighted him on the dais from which he had declared open its 71-acre dock.[11]

---

[11] *RM* vol 30 (1912), 441-86.

The branch from Woodford enabled the Great Central to compete for passenger traffic between Banbury and London. The distance from Banbury via Woodford and Aylesbury to Marylebone was 80¼ miles, and until 1910 Great Western trains still followed the 86¼ mile route to Paddington through Oxford and Reading. In 1904 the best up service from Banbury to Marylebone took 1 hour 50 minutes with a 13-minute wait at Woodford, and the best down service 2 hours 5 minutes. The fastest the GWR offered was a down service by slip coach in 1 hour 45 minutes. Even after the opening in 1910 of the Bicester cut-of there were times in the day when a passenger from Banbury might reach London more quickly via Woodford to Marylebone than by waiting for a train to Paddington.[12]

Anywhere to anywhere

In the first fourteen years of the twentieth century Sam Fay established a skein of services through Woodford and Banbury that linked most of the cities of northern England and the East Midlands with South Wales, the south coast and the south-west peninsula. The ambitions of the Great Central were summarised by the board at Woodford station which proclaimed 'WOODFORD: junction for the Great Western Railway, Banbury, Oxford, Reading, Aldershot, Southampton, Portsmouth, Weymouth, Cheltenham, Bath, Cardiff, Exeter, Plymouth, Dover, Folkestone and Stratford-on-Avon'. Until 1954 there was a refreshment room at the station for passengers awaiting connections.[13] The *Railway Magazine* remarked as early as 1902 that Fay had 'displayed quite a talent for through services between the Great Central and other railways'. There was a market for this kind of service. The appearance of Aldershot, Plymouth and Portsmouth on the board at Woodford indicated the significance of military and naval custom, and popular wisdom held that many merchant seamen travelled between Southampton, South Wales and the northern ports. To families and individuals with limited knowledge of railway connections, travelling with large amounts of luggage, the provision of through carriages proved attractive. The apparent success of the Great Central was flattered by imitation, by services inaugurated by other companies, reaching the south coast by the Midland & South Western Junction Railway from Cheltenham, the Somerset & Dorset Joint from Bath, through the Widened Lines from King's Cross to Blackfriars or along the West London lines from Willesden Junction.[14]

---

[12] *RM* vol 15 (1904), 173.
[13] *RM* vol 76 (1935), 66; J M C Healy, *Echoes of the Great Central* (London: Greenwich Editions, 1996), 14.
[14] *RM* vol 11 (1902), 23.

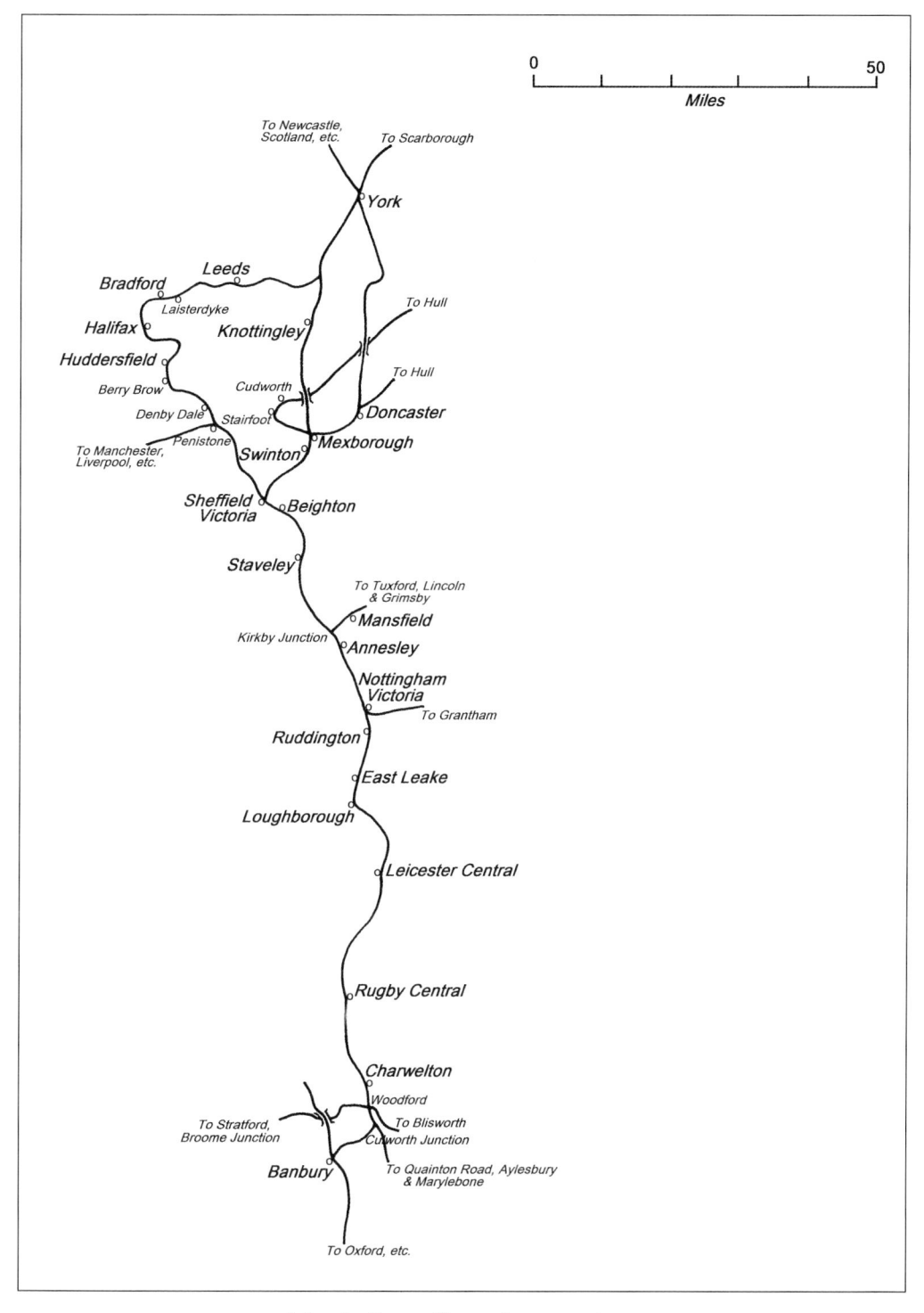

Map 3. Great Central connections.

The Great Central's route to the south through Banbury had advantages over those of its competitors. After a southbound train left Nottingham Victoria and crossed the River Trent it was clear of restrictions caused by colliery subsidence or suburban commuter networks. It could take water from the troughs at Charwelton. It faced neither severe gradients, nor speed-restricting curves, and was able to run at high speed over the London Extension and then over I K Brunel's gently graded lines to Basingstoke, before passing on to Joseph Locke's equally well-engineered LSWR main line to reach Southampton and Bournemouth. From Foxcote Junction at Didcot, trains for the south-west could follow Brunel's lines to Bristol and beyond. With two exceptions cross-country services from the Great Central followed routes without single line sections involving waits to cross trains coming in the opposite direction. While the loading gauge on the LSWR prevented the use of some Great Central coaches on through trains, there were virtually no restrictions on locomotive availability, and even the new Great Western four cylinder 4-6-0s were able to work north to Nottingham Victoria and south to Bournemouth. The North Eastern Railway was a willing partner at the northern end of the route, enabling trains to serve Newcastle, Sunderland and Scarborough.

Sam Fay used spectacular long-distance excursions to publicise the Great Central's cross-country services. Early in the life of the Woodford–Banbury branch, on Saturday 10 August 1901, it was traversed by a special train that left Bradford at 07.10, went through Penistone to Sheffield, reached the GWR at Banbury, and then, after reversing at Kidlington, proceeded to Blenheim & Woodstock where it arrived at 11.40. The nine coach train carried 194 guests of the Duke of Marlborough, who were served with breakfast on the southbound journey and dinner after departing for the north at 17.50. They arrived back in Bradford at 22.15.[15] In the following year Fay introduced day excursion trains which enabled passengers from Nottingham and Leicester to be on the beach at Bournemouth before midday.[16] On 28 October 1904 the Great Central publicised what was supposedly the longest run ever made by an engine in Great Britain without coming off its train. The Atlantic No 267 left Manchester at 22.30 and proceeded via Sheffield and Banbury to Plymouth, returning overnight on 30/31 October. On 20 April of the following year a similar train was run which carried 157 passengers beyond Banbury, but on this occasion engines were changed at Leicester. Another train followed the same route on 10 June 1905, and further 'Easter excursions' from Manchester to Devon ran in subsequent years.[17]

---

[15] *RM* vol 9 (1901), 287.
[16] *RM* vol 9 (1902), 382.
[17] Dow, *Great Central*, vol 3, 39-40, 99; *RM* vol 16 (1905), 522, vol 18 (1906), 439, vol 20 (1907), 429, vol 83 (1938), 219; D L Franks, *Great Central Remembered* (London: Ian Allan, 1985), 95-96; *GWE* No 113 (1991), 15; Dow, *Great Central*, vol 3, 40.

The Great Central's cross-country services were complex. Some were through coaches detached from or added to trains to or from Marylebone. Some were combined at Banbury or Oxford with Great Western services from Merseyside and the West Midlands. Some were, from the beginning, full-length trains. There were alterations in most timetables, especially to the routes trains followed through or round Sheffield. Here it is possible only to outline the development of the service.[18]

The initial success of the trains between Leicester and Oxford led the companies to extend one of them to Southampton by way of the Didcot, Newbury & Southampton Railway, ironically, one of those tortuous single-line routes of the kind used by rival services. The Great Western timetable for the first months of 1902 shows two trains in each direction running between Leicester and Southampton via Newbury, calling at Banbury at 13.49 and 18.25 southbound and 10.40 and 15.48 northbound. The following year the 07.05 from Southampton Docks was a Great Central corridor train carrying a breakfast car to York and in July and August continuing to Scarborough. Subsequently the GCR varied this service, sometimes making Woodford the northern terminus in the winter months. Nevertheless an early morning service from Southampton Docks to the Great Central via the DNSR continued until cross-country services were curtailed during the First World War. It was subsequently revived and only ceased on the outbreak of the Second World War.[19]

In the summer of 1902 the Great Central introduced a through train between Newcastle and Bournemouth calling at Banbury at 13.00 southbound. It included a kitchen car from which breakfast and luncheon were served to passengers in their compartments. Initially the train was combined at Oxford with a Great Western service from Birkenhead. The service proved popular, through coaches from Manchester and Bradford were added to those from the north-east, and by 1910 it was operated south of Oxford separately from the Great Western service from Birkenhead. In 1911 the Great Central built two six-coach sets for this service. The 56 ft long carriages had match-boarded sides, with illuminated glazed destination indicators set on the sides of the composite brakes at each end of the train. The company's initials, running numbers and class indications were denoted by brass characters. Metal fittings were of oxidised copper, and there were two-tiered luggage and parcels racks and extendable tables at each seat. An innovation in the timetable for 1914 was a through coach to Lymington for the ferry to the Isle of Wight.[20]

---

[18] J H Russell, *The Banbury and Cheltenham Railway 1887-1962* (Oxford: Oxford Publishing Co, 1977), 92; Dow, *Great Central*, vol 3, 31-32.
[19] *RM* vol 7 (1900), 305, vol 13 (1903), 71.
[20] *RM* vol 11 (1902), 23, vol 29 (1911), 78.

For several years from 1 October 1903 the Bournemouth services between Nottingham and Oxford conveyed through coaches from Manchester for Redhill, Dover and Deal which were added to the Great Western's train from Birkenhead to the Kentish ports and resorts. In the northbound direction coaches from Deal for both Manchester via Woodford and Birkenhead via Birmingham Snow Hill formed one train as far as Banbury. The service to and from the Great Central appears to have been abandoned before 1914.[21]

A Great Central presence remained at Banbury into the 1960s as evidenced by J11 ('Pom-Pom') class 0-6-0 No 64428 on a local train to Woodford in 1961.

Some trains from the Great Central turned west at Didcot on to Brunel's main line from Bristol. From July 1904 through coaches from Huddersfield and Halifax were worked through Banbury to Bristol where passengers bound for Devon and Cornwall could join the GWR's down *Cornishman*, and from 1 October of that year a train that left York at 06.45 and reached Banbury at 11.55 conveyed through coaches for Kingswear. Innovations in the summer timetable of 1909 included through coaches from Halifax, Huddersfield and Leeds to Ilfracombe, which for most of their journeys on GC metals were attached to trains running to or from Marylebone, and by 1912 the service included coaches to and from Manchester.[22]

---

[21] *RM* vol 13 (1903), 341, vol 14 (1904), 124, vol 84 (1939), 216.
[22] Dow, *Great Central*, vol 3, 32; *RM* vol 15 (1904), 355, vol 17 (1910), 318, vol 31 (1912), 65, vol 24 (1914), 77, 473-74.

Overnight trains between Bristol and York, operating by 1908, proved long-lasting. From an early date some were headed by Great Western engines as far as Leicester while Great Central engines worked to Swindon on other workings.[23] A Sunday service from Sheffield to Swindon and Cardiff and later extended to Swansea, was introduced in 1906, leaving Sheffield at 09.50 and reaching the Welsh capital at 15.42. In 1910 the GCR claimed that this was the only Sunday cross-country service of its kind. It regularly included non-passenger vehicles, including vans carrying theatrical scenery such as the Great Western MONSTER shown at the head of the train hauled by a Great Northern Atlantic passing Steventon in 1927.[24]

The most newsworthy of the Great Central's pre-First World War cross-country was the *Ports-to-Ports Express*, introduced in May 1906, which linked Swansea, Cardiff and Barry Docks with Newcastle and Hull. As the name suggests, potential customers included merchant seamen travelling in either direction to new ships. After it had been operating for a year the *Railway Magazine* reported that 'from the first these trains leapt into popularity'. Coaches to and from Hull, attached and detached at Sheffield, were introduced in 1909. The train followed the Great Central route from Sheffield to Banbury, but instead of proceeding to Didcot and Brunel's main line to the west, it diverged at King's Sutton on to the Banbury & Cheltenham Direct Railway. After passing Chipping Norton it took the Kingham avoiding line completed in 1906, and then the western portion of the BCDR which it followed to Cheltenham South; then passed through Gloucester and along the Severn Estuary through Chepstow to Newport and Cardiff. Fast running was impossible on the BCDR and the express took 84 minutes to cover the 45 miles from Banbury to Cheltenham South. The Great Central nevertheless regarded this as a prestigious service for which it provided special stock including a restaurant car.[25]

Fay's innovations made an impact. The *Railway Magazine*, when discussing the GCR's trains to Kent, commented in 1904 'Of the many improved and accelerated train services introduced within the last year or two, perhaps none merit wider and more favourable recognition that those affording through communication "across country"'. Nevertheless it may be doubted whether such an intricate network of through coaches was profitable. The *Railway Magazine* also commented in 1904 that 'this summer the number of through coaches between north and south seems to be almost as numerous as the through passengers'.[26]

---

[23] *RM* vol 23 (1908), 468, vol 45 (1919), 287.
[24] *RM* vol 18 (1906), 263, vol 17 (1910) 318.
[25] Dow, *Great Central*, vol 3, 100; C J Allen, *Titled Trains of Great Britain* (3rd edn, London: Ian Allan, 1953), 167; *RM* vol 18 (1906), 440, vol 20 (1907), 141, vol 25 (1909), 64, vol 24 (1914), 473-75, vol 76 (1935), 292; Russell, *Banbury & Cheltenham Railway*, 9-10, 65.
[26] *RM* vol 14 (1904), 124, vol 17 (1905), 174.

Banbury North Junction, a view from the GC line, which remains incomplete, to the GWR.
Record Office for Leicestershire, Leicester and Rutland

Freight

While cross-country trains drew publicity, freight traffic on the Banbury branch was of greater long term consequence. Two sets of interchange sidings were laid out at Banbury North Junction, on the up side of the GC line just short of the junction, and seven on the down side west of the Great Western through lines. The sorting sidings north of the station were increased in number from five to eleven, and the throat was moved about 400 yards north. The lines from Banbury provided the best connection from the north to a swathe of southern England from Sussex to Dorset. The Nottinghamshire and South Yorkshire coalfields were expanding and continued to grow. Sheffield, Rotherham and Scunthorpe were sources of steel, and with the co-operation of the North Eastern Railway the Great Central could carry iron from Co Durham and Teesside. The GCR controlled the fish docks at Grimsby, and in co-operation with the Hull & Barnsley Railway had access to those at Hull, and the company was well-placed to handle merchandise traffic to and from the cities of the West Riding and the East Midlands. Northbound traffic on the Banbury–Woodford link, in addition to merchandise, and empty coal wagons and fish vans, included fruit and vegetables from the Vale of Evesham, worked via Stratford, Hatton and Leamington, which reversed at Banbury Junction. In the first six months of operation the GWR and GCR exchanged 60,796 wagons over the

Woodford–Banbury link. The level of traffic had increased by 50 per cent by 1904 and by 1913-14 had reached 232,000 wagons per year.[27]

The carriage of fish from Grimsby was of particular importance to the Great Central. Most fish for stations south of Banbury was conveyed in a long tail of vans attached to the rear of a lunchtime train from Grimsby to Nottingham Victoria, where they were added to southbound trains to Banbury. After the completion in 1916 of the Mansfield Railway to Kirkby Junction north of Nottingham, southbound fish trains were able to reach the London Extension via Lincoln and the former LDECR line. In 1925 the 12.59 ex-Grimsby, which then ran to Leicester, customarily consisted of three passenger coaches and a tail of up to 30 fish vans, headed by one of the former GCR's large 4-6-0s. The equivalent train from Hull was worked by the Hull & Barnsley Railway from the docks to Cudworth, then by a GCR locomotive from Mexborough to Rotherham where the vans were added to the overnight train from York to Bristol.[28]

Reflections

It can be argued that the construction of the Great Central London Extension was a mistake, that it never offered realistic prospects of generating returns on the capital expended on its construction. It is true that traffic on the Extension never matched the intensity of that on the East Coast, Midland or West Coast lines. The social and economic circumstances of the decades after 1923 were not foreseen in the early 1890s when the decision to build the London Extension was taken, and in other circumstances the flair displayed before 1914 by the GCR management might have enabled the company to prosper amongst its larger competitors. Certainly the GCR's move southwards had a favourable influence on the overall development of railways in Britain. The quality of the services to and from Marylebone drove up standards on competing lines. Sam Fay's trains through Banbury inspired the development of new patterns of cross-country trains. The Woodford–Banbury branch for sixty years proved an effective way of moving freight between northern and southern England, and its usefulness became clear during the war that began fourteen years after it opened.

---

[27] Dow, *Great Central, vol 3*, 17-18; J Copsey, 'Goods Operations at Banbury', *GWRJ*, 92 (2014), 187.

[28] Dow, *Great Central, vol 3*, 17-18, 303; *RM* vol 25 (1914), 357; Franks, *Great Central Remembered*, 176-77.

9. The Great War and after 1914-23

The railway companies ... have more than justified the complete confidence reposed in them by the War Office, all grades of railway services having laboured with untiring energy and patience.
Lord Kitchener, 25 August 1914[1].

The beginning of the First World War in 1914 was shaped by railway timetables, notoriously by those compiled by Field Marshall Alfred von Schlieffen for the German high command but also by the arrangements made from 1912 by the British armed forces in collaboration with the Railway Executive Committee. Once war was declared in August 1914 it became clear that there was no alternative but to adhere to plans to send the units of the regular army that were in the United Kingdom to assemble before Mauberge in northern France.[2] Mobilisation began on 4 August 1914 and within the next few weeks some 1,408 special trains, of which 632 ran wholly or partly on the Great Western, took the men and horses of the British Expeditionary Force to embarkation points for France, principally to Southampton. Other trains took reserve forces to training depots, many of them around Aldershot, and returned some units from summer camps to their home towns. This obviously involved many movements through Banbury, but they are not well-documented.[3]

By the end of September 1914 it was evident that the war would follow patterns that had not been anticipated. Both sides realised that men in trenches with machine guns could withstand almost any form of assault, whether by artillery, infantry or cavalry, and the allied and German armies met along a front that extended from the Belgian coast to Switzerland. For the next four years soldiers, guns, ammunition, vehicles and supplies, were despatched in great numbers to the Western Front. It was the prime task of the railways to deliver supplies to the Channel ports, a task which placed the network under increasing strain, dictating severe cuts to services. Much of the traffic from north-west England and Scotland followed the route through Cannock Road Junction at Wolverhampton, Banbury and Basingstoke. Such movements were joined at Bordesley Junction, Birmingham, by trains from the Midland Railway, and at Banbury North by workings from the Great Central.[4]

---

[1] Quoted in J A B Hamilton, *Britain's Railways in World War 1* (London: Allen & Unwin, 1967), 23.
[2] A J P Taylor, *English History 1914-45* (Oxford Clarendon Press, 1965), 1-8.
[3] Hamilton, *Britain's Railways in World War 1,* 32; H J Dyos & D H Aldcroft, *British Transport: an economic survey* (Leicester University Press, 1971), 277 seq.
[4] G Dow, *Great Central, vol 3* (2nd edn, Shepperton: Ian Allan, 1971), 303; E T MacDermot, *History of the Great Western Railway* (1927, rev edn ed C R Clinker, 3 vols, London: Ian Allan, 1964), vol 2, 239.

Some excursion trains were withdrawn in the autumn of 1914, but specials for race meetings continued, and the demand for recreational travel remained substantial. Cross-country services were gradually curtailed. The York–Bournemouth was amongst trains withdrawn in the autumn of 1915, and the Great Central Sunday service between Sheffield and Swansea ran only to and from Didcot from 1 November 1915. Most restaurant cars were withdrawn from 1 May 1916, and the Great Western increased the timings of its London–Birmingham service in line with the deceleration of trains on the LNWR. Further changes, withdrawals of restaurant cars and slip coach services, were imposed from 1 January 1917 as the need to supply coal to France and Italy led to shortages in Britain. Some outlying parts of the system, twigs rather than branches, were closed, including the Alcester line, which was subsequently re-laid, and the branch from Rowington to Henley-in-Arden. Rails were removed from the disused section of the Stratford & Moreton Railway and in 1917 from the connection at Roade between the SMJR and the LNWR main line.[5]

The Rest Station

Banbury station was celebrated during the war for the hospitality it extended to servicemen travelling on troop or ambulance trains. This was largely the accomplishment of Sidney Mawle, ironmonger, town councillor and commandant of the local Red Cross. A letter in the *Banbury Guardian* related that on 10 September 1914 soldiers on a troop train that stopped at Banbury were so thirsty that they drank water from fire buckets. Miss Freda Day of Hightown Road persuaded Sidney Mawle, her grandfather, that refreshments should be provided for troops on similar trains, and he formed a committee to organise a canteen. The venture was supported by the St John Ambulance Brigade and the Early Closers' Association and the stationmaster placed the general waiting room at the committee's disposal. Banbury was recognised as an official rest station for ambulance trains, but refreshments were also provided for troop trains that stopped, usually to change engines, and for servicemen travelling on time-tabled services. On the first occasion that the rest station functioned some five hundred troops were served with lemonade, but the committee later provided later tea, coffee and sandwiches.

It became the normal procedure for military authorities to inform Mawle when ambulance trains were leaving Dover or Southampton, giving anticipated times of arrival at Banbury, and the numbers of wounded who needed attention. Ambulance trains normally carried between 100 and 350 patients, and halted at Banbury for 20 minutes. Two or three trains a day might pass after spells of heavy

---

[5] Hamilton, *Britain's Railways in World War 1*, 32, 139, 148; *RM* vol 26 (1915), 325, vol 27 (1915), 415; R C Riley & B Simpson, *A History of the Stratford-upon-Avon & Midland Junction Railway* (Witney: Lamplight Publications, 1999), 31.

fighting on the Western Front such as the launching of the offensive on the Somme in July 1916. Wounded soldiers were given cardboard trays with fruit, chocolate, a newspaper and cigarettes, together with postcards which could be written and posted to their families by members of the Red Cross. It was estimated that some 200,000 men on ambulance trains received refreshments at Banbury, apart from those travelling on troop specials or ordinary passenger services. The Rest Station served men of many nationalities, Canadians, Indians, Serbs, Italians and Australians. It was normally open from 04.00 until midnight, and the organisers calculated that in the course of the war they served some two million men. After the Armistice they greeted returning Banburian servicemen by raising signs saying 'Welcome home' and 'Welcome back to Blighty'.[6]

From the autumn of 1915 the station was the point of arrival for patients brought to Banbury for treatment in a hospital established in the extensive premises of the Wesleyan Methodist society in West Street, Grimsbury, although some serious cases were initially sent to the Horton Hospital. The first 26 patients arrived at 10.52 on Monday 25 October 1915. The hospital was extended by the erection of marquees on land provided by the Stroud family, farmers of Grimsbury. By the autumn of 1917 the hospital had access to 115 beds, a total that increased to 130 a year later.[7]

Troop specials deviously routed

Northover has traced workings that brought to Banbury military units that were accommodated in billets for short periods before moving to theatres of operation. The first battalion of the Essex Regiment was in Mauritius at the outbreak of war, but returned to England in December 1914, disembarking at Harwich. During the afternoon of Monday 18 January 1915 they travelled to Merton Street station where they were greeted by cheering crowds. A territorial band led them to the Horsefair where they dispersed to their billets guided by members of the Boy Scouts. A second train brought a further 924 men including the battalion's bugle band which led them to the Cross, and to the Drill Hall in Crouch Street where they established their headquarters. The battalion left for Avonmouth *en route* for Gallipoli on 21 March 1915.[8]

On 2 February 1915 the fourth battalion of the Worcestershire Regiment travelled to Banbury from Avonmouth where their troop ship had docked the

---

[6] The source for the rest station is an article 'The Banbury Rest Station and Canteen', *BG* 14 Aug 1919, summarised in B Adkins, 'Banbury Rest Station and Canteen, 1914-19', *C&CH* vol 8 (1979), 13-16 and K Northover, *Banbury during the Great War* (Witney: Prospero, 2003). 27-28. See also F Dummelow, 'Banbury as a Railway Centre' *RM* vol 50 (1922), 85; F Booker, *The Great Western Railway: A New History* (Newton Abbot: David & Charles, 1977), 118.

[7] Northover, *Banbury during the Great War*, 33-9; *RM* vol 26 (1965), 261.

[8] Northover, *Banbury during the Great War*, 21-22.

previous day. They established their headquarters in the Wesleyan premises in West Street, and were guided to billets in the surrounding streets by Boy Scouts. Similar workings continued during the remainder of the war. The King's Royal Rifle Corps travelled from Andover to Banbury on 28 January 1916 and remained until 28 March, for example.

No details survive of the routes that were taken by the troop trains, but it is possible to speculate. Routes from Andover, Avonmouth or even Harwich are fairly straightforward, but on 10 January 1916, 800 men of the 17th battalion of the Rifle Brigade travelled to Merton Street from St Pancras. The most straightforward route would appear to be the Midland Main Line as far as Oakley Junction north of Bedford, then through Olney on the branch to Northampton, turning west on to the SMJR at Ravenstone Wood, before passing through Towcester, Green's Norton and Cockley Brake to reach Banbury.

Wartime freight

The ships of the Royal Navy were steam-powered, and their boilers were designed for steam coal from South Wales. One of the prime tasks of the railways during the Great War was the carriage of coal from the Valleys to the north of Scotland, where the capital ships of the Fleet were moored at Scapa Flow. The 'Jellicoe Specials' travelled by various routes. In the early days of the war all five of the Great Western's 2800 class 2-8-0s that were stationed in its northern division, including No 2851 at Banbury, were transferred to Severn Tunnel Junction or Pontypool Road in order to work Admiralty coal trains over the North-and-West main line. Some naval units operated from east coast ports and four or five trains a day from South Wales travelled through Gloucester, Honeybourne, Stratford and Leamington to Banbury, where they were taken over by the Great Central Railway which took them to Immingham or other ports. Special trains carrying naval personnel between the bases at Invergordon and Rosyth in Scotland and Portsmouth travelled via the Waverley route, Carlisle, Crewe, Wolverhampton, Banbury and Basingstoke.[9]

With the encouragement of the Railway Executive Committee, Great Central and LNWR locomotives worked through Banbury to Reading, while LSWR and Great Western engines shared freight train workings between Leamington and Eastleigh. An LSWR T9 class 4-4-0 was photographed heading north on a freight train at Radley, and Great Western 'Bulldog' class 4-4-0s were recorded passing Betchworth on the SECR. Great Western engines worked over the Buckinghamshire Railway from Oxford to Bletchley and Cambridge. The link between the Great Western and the Great Central over the branch from Woodford

---

[9] RM vol 44 (1919), 64; J Copsey, '28XXs in the North during the Great Western era', *GWRJ No 11* (1994), 459-69.

A GWR 'Bulldog' 4-4-0 of the type that worked freight trains on to the SER during the First World War. This is probably No 3392 'New Zealand', receiving attention at Banbury shed before the installation of a workshop with a wheel drop during the Second World War. Great Western Trust Collection

proved particularly useful. The annual number of wagons exchanged exceeded 200,000 before the war, but it rose to 435,175 in 1915, 491,986 in 1916, and remained above 400,000 throughout the war.[10]

Banbury was on the direct route between munitions factories in the north and the Midlands and several of the military supply depots established during the war. The depot at Milton near Didcot opened in 1915, and had some 30 miles of railway sidings, shunted by pannier tanks with spark arrester chimneys which were a familiar sight in the area until the 1950s. Between Reading and Basingstoke, a depot at Bramley, also with some 30 miles of track, opened in 1917 and remained in use until 1987. The depot at Park Royal in north-west London could be accessed from Banbury via the Bicester cut-off, while many of the vehicles amassed at the base at Slough that did not become operational until after the Armistice must have passed through Banbury by rail.[11]

The increasing levels of freight traffic necessitated improvements to the infrastructure of the railway, although they were not on the scale of those carried

---

[10] *RM* vol 39 (1916), 365, vol 38 (1916), 409, vol 38 (1916), 340, vol 43 (1918), 355, vol 44 (1919), 381; G Dow, *Great Central, vol 3,* 303; Dyos & Aldcroft, *British Transport,* 284.

[11] MacDermot, *History, vol 2,* 239-40; M Stratton & B Trinder, *Twentieth Century Industrial Archaeology* (London: Spon, 2000), 95-96.

out during the Second World War. On 17 February 1915 a newly-constructed down loop for freight trains between the junction with the GCR and Cropredy came into use, although it had been authorised before the war in 1912. In 1917 a water crane was provided for locomotives on freight trains halted in the loop alongside the engine shed, and capacity in that area was increased by a new dead-end siding.[12]

The Filling Factory

The war brought changes to manufacturing industry in Banbury. The Britannia Works and other engineering concerns produced munitions that were certainly taken away by rail, although no details survive. The scale of extraction of ironstone increased, both in existing quarries along the line between King's Sutton and Hook Norton, and in new ventures around Wroxton and at Edgehill (see chapter 14)

At the outbreak of war the British army's only sources of explosives were the old-established works at Woolwich and Waltham Abbey. During the assault on Neuve Chapelle in March 1915 Sir John French, the British commander, complained about a shortage of shells. This was portrayed as a scandal by elements of the popular press, and led to the formation of a coalition government, in which David Lloyd George was appointed Minister of Munitions. The Munitions of War Act passed in May 1915 authorised the establishment of National Factories, of which some 240 had been opened by 1918. More than 20 were concerned with filling shells.[13]

National Filling Factory No 9 was built from 28 January 1916 in the parish of Warkworth east of Banbury where the Ministry of Munitions had purchased a 250-acre plot in the summer of the previous year. The site was extended and by the end of 1917 it consisted of 370 buildings, three miles of roads, nine miles of boundary fencing, 27 miles of narrow gauge track for internal movements of shells and components, and 3½ miles of standard gauge railway. The labour force was around 1,500, of whom about 40 per cent were women. It was estimated that in total some four million shells were filled at the factory. Many went to the Italian front where five British divisions were sent to shore up the Italian army after the battle of Caporetto in late October 1917. The factory also produced projectiles containing mustard gas that were used in the assault on the Hindenberg Line in September 1918.

The filling factory was accessed by rail from the Buckinghamshire Railway near Warkworth Crossing. A standard gauge system ran through the site extending across a level-crossing to storage buildings on the north side of the

---

[12] C R Potts, *An Historical Survey of Selected Great Western Stations, vol. 4* (Poole: Oxford Publishing Co, 1985), 12.
[13] Taylor, *English History 1914-45,* 26-32; Stratton & Trinder, *Twentieth Century*, 96-97.

road from Banbury to Overthorpe near the *Bowling Green* public house. The cases, explosives and other components of shells appear to have been delivered by rail, and all completed shells were despatched by train, as many as 30 wagon loads a day in busy periods. The sidings appear initially to have been shunted by an 0-6-0 saddle tank named *John*, built by Hudswell Clarke of Leeds in 1909. The regular engine, also an 0-6-0 saddle tank, then known as *Lidban*, was completed by the Avonside Engineering Co at Bristol in 1917. After the war *Lidban* was sold to the Brymbo Steel Co where she worked, carrying the name *Arenig*, until 1958. Precise procedures were drawn up by the LNWR for shunting at the filling factory, and people who worked on the line remembered that traffic was heavy. It was probably to enable the employment of larger locomotives on munitions traffic that the original turntable at Merton Street was replaced by a 42 ft turntable near the engine shed. Production at the factory ceased after the Armistice, and the site was cleared between 1919 and 1924 by Cohens of London.[14]

ROD class 2-8-0 No 3020 at Banbury shed on 26 April 1954, when its principal duty was on the 'Target' freight trains from the sidings by the shed to the down yard at Banbury North. Ian Stratford

---

[14] Northover, *Banbury during the Great War,* 41-54; B Simpson, *The Banbury to Verney Junction Branch* (Oxford: Oxford Publishing Co, 1978), 51-56. See also the film by Banbury Museum: *Banbury's Explosive Role in the First World War: National Filling Factory No 9.*

Post-war

A long-term effect of the war that had a considerable influence on railways at Banbury was the construction of more than 500 2-8-0 locomotives of J G Robinson's 8K class, introduced on the Great Central Railway in 1911. The engines were built, chiefly by private contractors, between February 1917 and the end of the war, and the majority were sent to work in France. After the Armistice they were returned to England and 498 were loaned to nine railway companies as compensation for the damage inflicted on the system during the war. They were then placed in storage and some were sold to the 'big four' companies. The GWR purchased 20 in 1919 and another 80 in 1925 and called them the ROD class. Eight were working from Banbury in January 1921, and RODs worked from the shed into the 1950s. The LNER, which already had 130 examples of the class inherited from the Great Central, bought another 273 between 1923 and 1927. They became the usual motive power for freight trains on the London Extension and took over from 0-6-0s most of the freight traffic to and from Banbury. The 'Tinies' as the 2-8-0s were known, were popular with locomen at Woodford,

The dispersal of the RODs marked a turning away from the consideration that had been given to the creation of a state-owned railway system in Britain, similar to those in other European countries. The ROD might have proved a suitable standard design, as might the 2-6-0 designed by R Maunsell and built at the Woolwich Arsenal (later the Southern Railway's N class), but the coalition government opted to re-organise the railway system under the control of four enlarged private companies.

10. Four great companies

'On that bright sunny morning long ago, looking out of the cab at the green meadows and leafy lanes in the heart of England gave one a feeling of elation. In such circumstances one sensed that it was not only great to be alive but Great to be Western'.[1]

John Drayton

It was sometimes possible in the 1930s to be optimistic about the prospects for railways in Great Britain, as on the day in 1935 when John Drayton, one of the most talented of GWR enginemen, then firing 2-6-0 No 8322 on a freight train from South Wales to Banbury, waited in a loop south of Leamington for 2½ hours watching the passing of seven excursions heading to London for King George V's Jubilee. The characteristic of the railways around Banbury in that period was continuity rather than change. There were innovations, but they did little to change established practices. From 1 January 1923 until the end of 1947 Britain's railways were owned by the four companies grouped by the Railways Act of 1921. The railways had expanded up to the outbreak of the First World War, but by 1920 their expenditure exceeded their revenues. State control, imposed in wartime, continued under the newly-established Ministry of Transport until 15 August 1921, a few days before the Railways Act became law. The Act was intended to eliminate wasteful rivalry, but competition remained, and in some activities, such as passenger traffic between London and Birmingham, it was probably beneficial. The permitted system of charging was modified, but common carrier obligations, amongst other factors, made it difficult for the railways to compete for freight traffic with growing numbers of lorries while motor coaches, buses and private cars provided alternatives for passengers. Most classes of freight traffic diminished between 1924 and 1937. All four companies became involved in bus services, deliveries by motor lorry and even in air passenger services. The tracks of three of the four companies met at Banbury while trains from the fourth passed through every weekday.[2]

Great Western

Substantial improvements were made between the two wars to the infrastructure of the Great Western's northern line. The tracks over the 9.5 miles between Olton and Lapworth south of Birmingham were quadrupled, and five stations were rebuilt. Automatic Train Control was completed by 1938 between High Wycombe and Wolverhampton, and the station at Leamington was

---

[1] J Drayton, *On the Footplate* (Truro: Bradford Barton, 1976), 56.
[2] M Bonavia, *The Four Great Railways* (Newton Abbot: David & Charles, 1980), 5-19; H J Dyos & D H Aldcroft, *British Transport: an economic survey* (Leicester University Press, 1971), 291-97; C L Mowat, *Britain between the Wars* (London: Methuen, 1955), 231-36, 260.

reconstructed from November 1937. The GWR intended to use money from the Government Guarantee Loan Scheme to rebuild Banbury station, sanctioning the expenditure of £167,250 in 1937. Preliminary work, including the construction of a new span carrying the road bridge north of the station over the River Cherwell, was carried out in 1938, but the outbreak of the Second World War brought operations to a close. Banbury's principal station remained a wooden structure of the 1850s to which additions had been made in the 1880s and in 1906. An official photograph of the down platform from the mid-1930s shows a confusion of milk churns, parcels trucks and a handcart, with piles of crates and parcels, alongside the Wymans newspaper stall, the refreshment room and a public telephone box.[3]

Services on the northern line improved in the 1920s. The 'Castle' class 4-6-0s were introduced in 1923 and at first worked to the West of England, but in 1925 two went to Stafford Road shed to haul trains between Wolverhampton and Paddington. Another six were working on the line in 1926, one of which was the first of the class No 4073 *Caerphilly Castle*, which many Banburians remembered as a familiar sight at the station. It was celebrated for its appearance on the GWR stand at British Empire Exhibition at Wembley in 1924, as the subject of one of the company's books for boys which sold 40,000 copies within a few months, and for its appearances on cigarette cards and jigsaw puzzles and in cardboard kits. In July 1927 the *GWR Magazine* announced the construction of the more powerful 'King' class. Their 22½ ton axle loading necessitated the strengthening of bridges in the Birmingham area in the spring of 1928, after which, in July of that year, two of the class went to Wolverhampton, to be followed by four more in 1930. Through the 1930s and until the early 1960s several 'Kings' from Stafford Road made daily return trips to Paddington, while one of the class from Old Oak Common worked the 09.10 from Paddington to Birkenhead as far as Wolverhampton, returning on the 11.45 ex Birkenhead, leaving Wolverhampton at 14.35 and calling at Banbury at 15.52. Banbury saw something of the GWR's attempt to join the fashion for streamlining. In February 1935 two express locomotives were rather inelegantly streamlined, one of which, No 6014 *King Henry VII*, worked a much-publicised Birmingham two-hour express on 2 August 1935.[4]

---

[3] C W Judge, *Thro' the Lens* (Poole: Railprint, 1985), Plate 56; R P & R P Hendry, *Paddington to the Mersey* (Sparkford: Oxford Publishing Co, 1992), 139-43; J Copsey, 'Banbury GWR: Pt 1: The Background', *BRJ No* 15 (1987), 223-35; C R Potts, *An Historical Survey of Selected Great Western Stations, vol. 4* (Poole: Oxford Publishing Co, 1985), 13.

[4] J Copsey, '"Kings" on the Northern Line', *GWRJ No* 3 (1992), 109-17; W G Chapman, "*Caerphilly Castle*" (London: Great Western Railway, 1924); *RM* vol 58 (1926), 83, vol 63 (1928), 254; *GWE* No 64 (1978-79), 6.

The cover of the Great Western Railway's book 'Caerphilly Castle' featuring a celebrated engine (No 4073) that was a familiar sight at Banbury in the 1920s and 30s.

Seven daily departures from Paddington for Birmingham and beyond via Bicester were standardised at ten minutes past the hour from the beginning of the summer timetable in 1924, although by 1938 some of the regularity of the clock face pattern had been lost. From 1934 the principal trains carried three-digit reporting numbers displayed on their engines' smokeboxes. The 'Midnight' from Paddington for Birkenhead departed in 1938 at 00.10 reaching Banbury at 02.40. It was followed by an *Isle of Man Boat Train* that left at 01.30 and reached Banbury via the Bicester cut-off only 18 minutes later. This train was regularly used by the bookmaker Horace Spencer Lester when he took friends and relations to ladies' nights at masonic lodges in London.[5]

Several down expresses served Banbury by slip coaches. The 09.10 from Paddington slipped a coach at Banbury at 10.25, but the following 10.20 *Cambrian Coast Express* and 11.05 *Isle of Man Boat Train* passed through non-stop. The 14.10 for Birkenhead served Banbury by slip coach, and the 16.05 *Belfast Boat Train* left a coach at Bicester which was worked forward by an auto-train to reach Banbury at 17.42. The late afternoon stopping train via the Bicester cut-off left Paddington at 16.40 in 1938 and arrived in Banbury at 18.25. The 18.10 departure, the principal businessmen's train to the West Midlands slipped

GWR No 102, 'La France', one of the three 4-4-2 locomotives designed by the French engineer Alfred de Glehn and purchased in 1903. The three were shedded at Oxford in the 1920s and worked through Banbury until their withdrawal in 1929. IGM

---

[5] *RM* vol 55 (1924), 138; M Lester, *Those Golden Days* (Banbury: privately published, 1992), 84-86.

a coach at Banbury at 19.22, but the 19.10 to Wolverhampton, passed non-stop. In the up direction expresses from Wolverhampton and further north called at Banbury at 08.40, 10.54, 15.54, 16.49 and 20.45. Banburians could also travel to Paddington via Oxford and Reading. Four services in each direction did the 86¼ mile journey in less than 2½ hours, the fastest of them, the 08.30 up train, reaching the capital in 1 hour 47 minutes. Paddington trains taking the Great Way Round and cross-country services were hauled by 'Castles', by the older 'Saint' and 'Star' class 4-6-0s, and by the mixed traffic 'Hall' class introduced in 1928, one of which, No 4967 *Shirenewton Hall* was allocated to Banbury when new in 1930. Until 1929 some trains were worked by the three French-built de Glehn compound Atlantics bought by the GWR in 1903-05 which were shedded at Oxford from 1913.

After the Grouping locomotives from the former North Eastern Railway reached Banbury from Woodford and continued to do so after Nationalisation. B16 class 4-6-0 No 61437, returns north after bringing a train for the south coast, 8 September 1956.

London & North Eastern

The absorption of the Great Central line into the LNER brought locomotives of the company's other English constituents to Woodford and Banbury, as well as those designed for the company by Sir Nigel Gresley. The allocation at Woodford on the day of the Grouping consisted of 27 of J G Robinson's 0-6-0s, classified as J11 by the LNER, 11 Atlantics, four of the 97-ton L3 class 2-6-4T tank engines, used on pick-up goods workings, and four B7 class 4-6-0s, employed predominantly on fast freight trains. From 1923 C1 class Atlantics of the former Great Northern Railway were allocated to the ex-GCR shed at Sheffield, and hauled cross-country trains to Banbury, sometimes continuing to Swindon. Great Northern 4-4-0s and 0-6-0s also worked on the London Extension, and in 1925 a Great Eastern 2-4-0 was observed near Woodford.[6] Sir Nigel Gresley's 'Sandringham' or B17 class 4-6-0s took fish and cross-country trains to Banbury from 1932, and the same engineer's class K3 2-6-0s and class J39 0-6-0s appeared on freight workings. By 1940 former North Eastern Railway locomotives, class C7 4-4-2s and class B16 4-6-0s were reaching Banbury on passenger trains.[7] Gresley's pacifics made appearances on the Great Central, as early as 1925, but by 1938 they were regularly working from Leicester as were Gresley's V2 class 2-6-2s. Nevertheless up to and during the Second World War the London Extension and its Banbury branch retained a predominantly Great Central atmosphere, with the majority of trains worked by locomotives designed by J G Robinson, his 31 Atlantics, his 'Director' class 4-4-0s and his various 4-6-0s on passenger workings, and his J11 0-6-0s and O4 class 2-8-0s on freight.[8]

The frontage of Merton Street station bearing the legend 'London, Midland & Scottish' which it retained into the 1950s. Ian Stratford

London Midland & Scottish

The most obvious consequence of the grouping on the former Buckinghamshire Railway was the appearance of gigantic letters on the wooden frontage of Merton Street station forming the legend 'London Midland & Scottish Railway'. The former LNWR engine shed at Banbury was closed on 11 April 1932 and demolished in 1935 and the line was thereafter worked from Bletchley.[9] The

---

[6] *RM* vol 53 (1923), 168, 334, vol 55 (1924), 502, vol 57 (1925), 444, vol 75 (1939), 27-29.
[7] *RM* vol 70, (1932), 76, 385, vol 86 (1940), 376; W B Yeadon, *LNER Locomotive Allocations 1st January 1923* (Oldham: Challenger, 1996), 39.
[8] *RM* vol 56 (1925), 165, Vol 73 (1933), 243, vol 83 (1938), 462, vol 86 (1940), 376.
[9] B Simpson, *The Banbury to Verney Junction Branch* (Oxford: Oxford Publishing Co, 1978), 112; A E Grigg, *Town of Trains* (Buckingham: Barracuda, 1980), 68.

passenger service was scarcely altered. One train in the early 1920s was a return evening trip by one of the steam rail motors used on the service between Oxford and Bicester from 1905 which was abandoned in 1926. The slip coach service from Euston to the branch was revived in 1923, but in some subsequent timetables was taken only as far as Buckingham. The connection to the Metropolitan Railway at Verney Junction, never practically useful to passengers from Banbury, was severed when passenger services to and from Quainton Road were withdrawn on 4 July 1936. Variations in services give some indications of passenger demand. 'Thursdays Only' trains to Banbury showed the magnetic power of the market, while trains from Bletchley that stopped short at Buckingham or Brackley suggest the diminishing importance of long distance traffic. In 1935 there were five return services from Bletchley to Banbury, with three shorter workings linking Bletchley with Brackley and Buckingham. In 1930 a through coach to Banbury was still carried by the 16.15 from Euston, returning on the next day's 09.05 from Merton Street, but these workings had been discontinued by 1935. In January 1933 pairs of new steel-bodied non-corridor coaches replaced ancient six-wheeled stock on most local trains from Bletchley. In 1935 two freight trains were scheduled to arrive at Banbury each morning. The engine of one of them made a return trip to Brackley at lunchtime and then hauled the evening train to Bletchley. The carriage of milk remained important, and cattle traffic was enhanced by the establishment in 1925 of the Midland Marts sale yard near the cattle docks at Merton Street and the removal of cattle dealing from the streets of Banbury in 1931.[10]

Most trains between Bletchley and Banbury were worked by F W Webb's 2-4-2T tank locomotives or by his 'Cauliflower' 0-6-0s, which 'afforded very little comfort', but some locomotives cascaded from main line duties appeared in the 1920s and '30s. In 1926 the 'Jumbo' class 2-4-0 No 5108 *Wyre* was observed, a member of a class of 166 locomotives introduced by F W Webb in 1887, one of which, No 790 *Hardwicke*, played a distinguished part in the Race to the North in 1895, and is now in the National Railway Museum. *Hardwicke* itself frequently worked to Oxford in the late 1920s. The 'Precursor' 4-4-0 No 5246 *Adjutant* was observed at Buckingham in 1930, one of a class designed by George Whale of which 130 were built between 1904 and 1907. Locomotives from other constituent companies of the LMSR appeared on the line including 0-6-0s from the Lancashire & Yorkshire Railway, nicknamed 'Gracie Fields' after the singer. Their exposed cabs made them unpopular with enginemen. The 0-6-0s of the

---

[10] Simpson, *Banbury to Verney Junction*, 60-63; L Waters, *Oxfordshire Railways in Old Photographs* (Gloucester: Sutton, 1989), 65; *RM* vol 76 (1935), 151, vol 79 (1936), 222, 456; W Potts, *Banbury through One Hundred Years* (*Banbury Guardian*, 1942), 42; R Griffiths, & P Smith, *The Directory of British Engine Sheds, vol 1* (Shepperton: Oxford Publishing Co, 1999), 109.

Midland Railway were used on most parts of the LMSR. Locomotives of the 2F and 3F classes, introduced by Samuel Waite Johnson in 1875 and 1885, worked on both lines into Merton Street. From 1926 the 4F 0-6-0s Nos 4071 and 4074, of a class introduced in 1924, a post-grouping development of Henry Fowler's design of 1911, began to work from Bletchley. They subsequently appeared regularly on freight trains to Banbury, and on the former SMJR. Bletchley shed was well-supplied with the 0-8-0 freight locomotives of the former LNWR, which sometimes reached Banbury. Sam Grigg recalled an incident in the late '30s when he was firing No 9005 when the brakes failed near Swanbourne while hauling a train from Banbury that included iron ore wagons.[11]

The Banbury branch lay in the shadow of the route from Bletchley to Oxford which was in effect a secondary main line in the 1920s and 30s. Through trains linked Oxford with Cambridge and excursions from the Midlands and the north were hauled to Oxford by main line locomotives. Parcels and mail traffic was exchanged between the GWR and the LMSR at Oxford in vans bearing the inscription 'Glasgow Central and Southampton'. Experimental vehicles ran to Oxford, a Michelin railcar in April 1932, and the diesel hydraulic set, Nos 80000-02, in September 1938. By 1938 trains of iron ore from Irthlingborough for the steel works at Ebbw Vale travelled through Northampton and Bletchley to the Yarnton loop where they were handed over to Great Western motive power. In the opposite direction four daily trains of coal from South Wales passed through Yarnton to stations on the LMSR.[12]

Cross-country

Cross country services were restored after the Armistice but the companies offered a more limited selection than before the war, with full-length trains linking big cities and popular resorts rather than through coaches 'from anywhere to everywhere'. The *Railway Magazine* in 1920 doubted the utility of the latter, commenting that before 1914 'many of them were, on the average, poorly patronised, and must have proved a substantial loss on the year's working, taking into account the cost of their haulage and the time and trouble occasioned in marshalling them on and off trains'.[13]

The daily train from Merseyside and the West Midlands to Kent was revived with some ceremony in October 1922 when the first southbound train was officially photographed at Guildford, its GWR clerestory coaches carrying boards

---

[11] Griffiths & Smith, *Directory*, 109; *RM* vol 58 (1926), 166, vol 59 (1926), 166, vol 67 (1930), 82, 249, vol 69 (1931), 89-92; A E Grigg, *Country Railwaymen* (Buckingham: Calypus, 1982), 48-50, 86.

[12] *RM* vol 78 (1936), vol 56; vol 83 (1938), 462; vol 84 (1939), 68, 227; T Middlemass, ed, *Railway Reflections* (Wellingborough: Patrick Stephens, 1989), 68; Waters, *Oxfordshire Railways*, 63, 70-71.

[13] *RM* vol 47 (1920), 51.

marked 'Birkenhead, Chester, Birmingham, Oxford, Reading, Folkestone, Dover and Deal'. From 1923 the trains carried through coaches for Hastings via Brighton and Eastbourne, attached and detached at Redhill, and by April 1925 a restaurant car of LSWR origin was included in the Southern Railway's train. The Southern's rationalisation of its inherited lines in the Isle of Thanet enabled the train to run to and from Margate from 1926. By 1939 the pattern of operation was for two coaches to leave Margate passing through Ramsgate, Deal, Dover and Folkestone *en route* to Ashford. There they were added to the main train with its restaurant car which departed from Margate 40 minutes later travelling via Ramsgate and Canterbury West. The combined train followed the old main line of the SER through Tonbridge to Redhill, where coaches from Hastings via Eastbourne and Brighton, were added. The whole train reversed and was worked by a Southern Railway engine to Reading from where it was taken north by the Great Western. From 1924 a relief train on Mondays and Saturdays ran between Birmingham (Snow Hill) and Dover Marine. However, the following year its path on the Great Western was taken over by a weekend Wolverhampton–Brighton, Eastbourne and Hastings train on which GWR locomotives worked to and from Redhill.[14]

The service between Birkenhead and Bournemouth through Banbury carrying Great Western coaches from Manchester was revived in the summer of 1919 with restaurant cars provided by the SR and the GWR on alternate days. From the mid-1920s weekend relief trains ran between Wolverhampton and Bournemouth. Great Western 'City' class 4-4-0s travelled to the south coast on Fridays, returning on Saturdays, while ex-LSWR 4-4-0s of classes D15 and T9 worked through Banbury to and from Wolverhampton. By 1922 there were also seasonal workings from Birkenhead and Birmingham to Portsmouth. On peak Saturdays in the last full summer of operation before the Second World War eight trains ran from Portsmouth and Bournemouth to Birkenhead, Manchester, Wolverhampton and Birmingham.[15]

The train linking Wolverhampton with Weymouth Town was revived and in 1922 called at Banbury at 13.27 southbound and 14.58 northbound. With the summer timetable of 1929 new trains were introduced for Channel Islands passengers, leaving Snow Hill at 08.10 and returning from Weymouth Quay at 16.35. Much of the route of the Weymouth trains, from Banbury, round the north curve at Didcot and through Swindon and Trowbridge to Westbury, was followed by a train introduced in the summer timetable of 1936. This left Birmingham

---

[14] K M Beck, & N Harris, *GWR Reflections* (Wadenhoe: Silver Link, 1987), 46; *RM* vol 55 (1924), 138, vol 57 (1925), 167, vol 82 (1938), 176, vol 84 (1939), 431; C F Klapper, *Sir Herbert Walker's Southern Railway* (London: Ian Allan, 1973), 117-18.

[15] *RM* vol 44 (1919), 24, vol 62 (1927), 67, vol 64 (1929) 331, vol 71 (1932) 295, vol 72 (1933), 184; Waters, *Oxfordshire Railways*, 36; *SD* January 2016, 15.

Snow Hill at 10.10, picked up passengers at Leamington but not at Banbury, and from Westbury ran down the West of England main line to terminate at Paignton.[16]

The First World War ended the prospect of travelling 'From Anywhere to Anywhere by the Great Central'. Regular trains to the south through Banbury from Manchester via the Woodhead Tunnel were never revived, nor were there services from the GC to the former SER lines in Kent and Sussex, nor to Ilfracombe. Four daytime long-distance passenger trains travelled the Banbury–Woodford link in the last year of the Great Central in 1922, and three, after fifteen years of LNER operation, in 1938. The two overnight trains between Swindon or Bristol and York, principally for parcels and mails, continued, one in each direction conveying Aberdeen–Penzance coaches.[17] The GWR and LNER agreed in the 1920s that the latter's engines would work through to Swindon with one of the night services and the daytime service on Sundays for a two-year period, and that for the next two-year period the trains would be worked south of Leicester by the GWR.[18] The Newcastle–Bournemouth trains continued with slight variations. Sir Nigel Gresley designed a new set of carriages for the service in 1927 and from 1930 the train carried coaches to and from Bradford via Penistone, attached and detached at Sheffield.[19]

The most curious feature of the Great Central service was the 07.32 from Southampton Terminus to Glasgow and Scarborough, two coaches for each, which set off, as it did before 1914, as a local service via Newbury to Didcot where it arrived at 10.06. It continued to Oxford where a restaurant car and more coaches were added, and after arrival at Banbury at 11.25, it was taken over by an LNER locomotive for the journey north. The return working which passed Banbury at 19.25 dropped its restaurant car at Oxford. In 1929 the remainder of the train went south by the DNSR but by 1938 it was routed via Basingstoke reaching Southampton Terminus at 22.53, to make connections with steamers for Le Havre and the Channel Islands. A traveller from Slough to Coventry in 1939 went by streamlined diesel railcar to Didcot, where the 07.32 from Southampton arrived with a Great Western 0-6-0 hauling a mixture of GWR and LNER coaches. A Southern Railway 2-6-0 No 1621 took it to Oxford, and was replaced by Great Western No 5955 *Garth Hall*. At Banbury the train was taken over by the ex-GCR B3 class 4-6-0 No 6164 *Earl Beatty*.[20]

---

[16] *RM* vol 65 (1929), 142, vol 79 (1936), 371.
[17] *RM* vol 53 (1923), 168, 334.
[18] *RM* vol 70, (1932), 76, vol 77, (1935), 456.
[19] *RM* vol 60 (1927), 301, vol 63 (1928), 149, vol 66 (1930), 404.
[20] *RM* vol 13 (1903), 71, vol 35 (1939), 310; A Vaughan, *The Great Western at Work 1921-1939* (Sparkford: Patrick Stephens, 1993), 72.

The *Ports-to-Ports Express*, revived from 12 July 1919, was extended to Swansea in 1920. It ran until the outbreak of the Second World War over the Banbury & Cheltenham Direct Railway via Kingham, according to Banbury enginemen passing 'over the Alps'. They worked it as a double-home turn, lodging overnight at Swansea. The passage of 'the express' along the BCDR was not speedy and when the tunnel at Hook Norton was repaired during the first days of 1935 the service was diverted 'round the Gold Coast' through Leamington, Stratford and Honeybourne, with scarcely any loss of time. The train usually consisted of seven corridor coaches but was strengthened at peak periods, and passenger demand sometimes necessitated the running of reliefs. On Saturday 5 August 1933 an observer noted the second part of the Swansea–Newcastle train at Rugby Central, with LNER 4-4-0 No 6037 hauling a load of 315 tons. In 1938 the first of the 'Manor' class 4-6-0s No 7800 *Torquay Manor* was allocated to Banbury, and rostered to the *Ports-to-Ports Express*, but its performance was disappointing. It was only when the second batch of the class was completed later that year that 'Manors' regularly worked the train. Loads sometimes taxed the capacity of the new locomotives, and on Saturday 22 July 1939 a photographer recorded the train leaving Banbury with No 7810 *Draycott Manor* piloted by 'Bulldog' class 4-4-0 No 3417 *Lord Mildmay of Fleet*. The service obviously attracted custom, although the opinion of the revered railway commentator Cecil J Allen that this was 'one of the most important of all cross-country expresses' seems exaggerated.[21]

The *Aberdeen–Penzance Express*, the principal post-war innovation in cross-country travel by the Great Central, had a publicity value comparable with the innovations of Sir Sam Fay before 1914. To call it an express was fanciful, and while passengers could transfer to sleeping cars beyond York northbound, and southbound beyond Swindon, implications that it provided through sleeping cars were misleading. The service was introduced on 3 October 1921, a collaboration between the Great Central, Great Western, North Eastern and North British railways. The southbound coaches left Aberdeen at 09.45 on an existing service which conveyed them to York. They travelled through Banbury to Swindon where they were placed on a Paddington–Penzance sleeper, completing the 785-mile journey in 21 hours. The northbound coaches went to Westbury on the 11.00 Paddington train from Penzance, then passed through Trowbridge and Chippenham to Swindon. They were added to the first of the evening trains to York where they were placed on an overnight service from King's Cross. The northbound service left Banbury at 19.42 both in 1922 and 1938, while the southbound departed at 22.00 in 1922 and 22.15 in 1938. The boards

---

[21] H. Household, *Gloucestershire Railways in the Twenties* (Gloucester: Sutton, 1986), 36; C J Allen in *RM* vol 47 (1920), 153; *RM* vol 82 (1938), J Copsey, '78XXs in Traffic', *GWRJ* No 15 (1995), 637-48, C J Allen, *Titled Trains of Great Britain* (3rd edn, London: Ian Allan, 1953), 166-73.

on the carriages read 'Aberdeen and Penzance via Edinburgh, York, Sheffield, Leicester, Swindon and Plymouth'. Another carriage ran from Penzance to York, and the three-car rake travelling between York and Swindon included a dining car. In the mid-1920s the Great Western was perturbed about losses, but the LNER was pleased to continue the service and from January 1926 provided the restaurant cars in both directions. Surveys at Oxford revealed averages of 50 northbound passengers, and 14 southbound in 1929, and 49 northbound and 16 southbound in 1937. In 1939 the LNER built new refreshment cars for the service, with a kitchen and buffet at one end, an open third class saloon seating 18, separated by Perspex panels from a first class saloon with seats for 12 people.[22]

Stopping trains

Local services on the seven lines into Banbury in the 1920s and '30s followed patterns set before 1914 but the railways now faced competition from motor buses. The Birmingham & Midland Motor Omnibus Company (Midland Red) opened a garage in Canal Street, Banbury, in October 1919, initially with two buses that worked to Hook Norton, Chipping Norton and Brackley, routes on which they competed directly with the railways. By 1921 buses were also running to Bicester, Kineton, Leamington and Buckingham. Other routes were worked by private operators.[23]

Six stopping trains ran between Leamington and Banbury on weekdays in 1922, and five in 1938. There were six all-stations services to and from Princes Risborough, some of which waited at Bicester to be overtaken by expresses. Halts on the line were opened at Ilmer in 1929 and Dorton in 1937. There were six return services between Banbury and Kingham in 1922 with one on Thursdays for the benefit of people attending Banbury market. The Great Western began its own express road service from 1 July 1929 from Banbury through Chipping Norton and Burford to Swindon, together with services linking Chipping Norton with Kingham Station. Meanwhile the Midland Red operated seven buses a day to Hook Norton and Chipping Norton which were integrated with local trains in the timetable of 1934. The survey *Country Planning* found in 1943 that the villages in that area depended almost entirely on buses, and that the BCDR brought few benefits, an observation that is confirmed by the numbers of passengers booking tickets at Adderbury in the 1930s which varied from 12 to 18

---

[22] Allen, *Titled Trains*, 9-11; *RM* vol 49 (1921), 33, vol 75 (1939), 228; Vaughan, *Great Western at Work*, 72; Dow, *Great Central, vol 3* (2nd edn, Shepperton: Ian Allan, 1971); 342; *RW* December 1977, 512-13; J Copsey, 'The Ports to Ports Services', *GWRJ* No 45 (2002), 274-84.
[23] W Potts, *One Hundred Years*, 63-64.

An auto-train of the kind that operated local services over the Bicester cut-off for most of its existence leaves Banbury behind 0-6-0PT No 5407 on 31 December 1955.

Ian Stratford

per week. The ticket office at Hook Norton, which had a population of 1,153 in 1931, sold between 40 and 64 tickets per week.[24]

On the line from Oxford, on which a halt at Tackley opened on 6 April 1931, there were six all-stations services in each direction both in 1922 and 1938. Morris Cowley passenger station, alongside Lord Nuffield's car factories on the route from Kennington Junction to Princes Risborough, opened in 1928. A return workmen's service from Banbury to Morris Cowley for men employed at the factories, stopping at all stations to Oxford, was inaugurated in 1933. In 1935 this working was for a five-coach set (No 241) which left Banbury at 06.05, arrived at Morris Cowley at 07.06½, then continued to Princes Risborough, arriving at 07.55, and returned to Oxford at 08.10. At 16.40 the locomotive took the stock from Oxford to Morris Cowley, and departed for Banbury at 17.10. For a time this was regular employment for No 2921 *St Dunstan*. Similar workmen's trains served Morris Cowley into the 1960s.[25]

---

[24] Mowat, *Britain between the Wars*, 233-34; W. Hemmings, *The Banbury & Cheltenham Railway, vol 1* (Didcot: Wild Swan, 2004), 185; *RM* vol 65 (1929), 243; Waters, *Oxfordshire Railways*, 67; Agricultural Economics Research Institute, Oxford, *Country Planning* (Oxford University Press, 1944), 13. See also the accompanying film *Twenty Four Square Miles*.

[25] *RM* vol 68 (1931), 418, vol 73 (1933), 323; R Lingard, *Princes Risborough–Thames–Oxford Railway* (Oxford: Oxford Publishing Co, 1978), 112, 114-16, 120.

Great Western diesel railcar No 14 on shed at Banbury. It was of similar design to No 9 which was destroyed by fire near Heyford on 24 September 1945. G W Trust Collection

The Great Western introduced its first streamlined diesel railcars in 1933. It was anticipated that they might operate from Swindon through Oxford to Banbury and replace steam-propelled auto-trains on the Banbury–Kingham and Banbury–Princes Risborough services. These proposals did not materialise, but some railcars were allocated to Oxford in 1935 and made journeys to Banbury. An itinerary for one car in 1944 involved leaving Oxford at 07.30 for Princes Risborough, travelling back through Oxford to Kingham and Chipping Norton, returning at 15.40 all the way to Princes Risborough: making a return trip to Thame, and then departing via Oxford for Banbury which was reached at 20.45. The railcar was scheduled to return empty five minutes later, arriving in the bay platform at Oxford at 21.28. Railcar No 9 was employed on this working on 24 September 1945 when it caught fire near Heyford on its late evening return to Oxford. Two days later its charred skeleton reposed in a siding in Oxford, and it was soon hauled to Swindon and scrapped.[26]

On the Northampton & Banbury line there were two return workings in 1922 and in 1938. On the branch from Woodford four return workings served the halts at Eydon Road and Chacombe, and some long-distance trains also linked Woodford and Banbury. Some trains were hauled by main line engines, but a particular locomotive was allocated to work the 'Banbury Motor'. A photograph of 1930 shows that this was then an ex-Great Central C13 class 4-4-2T No 6063, hauling a bogie vehicle and a six-wheel coach.[27]

[26] *RL* No 1.3 (Oct 1945); *RO* vol 21 (Sep 1945); *GWE* No 36 (1971), 6.
[27] S C Jenkins, *The Great Western & Great Central Joint Railway* (Tarrant Hinton, 1978), 28.

Excursions

The railways at Banbury regularly offered cheap fares on certain trains to Paddington, Oxford, Birmingham, Leicester and other towns served by their principal services, as well as special trains to London and conveniently situated seaside and inland resorts on Bank Holidays.

Some excursion trains linked towns on the Great Central main line with resorts on the Southern Railway. An annual summertime excursion ran from Sheffield to Bournemouth Central. Its eight coaches, including an ECJS 12-wheeler, were well filled in 1931, and in some years demand was such that the train had to be duplicated.[28] In two successive weeks in the summer of 1934 Great Western 'Hall' class 4-6-0s worked excursions from Brighton between Reading and Nottingham Victoria. On St Valentine's Day 1937 No 5006 *Tregenna Castle* and No 5045, then named *Bridgwater Castle*, hauled to Nottingham Victoria excursion trains originating at Bournemouth and Brighton that were too heavy to be handled by two-cylinder engines. No turntable on the LNER at Nottingham could accommodate them and they were turned on the triangle at Grantham. Later that year No 4004 *Morning Star* worked to Sheffield Victoria with an excursion from the Southern Railway, while on 30 April 1937 No 4052 *Princess Beatrice* took a special from Bournemouth to Nottingham.[29]

Special trains were organised for many football matches. In 1928 a Great Central Atlantic took a football excursion from Leicester to Reading, while three GWR 'Saint' class 4-6-0s headed specials to Nottingham Victoria. On 18 January 1930 No 4072 *Tresco Abbey* hauled Reading supporters to the same destination. In February of that year six specials took Newcastle United fans to a cup tie at Brighton, all of them routed via the Great Central line, Banbury, Princes Risborough and Kensington Olympia. One was hauled from Banbury to Kensington by No 4073 *Caerphilly Castle*.[30]

Race meetings also attracted special trains. It was a well-established practice for engines from Banbury to take excursions originating on the Great Central line to Royal Ascot. The Great Western was accustomed to run an annual train from Paddington to Merseyside for the Grand National, but more complex arrangements were made for an excursion from Aldershot in 1931. The train, of eight LNER coaches including two sleeping cars, was routed via Ash Junction and Wokingham to Reading, then through Banbury and on the GCR line to Sheffield, through the Woodhead Tunnel to Godley Junction then via Glazebrook into Liverpool Central. One of the most substantial rail movements for a sporting

---

[28] *RM* vol 68 (1931), 271, vol 69 (1931), 231, 271.
[29] *RM* vol 75 (1934), 151, vol 80 (1937), 308, vol 81 (1937), 464; *Locomotives Illustrated* No 86 (1992), 29.
[30] *RM* vol 62 (1928), 336, 502, vol 66 (1930), 242, 332.

occasion was for the rugby match between Scotland and Wales at Murrayfield in 1936. The LMSR organised 15 specials, running via the Central Wales line and Shrewsbury, while the GWR arranged 20, of which 12, originating at Swansea, Port Talbot, Llanelli, Hirwaun, Treherbert (3 trains), Treorchy, Blaina, Abergwnfi, Ferndale and Cwmmer, travelled via Banbury and the Great Central.[31]

Some excursions arranged for particular organisations, including schools, incorporated rail travel and cruises on the River Thames in Salter's steamers. Others took passengers to Reading for tours of the Huntley & Palmer biscuit factory. One excursion in 1938 ran from Durham via Banbury to Marlow, and was headed on the GWR by 2-6-0 No 8313. Another 2-6-0 in 1933 took over a special from Hull to Waddon, for Croydon Airport, which was hauled to Banbury by pacific No 4477 *Gay Crusader*. The LMSR occasionally offered excursions from Merton Street, and a pupil of Grimsbury Council School, aged 12 in 1924, had good memories of travelling on a special to Wembley Central for the British Empire Exhibition.[32]

An unusual special working on Sunday 20 March 1932 carried the cast of J B Priestley's 'The Good Companions' from Leeds Central via Doncaster, Retford, Edwinstowe, Mansfield and Nottingham to Banbury, where the train reversed and proceeded to Birmingham (Snow Hill). It was powered from Doncaster to Banbury by the B17 4-6-0 No 2835 *Milton*.[33] The most spectacular excursion of the period was the treat for the people of Rochdale arranged by the singer Gracie Fields at the time of the coronation in 1937. Some 9,000 people travelled on 20 special trains to Windsor, returning from London termini. Seven went via the Midland Main Line, six via the Western Section of the LMSR travelling through Banbury after being handed over to the Great Western at Leamington, and seven reached Banbury along the Great Central line.[34]

Milk, Post, Parcels and Pigeons

Many and varied commodities were conveyed by the railways in the inter-war period as 'passenger-rated traffic'. Banbury's newspapers were delivered by the 03.35 (in the 1950s, 03.30) train from Paddington. The front vehicle was a half brake coach with three compartments, sometimes occupied by locomen returning home 'on the cushions'. Newspapers for Banbury and village stations were in the luggage portion behind which were vans for Reading, Didcot and Oxford carrying sorters employed by the newspaper distributers. From Oxford the engine went forward with the leading brake coach stopping at Kidlington, Heyford,

---

[31] *RM* vol 68 (1931), 418.
[32] *RM* vol 83 (1938), 18, vol 73 (1933), 243; S Wenham, *Pleasure Boating on the Thames* (Stroud: The History Press, 2014), 127.
[33] *RM* vol 70 (1932), 383.
[34] *RM* vol 81 (1937), 5, 38.

Fritwell & Somerton and Aynho, reaching Banbury, where it was awaited by the town's wholesale newsagents, at 06.10.[35]

About half-a-dozen parcels or 'stores' trains passed Banbury in each direction every 24 hours, in addition to night-time trains such as the 'Midnight' from Paddington and the Swindon–York services which conveyed passengers but were primarily concerned with parcels and mail. The daily 'stores' trains between Wolverhampton and Swindon were running as early as 1876.[36] Much of the traffic was conveyed in the inter-war period in vans known on the GWR as 'Siphons', said to be 'among the most useful all-round vehicles to be found on a railway'. They were originally four-wheelers introduced for milk traffic in 1873 and evolved into gangwayed bogie vehicles that could run in fast passenger trains. Some Siphons passed Banbury with traffics for which they were specifically branded. In 1929-32 ten were fitted with roof boards proclaiming 'Rabbit Traffic: Helston to Sheffield via Banbury'. The rabbits, caught in the Lizard Peninsula, were conveyed to butchers in Sheffield. The vans were carried on the 23.20 Taunton-Wolverhampton parcels which called at Banbury between 04.38 and 04.55, and then forwarded on the 06.50 Banbury–York parcels which, in consequence, was known to railwaymen as 'The Rabbits'. The same trains might also have conveyed Siphons with general parcels traffic branded 'Penzance and Nottingham LNER' while trains to and from London included vehicles labelled 'Baschurch and Paddington', carrying milk in churns from the creamery at Ruyton-XI-Towns. Other Siphons were dedicated in 1934 to traffic from the works of C & T Harris at Calne, on the branch line from Chippenham. One was branded 'Harris Bacon and Wiltshire Sausages: Calne and Newcastle via Banbury'. Siphons branded 'Enparts' distributed locomotive spares from Swindon to depots across the Great Western. Siphons and similar vans might also be used to deliver a scout troop's equipment in advance to a station near the site of an annual summer camp. Traffic in racing pigeons was substantial. Small consignments of pigeon baskets might be conveyed in the guards' compartments of passenger trains or in vans for general use in parcels trains, but lengthy pigeon specials ran at weekends. When races began at Banbury walls of baskets would be erected on the platforms from which, at appointed times, whirlwinds of pigeons would be released before the empties were re-loaded to be returned to their stations of origin. Horseboxes were commonly conveyed on parcels trains or sometimes on passenger services, but from time to time horsebox specials passed Banbury bound for Ascot or Newbury.[37]

---

[35] R Tolley, *Steaming Spires* (Newton Abbot: David & Charles, 1987), 61.
[36] J Copsey, 'Goods Operations at Banbury', *GWRJ* No 92 (2014), 184.
[37] *RM* vol 40 (1917), 88; J N Slinn & B K Clarke, *Great Western Railway Siphons* (Penryn: Atlantic, 1986), 8-39, 44, 69-89; R Robotham, *Great Central Railway's London Extension* (Shepperton: Ian Allan, 1999), 149; R Robotham & F Stratford, *The Great Central from the Footplate* (London: Ian Allan, 1988), 12.

The trade in milk in churns increased in the second half of the nineteenth century as the numbers of insanitary cow houses in city centres diminished. The nine million gallons delivered to London by the GWR in 1889 increased to eleven million by 1900, while the total carried by the LNWR rose from seven million to nine million. Some of this traffic originated from stations in Banburyshire, but many of the churns handled on local trains travelled short distances to dairymen in Banbury or Oxford or to the factory at Buckingham. In the 1920s the railways faced competition for milk traffic from road hauliers, in response to which the four companies began in 1927 to carry milk to London in 3,000 gallon glass-lined tanks, owned by the dairy companies and mounted on chassis (originally four-wheel but from 1933 six-wheel) which they themselves built. The first such service on the GWR, from Wootton Bassett to Mitre Bridge in west London, began on 19 October 1927.[38]

Banbury's 'Modified Hall' class No 6976 'Graythwaite Hall' has collected the milk train for Marylebone at the Dorrington creamery and is approaching Shrewsbury in 1954.

Russell Mulford

The principal milk train through Banbury had no connections with local farmers or dairymen. A new dairy company, Independent Milk Supplies (IMS), was established in London in 1928 in competition with the two principal suppliers, United Dairies and Express Dairies. In 1934 IMS built a depot at

---

[38] Vaughan, *Great Western at Work*, 106-11; *RM* vol 62 (1928), 72, vol 73 (1933), 308-09; H C Webster, *British Railway Rolling Stock* (Oxford University Press, nd *circa* 1946), 144-45.

Rossmore Road adjacent to Marylebone station. The following year the company took over and rebuilt a creamery, established by a farmers' consortium in 1921, at Dorrington, 9½ miles south of Shrewsbury alongside the line to Hereford. In June 1936 IMS purchased ten six-wheel tanks (Nos 2567-76) built by the GWR at Swindon and the Dorrington–Marylebone (sometimes the Dorrington–Banbury) milk train began to run soon afterwards. The full tanks were worked to Banbury during the afternoon then attached to the 20.12 departure for Woodford where they were added to the 20.50 for Marylebone, arriving at 23.11. The empty tanks for Dorrington left Marylebone at 14.09 and reached Banbury at 16.50.[39]

Fish traffic from Grimsby and Hull increased during the inter-war period. Great Northern Atlantics, class K3 2-6-0s and 'Sandringham' class 4-6-0s worked the trains over the Great Central. One train left Grimsby around 13.00 for Leicester and Banbury. The 15.32 from Doncaster to Swindon, carrying traffic from Hull, arrived at Banbury at 19.28 and the 18.27 from Grimsby just after midnight. The 20.17 from Doncaster arrived at Banbury Junction at 00.33 and, after detaching a few vans for the south, reversed and departed for Hockley depot at Birmingham. The principal workings of empty vans in 1938 were the 15.20 from Swindon which reached Banbury just after 17.00 and left about two hours later, and a train that left Banbury station at 01.10, and picked up further wagons during a 25 minute stop at the junction before proceeding north.[40]

Freight

The aristocrats of Great Western freight trains were the vacuum-braked class 'C' and 'D' services that ran through the hours of darkness and bore nicknames that gained some official recognition. Trains passing through Banbury, most of them stopping to attach and detach wagons, included the 21.10 Paddington–Birkenhead, *The Northern Flash*, the 23.05 Paddington–Wolverhampton, *The Hampton*, the 00.10 Park Royal–Stourbridge Junction, *The Stour*, and the 01.30 Wolverhampton–Basingstoke, *The Southern Docker*. On any one night several of these trains would be headed by the giant 4700 class 2-8-0s introduced in 1919. John Drayton recalled that on Monday 25 March 1935 the fireman fell off No 4702 while it was detaching wagons at Banbury and could not continue. Drayton had never fired one of the big 2-8-0s, but was nevertheless instructed to climb on to the footplate, and, with help from the driver, Alf Simpson of Old Oak Common, successfully raised steam for No 4702's journey to Paddington.[41]

---

[39] *RM* vol 84 (1939), 372, vol 85 (1939), 302; B Trinder, *The Industrial Archaeology of Shropshire* (2nd edn, Logaston: Logaston Press, 2016), 34-35.
[40] *RM* vol 56 (1925), 166, 250, 334; vol 69 (1931), 463; vol 70 (1932), 131, 385; vol 73 (1933), 143; Drayton, *On the Footplate*, 51; J Copsey, 'Goods Operations at Banbury, part 2', *GWRJ* No 93 (2015), 265.
[41] Drayton, *On the Footplate*, 53.

The reception sidings of the hump marshalling yard. Class K3 2-6-0 No 61804 is entering the yard in 1961 with a trip working from Woodford that included wagons from an overnight train from the North East. The wagons in the sidings are evidence of the variety of traffics then conveyed by rail.

Other freight train operations through Banbury were transformed by the opening of the hump marshalling yard on 27 July 1931. The project was one of sixteen proposed by the Loans, Guarantees and Grants Act of 1929 in an attempt to relieve unemployment. The reception sidings were laid out east of the GWR main line south of the junction with the GC line and led to a hump south of the Old Grimsbury Road bridge, whose points were controlled by an electro-pneumatic system from an adjacent signal box. Below the hump were more than 20 reception sidings with capacity for 1,600 (later 2,000) wagons in which trains for the south were marshalled. There were no retarders, as there were in contemporary yards at Toton and Whitemoor, and it became the practice for shunters to ride dangerously on cuts of wagons before pushing down brake levers. An escape road enabled main line locomotives to make their way to the engine shed without going over the hump. The GWR forecast that the yard could handle 38 trains a day, and that a train of 60 wagons would be able to pass the hump in 12 minutes. The *Banbury Guardian* commented that the yard 'will considerably increase the railway work at Banbury and its importance as a railway centre'. The new yard drew to Banbury men made redundant by the GWR at Aberdare and other places in South Wales. John Drayton recalled that when traffic dwindled in the small hours of the morning Welsh songs in four-part harmony issued from the cabins where men assembled. The yard initially required three shunting engines for 24 hours a day. By 1938 there were 53 down

One of the few trains headed by class 4700 2-8-0s that could be seen in daylight was a working of meat vans from Smithfield to Birkenhead, seen here passing Banbury in 1954 behind No 4705.

and 58 up freight movements through Banbury, and daily duties for eight shunting engines, with an additional one at the cattle docks on Wednesdays and Thursdays. Almost every freight train from the north other than the overnight fitted workings terminated in the reception sidings, and every train for the south, whether a through service to the West of England, or the pick-up for Kingham, began its journey in the up sidings below the hump. By contrast, while some long-distance down trains terminated at Banbury, the majority were bound for Bordesley Junction or Oxley, and exchanged wagons in the down sidings on the opposite side of the main line from the hump reception yard.[42]

---

[42] B Trinder, 'Fifty years on – Banbury in 1931', *C&CH* vol 8 (1981), 117-37; M Rhodes, 'The Rise and Fall of the British Marshalling Yard: part 1', *RM* No.1351 (Nov 2013), 35; B Simpson, 'Banbury: All Changes', *Backtrack*, vol 4 (1992), 173-180; J Copsey, 'Banbury GWR', 231; J Copsey & M Clifton, 'Banbury – The Shed, the Engines and the Men', *GWRJ* No 3 (1992), 95; Copsey, 'Goods Operations at Banbury' (2014), 193-200; C R Potts, *Historical Survey*, 13.

Freight

Freight traffic on the former Great Central branch increased steadily. The number of wagons handed over by the GCR to the GWR at Banbury reached a wartime peak of 491,896 in 1916, but fell to just over 300,000 in 1919, and did not exceed 400,000 until 1927. It subsequently remained above that level until figures ceased to be kept in 1956, exceeded the wartime peak by reaching 499,799 in 1935, and in 1936, 1937 and 1938 exceeded half a million, before reaching even higher figures in the Second World War. In the summer of 1939 there were 21 daily transfer freights from Woodford to Banbury and 20 in the opposite direction. Others included the 21.16 Sheffield Bridgehouses via Staveley to Banbury Junction which arrived at 01.55, and the 19.20 from Stairfoot via Shirebrook which reached Banbury Junction at 04.45. The northbound 04.05 Banbury via Staveley to Sheffield Victoria and the 18.05 Banbury via Staveley and Darnall to York both carried perishables traffic.[43]

There were two class K workings on the Kingham line, the 10.40 Banbury–Kingham which arrived at 18.00, ran across the loop line, reversed into the station and then set off for Banbury at 18.40 with the engine facing in the right direction. It eventually reached Banbury Junction at 22.57. The second train, which principally served ironstone quarries, left Banbury at 14.05 for Hook Norton where it arrived at 15.31, and having picked up loaded wagons, left at 16.55 to reach Banbury at 19.55. The Hook Norton services ran only when required, and the return working from Kingham was specifically for 'iron ore and goods'.[44]

The construction of the marshalling yard necessitated the removal of a footbridge that had enabled residents of Grimsbury to cross the railway from the north end of West Street towards the town centre. As compensation the Great Western subscribed towards the purchase of the Moors, the field alongside the most easterly of the reception sidings, and it was dedicated by the Borough Council in December 1932 as a recreation ground.[45]

The railways continued to handle goods for Banbury's shops, whose volume increased with the opening of the F W Woolworth store on the site of the *Red Lion* hotel in 1931. From 1936 the GWR took responsibility for all small consignments, loaded vans arriving at Merton Street were shunted across the exchange siding, and the wooden shed was inscribed 'GW and LMS Goods Station'. Construction of a brick goods shed began in January 1939, but it was

---

[43] M Smith, 'Avoiding Banbury ... and Acton', *BRI* No 6 (1992), 322-23; G Goslin, *Goods Traffic of the LNER* (Didcot: Wild Swan, 2002), 85.

[44] B Trinder, 'The Railway Marshalling Yard at Banbury', *C&CH* vol 4 (1970), 131-36; J H Russell, *The Banbury and Cheltenham Railway 1887-1962* (Oxford: Oxford Publishing, 1977), 123.

[45] B Little, *The Changing Faces of Grimsbury* (Witney: Robert Boyd, 1999), 19; W Potts, *One Hundred Years*, 100.

unfinished when it was destroyed by bombs in October of the following year. The Northern Aluminium works on Southam Road, opened in 1931, installed a rail siding in 1937 that was connected to the lines of the Oxfordshire Ironstone Company. The factory received aluminium pig imported from Canada as well as some coke by rail, but its products, aluminium sheets and extrusions, were despatched by road.[46]

The most substantial outward traffic was ironstone from the quarries of the Oxfordshire Ironstone Company and those along the BCDR, discussed in chapter 14. The railside depot of the Britannia Works was demolished by 1929. The works was revived in 1931, but appears not to have provided significant traffic for the railways before its final closure two years later.[47]

Many cattle were transported by rail in the inter-war period, particularly after the dealers' market was removed on 12 November 1931 from the town's streets to the auction rooms built by Midland Marts Ltd close to Merton Street station. The GWR provided a shunting engine specifically for its cattle docks on market days. Cattle for the market were regularly loaded at stations along the BCDR, and John Drayton recalled working after-market cattle specials on Thursdays to Southam Road & Harbury and to Bicester in 1934-35. There were also long-distance cattle specials on Thursdays, some on the Buckinghamshire line, and an 18.25 departure for Sheffield on the Great Central.[48]

The Morris Motors plant at Cowley was the origin and destination of much of the freight that passed through Banbury. William Morris, who had a cycle, motorcycle and car business in Longwall Street, Oxford, purchased the Military Academy at Cowley where he assembled his first car in April 1913. He secured munitions contracts during the First World War and the business expanded in the 1920s. Sidings linking the Oxford–Princes Risborough line with Morris's works and the adjacent factory of the Pressed Steel Co, were laid in 1927, and a signal box and goods yard were constructed in 1928. Inward wagon-load traffics included steel, coal and oil. The outward traffic in completed cars, or vehicles 'knocked down' in crates for export to countries where import duties on assembled cars were high, was seasonal, lasting from October until May. Cars exported from the Port of London, were conveyed by rail to Brentford then by barge to the Docks, but others went through northern ports and passed through Banbury. An annual special for the Scottish Motor Exhibition was despatched every November, and empty car-carrying vans, ASMOs or MOGOs appear in

---

[46] Copsey, 'Goods Operations ... pt 2', 265, 269; R Hartree, 'The Banbury Aluminium Works 1929-2009', *C&CH* vol.20 (2015), 6-7; *BG* 1 Oct 1931; Simpson, *Banbury to Verney Junction*, 59.
[47] Copsey, J, 'Goods Operations, 92 (2014), 201; W Potts, *One Hundred Years*, 38-39.
[48] W Potts, *One Hundred Years*, 42; Trinder, 'Fifty years on', 136; Drayton, *On the Footplate*, 15, 53; Copsey, 'Goods Operations at Banbury pt 2', 265.

many photographs of freight trains heading south towards Banbury. Car bodies for manufacturers in Birmingham were conveyed from the Pressed Steel factory to Bordesley in a daily train of BOCARs, made by stripping bogie steel wagons of their bolsters and erecting light frameworks covered with old tarpaulin wagon sheets. Later vehicles were adapted from redundant passenger carriages. In 1938 the 22.10 from Morris Cowley to Bordesley Junction passed Banbury a few minutes after Midnight, and was followed by the 23.42 departure which was handed over to the LMSR at Leamington.[49]

Just like a Hornby train set: a 5600 class 0-6-2T climbs Cropredy bank with a local freight train from Banbury to Leamington in 1956. The third van is purpose-built for carrying cement and would be destined for Greaves's Sidings.

Two cement works north and south of Banbury generated traffic. The factory of Greaves, Bull & Lakin was established near Southam Road & Harbury station in 1855, and was producing Portland Cement by 1864. The railway supplied the works with coal and carried away its products on sufficient scale to merit the construction in 1899 of a signal box to control the sidings. In 1927 the works was purchased by Allied Cement Manufacturers (ACM, Red Circle) which went bankrupt in 1931 after which it came under the control of the Associated Portland Cement Manufacturers (APCM, Blue Circle). Cement in bags was despatched to customers in vans, some of them purpose-built. Wagons for Greaves's Sidings, as

---

[49] Lingard, *Princes Risborough–Thames–Oxford*, 26, 72-4, 79, 112; C W Judge, *Thro' the Lens* (Poole: Railprint, 1985), plate 182; *GWE* No 59 (1977), 13.

the works was known, were forwarded from Banbury on the daily pick-up freight, while coal was delivered on the southbound local goods from Leamington. The Washford Works (SP 493199) near Bletchingdon was established about 1907, and used the Oxford Canal to send cement to Bletchingdon station for despatch by rail. Its technology was obsolete by the 1920s and it was replaced by the works of the Oxford & Shipton Cement Co, at Bunkers Hill, Shipton-on-Cherwell, opened in 1929, whose sidings were sufficiently extensive to justify the employment of standard gauge shunting locomotives. The pick-up from Banbury delivered coal, and gypsum from quarries near the Great Central line at East Leake, Nottinghamshire.[50]

---

[50] L Waters & T Doyle, *British Railways Past and Present: Oxfordshire* (Wadenhoe: Past & Present, 1994), 119; S A Leleux, *Warwickshire Lime and Cement Works Railways* (Usk: Oakwood, 2014), 31-35, 51; C Dodsworth, 'The Early Years of the Oxford Cement Industry', *Industrial Archaeology*, vol 9 (1972), 285-95.

11. The Second World War

In peace-time railways could explain
When fog or ice held up your train,
But now the country's waging war
To tell you why's against the law....

The censor says you must not know
When there has been a fall of snow.

War-time poster issued by the four railway companies.

The armed forces, their supplies, and civilians taking journeys that may or may not have been really necessary travelled by rail during the Second World War. The railways were controlled by the government under the Emergency (Railway Control) Order of 1 September 1939 from a headquarters in the former Down Street station on the Piccadilly Line between Green Park and Hyde Park Corner. The junctions at Banbury formed one of the hubs around which wartime railway activity rotated. The town's railwaymen were involved in the first two transport crises of the war, evacuation and mobilisation in 1939, played a crucial role in the third, Operation Dynamo, in 1940, and for the next five years sustained an unrelenting slog, driving, firing, guarding, signalling and shunting trains supplying British and allied forces at airfields, ports or assembly camps. While additions were made to the railway infrastructure and new locomotives were built, line capacity was strained, engines were ill-maintained, crews worked excessively long hours, and routes were sometimes blocked by enemy action.

The atmosphere of the railways in wartime was memorably captured by George Behrend, describing Oxford in 1940-41 during his shortened spell as an undergraduate:

'Oxford struggled manfully with far more traffic than that for which it was designed in peacetime...(the line) between Wolvercote Junction and Oxford was filled to capacity with freight trains queuing buffer beam to brake van for a path through the station, a common sight from Oxford's famous Port Meadow. Somehow these trains became very reassuring landmarks of stability as the BBC news nightly announced the bombing of marshalling yards in Germany .... Oxford was said to be safe from air raids ... but the bombers wumped over nightly, and their loads fell on Birmingham and more especially on Coventry, yet next morning the procession of 28XXs, dirty and dishevelled, would always be there, from OXleY and TYSeley or sometimes BANbury, sizzling on the loop waiting for the signal for anything up to a couple of hours or more'.[1]

---

[1] G Behrend, *Gone with Regret* (Sidcup: Lambarde Press, 1964), 93. The capitals relate to GWR shed codes: Oxley (Wolverhampton), Tyseley (Birmingham) and Banbury.

The evacuation of children from London to areas less threatened by bombing was managed by an outstanding railwayman, Frank Pick, once of the North Eastern Railway and, from 1933, of London Transport. Of necessity much of what happened went unrecorded. The Great Western took 112,944 evacuees away from London, most of whom entrained at Ealing Broadway. On the first day, September 1, the 12.28 departure carried to Banbury some 800 children with 80 teachers from West Ham, Camberwell and Dagenham. It was followed after 37 minutes by a twelve coach train for Chipping Norton via Kingham, and later by the 14.36 departure for Bicester. No record remains of the arrival of the evacuees at Banbury, but a local photographer produced compelling images of their disembarkation at Chipping Norton. [2]

Similarly there are few records of Operation Dynamo, the dispersal of troops from the Channel ports in late May and early June of 1940 after their rescue from the beaches of Dunkirk. Some much-screened clips of film show trains reversing at Redhill, and there are photographs of cups of tea being passed to troops during station stops. The hub of operations was Redhill from where about half the trains from the coast were directed to destinations on the Southern Railway, mostly around Aldershot and on Salisbury Plain. Of the remainder, 37 per cent passed to the Great Western and 13 per cent to the LNER and LMS, many of which took the line for Guildford and Reading before proceeding north to Banbury. George Behrend saw the passage through Oxford of troop train after troop train, loaded with soldiers without weapons, many hauled by 4300 class 2-6-0s and some by ancient 'Aberdares'.[3]

Merton Street station was the wartime setting for several army exercises, and in March 1941 part of the LMSR film *Carrying the Load* was made there. A 4F 0-6-0 brought in a train of modern corridor stock with two bogie brake vans, while a similar rake occupied the parallel platform, and Bren gun carriers were unloaded from LNER flat wagons in the cattle docks. There were many special workings. On 15 February 1945 a train consisting of a Pullman car named *Joan*, painted red, and an LNER sleeping car was observed at Leamington carrying a United States army general. A more humble passenger was a German ex-prisoner-of-war employed at Barby who recalled arriving at Byfield on a special train from Colchester.[4]

The railway at Banbury was targeted by a solitary Luftwaffe Dornier 215 bomber on 3 October 1940. The GWR demolished the old timber goods shed in

---

[2] W. Hemmings, *The Banbury & Cheltenham Railway, vol 1* (Didcot: Wild Swan, 2004), 194-96; F Booker, *The Great Western Railway: A New History* (Newton Abbot: David & Charles, 1977), 151-53.
[3] Behrend, *Gone with Regret*, 99; Booker, *Great Western*, 151.
[4] B Simpson, *The Banbury to Verney Junction Branch* (Oxford: Oxford Publishing Co, 1978), 66-68: *RR* No 1.10 (1945).

preparation for rebuilding the station. Its partially-built replacement was destroyed by bombs which killed six railwaymen taking their lunchtime break. The nearby gasworks was severely damaged, although there was no loss of life there. Plans for a new passenger station were abandoned on the outbreak of war but a small extension, a timber-framed, asbestos-clad, single-storey structure housing a parcels office and a cloakroom, was added north of the existing buildings.[5]

There was much investment elsewhere. An eight-road flat yard was built at Banbury Junction between December 1940 and February 1941 alongside the existing sixteen-road down yard. A new reception line was added to the down layout, and two further reception sidings for the up hump yard which necessitated an extension to the steel road bridge built in 1931 to carry the road to Old Grimsbury. Extra sidings were added at the engine shed between April and August 1943, together with a second coal stage, two camouflaged ash shelters and a lifting shop with a 68-ft pit and a 50-ton engine hoist.[6]

Improvements between 1940 and 1943 increased capacity for freight trains on the routes to the south. Marshalling yards were extended at Annesley (Nottingham), Woodford, Yarnton, New Hinksey (Oxford) and Moreton Cutting (Didcot). On the Great Central line loops were constructed at Charwelton, Rugby, Quorn, Ashby Magna, Swithland, Loughborough, Ruddington and Hucknall, and on the Great Western at Wolvercote Junction, Kennington, Radley and Didcot. Chords linked the LMSR route from Oxford to Cambridge with the Great Central main line at Calvert and the Great Northern at Sandy. A double junction between the GWR and LMSR lines at Oxford was opened in November 1940, and a new link at Reading connected the Great Western with the Southern Railway's route to Feltham marshalling yard, Guildford and Redhill. An east-south chord at Broom Junction enabled trains from the former SMJR line to head south towards Gloucester. The line from Didcot to Newbury was doubled by American military engineers, and loops and a new junction were installed on the southern portion of the former DNSR.[7]

---

[5] G C J Hartland, 'Gas-Making in Banbury', *C&CH* vol 4 (1969), 47-54; B Simpson, 'Banbury: All Changes', *Backtrack*, vol 4 (1992), 174-79; J Copsey, 'Banbury GWR: Pt 1: The Background', *British Railways Journal*, 15 (1987), 237; J Copsey, 'Goods Operations at Banbury, part 2', *GWRJ* No 93 (2015), 265.

[6] Copsey, 'Banbury GWR Pt 1', 233; Copsey, 'Goods Operations at Banbury, part 2', 281; C R Potts, *An Historical Survey of Selected Great Western Stations, vol. 4* (Poole: Oxford Publishing Co, 1985), 13; M Stratton & B Trinder, *Twentieth Century Industrial Archaeology* (London: Spon, 2000), 116.

[7] C I Savage, *The History of the Second World War: Inland Transport* (London: HMSO-Longman, 1957); Stratton & Trinder, *Twentieth Century*, 115-17; G Goslin, *Goods Traffic of the LNER* (Didcot: Wild Swan, 2002), 85.

The nature of wartime activity on the railways is captured in this image of an American S160 class 2-8-0 crossing the new junction between the GWR and LMSR lines north of Oxford. A GWR 2-8-0 waits to proceed south through the station, while the down sidings in the distance are crowded with wagons.   Great Western Trust Collection

    The goods yard at Adderbury on the BCDR became intensely busy. A private siding previously used by the owners of an ironstone quarry was taken over by the Ministry of Aircraft Production from May 1941. The Ministry set up a 'shadow factory' managed by Northern Aluminium from Banbury, which reprocessed aluminium from crashed aircraft, much of which arrived by rail. The scrap was mixed with pig aluminium and cast into ingots to be despatched to Birmingham and Rogerstone by road. The factory also produced extrusions and powder for flares. The goods despatched from Adderbury reached a peak of 10,545 tons in 1944, an average of over 200 tons per week, while 10,024 tons of coal arrived in that year.[8] On the Buckinghamshire Railway a marshalling yard with three reception and ten sorting sidings was laid out at Swanbourne west of Bletchley, and became the focus for freight operations on the line until they ceased in the 1960s.[9]

---

[8] Hemmings, *Banbury & Cheltenham Railway, vol 1*, 253-59; R Hartree, 'The Banbury Aluminium Works 1929-2009', *C&CH* vol.20 (2015), 17.

[9] A E Grigg, *Town of Trains* (Buckingham: Barracuda, 1980), 78; B Simpson, *Oxford to Cambridge Railway, vol 1, Oxford to Bletchley* (Oxford: Oxford Publishing Co, 1981), 118-120.

The war brought the railway a new customer, a rail-connected food storage depot built in 1942 east of the hump reception sidings. The Ministry of Food built nearly fifty such cold storage depots for meat and dairy products, almost unfenestrated structures, constructed of Fletton-type bricks around steel frames, with adjacent ranges of Nissen-type huts accommodating dry foodstuffs. Many survived into the twenty-first century, but most, including that at Banbury, have been demolished within the last 17 years.[10]

Passenger services

Wartime services on the Great Western main line diminished but loads increased, and it was commonplace by 1943 to see 'King' class locomotives hauling trains of 17 coaches, which caused difficulties at Banbury's 640 ft long down platform which could only accommodate about ten. The need for assistance was sometimes anticipated, as in the closing months of 1944, when 'Bulldog' No 3442 *Bullfinch* was kept in the down bay at Leamington to double-head the heavily loaded 14.10 from Paddington up Hatton Bank.[11]

The service was sparse. There were trains via Bicester from Paddington to Birmingham and beyond at 09.10, 11.05, 14.10, 16.05 and 18.10, most of them, after slip coaches were discontinued, stopping at Banbury, while services to Banbury and beyond via Oxford departed from Paddington at 06.20, 09.45, 13.45, 15.18 and 19.40. The midnight departure for Birkenhead via Oxford was scheduled to run almost as it did in peacetime although it was often delayed by bombing alerts.

Local services were little changed probably because workers in essential industries relied on them, and fuel could not be spared for buses. In the absence of a convenient bus two sisters with small children travelling from Wigginton to Banbury in 1944 pushed two prams to Hook Norton in order to catch the 17.20 auto-train from Kingham, which to a child appeared the most curious of trains, with a small locomotive at the back and a tall man standing in a cab at the front manipulating levers with each hand. A soldier on leave could take his children to expend precious clothing coupons at a department store in Northampton, by catching the 10.40 train from Merton Street whose connection reached Northampton at 11.50, returning to Banbury on the 18.00 from Blisworth. The organisers of a Sunday School could take children for a summer treat in 'Mr Cherry's field' at Cropredy on the 14.15 local to Leamington returning on the 17.15 ex-Leamington. These were not necessarily comfortable journeys but they were possible. Aspiring passengers elsewhere in Europe were less fortunate.[12]

---

[10] Stratton & Trinder, *Twentieth Century*, 113, 115; Copsey, 'Goods Operations at Banbury, part 2', 281; B Little, *The Changing Faces of Grimsbury* (Witney: Boyd, 1999), 54.
[11] *RM* vol 89 (1943), 250-51; *RR* No 1.8 (1945).
[12] Great Western Railway, Working Timetable for passenger &c trains, from 22 May 1944.

The comfortable interior of a Great Western auto-coach of the kind used on services from Banbury to Kingham and Princes Risborough. Great Western Trust Collection

Troops usually travelled significant distances by train rather than by road. Units of the British Expeditionary Force were conveyed to Southampton on 261 trains in the 27 days between 9 September and 5 October 1939. Banbury's 'Manor' class locomotives, the largest GWR engines permitted on the line from Reading, were utilised during mobilisation in the first weeks of the war to work troop trains for the Kentish ports as far as Redhill. Most movements were necessarily unrecorded, but some leave (or as the GWR timetable expressed it, 'furlough') trains, and some linking camps with market towns for Saturday evening rest and recreation were listed in the timetable. One such was the Monday 00.05 from Paddington which ran via Bicester to Cosford (Shropshire) for the RAF station opened just before the war. On Saturdays the 13.05 from Cosford, calling at Banbury between 14.53 and 15.00, took homeward-bound airmen in the opposite direction.[13]

---

[13] J Copsey, '78XXs in Traffic', *GWRJ* No 15 (1995), 637-48. See also L Waters, *Great Western Manor Class* (Barnsley: Pen & Sword, 2016).

Troop trains could not be photographed during the Second World War but servicemen continued to travel by rail into the 1960s. This train from the Nottingham area has been hauled to Banbury by K2 class 2-6-0 No 61753 from Colwick shed, which has been replaced by a WR locomotive and is returning tender first towards the Great Central line, 26 June 1954.

Cross-country services were abandoned except for the two night-time trains linking Swindon with Sheffield and York, and the Sunday service between Sheffield and South Wales, which was heavily patronised in wartime. An LNER engine took the southbound train to Swindon and returned with the northbound service. The train loaded to as many as 14 or 15 coaches, and often required piloting north of Banbury. Two LNER locomotives visiting Swindon broke down there, and were repaired in the Great Western works. One, in 1943, was ex-North Eastern Railway class D21 4-4-0 No 1241, the other the familiar Woodford-based class B1 (later B18) class 4-6-0 No 5195 (No 1479 from June 1946) which entered the works on 17 December 1944, while its train returned northwards behind No 5072 *Hurricane*, one of a dozen 'Castles' re-named after RAF aircraft. The night time trains were also heavily loaded and on one occasion in 1945 the first of them left Banbury double-headed by two ex-GCR 'Lord Farringdon' class 4-6-0s, Nos 6167, once called *Lloyd George*, and 6168 *Lord Stuart of Wortley*, a total weight of 254 tons.[14]

From 23 September 1940 the Railway Executive began a weekday cross country service, primarily to carry troops based in Kent and Surrey to and from leave in the north of England, departing from Ashford at 08.45, travelling via

---

[14] *RM* vol 85 (1939), 377, vol 89 (1943), 250-51, vol 91 (1945), 118; *RR* No 1.8 (1945); *IRB* (1945); W B Yeadon, *Yeadon's Register of LNER Locomotives, vol 22* (Nottingham: Booklaw/Railbus, 2001), 10-15; C J Allen, 'Last Main Line into London', *Trains Annual 1955* (London: Ian Allan, 1955), 36-47, 112.

Redhill and Reading, reaching Banbury at 13.13, then following the Great Central route to Sheffield and on to Newcastle where it arrived at 20.45. Initially it was one of the few wartime services to carry a buffet car, although that was withdrawn from 18 May 1942. It was always heavily loaded and usually included some of the LNER tourist coaches, once painted green and cream. It was worked from Redhill to Banbury by a Southern Railway locomotive, almost invariably one of the ten U1 class 2-6-0s, Nos. 1890-99 then allocated to Redhill. On one occasion in 1941 No 1897 arrived at Banbury with 16 LNER carriages and three vans, totalling 550 tons. It was replaced by a Woodford engine, the powerful if coal-hungry ex-GCR B7 class 4-6-0 No 5461. On 11 April 1942 the U1 No 1896 handed its train to a V2 class 2-6-2, No 4887. The return service left Newcastle at 08.12, changed engines at Banbury between 15.42 and 15.55, and reached Ashford at 20.32. In the summer of 1944 a relief train, the 10.35 North Camp (near Aldershot) to Sheffield, passing Banbury at 12.45, ran when required. Shortly before D-Day, on 15 May 1944, the service ceased. It was restored from 4 September 1944 when the southern terminus was altered to Southampton, and Southern Railway locomotives, 'King Arthur' class 4-6-0s and 'Schools' class 4-4-0s took it through Banbury to Woodford.[15]

The Long Slog: Freight

The principal concern of the Railway Executive was the movement of freight consigned to southern England from the north and the midlands, including coal, imports from west coast ports, and supplies for troops. The threat of bombing made it desirable to route this traffic away from London, and much of it was passed from the LMSR to the GWR at Wolverhampton or Bordesley Junction, or from the LNER at Banbury North.

The pattern of railway movements was shaped not only by old-established industries and military installations but also by new bases built to provide munitions on an unprecedented scale for an army that until D-Day was largely based in Britain, to sustain the airfields of Bomber Command, and, from early 1942, to build up the resources of United States forces as they prepared for the invasion of Europe. None of the Royal Ordnance Factories built during the war was near Banbury, but traffic from Chorley, Birtley, Thorpe Arch, Ruddington and Swynnerton, passed through *en route* to the south coast.[16]

The largest of the military storage depots established during the war was at Bicester. Construction began in the month after Dunkirk of 'the most ambitious single project every attempted for military purposes in the United Kingdom', which cost £5 million. The depot lies south of the town. Civilian contractors built

---

[15] *RM* vol 87 (1941), 139, 268, 332, 380, vol 91 (1945), 117, vol 92 (1946), 989; Great Western Railway, Working Timetable, 1944; *BT*, vol 8 (1994), 41-43; 166; *GWE* No 127 (1994), 6.
[16] Stratton & Trinder, *Twentieth Century*, 103-06, 212-14.

the store houses while Royal Engineers constructed the roads and the 47-mile internal railway system which in wartime included six halts and employed 90 staff. The depot was connected with the national railway network by a siding from the Bletchley–Oxford line, but some leave trains ran from Bicester North station on the GWR, and soldiers going to Banbury for rest and recreation on Saturday evenings could return to their base by an auto-train that left at 23.00 and stopped at Bicester North and Blackthorn before terminating at Brill. Rather more men went into Oxford on trains hauled by GWR 'Dean Goods' 0-6-0s and a 'Jubilee' class 0-4-2 from the Southern Railway. From 1942 troop trains could run into the depot and a twelve-coach Sunday evening leave train from Euston split into six-coach portions for Arncott and Piddington and for Graven Hill and Ambrosden. Immediately before D-Day some 24,000 troops were accommodated there.[17]

Another large depot lay north of Banbury. Construction began in October 1940 of Marlborough Farm Camp, alongside the SMJR line close to its junction with the Edge Hill Light Railway, parts of whose track were requisitioned by the War Department in 1941 and 1943. The depot included 252 storehouses for explosives and 64 miles of railway track linked to the SMJR at Burton Dassett. Nine locomotives were working on the system on 18 February 1945. A depot, at Barby, ten miles north of Woodford, had siding connections from the London Extension. Eight WD 0-6-0STs were employed there in the autumn of 1944.[18] Other depots that generated traffic through Banbury were establishments built during the First World War at Milton and Bramley and new depots at Donnington and Nesscliffe in Shropshire.

Many premises in the Banbury area were adapted as bases at first for the British and then for the United States Army, including the yet-to-be-opened roadhouse pub, the *Blacklocks Arms* on the Middleton Road, part of the Methodist premises in West Street, and the mansion at Wykham Park, once the home of the wealthy William Mewburn. Banbury was ringed by RAF airfields and communications centres: Upper Heyford which dated from 1916, Croughton which opened in 1938, Greatworth which also pre-dated the war, and Barford St John, Chipping Norton, Chipping Warden and Gaydon which were commissioned in 1940-42. Most of the airfields were concerned with operational training. All generated freight traffic and passenger movements. The arrival of 'tar' (probably asphalt) at Bloxham station for the runways at Barford St John was well-remembered. Railway staff sometimes encountered difficulties with servicemen who objected to paying for tickets for evening journeys into Banbury.[19]

---

[17] Stratton & Trinder, *Twentieth Century*, 110; R T Munns, *Milk Churns to Merry-go-round* (Newton Abbot: David & Charles, 1986), 22.
[18] *RR* No 10 (1945); *IRB* No 6 (1944).
[19] W Hemmings, P Karau & C Turner, *The Banbury & Cheltenham Railway, vol 2* (Didcot: Wild Swan, 2004), 275.

The best measure of freight traffic through Banbury in wartime is provided by figures for the exchange of wagons with the LNER via the line to Woodford. In 1940 some 689,986 wagons, an average of 13,262 per week were exchanged at the junction with the LNER, the highest total recorded in the history of the line. The daily average of wagons moved south to Banbury increased from 1,148 (or 23 trains of 50 wagons) in 1942 to 1,220 in 1943, a rise of 6.3 per cent.[20]

Trains to and from Woodford comprised less than half the total handled at Banbury during the war. In 1943, 21 scheduled freight trains arrived at Banbury Junction from the ex-GCR line, 17 of which were trip workings from Woodford, the others originating from Stairfoot (near Barnsley), Sheffield, Nottingham and Leicester. In the opposite direction 21 trains left the down marshalling yard for the north, all trip workings to Woodford except for the 18.05 perishables to York, carrying wagons from the 13.00 class 'C' train from Worcester that reached Banbury via Stratford-upon-Avon at 17.25. Some 33 trains arrived from the Leamington direction, including six loads of iron ore empties. Of the general goods trains, six originated in South Wales at Cardiff, Newport, Copperworks Junction (Margam) and Rogerstone, two at Worcester and two at Gloucester. All the long-distance freight traffic from South Wales travelled via Stratford and Hatton. Most other trains came from the Black Country and Birmingham, although one originated at Crewe. Overnight between 20.45 and 05.15 six southbound fast goods trains passed Banbury without entering the yard, four of them classified C or D linking Wolverhampton and Birkenhead with Paddington, the others an express freight from Oxley to Basingstoke and a coal train from Leamington to Oxford. A similar number of express freights passed northwards. There were 36 daily southbound departures from the sidings of the hump yard, including pick-up workings to Brill, Hook Norton, Kingham and Old Oak Common, trains for the Morris Motors factory at Cowley and the cement works at Shipton-on-Cherwell, and workings as far afield as Bristol, Newton Abbot and Tavistock Junction. Most traffic for the Southern Railway was tripped to Didcot. Sixteen trains from the south terminated in the down yard at Banbury, including return workings of the local pick-up trains, while 23 northbound trains called at the yard to collect or set down wagons. Thirteen terminated at Oxley Sidings, Wolverhampton, five in Birmingham, two at Leamington and one at Crewe, while two were rakes of empty coal wagons bound for Woodford. Twenty one northbound trains began their journeys at Banbury station or the down yard, twelve of them carrying iron ore, one a livestock train running when required to Kingswinford in the Black Country, pick-up trains for Fenny Compton and Tyseley and two long-distance goods trains for Cardiff and Severn Tunnel Junction.[21]

---

[20] J Copsey & M Clifton, 'Banbury – The Shed, the Engines and the Men', *GWRJ* No 3 (1992), 96-102; M Smith, 'Avoiding Banbury … and Acton', *BRI* No 6 (1992), 322-23; Munns, *Milk Churns to Merry-go-round*, 69.

[21] B Trinder, 'The Railway Marshalling Yard at Banbury', *C&CH* vol 4 (1970), 131-36.

The WD class 2-8-0s built during the Second World War worked all over British Railways during the 1950s when they were the principal freight motive power at Woodford and hauled virtually all the trip workings to Banbury. Here No 90491 heads south on the London Extension at Helmdon, 3 April 1956.

The importance of freight movements through Banbury was indicated by the concentration in the area of many of the GWR's 2800 class 2-8-0s, of which there were 18 at the shed in 1941, 25 in the following year, and 24 in January 1944. Nevertheless wartime freight movements on the GWR were sustained by antiquated locomotives, some borrowed from other companies. One of the first loans from the LMSR was a batch of ex-Midland Railway class 2F and 3F 0-6-0s. An observer at Leamington in 1940 saw a freight train heading for Banbury hauled by a GWR 'Bulldog', No 3391 *Dominion of Canada* and LMS 3F No 3585. It became a regular practice in the area to couple two freight trains together, and one was seen between Leamington and Banbury in 1940 headed by another 'Bulldog', No 3366 *Earl of Cork* with 3F No 3387 in the middle. Late in 1940 Banbury shed received from the LNER five 2-8-0s of class O4, of the same design as the GWR's ROD class. The O4s left during 1942 but the LNER then provided a batch of class J25 0-6-0s, designed in 1898 for the North Eastern Railway by Wilson Worsdell. The LMSR loaned the Great Western some of its modern 8F class 2-8-0s, and in the course of the war 80 more of the class were built at Swindon. None of the wartime locos was officially allocated to Banbury although they worked into the marshalling yard from elsewhere. The Swindon-built 8Fs were returned to the LMS from late 1946. From the Southern Railway the GWR borrowed all seven 'Remembrance' class 4-6-0s, and five H15s of the same wheel arrangement. The variety of locomotives active on freight trains in 1941 is illustrated by an observer at Didcot on 18 April of that year who saw two LMSR class 3Fs based at the local shed, an O4 working from Reading and an 8F returning towards its temporary home at Severn Tunnel Junction.[22]

The growth in traffic was partially matched by the introduction of new locomotives. In 1942-44 some 398 2-8-0 locomotives, designed and built in the United States and classified S160, were shipped to Great Britain, unloaded at Newport, and used by the four companies. The LNER had 166 of them, and the pressure of traffic on the former GCR is indicated by the allocation of 14 of them to Woodford by May 1944 and 26 by August of that year. The GWR was allocated 175 of the class ten of which were working from Banbury by January 1944. More were sent to the shed in the following months to assist with the build-up to D-Day.[23]

Once the allied forces had established their beachhead in Normandy the military began to transport the S160s to the continent. Many were hauled to Newport for shipping and some made their way to South Wales under their own steam. Three that had been working on the LNER were observed at Banbury on 23 September 1944. They had been painted grey with white numbers, 'a very pleasing contrast', according to one observer, 'to the more general filthy conditions these locos were kept in while running on our metals'.[24]

Two further classes of freight locomotive appeared during 1943, designed for the Ministry of Supply by Robert Riddles, and usually called the WD (War Department) or Austerity classes. Some 935 2-8-0s and 150 2-10-0s were constructed by private builders. The North British Locomotive Company in the autumn of 1944 was completing one a day at its factories in Glasgow. By September 1944 the WDs were working from most of the sheds that powered freight trains through Banbury as well as from Banbury itself but before the end of 1944 they followed the S160s to the continent and few remained in England by February 1945.[25]

In 1944 an observer at Saunderton between Princes Risborough and High Wycombe found the line from Banbury busy with freight trains, some hauled by

---

[22] Copsey & Clifton; 'Banbury – The Shed', 96-102; B Brooksbank, *Train Watchers No 1* (Burton-on-Trent: Pearson, 1982), 29-31; *GWE* No 56 (1976), 13-14.
[23] Copsey & Clifton, 'Banbury – The Shed', 96-102; *FD* May 1944; *IR3* Aug 1944.
[24] *IRB* Nos 4 & 5 (1944).
[25] *IRB* Nos 4, 5, 6 (1944), No 7 (1945).

WDs or 8Fs or by the GWR's own 2-8-0s, but one by an 'Aberdare' and another by 'Bulldog' class No 3407 *Madras*. A visitor to Banbury shed on Boxing Day 1944 found it remarkably empty, with most of its locomotives out working freight trains. Engines on loan included an LMSR 3F, two 8Fs and a North Eastern J25.[26]

Railwaymen – and women

The strain of wartime working is conveyed in the memoirs of a Shropshire railwayman, Ken Jones, who as a young fireman moved to Banbury on 22 July 1940 and lodged for 14 months with Arthur Walton, a fellow engineman, at 'Penryn', a semi-detached house in East Street. He recalled the tedium of night work with a 'Dean Goods' 0-6-0 pushing wagons over the hump and the difficulties of rigging tarpaulins to hide the fires on locomotives with open cabs. He endured the discomfort of firing an ill-maintained ROD class 2-8-0 on a freight train to Didcot. An Oxford enginemen recalled shifts lasting several days: 'Oxford to Paddington to Birmingham to Southampton to Oxford. Away three days after leaving for an 8-hour shift'.[27]

As in other parts of England women took over railway jobs. Mrs Beer from Howard Road, passenger guard, worked on the BCDR in wartime, and regularly took the Newcastle–Bournemouth train to Oxford into the 1950s, while Miss Spittle from Middleton Road, passenger porter, was a familiar figure on the station platforms. The signal box at Bloxham was staffed by women during the war.[28]

The summer of 1944 saw the peak of wartime railway activity. The signal boxes at Banbury North, Banbury South and Banbury Junction were open continuously while the Ironstone Sidings box was closed only between 06.00 on Sundays and 06.00 on Mondays. Between April and June the Great Western alone operated more than three thousand special trains carrying troops, stores and equipment ready for the invasion, many of which passed through Banbury. After D-Day ambulance trains passed northwards with wounded from the battlefields, and between June and August the GWR put on 167 trains to take prisoners-of-war away from the coast. Urban myths circulated about American GIs escorting prisoners on such a train, sitting by open windows in the corridor of the leading carriage and being drenched when it passed over the water troughs at Aynho. The Army Post Office at Nottingham which handed mail bags to the LNER at the city's London Road station from where trains departed via Banbury to a south coast port were given priority over other workings.[29]

---

[26] *IRB* No 1 (1944), No 8 (1945); *WRL* No 2.22 (1944).
[27] K B Jones, *The Wenlock Branch* (Usk: Oakwood, 1998), 208-09; A Vaughan, *The Heart of the Great Western* (Wadenhoe, Silver Link, 1994).
[28] Hemmings, Karau & Turner, *Banbury & Cheltenham Railway, vol 2*, 274-77.
[29] Booker, *Great Western Railway*, 155-56; *RO* vol 21 (1945); Potts, *An Historical Survey, vol. 4*, 13.

Star class 4-6-0 No 4003 'Lode Star' travelled from Swansea to Banbury and back with the successor to the 'Ports-to-Ports Express' on the first occasion on which it ran after the war, 6 October 1946. George Behrend travelled on the train and recalled the change of engines at Banbury. Great Western Trust Collection

Relief

The legacy of the war lingered for many years over Britain's railways. The sense of relief at the end of hostilities is captured in George Behrend's description of his return home from military service to his home near Newbury. Having been demobilised at York on 6 October 1946 he discovered that there was a train to Swansea via Banbury, the first revival of the former *Ports-to-Ports Express* after the war. Platform staff knew little about it and the ticket collector was uncertain of its route. Behrend describes the train's passage through Yorkshire and southwards from Sheffield behind a V2 class 2-6-2, passing at Leicester Central the northbound service with Great Western coaches adorned with boards proclaiming 'Swansea, Cardiff, Banbury, Leicester, Sheffield, York and Newcastle-upon-Tyne'. Having taken water at Woodford the V2 approached the Great Western at Banbury, giving Behrend what he described as a 'Banbury feeling', similar to that encountered when he crossed the Rhine at Basel, entering a region where every feature was familiar, the distant prospect of Edge Hill, ex-Great Central O4 class 2-8-0s on freight trains and the inscription 'Banbury Junction Signal Box'. He watched the change of engines at Banbury, finding that, as usual, the train was to be taken south by the Landore (Swansea) engine off the northbound service, which proved to be No 4003 *Lode Star* (now preserved) on whose footplate were two locomotive inspectors, enjoying the ride, as well as the fireman and driver. He was pleasurably astonished 'to know every little station after so much strangeness', and duly changed at Oxford on to a local for Didcot and then to a DNSR train that took him to his home on the Berkshire Downs.[30]

On closer examination Behrend would have found that much had changed at Banbury. Express passenger services were much reduced. In the last Great Western timetable that began in October 1947, following government restrictions on the use of coal, Banbury had only four services via Bicester to Paddington and four direct trains via Oxford, while the only cross-country services were the night-time trains between Swindon and York. Small extensions had been made at the station although the main structure was little changed. The roof was miraculously intact. The goods depot had been patched up after the bombing of 3 October 1940. Additional sidings had been installed around the marshalling yard. Camouflaged shelters hid locomotives arriving at the engine shed, obscuring the glow of discarded ashes from unfriendly aircraft, while crippled locomotives queued for attention in the new lifting shop. Women were working in signal boxes and as passenger guards and porters. Railwaymen returned from working Dean Goods 0-6-0s fitted with Westinghouse air brakes from depots in the Mezzogiorno that were christened, in Great Western style, FoGgiA or TaranTO, or from riding with German crews between the shattered marshalling yards of the Ruhrgebiet. Others had suffered worse experiences in the Far East. At Banbury, as elsewhere, the railway system survived the conflict, but those who operated it had undergone much pain, and the war left a legacy of exhaustion, of men, women and equipment.[31]

---

[30] Behrend, *Gone with Regret*, 152-59.
[31] Behrend, *Gone with Regret*, 110-11. Vaughan, *Heart of the Great Western*, 57.

12. Nationalisation and After, 1948-1960

One of those peaks in particular is causing the Railway the deepest concern: the summer holiday peak which rises to a nightmare intensity at the August Bank Holiday weekend.
Great Western Railway, *Next Station* (1947).[1]

The general election of July 1945 resulted in the defeat of Winston Churchill's Conservative Party and the installation of a Labour government under Clement Attlee with a substantial majority. Locally, the Labour candidate came close to taking the Banbury seat, and the following November Labour secured seven of the twelve seats contested in the town council election. The Labour manifesto pledged that the commanding heights of the economy would be brought into public ownership and from New Year's Day 1948 the railways were nationalised. The system was divided into six regions. The main line through Banbury formed part of the Western Region, but it was joined at Banbury North Junction by the former LNER tracks of the Eastern Region, on which, from 1 November 1948, trains ran to *Woodford Halse* station, rather than to Woodford & Hinton. Merton Street station was part of the London Midland Region, successor to the LMSR. There was some co-ordination of management. By 1950 A W Moll was station master for the two stations and W H Daffurn served as goods agent for both the Western and London Midland regions. The principal local investments in the early years of Nationalisation were the construction of a hostel for locomotive crews off Middleton Road and the building of houses for railwaymen in Western Crescent and Lime Avenue. The new passenger station planned by the GWR when war intervened in 1939, with two island platforms, high-level access from the Middleton Road bridge, and bays at the north for LNER locals and at the south for LMSR trains, was further postponed, although the old station's overall roof was removed in 1953. A new station was finally constructed in 1956-58, providing a second through down platform, but no equivalent up platform, and no facilities for trains from Merton Street. The marshalling yard could scarcely cope with the traffic of the immediate post-war years, but congestion was mitigated by re-routing some services. The engine shed was home to diminishing numbers of locomotives, 90 in 1945, 64 in 1950 and 51 in 1955.[2]

---

[1] C Barman, *The Great Western Railway's last look forward* (1947, Rep Newton Abbot: David & Charles, 1972), 10.
[2] J R Hodgkins, *Over the Hills to Glory* (Southend: Clifton Press, 1978), 10-13; C R Potts, *An Historical Survey of Selected Great Western Stations, vol. 4* (Poole: Oxford Publishing Co, 1985), 13; Barman, *The Great Western Railway's last look forward*, 58-59, 67-68.

The new Banbury station built in 1956-58.

A shock disturbed the railway system on Thursday 2 July 1953. The 17.12 semi-fast from Banbury to Paddington (14.35 ex-Shrewsbury) was handled by a Banbury crew, and on that day was hauled, unusually, by a Banbury locomotive, No 5930 *Hannington Hall*. The driver was the jovial, rotund George Hambridge, inspiration of the locomen's mutual improvement society. The train, due to reach Paddington at 19.40 after stopping at Oxford, Didcot, Reading and Ealing Broadway, provided the fastest service from Banbury to London at that time of day – the 19.03 departure via Bicester did not reach the capital until 20.35. As the train approached Fritwell & Somerton Hambridge noticed a USAF B47 jet bomber approaching the runway at Upper Heyford and obviously in trouble. He shut off steam bringing his train to a gentle stop. The aircraft hit the ground about 300 yards from the railway, cut a swathe across a cornfield, and exploded, killing the crew, as it hit the embankment 200 yards ahead of the train. The signalman at Fritwell & Somerton also saw the crash and set signals at danger. The crisis was handled expeditiously. George Hambridge ran 5930 round the train and took it back tender first to Banbury where a 4300 class 2-6-0 was ready to haul it towards Oxford via Kingham. Other trains between Banbury and Oxford were cancelled or diverted. Wreckage was strewn across the line but the damage to the permanent way was soon repaired, and normal working was restored before the following morning.[3]

---

[3] *Bicester Advertiser* 10 July 1953.

By 1950 Banbury shed had lost all its 'Dean Goods' 0-6-0 locomotives, but No 2513 from Chester was waiting to leave the shed to pick up a northbound freight train on 26 April 1954.   Ian Stratford

Motive power

Wartime operations bequeathed a legacy of elderly, ill-maintained locomotives. The first 'Aberdare' class 2-6-0 freight engine to be withdrawn since the beginning of the war was scrapped in 1944 when 31 members of the 81 engines in the class, introduced in 1901, were still running. Three were then working from Banbury of which two remained at Nationalisation. They were soon scrapped and the last of the class was withdrawn from Worcester in November 1949. There was still a 'Dean Goods' 0-6-0 at Banbury at Nationalisation, which soon departed for Oswestry, but 54 of the class remained and engines from Oxford, Didcot, Reading and Swindon continued to pass through before the last was withdrawn in 1957. The last of the pre-World War I pannier tanks were also scrapped. Banbury's 2753 was withdrawn in December 1945, but 2065 remained on the shed's allocation at Nationalisation. The outside-framed No 1287 of the 'Sir Daniel' class, built in 1887, was overhauled at Swindon and returned to its shed at Leamington in May 1944. It was withdrawn two years later, and after service as a stationary boiler was hauled south in 1953, and lodged in the down yard at Banbury before resuming its journey to Swindon. On the evening of 20 May 1955 No 2183 from Croes Newydd, one of the ten 2181 class pannier tanks of 1897 fitted in 1939 with increased brake power, followed the Grimsby fish train out of Banbury on its last journey to Swindon.[4]

---

[4] *TI* vol 3 (1950), 34; *IRB* No 1 (1944); *LE* No 23 (1946).

'Duke' class 4-4-0 No 3083 'Comet' (previously 3315, 3283), built in 1899 was still working freight trains after the Second World War. It was observed at Tyseley in April 1946 with its nameplate amended to 'InCOME Tax'. Great Western Trust Collection

Several passenger engines well known to generations of travellers from Banbury disappeared. The 'Duke' class 4-4-0 No 9083 *Comet* (previously 3315, 3283), completed in March 1899, was regarded with particular affection and in April 1946 was observed at Tyseley with its nameplate amended to *InCOMETax*. By 1950 it was shedded at Swindon and used only on freight trains. It made a last appearance at Banbury in November 1950, arriving from the north about noon and taking on coal at the shed before leaving for Swindon with a freight train. It was scrapped the following month.[5]

The 'Saint' class No 2981 *Ivanhoe* was built experimentally as a 4-4-2 in 1905 and converted to a 4-6-0 in 1912. The zenith of it distinguished career came in January 1932 when it was substituted at Swindon for Castle class No 5000 on the up *Cheltenham Flyer*, and ran the 77.25 miles to Paddington in 64 minutes. Less gloriously it was photographed on 22 July 1939 shunting coaches at Banbury station, in filthy condition with steam oozing from every joint. In wartime it worked from Stafford Road, Wolverhampton, but was overhauled at Swindon in the closing months of 1945 and transferred to Banbury in 1946. *Ivanhoe* was soon

---

[5] G Behrens, *Gone with Regret* (Sidcup: Lambarde Press, 1964), 40; T Middlemass, ed, *Railway Reflections* (Wellingborough: Patrick Stephens, 1989), 105; *RM* vol 94 (1948), 274; *RL*. No 1.10 (1946).

2181 class 0-6-0PT No 2183 leaves Banbury en route for scrapping at Swindon, 20 May 1955.

fit only to be used on the 'Target', the haulage of down freight trains left in the loops alongside the shed to the down sidings near the North Junction. When several trains were coupled together the loads could approach a hundred wagons and the sound of the veteran being thrashed through the station remains memorable. *Ivanhoe* was withdrawn in March 1951 and was succeeded on the 'Target' by ROD class 2-8-0 No 3020 whose journeys through the station were equally thunderous.[6]

'Saint' No 2933 *Bibury Court*, a Leamington engine once familiar on local trains, ended its days as a Hatton banker, until on 17 January 1953, she worked the 09.05 freight from Leamington to Banbury and then the 14.20 departure for Swindon. Other members of the class continued to undertake main line duties. No 2927 *Saint Patrick* for a lengthy period in 1950 hauled the evening Swindon–Sheffield service as far as Banbury. The contemporary 'Star' class four-cylinder 4-6-0s were particularly evident on weekend reliefs to and from Paddington. One of the last survivors, No 4061 *Glastonbury Abbey*, hauled the up *Inter City* on 16 November 1951, and for a spell in 1955-56 served as station pilot at Banbury. She worked a Stephenson Locomotive Society excursion from Birmingham to Swindon on 11 September 1955, passing through Banbury on the return journey, and was withdrawn in March 1957.[7]

---

[6] *RM* vol 70, (1932), 383; *LE* No 2.6 (1945), 24; *RW*, Dec 1977; *TI* June 1951.
[7] *TI* vol 6 (1953), 32; *RO* Vol 21 No 274 (1951).

A faraway accident deprived Banbury shed of one of its locomotives. The 2-6-0 No 6315, far from its normal haunts, was hauling a night mail train from Ruabon to Barmouth on 8 September 1945 when, between Llangollen and Sun Bank Halt, it plunged into a 40 ft gap in the track caused by the bursting of the bank of the adjacent canal. The engine was so severely damaged that it was cut up on the spot.[8]

Banbury was involved with the experiment in 1946-48 using oil for firing steam locomotives. In August 1946 the Ministry of Transport announced that 1,217 locomotives would be converted, and that re-fuelling facilities would be installed at 16 Great Western depots, which included Banbury, where two 10,300-gallon tanks were erected west of the coaling stage. Alongside was a cabin with a boiler and pump, later used as a mess room and a first aid post. Eighteen GWR locomotives had been adapted for oil burning by February 1947. A further 19 were converted during the following twelve months but the Ministry of Transport withdrew the scheme during 1948, and by the December all the locomotives concerned were re-adapted for coal firing. The fuelling installation at Banbury appears scarcely to have been used. Oil-fuelling facilities were also installed at Woodford, but similarly they saw little use, and were demolished in 1957.[9]

The Great Western Railway renewed much of its locomotive stock in its fading years between VE-Day and Nationalisation. Banbury received two of the last batch of 2251 class 0-6-0s completed in 1948, and used them on pick-up freights to Old Oak Common. The first of F W Hawksworth's 'County' class 4-6-0s introduced in 1945, No 1000 *County of Middlesex*, worked the 09.10 from Paddington to Birkenhead and its usual return service, the 14.35 from Wolverhampton, for a long spell in September and October 1945, but the class became more familiar on cross-country turns than on London expresses. New 'Castle' class engines continued to appear through the summer of 1950. Banbury shed was allocated its first WD 2-8-0 of the peacetime years, No 77408 (later 90284), in June 1947, and two or three of the class were allocated there for most of the next 17 years. The autumn of 1949 saw the arrival of new 9400 class 0-6-0 panier tanks, which worked the hump yard until 1955. Shortly before Nationalisation the GWR placed an order for 200 of the class with private builders in Darlington, Leeds and Stafford, and on the Wednesdays or Thursdays of most weeks in the early 1950s new locomotives arrived dead at Banbury, from W G Bagnall of Stafford in coal trains from Nuneaton, or from Robert Stephenson & Hawthorn or the Yorkshire Engine Co on trip workings

---

[8] *RL* No 1.3 (1945); *RO* vol 15 No 200 (1945).
[9] J M C Healy, *Echoes of the Great Central* (London: Greenwich Editions, 1996), 105; C W Judge, *Thro' the Lens* (Poole: Railprint, 1985), 202; *SW* No 337, July 2015, 26-29; J Copsey & M Clifton, 'Banbury – The Shed, the Engines and the Men', *GWRJ* No 3 (1992), 102-03; Barman, *The Great Western Railway's Last Look Forward*, 30-33.

from the GC line, before being hauled towards Swindon on a freight train departing about 19.30. The last of the class, No 3409, was brought down the branch from Woodford on 28 September 1956.[10]

Some of the inter-regional trains that reached Banbury from the Great Central line in the early 1950s were worked by pacifics such as No 60044 'Melton', waiting to leave the shed after arriving with the Newcastle–Bournemouth train in 1954.

This was a time of change on the former Great Central lines. The LNER's Chief Mechanical Engineer between 1941 and 1946, Edward Thompson, controversially embarked on a programme of standardised two-cylinder mixed traffic locomotives. His B1 class 4-6-0s from 1943 took over many of the duties of former Great Central locomotives on the London Extension and its branch to Banbury, while his L1 class 2-6-4T tank engines appeared on workings from Neasden. With the arrival of more pacifics and V2 class 2-6-2s the line lost its Great Central air.[11] The 27 Great Central Atlantics were particularly associated with the London Extension. Twenty remained at Nationalisation but they were concentrated in Lincolnshire and the last was withdrawn in 1950.

---

[10] *LE* No 2.4 (1945); *RL* No 1.3 (1945); *GWE* No 122 (1993), 13.
[11] *RM* vol 89 (1943), 165, vol 90 (1944), 316.

The Great Central's 4-6-0s made their final appearances on the London Extension in 1949. No 61482, named *Immingham* after it hauled the royal train to the opening of Immingham Dock in 1912, happened to be at Leicester on 25 June 1949 when an influential admirer ensured that it took to Banbury the twelve coaches of the Newcastle–Bournemouth train. Ten weeks later, on Saturday 10 September 1949, one of the last of the B7 class, No 61709, which had been based at Woodford during the Second World War, worked the Banbury Motor. Both locomotives were withdrawn during 1950. The two GCR B18 class 4-6-0s Nos 5195/96 that were particularly associated with wartime services over the Woodford branch were scrapped shortly before Nationalisation.[12]

Seventeen Great Central locomotives remained at Woodford in 1950, ten J11 or 'Pom-Pom' 0-6-0s, two of the 97½ ton 2-6-4T tank locomotives of class L3, and five N15 class 0-6-2T tank locomotives which shunted the yards. All three classes, particularly the 'Pom-Poms', occasionally worked the 'Banbury Motor'. The L3s were scrapped in the summer of 1953 and the N5s departed from Woodford after the arrival of diesel shunters in 1954. Immediately after Nationalisation the Banbury Motor service, involving two trips with three coaches from Woodford to Banbury, returning at 10.04 and 13.16, was worked by Woodford's four B17 4-6-0s, which were in too bad a condition to undertake more strenuous duties. The engine nominally allocated for this service was an ex-Great Northern N2 class 0-6-2T, No 69560, which was unpopular with its crews. It was replaced in 1952 by a Great Central engine, Class C13 4-4-2T No 67408, which was in turn supplanted in 1953 by a former Great Eastern engine, N7 class 0-6-2T No 69621. The duty was sometimes undertaken by locomotives resting between turns at Woodford, including ex-North Eastern Railway class B16 4-6-0s, class L1 2-6-4Ts and ex-Great Central class A5 4-6-2Ts from Neasden, and by two Ivatt 4MT 2-6-0s transferred from South Lynn in 1956. In the closing months of the war Woodford's passenger engines were 16 class K3 class 2-6-0s but during 1949 they were replaced by ten V2 class 2-6-2s, which became the characteristic Woodford express locomotives of the 1950s. Passenger services on the branch were distinguished by the allocation to Leicester shed of No 60103 *Flying Scotsman*, which for several years worked cross-country trains and balancing locals. The WD 2-8-0s replaced ex-GCR class 04 2-8-0s and J11 0-6-0s on transfer freights and became the characteristic Woodford freight engines. The first were allocated to Woodford in January 1946 and more than 20 were at the depot before the end of that year. Like many other sheds Woodford was short of staff and had 33 vacancies for cleaners in the summer of 1951.[13]

---

[12] *SD* No 121 (1999), 574; *RO* vol 21, no 263, Jan 1951.
[13] *TI* April 1952, May 1953, May 1960; R H N Hardy, *Steam in the Blood* (London: Ian Allan, 1971, 1975), 105-06, 108; *RO* Vol 21 No 274 (1951).

A 7F class 0-8-0 approaching Banbury shed having brought a coal train from the Warwickshire Coalfield, 1954.

Inter-regional co-operation

Nationalisation stimulated an increase in inter-regional workings. On most weekday afternoons from 1950 a London Midland Region 7F 0-8-0 from Warwick (usually No 49120) and an 8F 2-8-0 (usually No 48020) from Nuneaton hauled coal trains from the Warwickshire coalfield through Leamington to the reception sidings at Banbury hump yard. From 1951 Southern Region Q1 0-6-0s worked as far as Banbury with the 05.50 from Eastleigh, consisting in season of coal wagons filled with sugar beet from the Chichester area, consigned to the sugar factory at Colwick near Nottingham. Another Southern Region working in the 1950s was the summertime 16.20 Southampton–Crewe perishables which reached Banbury at 22.30. 'King Arthur' and 'Remembrance' class locomotives were employed but it became a regular turn for Eastleigh's standard class 4MT 2-6-0s. In the summer of 1951 the Western Region borrowed six O4 class 2-8-0s from the Hull depots of the North Eastern Region, most of which appeared at Banbury in the following months. From 1957 locomotives from Saltley on the London Midland Region in Birmingham began to work the 12.15 Washwood

Heath–Eastleigh fitted freight through Banbury as far as Hinksey Yard, Oxford, returning on the 16.40 Hinksey–Water Orton.[14]

There were also through passenger workings. In the summer of 1949 the Saturday Poole–Bradford train was worked to Banbury by a Southern Region locomotive from Basingstoke, usually a 'Remembrance' class 4-6-0. This working ceased in 1953, but in most subsequent summers Southern locomotives made sporadic weekend appearances at Banbury on passenger trains. Two light engine movements between Woodford and Banbury were eliminated from September 1953 when the Banbury 'Hall' which brought the Bournemouth–Newcastle train from Oxford to Banbury continued to Leicester, and returned with the first fish train from Hull. From November 1960 the Banbury engine that took over the daily Newcastle–Bournemouth continued to Bournemouth instead of coming off at Oxford.[15]

The route of the Dorrington–Marylebone milk train was rationalised after Nationalisation. An Eastern Region locomotive from Neasden left Marylebone with the empties at 19.35, ran direct to Banbury through Princes Risborough and Bicester, and placed the tanks in the down bay around 21.30. It was turned at the shed, then took over the up train at 23.00. From the mid-1950s the up train, departing from Birmingham Snow Hill at 22.00, carried a passenger carriage to Banbury, introduced at the instigation of Councillor Harry Price, mayor in 1952-53, railwayman, and native of Stourbridge. This was a popular innovation since the last train from Snow Hill to Banbury was previously the 20.10 departure for Paddington. The Dorrington milk train was still running in 1965, when it was hauled by 'Western' class diesels, but ceased soon afterwards when the creamery closed.

The standard class steam locomotives introduced by British Railways in 1951 made only a limited impression at Banbury. The Western Region received 15 of the 'Britannia' class pacifics built at Crewe which slipped quietly through Banbury *en route* to Swindon during the summer of 1951. In the autumn of that year several of the class allocated to Old Oak Common worked the 09.10 from Paddington and its customary return working, but the pacifics were later concentrated at Cardiff and only occasionally reached the Midlands. The standard 4-6-0s of class 5MT and 4MT were regarded on the Western Region principally as freight locomotives and only occasionally worked through Banbury, although by the late 1950s 5MT locomotives allocated to Weymouth, then on the Southern Region, hauled trains from the coast through to Wolverhampton, and those at Neasden occasionally arrived from Woodford. Class 4MT 2-6-0s from Neasden sometimes worked the Dorrington milk train and members of the class from Eastleigh hauled seasonal fruit trains from Southampton. Otherwise few standard locomotives were seen at Banbury General until the late 1950s.

---

[14] *RO* Vol 21 (1951); 269; M Page, 'We're off to Leamington', *SD*, No 313 (2015), 9-10.
[15] *TI* January 1961.

The British Railways Modernisation Plan released in 1955 envisaged a change from steam to diesel and electric traction. It was followed by the introduction of diesel locomotive and multiple units, but their impact on operations through Banbury before 1960 was limited, indeed, the experimental Bo-Bo diesel No 10800 which worked freight trains into Merton Street was the only main line diesel locomotive to work regularly to Banbury in that decade. In February 1954 a 3ft 6in gauge 950hp Bo-Bo diesel built by the Birmingham Railway Carriage & Wagon Co at Smethwick and intended for export was placed on standard gauge bogies and worked five-coach articulated sets of ex-LNER air-braked suburban stock to Banbury on trials. The Western Region's second gas turbine locomotive No 18100 probably travelled via Banbury on its way to Swindon from Trafford Park where it was built by Metropolitan Vickers. On 1 April 1952 it certainly passed through with a 13-coach test train from London to Wolverhampton, but it never worked regularly on the northern line, nor did No 18000 its Swiss-built counterpart. No 18100 was re-incarnated in the late 1950s as an electric locomotive, No E2001, for crew-training on the West Coast Main Line. By 1969 it was stored in the open at Akeman Street between Ashendon and Grendon Underwood junctions. It was scrapped in November 1972.[16] Diesel multiple units were responsible for only three or four return semi-fast workings through Banbury by the end of the decade, all working to or through Oxford and following rosters designed for steam trains.

Nos 13106/08, two of the batch of six 350 hp diesel shunters that worked at Banbury from the spring of 1955. 6 April 1955. Ian Stratford

Banbury shed received six standard 350hp 0-6-0 diesel shunters (class 08) in the spring of 1955, making redundant the shed's 9400 class panier tanks, while new engines of the same class were still being delivered. Woodford received a similar allocation early in 1954.

---

[16] Page, 'We're off to Leamington', 12.

The Main Line

Services on the GWR northern line reverted to their pre-war pattern, although timings were slower. The principal trains were hauled, as they had been before 1939, by 'King' class 4-6-0s from Old Oak Common and Wolverhampton Stafford Road, which between 1949 and 1952 bore the standard blue livery.[17]

'Princess Coronation' class 4-6-2 No 46257 'City of Salford' passes Banbury shed with the 09.10 ex-Paddington on 20 February 1956. Ian Stratford

A new express leaving Paddington at 09.00 for Birmingham and Wolverhampton, and returning at 16.35 was inaugurated on 4 March 1946. It was soon restricted to a Mondays Only service, then reinstated, and was named the *Inter City* from 25 September 1950. On 5 May 1951 another named train, the *William Shakespeare*, was introduced, one of five services marking the Festival of Britain that were made up of Mark I standard coaches. It left Paddington at 10.10 and was principally a train for Wolverhampton, but carried three coaches for Stratford detached at Leamington. The *William Shakespeare* was not well publicised and ceased to run in September 1951. Stratford was then served, as previously, by a coach carried to Leamington on the tail of the 09.10 from Paddington, returning on the 17.35 ex-Wolverhampton. A more lasting innovation was the introduction of sleeping cars on the overnight services between Paddington and Birkenhead from the start of the winter timetable in 1954.[18]

---

[17] R C Riley, *Great Western Album* (London: Ian Allan, 1966), 20; J Copsey, '"Kings" on the Northern Line', *GWRJ* No 3 (1992), 109-17; *RO* vol 21 (1951).

[18] Barman, *The Great Western Railway's last look forward*, 9; *TI* July 1951; R P & R P Hendry, *Paddington to the Mersey* (Sparkford: Oxford Publishing, 1992), 105; *RO* vol 21 (1951), 294 (1953); *SC* 3 Dec 1954.

London Midland Region power appeared on the main line for two short spells. For several weeks in May 1955 the Stanier pacific No 46237 *City of Bristol* experimentally worked the 09.10 from Paddington. The following January the 'Kings' were temporarily withdrawn from traffic to have bogie faults checked and four LMR pacifics, Nos 46207/10, and 46254/57 were borrowed for Paddington–Wolverhampton workings.[19]

LMR 'Princess Royal' class 4-6-2 No 46207 'Princess Arthur of Connaught' heading the 09.10 Paddington–Birkenhead near King's Sutton while the 'Kings' were out of service early in 1956.

---

[19] *SD* January 2016, 19.

Slip coach services, a feature of operations at Banbury in the 1930s, were not resumed there after the war, but the principal businessmen's train to the West Midlands, the 17.10 from Paddington, dropped a coach at Bicester which was carried forward on a local train. This was a popular service with Banburians, although they could not access the 17.10's lavish dining facilities. The Bicester slip continued until Friday 9 September 1960 when it was the last such service in Britain.[20]

The coastal resorts of mid-Wales were linked with Paddington in the early 1950s by through coaches on the 11.10 Birkenhead service and the 14.35 ex-Wolverhampton, and by a through train to Aberystwyth and Pwllheli that ran on peak Saturdays from July 1946. In 1956 a new daily *Cambrian Coast Express* was introduced, leaving Paddington at 10.10 for Aberystwyth and Pwllheli and stopping only at Banbury before Birmingham.[21] The up service at 16.00 from Birmingham did not stop at Banbury. When Banbury acquired a public address system, with the completion of the new station in 1958, a Welsh-speaking platform inspector gained and gave much pleasure from his daily announcement that the *Cambrian Coast Express* would call late in the afternoon at Llwngwril, Duffryn–Ardudwy and Penrhyndeudraeth. The down locomotive working from Paddington to Shrewsbury was demanding and was handled for long periods in 1956 by No 7010 *Avondale Castle*.

Cross Country

Some cross-country trains through Banbury were restored after the war but apart from the overnight trains from Swindon to Sheffield they were withdrawn as a result of coal shortages in the winter of 1947-48. They ran again in the first summer of Nationalisation and continued until the mid-1960s, although some had their journeys shortened or were confined to weekend operation as cuts took effect after 1958.[22]

The daily through train from Merseyside to the Kent and Sussex coast was reinstated in September 1948, but no longer faced weekday competition from trains using the route of the *Sunny South Express*. In the post-war period it was worked between Reading and Chester by locomotives from those depots, most commonly 'Castle' and 'County' 4-6-0s.[23] The principal change in services between the north and the Midlands and Southampton, Portsmouth and Bournemouth was the abandonment of workings to and from Manchester, which

---

[20] L Waters, & T Doyle, *British Railways Past and Present: Oxfordshire* (Wadenhoe: Past & Present Publishing, 1994), 88; *RM* vol 106 (1960) 675; S C Jenkins, *The Great Western & Great Central Joint Railway* (Tarrant Hinton: Oakwood, 1978), 20.
[21] C J Allen, *Titled Trains of Great Britain* (3rd edn, London: Ian Allan, 1953), 31-32.
[22] *RO* vol 69 (1999), 267.
[23] *RM* vol 96 (1950) 679, 714.

was served by trains to the south coast by other routes. Most timetables until 1964 included weekday trains between Birkenhead and Bournemouth that passed just north of Banbury, the northbound train calling (in 1959) at 13.19 and the southbound at 13.47. The daily service between Wolverhampton and Weymouth calling at Banbury about 12.35 southbound and shortly before 15.00 northbound ran in most timetables between 1945 and 1964 but was withdrawn in January 1947 on account of the coal shortage and by 1959 ran only on Fridays and Saturdays. The Saturday service between the West Midlands and the Torbay resorts via Oxford was restored and called at Banbury in both directions. For several years in the 1950s the Sunday equivalent of the *Cornishman*, the 09.00 from Wolverhampton to Penzance and Kingswear, ran via Banbury and the Didcot north curve calling (in 1954) at Banbury at 10.44 southbound and at 20.46 northbound.

The Newcastle–Bournemouth trains were reinstated, although in some timetables they ran only to and from York. The Swansea–Newcastle train, once the *Ports-to-Ports Express*, was revived in the autumn of 1946 but ran between Banbury and Newport through Didcot and the Severn Tunnel rather than via the BCDR. With the introduction of services between Birmingham New Street, Gloucester and South Wales in the early 1950s, it was restricted to a weekend through working in summer, and a weekend service between Banbury and Sheffield in winter. The two night time trains linking Swindon and Bristol with Sheffield and York continued, but no longer conveyed through coaches between Penzance and Aberdeen.

Cross-country trains of this sort were a feature of railway operation in Britain for a little more than 50 years. They originated in the first decade of the twentieth century, were interrupted by two world wars and revived in the early years of Nationalisation. Most were culled during the Beeching cuts, although the survivors multiplied a little in the 1970s and more in the 1980s, and the present-day cross-country service through Banbury is more lavish than any in the twentieth century. Most such services originally consisted of one train in each direction per day. Some carried titles, the *Pines Express* from Manchester via Bath Green Park to Bournemouth West, the *Devonian* from Bradford Forster Square to Kingswear, the *Cornishman* from Wolverhampton Low Level to Penzance. Such services also included the afternoon train from New Street that traditionally took honeymooners from Birmingham and Leicester via Melton Constable to Cromer, Sheringham and Yarmouth, and the service between Cheltenham and Southampton via the Midland & South Western Junction Railway. Scarcely any data about the users of such trains survives, although those through Banbury were generally well-filled. The complement of the Newcastle–Bournemouth trains in the 1950s might include National Service Light Infantrymen travelling between Yorkshire or Co Durham and the barracks at Winchester and students from the

In winter from the early 1950s the former Ports-to-Ports Express working was no more than a Friday and Saturday service between Banbury and Sheffield, for which a set of ER coaches was left in a siding by Banbury shed for the rest of the week. B1 No 61225 couples up to the coaches before leaving for the north, 1954.

south bound for universities at Leicester, Nottingham, Sheffield, Durham or Newcastle, or from the north heading for Oxford, Reading or Southampton. Elderly people encumbered with luggage requiring portering would exchange visits with relations, or take sedate holidays in the quieter Bournemouth hotels. Merchant seamen might travel between ships at Southampton and Newcastle. Long-distance travellers might be joined for half an hour by Banburians going to the nearest branches of Marks & Spencers in Leamington Spa or Oxford, with business at the County Council offices, or with the intention of enjoying the Jephson Gardens. The services from Birkenhead to Kent and Sussex and from the North East to Bournemouth served many needs.

Local services: foretastes of decline

Both portions of the route through Banbury from east to west lost their passenger trains in 1951. Auto-train services between Banbury and Kingham were withdrawn from 4 June 1951. A picture of Adderbury station with a chicken run on the up platform taken ten days earlier encapsulates a charmingly rustic but obviously unprofitable railway. On 30 June 1951 the last services between Merton Street and Blisworth were worked by class 3F 0-6-0 No 43568 with a chalk inscription on its smokebox, 'Last Train to Banbury', and class 4F No 44204 with a Union Jack on its tender. Freight services ceased on 29 October 1951. On 5 April 1952, passenger services ended, with more ceremony, on the 'main line' of the former SMJR between Stratford and Blisworth. At the time of closure to freight, coal traffic to Wappenham amounted to only 1,000 tons pa (less than two wagon loads a week) while Helmdon received only 1,800 tons. Passenger numbers on the single coach trains rarely reached double figures.[24]

On the Western Region main line the stations at Blackthorn and Cropredy were closed respectively in 1953 and 1956, and Brill & Ludgershall became an unstaffed halt in 1956. The halts at Chacombe and Eydon Road on the Woodford branch were closed in 1956. There were six or seven all-stations trains between Banbury and Oxford in most timetables during the 1950s, and five or six auto-train stopping services on the Bicester cut-off. Only two local trains were running between Banbury and Leamington by 1960.

Merton Street station after it was re-painted for the launch of the diesel car service to Buckingham in 1956. Ian Stratford

---

[24] *Railphoto Album* 1951, 30; Jenkins, *Great Western & Great Central*, 101; *RO* vol 21 (1951), 271.

The terminus of the former Buckinghamshire Railway passed into the management of the Western Region in April 1950, and the inscription on the front was changed to 'Banbury Merton Street Station'. Proposals made in 1938 to divert passenger trains from Bletchley into the GWR station were revived but were never implemented. The post-war service on the Bletchley line was scarcely attractive to passengers from Banbury who could travel more conveniently to Brackley and Buckingham by Midland Red bus. The last down train at 17.28 from Bletchley was made up of a pair of steel-bodied non-corridor coaches and a non-vestibuled corridor coach with lavatories for each compartment, whose fittings were inscribed WCJS (i.e. West Coast Joint Stock). The venerable vehicle was left at Banbury to form, with the engine and brake guard of an incoming mail and parcels train, the following morning's 07.15 departure for Bletchley, which rarely carried more than ten passengers. Other trains for Bletchley left at 13.40, 15.42 and 19.00. Packages of clothes for dry cleaning and dyeing were despatched from Merton Street to Pullars of Perth, while inward traffic included mail order parcels from Littlewoods of Liverpool and GUS of Manchester, cakes from Merseyside for F W Woolworth, and a weekly consignment of fish from Aberdeen for W A Truss at 41 Parson's Street.[25] Passenger services were taken over during the Second World War by LMSR class 4MT 2-6-4T tank engines, ten of which were working from Bletchley in 1945. They could easily handle trains of three coaches. From the summer of 1952 they were supplemented and then replaced by the similar Standard class 4MT 2-6-4Ts built at Brighton.

The passenger service from Merton Street was transformed from 13 August 1956, when British Railways began an intensive service of four daily trains to Bletchley and five to Buckingham, using single unit diesel railcars of the 'Derby Lightweight' type. New halts were opened at Water Stratford and Radclive, cosmetic improvements were made at Merton Street and the service was brilliantly marketed. The *Times* applauded 'these little olive green railcars gliding about pleasant countryside'. On most services passengers for Bletchley and beyond had to change at Buckingham into steam-operated push-and-pull trains. Early morning and late evening trains enlarged opportunities for long-distance travel, particularly to eastern England via Cambridge, but most of the new passengers were shoppers and there were complaints that the busiest trains were overcrowded, and that the railcars had insufficient capacity for prams. On market days the two railcars were coupled together, and sometimes arrived at Merton Street with as many as 120 passengers.[26]

---

[25] J M Dunn, *The Stratford-upon-Avon & Midland Junction Railway* (Lingfield: Oakwood, 1952), 12.
[26] B Simpson, *The Banbury to Verney Junction Branch* (Oxford: Oxford Publishing Co, 1978), 144-62; B Simpson, 'The Banbury Branch (LNWR), *Back Track*, vol 1 (1987), 106-13; M G D Farr, 'The Banbury-Buckingham railcar experiment', *TI*, vol 12 (1959), 594-95.

A diesel railcar from Merton connects at Buckingham with a steam auto-train for Bletchley headed by Standard Class 2MT 2-6-2T No 84004. 1956. Ian Stratford

Freight

Freight services on the Great Central line were revolutionised on the eve of Nationalisation. From 30 June 1947 the LNER introduced a scheme by which southbound trains from Annesley with up to 55 loaded wagons or 60 empties were worked to Woodford by Annesley crews who were relieved on arrival by Woodford men who took their locomotives for servicing, while they moved straight to fresh engines for the return journey. The trains, known as the 'Runners' but more recently called 'Windcutters', ran approximately hourly, but there were paths for up to 30 workings per day. Most were headed by O1 class 2-8-0s, rebuilt by Edward Thompson from the Great Central engines classified O4 by the LNER, although some unmodified O4s shared the workings. The service was transformed from 1957 by the transfer to Annesley of Standard class 9F 2-10-0s, four arriving at the shed in February of that year, 18 in March, two in April and six in June.[27]

There were also changes in workings south from Woodford. The freight depot at Marylebone, severely damaged by bombing on 16 April 1941, closed in 1952, which reduced the amount of merchandise traffic on the London Extension, although there were more through workings of coal to the gasworks at Kensal Green, Slough and Southall reached via Greenford. These trains and the roughly

---

[27] *RM* vol 98 (1952) 494; M Williams, *Steaming to Victory* (London: Preface, 2013), 195.

hourly trip workings to the hump yard at Banbury were almost entirely taken over by WD 2-8-0 locomotives. Sidings at Woodford were used to store these locomotives when they were returned from the continent to Britain from the closing weeks of 1945. The LNER purchased nearly 200 of them, and classified them O6, and 26 were working from Woodford by February 1946. More than 20 of the class remained at Woodford into the 1960s.[28]

A partially-fitted freight train that left Banbury for Bristol about 14.20 conveyed wagons brought south on overnight trains from York and further north. Here the train approaches King's Sutton in 1957 behind No 5947 'St Benet's Hall'.

The number of freight wagons exchanged via Woodford and Banbury between the LNER and the GWR and then the Eastern and Western regions of British Railway diminished with the end of hostilities, from 615,943 in 1944 to 571,837 in 1945, but then revived, totalling 687,191 in 1950. There was congestion in the yards at Banbury, and from 4 June 1951 four return workings, chiefly of semi-finished steel southbound and empty steel-carrying wagons northbound, were

---

[28] R Partridge, 'Woodford Halse: a Railway Community recalled', N Harris, ed, *Railway World Annual 1987* (Shepperton: Ian Allan, 1986), 8; Hardy, *Steam in the Blood*, 105, 108-110; J W P Rowledge, *Austerity 2-8-0s and 2-10-0s* (London: Ian Allan, 1987), 78, 87; *LE* No 23 No 2 (1946); M A Vanns, *Rail Centres: Nottingham* (Shepperton: Ian Allan, 1993), 98, 104; R Irons and S C Jenkins, *Woodford Halse* (Usk: Oakwood, 1999),106; J M C Healy, *Echoes of the Great Central* (London: Greenwich Editions, 1996), 73; R T Munns, *Milk Churns to Merry-go-round* (Newton Abbot: David & Charles, 1986), 96-98.

routed between Woodford and Newport via the SMJR and the south curve at Broome Junction. By 1956 some 30 trains a week in each direction were using this route. Some services to and from Stoke Gifford (Bristol) continued to go through Banbury but avoided the marshalling yard. Consequently traffic between Woodford and Banbury declined, and only 401,810 wagons were handled on the 95 freight trains per week that travelled on the line in 1956. In 1958 there were 18 trip workings from Woodford to Banbury and 17 in the other direction. From 1 June 1960 new connections were opened at Fenny Compton and Racecourse Junction at Stratford that shortened the route of trains from Banbury bound for South Wales, as well as those from Woodford.[29]

Overall freight traffic at Banbury was buoyant until the late 1950s. In 1958 there were 52 daily down movements, and 74 up movements, including 32 trains terminating in the Hump reception sidings and 28 departing from the yard below. Chiefly in the hours of darkness, class C and class D fitted freight trains linking Merseyside and the West Midlands with London and the south coast, continued to pass through, some of them exchanging wagons in the up sidings.[30]

Fish traffic reached a peak in the early 1950s when four nightly trains, two from Grimsby and two from Hull passed from the GC line to the WR at Banbury. The first of them, the 13.04 from New Clee, was worked through from Grimsby by a K3 2-6-0 locomotive from Immingham depot that usually, with the characteristic clanking valve gear of a Gresley three-cylinder locomotive, followed the 19.01 express for Paddington from Banbury North Junction into the station. This lengthy train almost filled the 1010 ft platform, with wagons consigned for stations from Hastings in the east to Plymouth and Whitland in the west. The aroma and the plop-plop-plopping of melting ice remain memorable. The K3 was replaced by the engine that had earlier brought a balancing train of empties from Swindon which was frequently a locomotive fresh from overhaul in the works. The Grimsby train was followed by the 12.30 from Hull, whose engine was changed at Leicester. Subsequent fish trains, the 16.30 from New Clee and 15.30 from Hull, were worked to Swindon by Leicester engines that returned coupled together in the early hours of the morning.

Freight trains at Merton Street also saw modern motive power. The first of the class 4MT 2-6-0 locomotives, designed by H G Ivatt and introduced in 1947, were allocated to Bletchley and for some years worked to Banbury. No 43002 of the class departed late with the daily freight train on Saturday 13 May 1950 when the royal train delivered King George VI and Queen Elizabeth to Brackley on their way to the first post-war Grand Prix at Silverstone.

---

[29] *RO* vol 21 No 269 (1951), 156; M Smith, 'Avoiding Banbury … and Acton', *BRI*, No 6 (1997), 312-23; Munns, *Milk Churns to Merry-go-round*, 22.

[30] J Copsey, 'Goods Operations at Banbury, part 3', *GWRJ* No 94 (2015), 356-57.

After the closure of the SMJR line to Blisworth, a cattle special was worked to Northampton via Bletchley every Thursday evening. It had a variety of motive power. Class 2P 4-4-0 No 40677 waits to leave Merton Street yard on 17 June 1954.

From 8 January 1951 an experimental diesel locomotive, No 10800, built in Glasgow by the North British Locomotive Company, was tried on the branches from Bletchley, and worked the daily 06.25 freight train from Swanbourne Sidings to Banbury, returning at 11.25 to Bletchley. In the summer of 1953 ten Standard Swindon-built class 4MT 4-6-0s, Nos 75030-39 were allocated to Bletchley and sometimes worked the morning freight. Nevertheless the majority of workings in the mid- and late 1950s were handled by 4F 0-6-0s. The most significant traffic was iron ore from the Oxfordshire Ironstone Co bound for

Wellingborough or Corby which was shunted from the WR lines into the sidings at Merton Street. When the load was heavy the train was piloted from Banbury to Brackley by the engine off the 08.22 arrival from Bletchley, whose return passenger working did not depart until 13.40. Cattle traffic remained substantial. After the line to Towcester closed to freight on 29 October 1951, a cattle train was worked every Thursday evening to Northampton via Bletchley. It was headed by varied locomotives, ex-Midland 2F 0-6-0s, a class 4MT 2-6-0 from Leicester, Northampton's class 2P 4-4-0s, and class 4F 0-6-0s from distant Midland Division sheds, and carried cattle consigned as far afield as Tutbury and Middlewich. Animal feed arrived at Merton Street from Merseyside while the local coal merchants Palmer & Sons, William Welford & Sons and Bernhard T Frost all received coal in the yard.[31]

Excursions

Excursions remained a feature of railway operation through the 1950s. British Railways regularly offered cheap day-return tickets to popular destinations. Banburians took advantage of them to travel to Saturday football matches at Birmingham on the 09.45 from Paddington via Oxford, leaving about noon, and returning on the 18.00 from Snow Hill, that also conveyed copies of the pink *Sports Argus* hurriedly conveyed to a Broad Street newsagent for queueing customers. On the last Sunday in July there was usually an excursion from Bournemouth calling at principal stations to Nottingham. On 29 July 1956 it was hauled throughout by 'King Arthur' class No 30789 *Sir Guy*, which needed assistance from WR and ER locomotives in both directions between Banbury and Nottingham Victoria. There were promotions for race meetings at Warwick and Wolverhampton, and Newbury meetings were sometimes served by special trains from the West Midlands. On most days of the Royal Ascot meeting in June specials passed through Banbury, some from the Great Central Line. The Western Region continued the GWR tradition of running an annual special from Paddington to Birkenhead for the Grand National. It also offered tickets from many of its stations, including Banbury, that enabled excursionists to travel to Oxford, Bourne End, Windsor or Henley, take a voyage on a Salters steamer on the River Thames, and return home, sometimes from another station. Chartered trains took parties on similar excursions that might involve guided tours of Oxford or Windsor Castle or visits to the spectator area at Heathrow Airport as well as steamer travel. On 20 July 1953 the staff and students of Banbury Grammar School celebrated the school's Diamond Jubilee by travelling to Bourne End and cruising on the Thames before watching Constellations and Vikings at Heathrow, and returning home from Windsor. The Western Region

---

[31] Simpson, *Banbury to Verney Junction*, 89; C Turner, 'Banbury Merton Street', *BRJ* No 70 (2001), 178-207; *TI* vol 4 (1951), 30; *RO* vol 21 No 264 (1951), 31-32.

SR No 30789 'Sir Guy', on the annual Bournemouth–Nottingham excursion on the last Sunday of July in 1956. The 'King Arthur' worked through to Nottingham Victoria, but needed assistance from WR and ER locomotives from and to Banbury Ian Stratford

provided Craven Arms set No. 2, a rake of ex-GWR 60ft 'Excursion' stock built in 1935, hauled by No. 7912 *Little Linford Hall*. In 1955 the Western Region arranged 133 such special trains for Salters, but in the 1960s an increasing proportion of excursionists cruising the Thames travelled to their embarkation points by coach.[32]

Many football excursions that passed through Banbury were unremarkable journeys of supporters of clubs in the West Midlands to matches in London or *vice versa*, but cup ties could produce unusual workings. The most notable resulted from the successes of Portsmouth football club in the FA Cup in 1952. In the third round, in early January, the club were at home to Grimsby Town, which brought two excursion trains hauled by B1 class 4-6-0s from Immingham shed as far as Banbury, whence Western Region power took them to the south coast.

---

[32] J H Russell, *A Pictorial Record of Great Western Coaches 1903-1948* (Sparkford: Haynes, 1990), 199-202; *The Banburian*, vol 11, No 2, (1953); R Lewis, *Anthony Burgess* (London: Faber, 2002), 175; S Wenham, *Pleasure Boating on the Thames* (Stroud: The History Press, 2014), 120-23.

A football excursion conveying supporters of Aston Villa FC to the FA Cup Final on 4 May 1957 is passed near King's Sutton by the pick-up goods from Oxford to Banbury headed by 7200 class 2-8-2T No 7236.

In the next round Portsmouth were away to Nottingham Forest, and four excursions, hauled to Banbury by 'King Arthur' class 4-6-0s Nos 30742 *Camelot*, 30783 *Sir Gillemere*, 30785 *Sir Mador de la Porte* and 30787 *Sir Menadeuke*, were taken north by B1s and V2s from Woodford. For the fifth round on 8 March 1952 Portsmouth were at home to Newcastle United. Eight overnight trains carried Newcastle supporters south, three via London and five via Banbury, two of which were made up of sleeping cars and restaurant cars that served breakfast. The trains reached Banbury behind three B1 4-6-0s, Nos. 61056, 61125 and 61258 from Doncaster, a V2 2-6-2 No. 60802 from Heaton (Newcastle) and the York-based pacific No 60501 *Cock o' the North*, the inelegant conversion by Edward Thompson of Sir Nigel Gresley's class P2 class 2-8-2. The trains were taken to the coast by five Banbury-based 4-6-0s, Nos 4918 *Dartington Hall*, 4980 *Wrottesley Hall*, 5954 *Faendre Hall*, 6819 *Highnam Grange* and 6833 *Calcott Grange*.[33]

---

[33] *TI* vol 5 (May 1952); *RO* Vol 72 (2002), 193.

The railway authorities in the 1950s organised several 'holiday expresses' on which stay-at-home holidaymakers could travel to five different destinations on Mondays to Fridays. Trains from Birmingham to the south coast or the River Thames regularly passed through Banbury. During the week beginning 13 August 1956 the *City of Leicester Holiday Express* was taken to Oxford and Windsor, hauled, appropriately by B17 'Footballer' class 4-6-0 No 61665 *Leicester City*, a Yarmouth engine that had just been overhauled at Gorton works, which reappeared on Saturday 18 August with the main portion of the Newcastle–Bournemouth train.

Increasing numbers of excursions for railway enthusiasts took place during the 1950s, many of them 'farewell tours' hauled by the last representatives of particular classes of locomotive. The last 'Bulldog' No 3454 *Skylark* took five coaches from Birmingham to Oxford and Didcot on 17 June 1951, the last 'Saint' No 2920 *St David* ran from Snow Hill to Gloucester and Swindon and returned through Banbury on 15 June 1952, and the last 'Star', No 4056 *Princess Margaret* ran from Birmingham to Hereford returning via Swindon and Banbury on 9 September 1956. The 4-4-0 No 3440 *City of Truro* was released from York Museum in 1957, worked regular trains from Didcot, and hauled numerous specials before its retirement in 1961, including an excursion from Birmingham to Swindon on 16 June 1957. [34]

The Talyllyn Railway Preservation Society regularly conveyed its members from London and intermediate stations to Tywyn for its annual general meeting. The first such excursion was undertaken on 26-27 September 1953 in ex-GWR diesel railcar No W13, which left Paddington at 06.45, and after a 45-minute refuelling stop at Leamington reached Tywyn at 14.34. After a return departure at 23.03 the railcar's engines failed at Lapworth at 03.28 on the Sunday morning. Fortunately 2-8-0 No 2830 was at hand on a freight train and towed the stricken vehicle into Leamington station at 05.25. One of Leamington's own railcars, No W22 took the party to Paddington which was reached at 07.54, only 95 minutes late. Longer trains were needed as the society grew. On 25-26 September 1954 the special was worked by railcars W33W and W38W, sandwiching an additional coach. On 24 September 1955 it was taken from Paddington to Shrewsbury by No 4061 *Glastonbury Abbey*, and on 22 September 1956 by No 4056 *Princess Margaret*. The 4-4-0 *City of Truro* was in charge on 28 September 1957, Midland Compound No 41123 on 27 September 1958, and 'Castle' class No 7007 *Great Western* on 25 September 1959.[35]

---

[34] *RO* vol 21 No 269 (1951), 155; R J Blenkinsop, *Locomotives Illustrated: 50: GWR Double-framed 4-4-0s* (Shepperton: Ian Allan 1986), 34-35.

[35] *RO* vol 23 No 297 (1953), 317; Blenkinsop, *Locomotives Illustrated 50*, 34-35.

For several years Alan Pegler of the Northern Rubber Company at Retford sponsored the 'Farnborough Flyer' which carried his employees to Farnborough (Hants) for the air show, reached through Banbury and Basingstoke where the train reversed. On 11 September 1954 the train was hauled by Great Northern Atlantic No 251 from York Railway Museum and ex-GCR 'Director' class 4-4-0 No 62663 *Prince Albert*. Their stop for water at Banbury on the return journey aroused much interest. A year later a similar train was worked by the 'Directors' Nos 62666 *Zeebrugge* and 62667 *Somme*, and on 7 September 1958 the *Flyer* was hauled by English Electric type 4 diesel No D 201, perhaps the first of its class to pass through Banbury.[36]

The 'Farnborough Flyer' with D11s Nos 62666 'Zeebrugge' and 62667 'Somme', makes its way south from Banbury, 11 September 1955. Ian Stratford

Summer Saturday pressures [37]

The prospects of meeting demands for travel to and from seaside resorts were a cause of serious concern to managers of the GWR as the war ended and subsequently operations on summer Saturdays were probably as stressful as any wartime railway activities. Northbound trains converged on Banbury from Torbay and Weymouth via Swindon and Didcot, from Bournemouth and Portsmouth via Basingstoke, from the resorts of Kent and Sussex via Redhill and Reading or through Kensington Olympia, as well as from Paddington via Bicester or Oxford.

---

[36] *TI* vol 7 (1954).
[37] Barman, *The Great Western Railway's last look forward*, 10-14. The times quoted in the paragraphs that follow are from the summer timetable for 1959.

North of Banbury holiday trains carried passengers from and to the West Midlands and Merseyside and the cities of the East Midlands, Yorkshire and further north, as well as taking holidaymakers from the south to and from mid- and north Wales. A pilot engine, usually a 4-6-0, was always available in a down bay platform, adding and subtracting parcels vans from through trains, shunting empty stock and being available to replace or assist failing locomotives on passenger trains, but on summer Saturdays a pilot was also provided at the south end.

Saturday workings, like those on other days, began at Banbury station with the arrival soon after midnight of the 18.40 York to Swindon. In the summer of 1959 this train, primarily for mail and parcels, conveyed through-coaches on Saturday mornings from Scarborough. An hour later between 01.01 and 01.37 came a flurry of overnight services bound for Portsmouth Harbour and the ferries to the Isle of Wight, the 22.00 from Sheffield, the 23.30 from Nottingham Victoria and the 00.30 from Birmingham Moor Street, all of which promised to land their passengers on the Pier Head at Ryde by 06.30. The sleeper from Birkenhead to Paddington paused for seven minutes from 02.10 before continuing its unhurried journey to the capital through Oxford and Reading, and was followed by another regular weekday train, the 22.22 York–Swindon which spent 14 minutes at Banbury from 03.34. The last of the southbound overnight holiday trains, the 21.40 Newcastle–Bournemouth arrived at 03.32. In the down direction the main event of the hours of darkness was the arrival at 02.35 of the 00.05 Paddington–Birkenhead sleeper. Its weekday business chiefly concerned mailbags and parcels, but on summer Saturdays early-rising Banburians joined it to reach resorts in mid- and north Wales via Ruabon or Chester. As the Midnight's 'Castle' class locomotive heaved its lengthy train out of the platform it was followed by the 23.00 Portsmouth Harbour–Nottingham Victoria which was allowed ten minutes to change engines before continuing northwards. The next few hours were relatively quiet although several parcels trains called, the 03.30 newspaper train from Paddington arrived just after six o'clock, and the station pilot shunted the vans that made up the 06.50 Banbury–York, perishables and parcels.

The tide of daytime trains to the coast began at 07.03 with the arrival of the 06.05 from Snow Hill to Bournemouth West, but the main preoccupation remained local services, together with the first main line service of the day, the 06.45 Wolverhampton–Paddington which called at 08.25, picking up Banbury holidaymakers travelling via London. It was followed by the 08.35 for Oxford that continued as a semi-fast to Paddington. A deluge began after its departure with the non-stop passage within twenty minutes of the 07.50 Snow Hill–Weymouth Town, the 08.00 Snow Hill–Weymouth Quay and the 07.28 Wolverhampton–Brighton, Eastbourne and Hastings via Kensington Olympia. The departure of the 09.12 all stations to Oxford was the prelude to twenty quiet minutes before the arrival of the 07.48 Wolverhampton–Portsmouth at 09.27 and the 08.40 Moor Street–Portsmouth at 09.37. On most Saturdays a non-stopping relief from Wolverhampton to Paddington preceded the rapid passage of a 'King' with the 07.30 Shrewsbury–Paddington at about 10.00. It was followed by the 09.05 Snow Hill–Portsmouth & Southsea, calling at 10.08, and the 08.43 Wolverhampton–Portsmouth Harbour at 10.20, before a short intermission for the handling of local trains prior to the arrival at 10.47 of the 09.25 Wolverhampton–Paignton via Oxford, Swindon and Westbury. This train was notoriously unpunctual and on 27 July 1957 its ten coaches hauled by 2-6-0 No 5385 reached Newton Abbot 163 minutes late. The first up train of the day to travel the length of the GWR's northern line, the 06.30 Birkenhead–Paddington stopped five minutes later. Services for Kent and Sussex occupied the next hour. At 11.10 the 10.10 from Birmingham (Moor Street) called *en route* via Kensington Olympia for the Thanet resorts, reaching Ramsgate at 15.20 after a theoretically non-stop run from Banbury. It was followed by the 10.20 from Snow Hill to Margate, which, after crossing the North Downs to Redhill, reached its destination at 16.33. The 10.40 from Snow Hill, calling at Banbury at 11.42, followed the 10.20 to Redhill, and then took the main line to Brighton, continuing, with reversals, to Eastbourne and Hastings. Its locomotive, a 2-6-0 or a 'Manor' class 4-6-0 from Tyseley shed, worked from Birmingham to Redhill. The sequence of trains to the south-east was concluded by the 07.35 from Birkenhead, usually hauled by the 'Castle' from Reading that had gone north with the balancing working the previous day. It ran in the path of the weekday train, but with only two portions, one for Margate via Canterbury West and Ramsgate, the other, detached at Ashford, serving Folkestone, Dover, Deal and Sandwich before reaching Ramsgate. The despatch of a local to Oxford at 11.57 dictated a lull in southbound holiday traffic before the arrival at 12.33 of the 11.05 Wolverhampton–Weymouth, followed by the advertised 09.20 Chester–Paddington relief which passed non-stop, and the 08.55 Birkenhead–Paddington which called at 12.52.

The morning service in the down direction was similar to that on weekdays with the addition of more trains from Paddington to mid-Wales. Whistling at about 10.20 heralded the non-stop passage of the 09.00 from Paddington, on weekdays the *Inter City* conveying businessmen to Birmingham and Wolverhampton, but on Saturdays a train to Pwllheli via Ruabon, taking expectantly happy Cockney campers to Butlin's at Penychain, with a restaurant car that served meals until it reached Barmouth at 15.28. It was followed by the 09.10 Paddington–Birkenhead, and by the first daytime trains from the south coast, the 08.05 Bournemouth Central–Newcastle whose WR engine passed non-stop to Leicester Central, and the 08.47 Pokesdown–Birkenhead, which called at 11.53. The Saturday *Cambrian Coast Express*, the 10.50 ex-Paddington, with portions for Aberystwyth and Pwllheli, called at 12.11 and the 11.10 from Paddington to Birkenhead at 12.32.

After 13.00 the focus of southbound holiday traffic switched from Kent and Sussex to Hampshire and Dorset, with the passage of the non-stop 12.10 Snow Hill–Bournemouth Central, and calls at 13.20 of the 09.20 Birkenhead–Bournemouth Central and at 13.44 of the 09.30 Birkenhead–Bournemouth West. At about 14.15 came the usually rapid flight of the 07.25 ex-Pwllheli, a short train almost invariably hauled by a 'King' running non-stop from Snow Hill to Paddington. The first daytime long-distance arrival from the Great Central line was the 10.15 Bradford Exchange–Poole, which in some years was taken through to Oxford by its Eastern (from 1958 London Midland) Region locomotive, and in other years changed engines at about 14.30. It was followed by the up *Cambrian Coast Express*, with portions that left Aberystwyth at 09.25 and Barmouth Junction (Morfa Mawdach) at 08.45, which ran non-stop to Paddington from Leamington. The main train from the Great Central, the 08.35 Newcastle–Bournemouth West arrived at 14.45 and its relief, the 12.10 Sheffield–Bournemouth Central at 15.04. This was the last of the holiday services for the south coast. The successor to the *Ports-to-Ports Express*, the 10.08 Newcastle–Swansea, called at 16.31. Another train from North Wales, the 09.45 Pwllheli–Paddington stopped at 16.50. Otherwise seaside traffic in the up direction was concluded by teatime, and evening services were similar to those on weekdays. Empty stock workings returned sets of carriages from the West Midlands to the Southern Region or to Western Region sidings in the London area. Strings of as many as three WR 4-6-0s might return to Banbury shed after taking trains to Leicester or Nottingham. Late on Saturday evenings in mid-July there might be 'trip' workings taking home employees at the Swindon railway works from holidays at Llandudno or Blackpool.[38]

The most stressful aspect of summer Saturday operations at Banbury was during the afternoon in the down direction. Until 1958 there was only one down platform and even when there were two, after the rebuilding of the station, congestion built up as some trains changed engines and others took water, since the short intervals between trains did not allow the troughs at Aynho to refill. The arrival of unscheduled relief trains was unpredictable. On 6 August 1960 eight northbound trains stopped in the station in the hour after 14.00. The down platform was usually crowded with passengers from the south coast taking the last opportunity to change from a train bound for the Great Central to one for the West Midlands or *vice versa*. In the absence of a public address system before the completion of the new station there was much confusion, and much passing of

---

[38] R Woodley, *The Day of the Holiday Express* (Shepperton: Ian Allan, 1996), 132.

blame. Lateness was invariably attributed to delays on the Southern Region. Passengers demanded to know about connections beyond the knowledge of Banbury's porters – the best place to change for Catterick Camp or Nantwich. Harold Sumner, platform inspector and Methodist local preacher, observed in sermons that while the Anglican University of Oxford might be a seat of learning, the knowledge of Oxford platform staff as to the destinations of trains often required correction by Dissenting Banburians.

Many trains were hauled by engines and crews that were engaged on weekdays on freight trains, whether the GWR 2-6-0s which worked many trains to and from the south coast, or the ex-LNER K3s or, later, class 9F 2-10-0s, which filled the atmosphere with the acrid stench of Nottinghamshire coal as they waited in the down bay for trains destined for the Great Central. Their Annesley crews sat on luggage trucks and gossiped in Nottinghamshire accents, while attendants patrolled the platform supplying Banbury Cakes and cartons of squash to parched passengers leaning from the windows of trains awaiting fresh locomotives or a northbound path. Sometimes unanticipated extras meant that a train bound for the GC arriving in Banbury from the south had no locomotive waiting to take it over, and a WR or SR engine had to continue northwards. On 28 August 1954 the SR 'King Arthur' No 30790 *Sir Villiars* with an extra from Portsmouth took its train as far as Leicester Central.[39]

The train that marked the beginning of the afternoon rush was the 08.10 Swansea–York which changed engines between 12.52 and 12.58. Hard on its heels, in theory arriving at 13.02, came the 09.25 Weymouth–Wolverhampton, then at an interval of seven minutes, the 08.50 Margate–Birmingham, nominally non-stop from Margate to Redhill and from Redhill to Banbury, which meant that it would invariably be hauled by an ex-GWR 2-6-0. Eight minutes after its nominal departure time the 09.30 Bournemouth Central–Wolverhampton arrived, and about a quarter of an hour later the 08.48 from Hastings via Brighton and Kensington Olympia passed non-stop, also bound for Wolverhampton. At 13.48 the main train from the south coast to Merseyside, the 09.30 Bournemouth West–Birkenhead called, hauled by the 'County' or 'Castle' from Chester that had gone to Oxford the previous day, and nine minutes later the 10.00 Weymouth Town–Birmingham Moor Street went through non-stop, followed by the 09.02 from Margate via Canterbury West, Ashford and Redhill, also terminating at Moor Street. A quarter of an hour later came the main train from the Kent coast, nominally the 09.10 ex-Sandwich and the 09.15 ex-Margate, consisting of the coaches from the weekday service, including the restaurant car, and the Chester locomotive that had taken the train to Reading the previous day. The 13.10 from Paddington to Chester, calling at 14.31, was scheduled to be followed by two

---

[39] *TI* Oct 1954; *RM* vol 100 (1954), 731; *GWE* No 118 (1992), 8.

characteristic holiday services. The 10.25 Poole–Bradford was due at 14.37 and usually changed locomotives. On most Saturdays in the late 1940s and early '50s it was hauled to Banbury by a Southern Region locomotive, a 'King Arthur' or a 'Remembrance'. It was scheduled to leave at 14.44 and two minutes later the 09.10 ex-Kingswear was due to arrive, but it was frequently delayed leaving Devon and on its devious journey via Westbury and Swindon. Five minutes after the departure of the Kingswear, 14.54, was the scheduled arrival time of the 10.20 Weymouth Town–Wolverhampton which followed it from Westbury. The departure of an all-stations local to Leamington at 15.00 was followed by a succession of trains for the Great Central line, the 11.00 Bournemouth Central–Sheffield and the 11.16 Bournemouth West–Newcastle were timetabled services, but there were often reliefs. The 14.10 Paddington–Birkenhead, almost always headed by a 'King' from Wolverhampton, was due at 15.31 and was usually preceded by a relief, the 13.58 from Paddington which in the early 1950s was often hauled by a 4700 class 2-8-0 from Oxley shed which had gone to London on a night time fast freight.

The frequency of trains heading north from the coast lessened a little with the 11.50 Bournemouth Central–Snow Hill calling at 15.38 but no other holiday service until the 13.11 Portsmouth Harbour–Birmingham Moor Street at 16.20. Another train that served holidaymakers from the Isle of Wight, the 13.28 Portsmouth Harbour–Snow Hill stopped at 16.56, and the service from Hastings, Eastbourne and Brighton via Redhill to Snow Hill at 17.14. The 16.10 Paddington–Birkenhead calling at 17.40 was followed, as usual, by a local service to Woodford worked by a main line locomotive that had been involved earlier in the afternoon with long-distance trains. It was followed by yet another train from the coast, the 15.02 Portsmouth Harbour–Wolverhampton. The next hour was devoted to local services, but at 19.07 the 15.40 Portsmouth Harbour–Wolverhampton called at Banbury with more passengers from the Isle of Wight, and after the passage of the 18.10 Paddington–Birkenhead and its relief, the 16.57 from Portsmouth Harbour pulled in at 19.55 exchanging its WR locomotive for one from the Great Central which took it to Sheffield. Even this was not the last of the down seaside specials, for 20.44 was the scheduled arrival time of the Birmingham portion of the 16.05 from Weymouth Quay, which detached coaches for Cardiff at Westbury. It was followed by the 19.30 Swindon–Sheffield, a train that ran every weekday and usually consisted of three or four passenger carriages and an assortment of parcels vans. It changed locomotives at Banbury and seemed a refreshing return to normality after the stress of the afternoon.

This pattern of Saturday operation extended from the immediate post-war years until 1964, with remarkably little change, although there were minor variations in timings and in locomotive workings. In 1958 many services to and from the Great Central line were worked by 9F class 2-10-0s newly allocated to Annesley shed but after some ran at high speeds the practice was discouraged by management. Subsequently London Midland Region locomotives, including 'Royal Scots' and 'Jubilees', worked some trains from the North until Great Central services ceased in 1965.[40] From September 1960 the pattern of Saturday workings was affected by the increased service between Paddington, Birmingham and Wolverhampton, and it changed again from August 1962 as those trains were taken over by diesel locomotives.[41]

Summer holiday trains could bring exotic coaching stock as well as exotic locomotives to Banbury. On 4 August 1951 the Bournemouth–Newcastle train included three khaki-painted coaches from the former Great Eastern Railway, as well as a composite brake once the property of the Manchester South Junction & Altrincham Railway. The bulky matchboard-sided 'Barnum' coaches of the former Great Central Railway sometimes appeared on trains from the north, while the Southern Region occasionally used wasp-waisted stock from the L&SWR, which usually worked around Portsmouth and Southampton, birdcage coaches from the SECR which normally formed local trains in Kent, matchboard-sided former Pullmans redundant on boat trains, and, on one occasion in 1954, No 7895 *At the sign of The Bull*, one of the outrageous tavern cars designed by O V S Bulleid. Trains of Western Region stock sometimes included saloons, coaches that were constructed for families or invalids so that private parties could have sole use of the vehicles, although on holiday trains such coaches were usually open to all.[42]

The two decades after the conclusion of the Second World War marked the zenith of the British seaside holiday, as most workers gained rights to holidays with pay, real wages increased, and holiday camp entrepreneurs as well as guest-house proprietors and families providing bed and breakfast increased the supply of accommodation. Such holidays were only made possible by the labours of railwaymen and women – at Banbury and elsewhere.

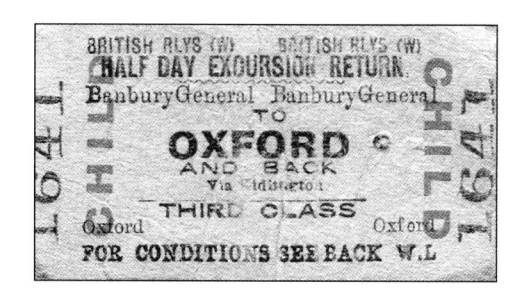

---

[40] *RM* vol 108 (1962), 508.
[41] *RM* vol 110 (1964), 805; J S Whiteley & G W Morrison, *The Great Western Remembered* (Poole: Oxford Publishing Co, 1985), 163.
[42] *RO* vol 21 (1951); Russell, *Pictorial Record,* 101, 104.

12a. To and from the seaside

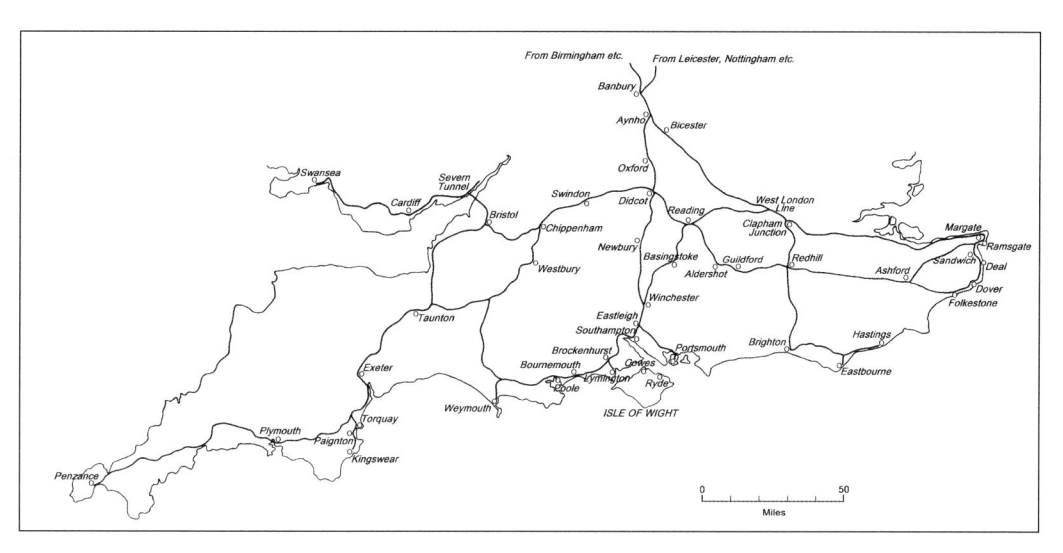

Routes to the South Coast.

Locomotives of all kinds hauled holiday trains in the post-war period. 'Castle' class 4-6-0 No 4086 'Builth Castle', a genuine express engine, heads a train of mixed stock north from Banbury in August 1961.

171

On a Saturday during the re-building of Banbury station in the summer of 1958 a K3 class 2-6-0 enters the station from the GC line, probably, since the coaching stock is so varied, a relief. In the background is a line of cattle wagons, while a stack of pigeon baskets occupies the up platform. Ian Stratford

On most summer Saturdays some locomotives from the GC line continued with their trains south from Banbury. B1 No 61061 heads the main portion of the Newcastle–Bournemouth train past Franklow's Knob in 1961.

Perhaps the most unusual motive power for the Newcastle–Bournemouth train was LMR class 8F 48508 from Rotherham (Canklow) which arrived at Banbury from the north in August 1958, while the station was being rebuilt. Ian Stratford

Standard class 5MT 4-6-0s from the Southern Region shedded at Weymouth passed through Banbury at weekends in the early 1960s with trains from the coast to the West Midlands. Here No 73017 is heading south on a Saturday having gone to Wolverhampton the previous day.

From 1958 some summer Saturday trains from the Great Central line were hauled to Banbury by class 9F 2-10-0s newly allocated to Annesley depot near Nottingham. No 92030 has just passed Banbury North Junction with a train of LMR carriages for the south coast.

Great Western 4300 class 2-6-0s were the characteristic motive power for trains between the south coast and the West Midlands. No 6385 heads a train of SR stock northwards from Banbury on 1 July 1961.

2-6-0 No 6320 powers a train of LMR stock from the coast on 25 June 1961.

Manor class 4-6-0 No 7816 'Frilsham Manor' retained the GWR emblem on its tender into the 1960s. It pauses at Banbury in 1961 with a train of SR stock which it probably took over at Redhill.

A 'Britannia' class pacific, No 70018 'Flying Dutchman', from Cardiff, having worked to Banbury in 1956 on the successor to the 'Ports-to-Ports Express', awaits the return train, while a 'Castle' class 4-6-0 passes with a train from the south coast.

B1 class 4-6-0 No 61399 heads towards Banbury North Junction with a train from the south coast, 25 June 1961

A typical summer Saturday scene at the new Banbury station in 1959. On the left a 'County' class 4-6-0 is heading for the West Midlands with a train of mixed stock from the south coast. A V2 class 2-6-2 waits in a bay platform for a train for the GC line, while a 'Hall' class 4-6-0 acts as station pilot. Ian Stratford

13. Shrinking: the 1960s

.... And we leave the old Great Central line
For Banbury and buns.[1]
John Betjeman, 'Great Central Railway Sheffield Victoria to Banbury'.

Banbury's railways changed slowly, during the 1950s. Expresses on the Western Region's northern line were accelerated and the quality of coaching stock improved. The *Cambrian Coast Express* made up of Mark I coaches in chocolate-and-cream livery headed by a green 'Castle' class locomotive, reaching Banbury (in 1959) in 72 minutes from Paddington, was a service in which any railway manager might have taken pride. Cross-country trains provided convenient services on weekdays and coped, if desperately, with surging demands on summer Saturdays. The passenger trains on the BCDR and the NBJR which ceased in 1951 had never been well-patronised, nor had the wayside stations and halts that closed later in the decade. The Bletchley line was re-invigorated by the introduction of diesel railcars in 1956. The new station, completed in 1958, had the potential to change the image of the railway in Banbury from a Victorian anachronism to a confident and efficient service attuned to the needs of the second half of the twentieth century. There were nevertheless grounds for pessimism. The failure of management to address the grievances of locomen led to strikes in which Banbury members of ASLEF were prominent, and strikes led to the loss of traffic. Diesel multiple units were introduced but they followed existing schedules, secured few operational economies, and made scarcely any marketing impact. The means of handling goods traffic were scarcely improved while new, continuously-braked iron ore wagons lay rusting in sidings at Merton Street. Nevertheless it was possible at the end of the decade for Banbury's railwaymen to be optimistic.

That optimism was not maintained. In part this was the outcome of a culture of contraction nationally, encapsulated but not instigated by the reports of Dr Richard Beeching, chairman of the British Transport Commission from 1961 to 1963, and of the British Railways Board between 1963 and 1966. In his first report published on 27 March 1963 Beeching demonstrated that a third of the system's route mileage generated only one per cent of total passenger miles, and that half the stations produced less than one per cent of total passenger receipts. The system was reduced by some 4,000 route miles under Beeching's direction, and by a further 2,000 miles by 1970. His second report, made public

---

[1] 'Great Central Railway Sheffield Victoria to Banbury', J Betjeman, *John Betjeman's Collected Poems* (London: John Murray, 1980), 316.

on 16 February 1965, argued that only 3,000 of the 7,500 route miles of main line should receive future investment, and that many routes, including the East Coast Main Line north of Newcastle and the lines through Cornwall should be closed. Most of its recommendations were rejected by government and Beeching returned to ICI in 1966.[2]

From 1 January 1963 the lines through Banbury, northwards from Ardley on the Bicester cut-off and Heyford on the line from Oxford, became part of the London Midland Region. The engine shed at Banbury was transferred to the London Midland Region, and was classified as 2D instead of 84C.

Contraction

The closure of lines in Banburyshire accelerated in the early 1960s. The railcar service on the Buckinghamshire Railway, introduced in 1956, survived for only the first year of the following decade. It was unprofitable by the accounting criteria then used by British Railways, making a loss in spite of a one-third reduction in running costs and a four hundred per cent increase in traffic. Peak time services were well-patronised, but other trains ran almost empty. An observer counted 104 passengers on the 13.26 arrival at Banbury on 5 December 1959 but the shoppers initially attracted by the service were precisely the customers likely to be lost as car ownership increased. There were only five passengers on the mid-morning departure from Merton Street for Bletchley on 6 September 1960, a further seven joined but six left the train at intermediate stations, leaving six on board when the railcar reached its destination. The last passenger trains ran on 31 December 1960. A new four-car class 115 diesel multiple unit, intended to work from Marylebone, provided the sparsely-occupied final service at 22.15 from Merton Street which the journalist Graham Wilton described as 'the bare-ribbed station appearing now like a stranded whale'. The inscription 'British Road Services' replaced 'Banbury Merton Street Station' on its frontage. Passenger services between Buckingham and Bletchley continued until 7 September 1964.[3]

The intermediate stations between Princes Risborough and Banbury were closed, with the exception of King's Sutton and Bicester, from 7 January 1963. Steam-powered auto-trains had been replaced by single car diesel units from June 1962, and on the last day services through snow drifts were provided by a three-car multiple unit. From 2 November 1964 trains ceased calling at Kidlington, Bletchington, Fritwell & Somerton, Aynho, Fenny Compton and Southam Road & Harbury, on the line from Oxford through Banbury to Leamington.[4]

---

[2] B Harrison, *Seeking a Role: the United Kingdom 1951-70* (Oxford: Clarendon Press, 2009), 141-42.
[3] M G D Farr, 'The Banbury-Buckingham railcar experiment', *TI*, vol 12 (1959), 594-95.
[4] B Simpson, *The Banbury to Verney Junction Branch* (Oxford: Oxford Publishing Co, 1978), 153-62; *RM* vol 107 (1961), 138; vol 109 (1963), 108-09, 140, 259; vol 110 (1964), 126; L Waters, & T Doyle, *British Railways Past and Present: Oxfordshire* (Wadenhoe: Past & Present Publishing, 1994), 138.

This was part of a wider pattern of contraction. The branches to Watlington and Wallingford had closed respectively in 1957 and 1959 and trains ceased to run to Fairford in 1962. The Abingdon branch and Oxford's alternative route to London via Thame and Princes Risborough closed to passengers in 1963, the southern part of the Didcot, Newbury & Southampton Railway in 1960 and the remainder in 1964. All might have been considered, in Beeching's words, as 'twigs with no sap in them'. The former LNWR line from Leamington through Warwick to Coventry lost its local services in 1965, but the sap in that twig proved resilient.

A sign that the Great Central line passed under the control of the London Midland Region in 1958 was the appearance of 'Black Five' 4-6-0s at Banbury. No 44691 heads south from the Junction with the Newcastle–Bournemouth train in 1961.

Great Central

The closure of the Great Central line was of a different order from that of branch lines and village stations. It was the kind of change envisaged in the second Beeching report of 1965, although it was anticipated much earlier. The London Extension was transferred from the Eastern to the London Midland Region with effect from 1 February 1958 and on some days in the following summer ex-LMSR Stanier 'Black Fives' hauled the Newcastle–Bournemouth train into Banbury. Eastern and North Eastern region locomotives continued to reach Banbury but by the summer of 1961 ex-LMSR express locomotives,

'Rebuilt Royal Scots' and 'Jubilees' were working holiday trains from the north – No 45656 *Cochrane* from Sheffield (Millhouses) and No 45739 *Ulster* from Leeds (Holbeck) on Saturday 12 August 1961, for example.[5]

Expresses on the London Extension from Marylebone to Sheffield and Manchester were replaced in 1960 by semi-fast trains that ran only to and from Nottingham. The Newcastle–Bournemouth service was reduced in the winter of 1961-62 to a return working between York and Banbury by a pair of two-car diesel multiple units, but was subsequently revived. Diesel locomotives took it from Sheffield to Banbury, from where it continued with steam traction to the south coast. Local trains between Banbury and Woodford ceased from Saturday 13 June 1964, the final train, the 18.55 from Woodford consisting of ex-LMSR 2-6-4T No 42251 and two coaches, carrying more than eighty passengers.

The local service between Woodford and Banbury ceased from 13 June 1964. Throughout its history some short trains had been hauled by main line locomotives, in this case, in 1961, by a class 9F 2-10-0 from Annesley.

Freight services on the Great Central were contracting by the spring of 1963 when ten WD 2-8-0s were in store at Woodford. The 'runners' between Annesley and Woodford ceased in March 1965 and the shed and yards at Woodford closed on 14 June 1965. Operations at Annesley shed continued until 3 January 1966. The semi-fast services between Marylebone and Nottingham descended into a spiral of embarrassing decline, with delays resulting from inadequate maintenance of locomotives or shortages of staff. For a short time from October 1965 trains were worked by eight 'Britannia' class pacifics (70045/6/7/50-54) based at Banbury, but from January 1966 the pacifics were re-allocated to Carlisle (Kingmoor) and most trains were then hauled by 'Black Fives'.

---

[5] *RM* vol 109 (1963), 143.

On 3 January 1966 as a result of the failure at Woodford of the train's locomotive, and then of its first replacement summoned from Banbury, the 08.15 from Nottingham reached Marylebone 208 min late.[6]

The deterioration in standards of management was evidenced by the progress on 15 August 1964 of Western Region 4-6-0 No 6858 *Woolston Grange* which replaced a Southern Region locomotive at Oxford on the 08.55 Bournemouth West–Leeds. Neither Banbury, Leicester nor Nottingham could supply a replacement. Nor could Sheffield Victoria where the cylinder casing of *Woolston Grange* touched the platform edge. After the driver refused to proceed a locomotive inspector drove it through Penistone, across the Denby Dale Viaduct and through Berry Brow where its cylinder casing clattered into the platform edge. At Huddersfield the 'Grange' was removed to Hillhouse engine shed, and remained there until 26 August when it returned to Oxley via Crewe as an out-of-gauge load. Such was the embarrassment caused that a respected railway photographer was unceremoniously ejected from the depot.[7]

The last workings between Aylesbury and Rugby, and on the Banbury branch, took place on 3 September 1966 and in the early hours of the following morning. 'The Rabbits', the 06.50 Banbury–York parcels, ran for the last time behind 'Black Five' No 45292 which returned south from Nottingham to Marylebone with empty newspaper vans. The Newcastle–Bournemouth service was hauled to and from Banbury by Brush diesel No D1572. The southbound train was taken from Banbury to Bournemouth by No 34005 *Barnstaple* while the northbound service arrived behind No 34034 *Honiton*. The two overnight services between Swindon and York had also ceased on 3 September 1966 when Hymek diesels Nos D7012/23 worked them from Swindon through Banbury to Leicester and back. The humiliation of the London Extension continued as woebegone diesel multiple units plied between Rugby Central and Nottingham (Arkwright Street) until 3 May 1969.[8]

Sidney Tyrrell of Eydon witnessed as a child the construction of the London Extension and as an old man mourned its passing. He observed, after the last 'Little Banbury' ran in June 1964, '*Sam Fay* no longer thunders along the bank, leaving a billowing plume of smoke on her way to Sheffield, a reminder that it's nearly tea-time. There are no expresses now, no ordinary goods trains, just a few trains go along the bank containing maybe half a dozen people … The friendly

---

[6] *MDR* vol 22, No 208 (1966), 60, vol 22, No 209 (1966), 117, vol 22, No 210 (1966), 229; *TI* vol 22 (1966), 61, 229.

[7] J S Whiteley & G W Morrison, *The Great Western Remembered* (Poole: Oxford Publishing Co, 1985), 163; *RM* vol 110 (1964), 805; *RO* vol 83 (2013), 273-74, vol 84 (2014), 720; P Atkins, 'Off the Beaten Track', *RM* vol 161 (2015).

[8] *RM* vol 108 (1962), 508; D Hucknall, *On Shed* (London: BCA, 1993), 127; D Pearce, 'The last weekend of the Great Central's London Extension', *SD* (2016), 9.

light of the signal box has gone out, so there is now no one in the parish keeping watch while we are asleep'. At 03.00 on 4 September 1966 Tyrrell saw the last newspaper train from Marylebone to Nottingham speed past Culworth Junction hauled by Class 2 diesel No D5085, followed by a diesel locomotive off the Banbury line that stopped at the junction signal box to pick up the signalman who put out the light and locked the door for the last time. 'This is the end' he wrote, 'the line is now deserted'. He and his neighbours found themselves unconsciously listening for trains.[9]

The opinions of professional railwaymen about the Great Central must be respected. Michael Bonavia, Richard Hardy and R T Munns thought its closure inevitable, and certainly the freight traffic that had sustained it was shrinking. Energy derived from Nottinghamshire coal was more efficiently carried south from power stations in the Trent Valley by the National Grid. Patterns of movement of finished and semi-finished steel were changing, the carriage of fish by rail ceased in 1964, and merchandise traffic was diminishing. None of the GC's passenger services to London was without competition. Nevertheless, with the admitted benefit of hindsight, the closure of the line was not the pruning of a sapless twig but rather the destruction of a national asset whose potential long-term benefits to the economy were never adequately assessed. Those who travelled on the Great Central in the mid-1960s were subjected to experiences that disposed many against rail travel for their lifetimes, while the embarrassment caused to the crews who worked the remaining services shattered the morale of railwaymen for a generation.[10]

The main line

The 1960s opened on the Great Western northern line with a majestic coda to the age of steam. The West Coast Main Line was in process of electrification and from September 1960 trains between Birmingham New Street and Euston were reduced in number, while the frequency of services between Snow Hill and Paddington was increased to approximately hourly. For a spell some trains detached portions for the south coast at Banbury, and three 'Castle' class engines, including No 7011 *Banbury Castle*, were allocated to the shed to handle this traffic. There were 15 weekday departures from Paddington to Wolverhampton and beyond by way of Bicester with an additional peak hour train on Fridays. From 12 September 1960 an eight-car 'Blue Pullman' unit operated up morning and down evening business services to and from Wolverhampton and made a

---

[9] S J Tyrrell, *A Countryman's Tale* (London: Constable, 1973), 121-22.
[10] M Bonavia, *The Four Great Railways* (Newton Abbot: David & Charles, 1980), 56; R H N Hardy, *Steam in the Blood* (London: Ian Allan, 1971, paperback edn, 1975), 114; R T Munns, *Milk Churns to Merry-go-round* (Newton Abbot: David & Charles, 1986), 21-22; see also H Jones, *The Chiltern Railways Story* (Stroud: The History Press, 2010).

When a Blue Pullman unit was unavailable its workings were undertaken by 'Western' class diesels with vintage Pullman coaches. No D1005 'Western Venturer' passes Banbury with a down working in August 1962.

No 6027 'King Richard I' at Banbury shed after breaking down while hauling an up express in the summer of 1962. It remained outside the repair shop for many months until it was hauled to Langley Green for scrapping the following June.

return trip to Snow Hill in the middle of the day. The film *Let's Go to Birmingham*, made by British Transport Films in 1962 is a record of a return midday journey between Paddington and Snow Hill completed in five-and-a-half minutes in a Blue Pullman unit. The 30 locomotives of the 'King' class were concentrated on the line, having been displaced by diesels from services to the West of England and South Wales. The experience in the summer of 1962 of watching the 'Kings', by then 35 years old, hauling heavy trains through the Chilterns, rolling across the Souldern viaducts and down to Aynho or barking up Cropredy Bank, remains memorable.[11]

In that summer Swindon works constructed a series of 2700 hp Co-Co diesel locomotives, with engines supplied by the German company, Maybach Motorenbau GmbH, and the hydraulic transmission that had been adopted as standard by the Western Region. In August the class began to work Paddington–Wolverhampton trains and took over the operation of the whole service from the beginning of the winter timetable in September, but proved unreliable. On the opening day of the service the 14.10 from Paddington reached Wolverhampton behind an 8F 2-8-0, and as late as 18 October 1962 No 6011 *King James I* worked the up *Cambrian Coast Express*. During 1962 the experimental diesel locomotive No D0260 *Lion*, built at Smethwick by the Birmingham Railway Carriage & Wagon Co, worked experimentally on the 07.25 Wolverhampton–Paddington and the 12.10 return. No 6027 *King Richard I* broke down near Banbury

---

[11] *RM* vol 106 (1960), 140, 533, 675; S C Jenkins, *The Great Western & Great Central Joint Railway* (Tarrant Hinton: Oakwood, 1978), 26-28.

shortly before the diesel takeover and remained derelict at Banbury shed until June 1963 when it was towed away by a 9F 2-10-0 to be cut up at Langley Green.[12]

Stanier 'Black Fives' and 8Fs gave an increasingly London Midland air to the shed at Banbury, which frequently had to find replacements for failed diesels. Banbury's No 6930 *Aldersley Hall* reached Paddington with the up *Cambrian Coast Express* on 24 January 1963 and again on 25 February 1963 with the up *Inter City*. On 9 June 1963 No 7905 *Fowey Hall* replaced No D1011 *Western Thunderer* on the 14.10 from Paddington. Crew-training between Paddington and Wolverhampton with Brush Type 4 diesel electrics (later Class 47) began on 4 November 1963, and from Monday 23 December of that year they took over the whole service, while the 'Westerns' were re-deployed in the West of England. Increasingly when there were breakdowns the replacements were diesel engines from freight trains such an English Electric type 4 (class 40), No D330, which took over the *Cambrian Coast Express* on 17 January 1967. On 17 February 1966 Southern Region pacific No 34017 *Ilfracombe*, which had worked to Banbury on a cross-country train, was commandeered to take over the 09.10 Paddington–Wolverhampton.[13]

The most positive change in main line services through Banbury in the mid-1960s was the introduction of Mark II coaches, the first of which were built in 1964. They were of semi-integral construction, had pressure ventilation and retained the LMS tradition of wood-panelled interiors. The former GWR and LMSR coaches that had been used on the Paddington–Wolverhampton interval trains gradually disappeared. The new coaches, and the Mark Is that continued in use, appeared in British Rail's new blue and grey livery, while the Brush Type 4 diesel locomotives were now painted in two shades of green. In 1965 the principal businessmen's service to Birmingham and Wolverhampton ceased to be called the *Inter City* when that name became the brand for the whole of British Rail's express network.

The semi-fast leaving Paddington for Banbury via Bicester in the late afternoon that until 1960 had collected the slip coach from the 17.10 express at Bicester, was operated by ex-GWR steam locomotives until 1965. The train, then the 16.15 Paddington–Banbury, was hauled on 11 June 1965 by No 7029 *Clun Castle*. This was the last train in normal service to be powered by steam out of Paddington. Some steam workings remained, and the extra parcels trains provided for the Christmas rush in 1965 were all headed by 'Black Fives'.[14]

---

[12] *SD* January 2016, 22; *Steam World*, 354 (December 2016), 22.
[13] K Jones, *Once upon a time by the Lineside* (Nottingham: Challenger, 1998), 4-5, 85; *RM* vol 109 (1963), 69, 294; vol 110 (1964) 264, 333, 466; Jenkins, *Great Western & Great Central*, 30; *TI* vol 22 (1966), 231-32, 398.
[14] *MDR* vol 22 (1966), 117.

Pictures of Banbury shed in its latter days show ranks of ill-maintained locomotives flanked by puddles bordered by thick black grease, and untidy piles of ash, clinker, litter and straggly grass. A visitor on 2 January 1966 was shocked by the rust-encrusted condition of the three 'Halls' on shed. An observer in September saw three Black Fives, an 8F, class 2MT No 46522 dead outside the main building, and B1 No 61306 in the lifting shop. The shed closed from 3 October 1966.[15]

Cross-country services contracted. The daily train from Birkenhead to the Kent and Sussex coasts ceased to operate during the winter months after 31 October 1959, and when restored in May 1960 ran south of Wolverhampton only. From the spring of 1962 the coaches serving the Sussex coast ran only to Eastbourne, not to Hastings. The Southern Region's class 33 diesels were employed on the train from the summer of 1962, but steam, in the form of 'Castle' class 4-6-0s, worked as far as Reading on most of the through trains to Kent and Sussex in the service's final summer which ended on 5 September 1964. By 1966 traffic had so diminished that on the first Saturday in August, once the busiest day of the year, only three relief trains were required at Birmingham Snow Hill.[16]

The *Pines Express*, from Manchester to Bournemouth West via Birmingham New Street, Gloucester, Bath and the Somerset & Dorset Joint Railway ran for the last time on Saturday 8 September 1962. From the following Monday the name was bestowed on a train that ran from Manchester via Crewe, Market Drayton, Wellington, and Wolverhampton to Banbury and thence via Reading and Basingstoke to Poole, taking the place of the established service from Birkenhead. From 17 June 1963 the *Pines* was diverted to run from Crewe to Wellington via Shrewsbury, and from January 1966 it was hauled in both directions between Poole and Crewe by class 47 diesels. The name was dropped from 4 March 1967. More Southern Region locomotives reached Banbury with cross-country trains and some went further north. On 8 August 1964, Southern Region diesels Nos D6516, D6518 and D6525 worked to Wolverhampton on trains from Margate, Eastbourne and Portsmouth Harbour. On 6 July 1963 No 34004 *Yeovil* arrived at Wolverhampton, and on 6 August 1965 34053 *Sir Keith Park* worked the 09.50 Bournemouth–Wolverhampton throughout. For a time in 1966 'Black Five' 4-6-0s and Southern Region locomotives hauled the Bournemouth–York trains on alternate days between Banbury and the south coast, and 'Merchant Navy' and 'West Country' 4-6-2s spent some summer evenings serving as Banbury's station pilot. On 23 February 1966 a failure

---

[15] F Booker, *The Great Western Railway: A New History* (Newton Abbot: David & Charles, 1977), 159; Hucknall, *On Shed*, 98; R Adley, *The Call of Steam* (Poole: Blandford, 1982), 194.
[16] *MDR* vol 22 (1966), 567; S Bartley, 'Indian Summer of Wolverhampton (Oxley) Castles', *SD*, No 308 (2015), 5-22.

resulted in the provision of class 8F No 48276, which lacked steam-heating facilities, to work from Banbury to Poole, and on 22 March 1966 'Black Five' No 44872 failed at Kidlington on the Poole–York and was replaced by 9F 2-10-0 No 92218.[17]

After the closure of Banbury shed on 3 October 1966 steam working of the Poole–Manchester trains ceased and the service was diverted to run north of Oxford through Worcester to Birmingham New Street while junctions in Birmingham were improved enabling trains to run between New Street and Banbury.[18]

Revolution

Over the weekend of 4-5 March 1967 the nature of the railways through Banbury changed utterly. On Saturday 4 March excursions were arranged marking the end of the Great Western's main line to Merseyside. 'Castle' class locomotives No 4079 *Pendennis Castle* and No 7029 *Clun Castle* headed specials from Paddington to Birkenhead. The following Monday saw the beginning of full electric services on the West Coast Main Line, including two trains every hour between Euston and Birmingham New Street. Banbury was subsequently served by seven trains in each direction that left New Street, followed the tortuous curves on to the Midland Railway's Camp Hill line past the St Andrew's football ground, and joined the line from Snow Hill at Bordesley Junction before heading for Paddington. For a spell in the following autumn Western Region 'Warship' class diesel hydraulics were used on some trains but they proved unreliable and Brush Class 47s were substituted.

The shed buildings at Banbury were demolished, and the site remained undeveloped until 2016. Diesel locomotives were stabled between turns in sidings alongside the Western Region's disused cattle docks until February 1984, when rostering of crews at Banbury formally ceased.[19] The disposal within a few years of thousands of unwanted steam locomotives involved many private companies. James Friswell & Son, having cut up the engines from the Edge Hill Light Railway in 1946, scrapped 14 main line locomotives at Banbury shed between November 1964 and March 1965, including six 'Halls', two 'Modified Halls' and 2-8-2T No 7207 which was considered unfit to be moved.[20]

The Great Western's main line to Merseyside was fragmented from 1967. The three miles from Paddington as far as Old Oak Common remained in intensive

---

[17] *RM* vol 98 (1962), 250, 514; vol 99 (1963) 509; *SVRN* 185 (2014); Hucknall, *On Shed*, 98; *MDR* vol 22 (1966), 175; *TI* vol 22 (1966), 117, 231-32.
[18] *MDR* vol 22 (1966), 567-68, 625, 679.
[19] B Simpson, 'Banbury: All Changes', *Back Track*, vol 4 (1992), 173-79.
[20] N Trevenna, *Steam for Scrap* (ed A Earnshaw, Penryn: Atlantic Transport Publishers, 1992), 75.

use. The section to Northolt Junction continued to carry trains from New Street to Paddington but increasingly they were diverted to run via Oxford and Reading. The joint GWR/GCR line beyond Northolt was served by suburban trains from Marylebone to High Wycombe and Princes Risborough, some of which continued from 1973 to Banbury. From Princes Risborough to Aynho Junction the line remained open but it was singled from 1968. The section from Aynho Junction to Bordesley remained busy but only a few trains from Leamington and Stratford continued to go into Snow Hill station, and they were cut back to Moor Street from 2 March 1968. A skeleton service of railcars served the intermediate stations between Snow Hill and Wolverhampton Low Level until 6 March 1972. From 1967 trains from Shrewsbury were diverted into the former LNWR High Level station at Wolverhampton. Apart from one daily train between Shrewsbury and Euston these were aging diesel multiple units, some of which worked through to Chester. Diesel multiple unit services on the final section from Chester to Woodside station at Birkenhead were cut back to Rock Ferry from 5 November 1967.[21]

Freight

When the new junctions at Fenny Compton and Stratford opened in 1960 traffic from Banbury and Woodford along the former SMJR line was heavy, but it soon diminished. The line west of the military depot at Burton Dassett ceased to be used from 1 March 1965 and was officially closed from 5 July 1965. In the last months of 1965, steam locomotives from Banbury were still hauling freight trains to Southall, although the depot had officially closed to steam. From 3 January 1966 the Western Region formally banned steam locomotives from its tracks. Traffic for South Wales that had passed through Woodford was diverted through Birmingham and Bromsgrove. From February 1965 freight from Nottinghamshire for southern England was worked from Toton to Banbury via Burton-on-Trent and Bordesley Junction. Other trains were routed from Bescot to Banbury through Berkswell or Coventry to Kenilworth, and over existing connections at Leamington. By February 1966 all freight trains using this route were diesel-hauled, but 9F class 2-10-0s were still working from Washwood Heath via Bordesley Junction to Banbury in March 1966. By that time oil trains from Fawley through Banbury to Bromford Bridge were being hauled by class 33 diesels from the Southern Region. On 22 March 1966 the 11.10 Banbury–Eastleigh freight had unusual power in the form of the A4 pacific No 60024 *Kingfisher* heading south to work enthusiasts' excursions. During May, June and July 1966 No 7029 *Clun Castle*, officially withdrawn prior to preservation, was hauling freight between Banbury and Bordesley. The marshalling yard at Oxley

---

[21] *MDR* vol 22 (1966), 623.

north of Wolverhampton, a staging point for traffic to and from Banbury for many decades, closed late in 1966, and in 1967 freight trains ceased to access Crewe through Wellington and Market Drayton. Training for Banbury locomen on class 24, 25 and 40 diesels began in September 1966, and after the closure of Banbury shed in October most freight trains were diesel-hauled.[22]

Diminishing loads on the daily freight trains to and from Merton Street were usually worked by 'Black Five' 4-6-0s until the line from Banbury to Buckingham was closed to all traffic in December 1964. Coal continued to be unloaded in the yard at Merton Street until the connection from the former Great Western line was removed from 2 June 1966. The track on the branch was lifted between December 1966 and February 1967. The rump of the BCDR, from the junction at King's Sutton to Adderbury, was closed on 18 August 1969, after which the removal of the track was completed on 3 October.[23]

The carriage of coal to gasworks fell away during the 1950s. By 1956 the works at Banbury was supplying Adderbury, Brackley and Woodford Halse which formerly had their own works. The works closed on 1 October 1958 when the completion of a pipeline enabled the local network to be supplied from the works at Oxford, which itself closed in 1960. The carriage of gas coal ceased completely as networks and appliances were converted to receive natural gas from the North Sea, a process completed in 1977. Banbury gasworks was occupied by the scrap merchants, James Friswell & Son, who for a time used the siding from the WR line to dispose of scrap iron by rail to the Ford foundry at Leamington.[24]

Cattle were still being despatched from Merton Street in 1961, and a photograph of No 7905 *Fowey Hall* taking over a southbound train on 10 October 1962 shows a long line of cattle wagons in the Western Region dock. During that year British Railways reduced the number of stations handling live cattle from over 2,500 to around 200, and by 1965 the only cattle movements were block trains from the ports for Ireland.[25]

In the mid-1950s four trains daily took fish from Hull and Grimsby to the south via the Great Central line and Banbury, and most trip workings from Banbury to Woodford included empty fish vans. In the early 1960s the Hull fish train was

---

[22] TI vol 22 (1966), 118, 623; R C Riley & B Simpson, *A History of the Stratford-upon-Avon & Midland Junction Railway* (Witney: Lamplight Publications, 1999), 111-12, 113/14/16/17/18/22/23/24/26/27/28; MDR vol 22 (1966), 61, 69, 118, 282, 398, 454, 510, 513, 567, 681-82.

[23] Simpson, *Banbury to Verney Junction*, 153-63; L Waters, *Oxfordshire Railways in Old Photographs* (Gloucester: Sutton, 1989), 122-23.

[24] G C J Hartland, 'Gas-Making in Banbury', C&CH vol 4 (1969), 53; Waters, *Oxfordshire Railways*, 122-23.

[25] RM vol 110 (1964), 126.

diverted to run from Woodford to Oxford along the London Extension to Calvert and then by the former Buckinghamshire Railway. Traffic from both ports was diminishing and in 1964 most of British Rail's fish traffic, including all of that which passed through Banbury, was handed to road hauliers.[26]

Another traffic that disappeared was the conveyance of bananas which travelled to inland depots in steam-heated vans from the ports of Avonmouth, Barry, Garston, Hull, Tilbury and Southampton. In 1964 there were conditional paths for five banana trains from Southampton that passed through Banbury *en route* for the Midlands and the North, and three from Avonmouth via Didcot, as well as a working from Barry via Stratford and Hatton, that reversed at Banbury Junction before going through Woodford to Laisterdyke. Most banana traffic moved to road transport during the 1960s, and rail carriage ceased altogether in 1979.[27]

Traffic to and from the cement works at Bletchingdon and Harbury had long been handled at Banbury. The works at Shipton-on-Cherwell received gypsum from East Leake as well as coal, by rail. Wagons were usually tripped from Banbury, but later from Woodford, and after the closure of the London Extension, from yards further north, until the works closed in 1987. From 1957 trains of 24-ton hopper wagons began to pass through Banbury conveying limestone from a re-opened quarry at Ardley to Greaves's Sidings, Harbury. The trains were worked by locomotives from Leamington shed which closed in June 1965. After that Banbury shed was responsible for the workings, some of which were undertaken by class 9F 2-10-0s. After Banbury shed closed the limestone trains were diesel-hauled until the factory ceased production in 1970.[28]

In 1964 ten trains were despatched every weekday from the Oxfordshire Ironstone Co, six, with continuous brakes, to South Wales, three unfitted trains to Bilston West, and one to Croes Newydd. After the closure of the SMJR line on 1 March 1965 diminishing numbers of iron ore trains from Banbury to South Wales were diesel-hauled by class 47s via Didcot and the Severn Tunnel, but the ironstone company ceased operations from September 1967. Its quarry at Alkerton was taken over by Peter Bennie Ltd, principally for the production of road stone, but from 1969 the company despatched up to five hundred tons per day of ironstone by road to Banbury station where it was loaded into railway wagons for the steelworks at Shelton and Bilston. Later, in 1977-78, some loads were sent to Llanwern in close-coupled bogie wagons of the kind that supplied the works from the import terminal at Port Talbot, but the traffic ceased from 16 June 1978.

---

[26] *RM* vol 109 (1963), 1; Munns, *Milk Churns to Merry-go-rounds*, 120.
[27] Western Region Working Timetable, 1964.
[28] C Dodsworth, 'The Early Years of the Oxford Cement Industry', *Industrial Archaeology*, vol 9 (1972), 285-95; S A Leleux, *Warwickshire Lime and Cement Works Railways* (Usk: Oakwood, 2014), 31-35, 51.

A limestone working from Ardley to Greaves's Sidings, headed by 5100 class 2-6-2T No 4112. 1961.

On weekdays in 1964 some seventy down freight workings were scheduled to start or terminate at or pass through Banbury. Ten were departures of loaded trains of iron ore. Another ten comprised class 4 fitted general goods trains, mostly running overnight, including workings from Basingstoke to Crewe, Paddington to Birkenhead, Eastleigh to Lawley Street (Birmingham), Exeter to Oxley (Wolverhampton), Severn Beach (Bristol) to Tees Yard and Southampton Docks to Edgehill (Liverpool). Eight partially-fitted class 5 or class 6 trains passed northwards to yards at Birmingham, Wolverhampton and Crewe, four of them originating in the London area, and there were three through workings to Woodford, two from Bristol and one from Tavistock Junction. There were three fully-fitted block trains, the 04.45 and 22.55 workings carrying oil products from the refinery at Fawley on Southampton Water to Bromford Bridge (Birmingham) and the 13.18 motor car and parts train from Morris Cowley to Bathgate in Scotland. The pattern of trip workings to Woodford was changing. Five class 7 trains worked from the down yard to Woodford, but there were additional trains of coal empties that fitted into the pattern of trip workings, two each from Reading and Didcot and one each from Hinksey (Oxford), Slough, Southall, North Acton and Shipton-on-Cherwell, the latter including gypsum empties for East Leake. Local freight trains of class 8 and class 9 were despatched to Leamington and Burton Dassett and arrived in the down yard from Hinksey (Oxford), Adderbury and Princes Risborough.

Some eighty up workings began or terminated at, or passed through Banbury in 1964. Six were return workings of iron ore empties. Six class 4 trains terminated at Banbury, two from Crewe, and one each from York, Carlisle, Saltney (Chester) and Oxley. Five passed through *en route* from Tees Yard to Bristol, Birkenhead to Paddington and Manchester and Washwood Heath (Birmingham) to Basingstoke, and Queens Head to Dartford, in addition to two empty tank trains from Bromford Bridge to Fawley. The return Bathgate–Morris Cowley class 3 working left its Scottish terminus at 12.00 and passed Banbury at 01.29. There were eight partially-fitted class 5 workings, three of them departures for the London area, terminating workings from Oldbury & Langley Green, Saltney and Leicester, and through workings from Washwood Heath to Eastleigh and from Victoria Basin (Wolverhampton) to Basingstoke. Most southbound unbraked workings from the GW line into the Hump Yard were from Oxley or yards in Birmingham. Nine trip workings from Woodford terminated in the hump reception sidings, but there were also three through workings from Woodford to Didcot and one to Bletchington. Local freight trains went south to Hinksey, Princes Risborough and Adderbury, with an option for the latter to continue to Hook Norton. Local freights worked into the hump yard from Leamington, Greaves's Siding and Burton Dassett and there were departures of long-distance unbraked trains for Stoke Gifford and Westbury. Two coal trains from Coventry and Nuneaton maintained the link between Banbury and the Warwickshire Coalfield. Some thirty trains were scheduled to terminate in the hump reception sidings every 24 hours.[29]

The hump marshalling yard was closed with the introduction of a new timetable on 4 May 1970, although the up sidings north of the station were used for sorting wagons until the early 1990s.[30] Traffic at Banbury's goods depot, like that in other towns, declined with the growth of the motorway system. Operations at the depot were taken over by National Carriers in 1969, but its future was already threatened.

Excursions

The railways continued to provide special trains for football matches, race meetings and other events through the early 1960s. A particularly notable excursion on 4 November 1961 carried more than 400 supporters of Banbury Spencer Football Club to an FA Cup match with Shrewsbury Town. The train was headed by one of Banbury shed's 'Hall' class 4-6-0s which carried a headboard

---

[29] Western Region Working Timetable, 1964.

[30] M Rhodes, 'The Rise and Fall of the British Marshalling Yard: part 1, The 19th century to 1963', *RM* 1351 (2013), 35; B Trinder, 'The Railway Marshalling Yard at Banbury', *C&CH* vol 4 (1970), 131; L Waters, & T Doyle, *British Railways Past and Present*, 137; C R Potts, *An Historical Survey of Selected Great Western Stations, vol. 4* (Poole: Oxford Publishing Co, 1985), 14.

'Banbury Spencer – Gay Puritans to Gay Meadow'. This was probably the only special train to have carried supporters of the Banbury club. Unfortunately for those supporters Shrewsbury Town were then enjoying a spell of success with the famous Arthur Rowley as player manager, and the Banbury team lost 7-1.[31]

The changeover from steam to diesel: in the summer of 1964 a Southern Region class 33 diesel heads a train carrying returning holiday makers to the West Midlands. To the right a second train from the coast is in charge of a 'Hall' class 4-6-0, another of which is on station pilot duties to the left.

On 7 May 1960 members of the 'King' class headed two of five excursions taking supporters of Wolverhampton Wanderers to the FA Cup Final against Blackburn Rovers, perhaps the last occasion on which Wembley-bound steam-hauled football specials passed through Banbury. After the 'Kings' had been displaced by diesels on the main line, No 6000 *King George V* hauled a 'Farewell to the Kings on the Birmingham line' excursion from Wolverhampton to Swindon

---

[31] B Little & D Shadbolt, *The History of Banbury Spencer Football Club* (Witney, Boyd, 2013), 109-13.

on 9 September 1962. The Locomotive Club of Great Britain organised a 'King Commemoration Tour' on 17 November 1962 hauled from Paddington to Wolverhampton by No 6018 *King Henry VI*, which subsequently made its way from Tyseley through Banbury to Swindon, while the train went by a devious route via the Bletchley flyover and Calvert to Marylebone. The same engine hauled a Stephenson Locomotive Society special from Birmingham through Greenford to Swindon on 28 April 1963.[32]

Special trains from London to Tywyn for the annual general meetings of the Talyllyn Railway Preservation Society continued to pass through Banbury. On 24 September 1960 the train was hauled by the mixed traffic 2-8-0 No 4701, which had just been through the shops at Swindon, and on 30 September 1961 by its sister engine No 4704. On 9 September 1962 the special was headed by No 6000 *King George V*. In 1963 the train included sleeping cars on the return journey, and was hauled between Paddington and Shrewsbury by SR pacific No 34064 *Fighter Command*. In 1964 Talyllyn members were taken from Paddington to Wolverhampton by No 7029 *Clun Castle*, and from Wolverhampton to Ruabon by No 1011 *County of Chester*. The train returned to the main line at Shrewsbury whence *Clun Castle* returned it to Paddington. In 1965 the special was hauled from Paddington to Shrewsbury and, on the return, from Tyseley to Paddington by No 4079 *Pendennis Castle*, with diesel haulage from Shrewsbury to Tyseley. This train attracted more than four hundred passengers in the belief that it would be the last steam-worked agm special. That proved not to be the case for on 24 September 1966 the train was hauled between Paddington and Banbury by diesels, but in each direction between Banbury and Shrewsbury by *Clun Castle*. In 1967 85 members of the Society travelled by service train from Euston to New Street where they transferred to a chartered diesel multiple unit.[33]

There were similar workings for the annual meetings of the Festiniog Railway Society. On 20 April 1963 No 4472 *Flying Scotsman* made its first run in its newly acquired LNER livery, and attracted huge crowds along its route to Ruabon. No 4079 *Pendennis Castle* hauled the equivalent train on 25 April 1964. On May Day 1965 the Festiniog special was due to be headed from Paddington by No 7029 *Clun Castle*, which failed in the platform. A diesel took the train to Banbury where No 6849 *Walton Grange* was substituted to continue the journey to Shrewsbury.[34]

Several tours marking the ends of locomotive classes or the impending closures of lines passed through Banbury in the mid-1960s. On 10 February 1963 'West

---

[32] K Jones, *Once upon a time by the Lineside* (Nottingham: Challenger, 1998), 82-83; *RM* vol 98 (1962), 801/878; vol 99 (1963), 144; vol 109 (1963), 35; vol 98 (1962), 801/878; vol 99 (1963), 144, 410; *RC* vol 99 (1963), 288,515.
[33] *SW* No 273, (2010) 62; *RM* vol 98 (1962), 801/878; *RC* vol 99 (1963), 664.
[34] *RM* vol 99 (1963), 519, vol 101 (1964), 600.

Country' class light pacific No 34094 *Mortehoe* headed a special organised by the Home Counties Railway Society from Marylebone via Birmingham Snow Hill to Crewe. The 'Thames Avon Severn Tour' on 12 October 1963 was hauled from Waterloo to Woodford through Banbury by Southern Region T9 class 4-4-0 No 120 (now 30120, preserved as part of the National Collection) and U class 2-6-0 No 31790. Western Region 2-6-0 No 6368 and 0-6-0 No 2246 then took it from Woodford over the SMJR through Stratford to Worcester. 'Jubilee' No 45552 *Silver Jubilee* hauled it over the Lickey Incline, the Camp Hill line and through New Street station, then to Cheltenham, before the train returned to London behind 'Castle' No 7005 *Sir Edward Elgar*. On 17 November 1963 No 46245 *City of London* passed through Banbury on the Wolverhampton–Paddington leg of a Euston–Crewe–Paddington special, and on 1 September headed an Ian Allan Locospotters' excursion from Paddington to Crewe. *Flying Scotsman*, then carrying the number 4472, took the Warwickshire Railway Society from Birmingham to Eastleigh Works on 16 August 1964, and hauled an excursion from Birmingham to the Farnborough Air Show on 12 September of that year. On 21 June 1964 the Locomotive Club of Great Britain organised a special between Shrewsbury and Paddington hauled by No 46251 *City of Nottingham*.

The Stephenson Locomotive Society bade farewell to the 'County' class by arranging for No 1011 *County of Chester* to head its annual trip from Birmingham to Swindon on 20 September 1964. The A4 Preservation Society arranged for No 60007 *Sir Nigel Gresley* to head the 'Paddington Streamliner' from Manchester via Banbury to Paddington on 23 October 1965. On 25 and 26 June 1966 'Merchant Navy' class 4-6-2 No 35026 *Lamport & Holt Line* passed on the outward and return journeys of an ambitious tour named 'The Aberdonian' which travelled over unusual routes in Scotland. Another 'Merchant Navy' visited Banbury on 12 November 1966 when No 35023 *Holland-Afrika Line* brought in the 'Shakespearian Rail Tour' from Waterloo. The train was handed over to No 7029 *Clun Castle* which took it on a tour of the West Midlands, after which No 35023 returned it to Victoria. The fledgling Great Western Society organised an excursion from Snow Hill through Banbury and Greenford to Taplow and Didcot headed by No 7808 *Cookham Manor* on 12 September 1966.[35]

The last passenger working into Merton Street was probably *The Banburian*, organised by the South Bedfordshire Locomotive Club which ran on 22 September 1962 from Luton through Leighton Buzzard and over the Bletchley flyover, headed by 'Super D' class 0-8-0 No 48930.[36]

---

[35] *SVRN* 185 (2014); *RM* vol 99 (1963), 442.
[36] R Coleman & J Rajczonek, *Railway Images around Northamptonshire* (Wellingborough: Wharton, 1992), 72; A E Grigg, *Town of Trains* (Buckingham: Barracuda, 1980), 58.

2-6-2T No 6111 takes water at Bicester Town station with 'Chiltern 200', the last passenger train to use several of the lines in 'Banburyshire', 14 September 1963.

Nearly a year later, on 14 September 1963 the Railway Enthusiasts' Club organised what was probably the last passenger train to traverse several lines in Banburyshire. Headed by 2-6-2T No 6111, *Chiltern 200* left Rewley Road station in Oxford and travelled to Bicester. It then reversed, crossed the north side of the triangle from Oxford Road Junction to Yarnton, and ran along the former OWWR through Kingham to Chipping Norton.

After running round, it returned to Kingham, reversed again, then went through Honeybourne to Stratford where it took the connection made in 1960 with the SMJR line which it followed to Fenny Compton. The train then passed through Banbury station and took the BCDR line at King's Sutton as far as the viaduct at Hook Norton. On returning to Banbury No 6111 took the train through the station before reversing into the sidings on its eastern side and propelling the coaches over the connection into Merton Street yard. A class 4MT 2-6-4T, No 42105 was waiting, coupled up to what had been the rear of the train, and headed for Verney Junction from where it propelled the train at low speed as far as was possible along the line towards Quainton Road. Once back at Verney Junction the train returned to Oxford.

The depths

The years around 1970 appear in retrospect as the nadir of railway fortunes in the Banbury region. Traffic had ceased on five of the eight converging lines, and one of the remaining three, the Bicester cut-off, was threatened. The closure of the engine shed and the marshalling yard reduced the numbers of railway employees. Traffic at the freight depot was diminishing. There were few through services to distant destinations other than London and Birmingham. Passengers could look back on much discomfort during the ill-managed transition from steam to diesel traction, which had been demoralising for railwaymen. Optimism about railways had been possible in 1960. It was difficult to sustain in 1970.

The ticket produced for Chiltern 200. The starting point of the tour should be Rewley Road not Beverley Road.

14. Mines of Precious Stone: Iron Ore

'Northamptonshire, during the last fifteen years, has become a very important district for iron ore'.
Samuel Griffiths, 1873.[1]

Banbury's railwaymen spent more than a century moving iron ore. The most useful feature of the line from King's Sutton to Hook Norton was the access it provided to quarries, while the five-mile railway from the Oxfordshire Ironstone Company's quarries at Wroxton, the last to be built of the of the eight lines that converged on Banbury, was nevertheless one of the busiest.

The mid-nineteenth century iron industry

Britain's iron industry grew at a prodigious rate between 1700 and 1870. The number of blast furnaces increased from 85 to 715 in the ninety years after 1791 while their total annual output expanded from about 80,000 tons of pig iron to more than 650,000 tons. Most of the ores consumed in those furnaces came from seams within the carboniferous measures. By 1870 the Black Country and South Wales, iron-working regions which grew to prominence between 1790 and 1810, had been joined by Scotland and Cleveland as significant centres of production.

There was concern in iron-making regions around 1850 about the supply of ore. The shortage of local ores in the Black Country was noted in 1854 by Harry Scrivenor, who remarked 'Is not this, as regards South Staffordshire, the beginning of an end?' Samples of Northamptonshire ironstone from Woodford near Kettering, displayed at the Great Exhibition in 1851, aroused widespread interest and quarrying for ironstone began soon afterwards at Blisworth and Wellingborough. In 1854 Thomas Butlin blew in a blast furnace at Wellingborough, where his company employed 120 men by 1861, but most Northamptonshire ore was despatched to the Black Country or the Erewash Valley. Owners of furnaces in South Wales secured supplies from the Forest of Dean and increasingly looked to the Basque Country for their ore. Many ironmasters were interested in the deposits of ironstone in north Oxfordshire and on the southern fringes of Northamptonshire. The fortunes of the quarries around Banbury were dictated by what was happening in the iron and steel industry nationally.[2]

The iron-bearing marlstone rocks of the Banbury region mostly lay beneath a shallow overburden and could be extracted relatively easily. The first quarries were worked without mechanical equipment and even mid-twentieth century

---

[1] S Griffiths, *Guide to the Iron Trade* (1873, rep Newton Abbot: David & Charles, 1967), 128.
[2] B Trinder, *Britain's Industrial Revolution* (Lancaster: Carnegie, 2013), 291-97, 343-44.

workings were relatively shallow. Oxfordshire ore was not rich in iron, but some types, when used in a blast furnace, could reduce the amount of limestone needed as flux. At several workings calcining kilns were used to roast the ironstone, driving off moisture, sulphur and carbon dioxide, and separating some waste rock, but in the latter decades of operation ironworks preferred to receive uncalcined ore, crushed or uncrushed.

The ironworking companies most closely associated with quarrying in the Banbury region were Richard Thomas & Baldwin in South Wales, Alfred Hickman & Sons (later Stewart & Lloyds) in the Black Country and the Brymbo Steel Co near Wrexham, although other concerns including the Earl of Dudley's Round Oak works on the western side of the Black Country, Clay Cross near Chesterfield and the furnaces at Corby and Wellingborough used some Oxfordshire ore.

The Brymbo ironworks, established by John Wilkinson in the 1790s, was revived in the 1840s by a partnership that included the engineer and politician Sir Henry Robertson and Charles and William Darby of Coalbrookdale, after whose deaths it was incorporated in 1884 as the Brymbo Steel Co. It was linked to the Minera branch of the GWR which joined the main line to Chester at Croes Newydd, south of Wrexham General station. The works was closed after bankruptcy between 1931 and 1934, but Sir Harry Beyer Robertson formed a new company which gained a lucrative contract to supply Rolls Royce with steel for aero engines. From 1948 Brymbo was part of Guest, Keen & Nettlefold (GKN). The blast furnace ceased operation in 1978 after which steel was made from scrap in electric furnaces until the works closed in 1990.

Sir Alfred Hickman, son of a colliery owner in Tipton, became one of the leading ironmasters in the Black Country. In 1866 his family acquired the Springvale Furnaces in Bilston, and in 1882 he opened the adjacent Staffordshire Steel Ingot & Iron Co to produce steel by the Gilchrist Thomas process. The two works were amalgamated in 1897 by the company then called Alfred Hickman & Sons Ltd. The Bilston site was accessible by rail from the OWWR south of Wolverhampton as well as from the LNWR main line.

Stewart & Lloyds Ltd was established in 1903, an amalgamation of the Birmingham company Lloyd & Lloyd which dated from 1859, and A & J Stewart & Menzies Ltd of Coatbridge in Scotland, makers of steel tubes. The company's policy was to take over the firms on which they relied for supplies and transport, and they acquired Alfred Hickman & Sons Ltd in 1921. At Corby, Stewart & Lloyds enlarged the furnace complex and built steel-making facilities and a tube mill in the early 1930s. The company continued to develop the works at Bilston, blowing-in *Elisabeth*, the Black Country's last blast furnace, in 1954.

Richard Thomas & Baldwin was formed in 1948 by a merger of Richard Thomas & Co with Baldwins Ltd. Richard Thomas, by leasing works in the Forest of Dean and South Wales, created one of the principal tinplate manufacturing companies in the region. In the 1930s the company acquired the derelict ironworks at Ebbw Vale, and constructed, with government assistance, a new works with blast furnaces, a steel plant, rolling mills and a mill producing strip for tinplate. The site lay 16 miles north of the GWR main line at Newport, up a steeply-graded railway, with no nearby supplies of ore, and the company would have preferred to build in Lincolnshire, but bowed to pressure from government and public opinion. Baldwins Ltd originated as E, P & W Baldwin of the Wilden Ironworks near Kidderminster. Alfred Baldwin bought out other family members in 1888 and introduced into the business his 21-year-old son Stanley, the future Prime Minister. The company was incorporated as E, P & W Baldwin Ltd in 1898, and gradually acquired tinplate works in South Wales. Richard Thomas & Baldwin was nationalised in 1951, but, alone among steel-making companies, was not privatised in the 1950s and remained in public hands at the time of re-nationalisation in 1967. The company installed the first continuous tinning line in Britain at Ebbw Vale in 1948, and in 1962 opened the Spencer Works, an integrated iron and steel plant, at Llanwern near Newport.

Workings along the main line

The first ironstone mining operations near Banbury centred on a quarry in Adderbury north-east of the present B4100, from where a narrow gauge tramway carried ore to the Oxford Canal. The quarry produced 3,410 tons of ore in 1859, which declined to 1,250 tons in 1860. A nil return was made the following year. Operations resumed in 1869 when 10,000 tons were produced from an expanded area. There were two distinct operations, one directed by John Angel, a Cornishman resident in Adderbury, the other by an engineer from Birmingham, both sending ore to the Parkfield Ironworks at Wolverhampton. The workings were purchased by the ironmaster Samuel Lloyd, and operated as the Adderbury Ironstone Company which from 1869 until 1877 leased wagons from the Birmingham Railway Carriage & Wagon Co. A tramway linked the quarries with a wharf on the west bank of the canal and with an interchange with the GWR south of King's Sutton station. On 12 August 1871 an ironstone train on the main line collided near the wharf with an 18-coach excursion train from Paddington to Birkenhead. About a dozen people were working in the ironstone quarries at Adderbury in 1871 and slightly fewer in 1881. Ore from these quarries was carried to Wolverhampton in 1876 by the 13.25 mineral train from King's Sutton and empties were returned on the 19.20 Wolverhampton–King's Sutton. Output diminished from 1877 and Samuel Lloyd's operation ceased from 1881. The workings were re-opened in 1889 by Alfred Hickman Ltd who carried ore to canal barges which took it to be loaded into standard gauge wagons at the wharf south of King's Sutton station that was later served by a railway from quarries on Sydenham Farm (see opposite). The quarries closed permanently soon after 1900.[3]

Workings in King's Sutton parish near Nell Bridge, about three-quarters of a mile south of the parish church, commenced about 1870 when permission was sought for the construction of a tramway which ran to an elevated tipping dock alongside a GWR siding. More than thirty men in King's Sutton were working at the quarries in 1871, most of them locally-born. The operation was short-lived and was mentioned for the last time in *Mining Statistics* in 1874.[4]

Alfred Hickman Ltd leased an area of 319 acres in King's Sutton for ironstone extraction in 1896 and the first ore was produced in July 1897. Workings ultimately extended about 1¾ miles to a quarry north-east of Buston Farm. A 2ft 1in gauge tramway carried ore to a transfer point alongside the GWR main line north of King's Sutton station, where there were initially three, and from 1898-99 five 64ft high calcining kilns. Tramway wagons crossed a viaduct to discharge their contents into the tops of the kilns and standard gauge wagons were filled from chutes at the kiln bases, although some ore was carried away in its raw state. Tramway wagons were hauled on an endless steel cable operated by a stationary steam engine alongside the kilns. By 1899 production had reached 100,000 tons pa, all of it conveyed to Hickman's Springvale Furnaces at Bilston. The scale of the operations is indicated by the presence of more than sixty ironstone quarry workers in King's Sutton parish in 1901. The lease expired in 1923, and was extended, but only for one year, after which the kilns were demolished. The connection to the main line was severed in November 1924 when the cabin that controlled it was renamed Astrop Signal Box.[5]

King's Sutton to Hook Norton

The construction of the Banbury & Cheltenham Direct Railway began in 1875 (as detailed in chapter 5), and by October of the following year tracks were laid from the junction with the GWR main line at King's Sutton station as far as Adderbury. By 1884 the line as far as Hook Norton was judged satisfactory, but it was not until 1887 that trains were able to progress as far as Chipping Norton and Kingham. Completion in 1906 of loops at Hatherley and Kingham enabled trains from the Banbury direction to progress southwards through Gloucester to South Wales. The most useful feature of the line was its ability to take away iron ore from quarries at Adderbury, Bloxham and Hook Norton.

---

[3] E Tonks, *The Ironstone Quarries of the Midlands, History Operations and Railways, Part 2, The Oxfordshire Field* (Cheltenham: Runpast, 1988), 26-33; *BG* 17 August 1871; J Copsey, 'Goods Operations at Banbury', *GWRJ* No 92 (2014), 184.

[4] Tonks, *Oxfordshire Field*, 16-18.

[5] J H Russell, *The Banbury and Cheltenham Railway 1887-1962* (Oxford: Oxford Publishing Co, 1977), 16; Tonks, *Oxfordshire Field*, 19-24.

The principal pits in Adderbury East were on Sydenham Farm about half a mile south-east of King's Sutton church, adjacent to the workings previously operated by the Adderbury Ironstone Co. The quarries were opened in March 1914 and developed during the First World War. A 2ft gauge tramway carried ore to kilns alongside Sydenham Sidings, served by a signal box on the BCDR. The kilns were similar to those at Astrop except that wagons were hoisted to the tops of the kilns rather than gaining access by a viaduct. Calcined ore was taken by the GWR to the Springvale Furnaces of Alfred Hickman & Co. Production declined after the war, when Hickmans had a half share in the Oxfordshire Ironstone Co, and the Sydenham quarries closed in June 1925. The kilns were demolished by James Friswell & Son about 1932.[6]

Prospecting for ore in Adderbury West began in 1890 south of Adderbury station, and workings may have begun in 1895, using a 20 in gauge tramway with a locomotive called *Florence*, brought from the colliery at Brora in Co Sutherland. Operations were intermittent, and the company went into liquidation in 1903. The quarries were taken over by Cochrane & Co of the Woodside Ironworks, Dudley, production re-commenced by 1911 and workings were extended west of the Banbury–Oxford road. Extraction continued during the First World War but the Woodside furnaces closed in 1922 bringing quarrying to an end. From 1928 the site was used by the Duffield Iron Corporation to test a process for reducing iron ore using pulverised coal. The government declined to support the project in 1940, after which the site was used for recovering scrap aluminium.[7]

Milton and Bloxham

One of many ironstone undertakings begun during the First World War was a series of quarries east of Bloxham church on land leased in September 1916. Operation began in 1918 under the management of Alfred Wassall and two directors of the iron company at Islip near Kettering. The ore was sold to companies in South Wales and the Black Country since the Islip furnaces were sufficiently supplied from adjacent quarries. Initially German prisoners-of-war were employed in the quarries. A standard gauge tramway carried ore for a mile and a half to sidings near Milton Halt on the BCDR. The quarries ceased working in 1921, but were re-opened spasmodically during the remainder of the decade before being closed formally from October 1929.[8]

Iron companies acquired ore-bearing land in Bloxham from the early 1880s, but, as at Milton, quarrying was stimulated by the First World War. The quarries

---

[6] Russell, *Banbury and Cheltenham*, 23; Tonks, *Oxfordshire Field*, 35-41; *BG* 11 June 1925; P Brookfield, 'Sydenham Quarries', *C&CH* vol 17 (2009), 287-95.
[7] Tonks, *Oxfordshire Field*, 43-47; Russell, *Banbury and Cheltenham*, 23-24.
[8] Russell, *Banbury and Cheltenham*, 26; Tonks, *Oxfordshire Field*, 49-56.

lay east of the village south of the road to Tadmarton. The Northamptonshire Ironstone Co built a standard gauge tramway which linked the workings to the BCDR near Bloxham station. Production began two months before the Armistice in 1918, and concluded when the company went into liquidation in 1925. The Clay Cross Co re-opened the workings in 1927, but operations were suspended in 1942. The quarries opened again in 1948 after the Clay Cross workings at Brixworth (Northamptonshire) were closed. They operated with a staff of three until 1954 when increased British Railways charges made them uneconomic. *Amos*, the quarry's petrol-electric locomotive was employed in 1955 in track-lifting on the Northampton & Banbury Junction Railway.[9]

Hook Norton

The BCDR approached the village of Hook Norton from the east, running north of the road from Milcombe, before turning south near the village station for about a mile, skirting the eastern edge of the village, crossing two tributaries of the River Swere on viaducts and approaching the north west corner of Swerford Park before turning west towards Chipping Norton.

The first significant iron ore workings in the parish were those of the Hook Norton Ironstone Partnership which acquired land for quarrying north and south-east of the station in 1889 and 1890. Extraction began in 1889 and workings were accessed by a 20 in gauge tramway which carried ore to a tipping dock on a standard gauge line that ran beneath the northernmost viaduct and up an incline to join the BCDR at the station. The latter line was worked by an 0-6-0T locomotive delivered that year by Manning Wardle and named *Hook Norton*. Up to twenty people were employed at the quarries in 1891. The company was wound up in 1903 after which *Hook Norton* passed into the ownership of the GWR who employed it until 1926 on Weymouth Quay.[10]

The Brymbo company's operations at Hook Norton lasted more than fifty years. Prospecting began in 1897 and in the following year the company leased the 12-acre Park Farm. Most of its ore was extracted from the high ground between the streams crossed by the two viaducts. The quarries were linked to sidings alongside the BCDR a mile east of Hook Norton station by 2 ft gauge tramways, the first locomotive for which was delivered in 1899. The company built two gas-fired continuous calcining kilns, with stone bases and coned steel sides encircled by galleries. Another kiln was constructed, probably during the First World War, and a fourth was added in 1922. The scale of the operation is indicated by the presence of about fifty quarry workers in Hook Norton in 1901. The first consignment of untreated ore was sent to Brymbo in September 1899 and the first load of calcined ore on 6 December of that year. Workings were

---

[9] Tonks, *Oxfordshire Field*, 57-65. Russell, *Banbury and Cheltenham*, 33.
[10] Russell, *Banbury and Cheltenham*, 33; Tonks, *Oxfordshire Field*, 73-81.

Calcining kilns at the Brymbo company's quarry at Hook Norton. These two kilns, fed by a 2 ft gauge railway system, probably date from soon after the company began operations in 1896. Two more were subsequently built but calcining on the site ceased in 1926. BHS Collection

extended and in 1909 the company acquired land for quarrying north of the railway, some of it formerly leased by the Hook Norton Ironstone Partnership. With increasing demand during the First World War workings extended over 300 acres, and employed about a hundred men. A Ruston Proctor steam excavator was used from 1916, and output reached 5,000 tons per week, some of which was despatched to works other than Brymbo. Production was reduced after the war and calcining ceased in 1926. Output varied with the state of the economy, averaging 806 tons per week in 1935, and 1,668 tons in 1937, but only 478 tons in 1938. By the 1940s a rotary tipper was transferring ore from trucks on the narrow gauge to standard gauge wagons. The quarries were intensively worked during the Second World War, when output reached 161,602 tons in 1943. A notable locomotive, the 2-6-2T *Russell* from the Welsh Highland Railway, was brought to Hook Norton in 1941 by the Ministry of Supply but its wheelbase proved too long for the curves of the quarry tramway. Only one locomotive was in use on 25 June 1945 and the quarries closed in June 1946. During the summer of 1949 the locomotives, with the exception of *Russell* which went to Dorset, were cut up on the spot, and the wagons went to Tanganyika for the groundnuts scheme.[11]

Quarries near Grounds Farm were owned by the Earls of Dudley whose principal ironworks was at Round Oak. Ore was calcined in a kiln under the viaduct and taken up a rope incline to sidings alongside the BCDR at the south end of the viaduct. Workings ceased in 1916 and the plant was dismantled for scrap in 1920.[12]

Other quarries at Hook Norton, the Top Pit on the road to Sibford Ferris and the Bottom Pit at East End, were worked from the 1890s by a local farmer Henry W Baker, who transported ore by horse-drawn carts to sidings at the station. It was sent to the Lilleshall Company at Priorslee, Shropshire, to Round Oak, and to works in South Wales. When Baker died in 1915 the quarries were almost exhausted and operations ceased in 1918 or 1919.[13]

The Dassett Hills

The first quarrying operations in the Dassett Hills, eight miles north-west of Banbury, began about 1868 and originally despatched ore by horse-drawn cart to Fenny Compton station on the GWR. By 1873 the owners utilised one of the first overhead ropeways installed by the Wire Tramway Co of London, the firm founded by Charles Hodgson, inventor of the technology. It carried ore from the quarries to a siding on the EWJR, at the point where it was crossed by the main road from Banbury to Warwick. The original ropeway was closed in the 1880s, but the quarries re-opened using a new installation in the mid-1890s. Fifteen quarry workers were recorded in Burton Dassett by the 1901 census. After a period when the plant stood still, working was resumed by the Willingsworth Iron Co of Tipton in 1908-09, but ceased by 1912. Production resumed briefly towards the end of the First World War, and after standing disused for about a decade, the plant was dismantled by James Friswell & Son in 1929. The depot became a public siding in March 1885, and an unofficial passenger station after the opening of the nearby ordnance depot during the Second World War.[14]

---

[11] Tonks, *Oxfordshire Field*, 84-102; Russell, *Banbury and Cheltenham*, 33; L Waters, *Oxfordshire Railways in Old Photographs* (Gloucester: Sutton, 1989), 129-32; *RL* No 1.10 (1946); *LE* No 2.4 (1945); W Hemmings, P Karau & C Turner, *The Banbury & Cheltenham Railway, vol 2* (Didcot: Wild Swan, 2004), 285, 295; G E Gardam, 'The Brymbo Ironworks, Hook Norton', *C&CH* vol 3 (1968), 226-27; G E Gardam, 'The Brymbo Iron Works, Hook Norton', *C&CH*, vol 4 (1970), 138-40; *BG* 22 Sep 1898.

[12] Russell, *Banbury and Cheltenham*, 33; R Gorton, 'The Hook Norton Ironstone Companies', *C&CH* vol 9 (1982), 14-22; Tonks, *Oxfordshire Field*, 103-07.

[13] Tonks, *Oxfordshire Field*, 82-83, Gorton, 'Hook Norton Ironstone', 14-22.

[14] *BG* 22 May 1873; R C Riley & B Simpson, *A History of the Stratford-upon-Avon & Midland Junction Railway* (Witney: Lamplight Publications, 1999), 65-67; Tonks, *Oxfordshire Field*, 232-41; for ropeways See W E Hipkins, *The Wire Rope and its Applications* (Birmingham: J & E Wright, 1896); A J Wallis-Taylor, *Aerial or Wire Rope Tramways* (London: Crosby Lockwood, 1898).

Other workings in the Edge Hill area, north of Ratley, were served by a line constructed under the terms of the Light Railways Act of 1894. The demand for iron ore increased during the First World War when Harry Wilmott of the SMJR estimated that 30 million tons could be exploited in the quarries on Edge Hill. A company was formed to work them. It gained authority to proceed at contested hearings in Banbury in November 1917, but it was not until a Light Railway Order was obtained on 28 January 1919 that work began. The engineer was the celebrated Colonel H F Stephens. An inclined plane, with its winding wheel under the road from Edge Hill to Warmington, lowered wagons of ore nearly 300 ft to the lower section of the railway that ran for almost two miles to a junction with the SMJR near Burton Dassett. The upper section of the line penetrating into the quarries was worked by a Manning Wardle 0-4-0 saddle tank called *Sankey*, while two 'Terrier' class 0-6-0Ts were acquired from the London, Brighton & South Coast Railway for the lower section.

Production commenced on 22 January 1922, and iron was supplied to several blast furnace complexes in the Black Country and North Staffordshire. The project proved unprofitable, and the last loaded wagons left on 27 January 1925. The line was abandoned in 1930, but since legislation was required for its formal closure the three locomotives and other plant remained *in situ*, attracting numerous visits by railway enthusiasts. The 'Terriers' survived wartime scrap drives and the establishment of Marlborough Farm Camp on the lower part of the line, but they were cut up by James Friswell & Son during 1946, and the Light Railway Company finally went into liquidation in 1957.[15]

Wroxton and beyond

The Oxfordshire Ironstone Company was also born in wartime, but proved vastly more profitable than the Edge Hill Light Railway. After the formation of the Ministry of Munitions in 1915 Colonel W C Wright, a director of Baldwins Ltd, was seconded to work under Sir John Hunter, who had charge of domestic iron ore production, and had the opportunity to encourage an increase in output of ore from Midlands quarries. Another leading figure in Baldwins, the mining engineer Alex Mackay, realised the shortcomings of the proposals for Edge Hill, and proposed large-scale quarrying north-west of Banbury with a direct connection to the GWR. While negotiations for leases were in progress he met his friend J S Hollings of the Brymbo Steel Co, as a result of which the two companies made a joint application to extract ore from 2,200 acres near Wroxton, and in June 1917 registered the Oxfordshire Ironstone Co Ltd, in which Baldwins held 60 per cent of the shares and Brymbo 40 per cent. The project was encouraged by the Ministry of Munitions which in May 1917 authorised the construction of a

---

[15] Tonks, *Oxfordshire Field*, 205-31; Riley & Simpson, *Stratford-upon-Avon & Midland Junction*, 31-38; *LE* 2.4 (1945).

One of the first quarries near Wroxton developed by the Oxfordshire Ironstone Co in 1919.   Historic England

railway to carry the ore. German prisoners-of-war were employed during its construction for which the contractors were Topham, Jones, Railton. The connection with the GWR was made on 17 August 1918. A touring cyclist in the summer of 1918 was surprised to see an unfinished bridge across the Southam Road outside Banbury. A signal box was built at the junction where the GWR laid out four 60-wagon sidings, and built a signal box, opened on 8 February 1920. It was known as the 'Ironstone Mines' box till 1958 when it was renamed the 'Ironstone Branch' box. Production began in 1919 but the enterprise did not initially flourish. In 1922 half the shares passed into the ownership of Alfred Hickman and Sons Ltd which by then was part of Stewart & Lloyd, and Hickmans became the company's principal customer.[16]

This was an operation on a different scale from other quarry railway systems. Eric Tonks, the authority on the subject, considered that 'At the time of its construction it was, from an engineering standpoint, the finest ironstone railway in the country'.[17] The line was equipped with quarter mile posts, gradient posts

---

[16] Tonks, *Oxfordshire Field*, 138-204; *RM* vol 43 (1918), 418; C R Potts, *An Historical Survey of Selected Great Western Stations, vol. 4* (Poole: Oxford Publishing Co, 1985), 12; see also F Scopes, *The Development of Corby Works* (Corby: Stewart & Lloyds, 1968).

[17] Tonks, *Oxfordshire Field*, 146.

and a railside telegraph. A signalling system was installed in 1921 and there were signal boxes at the principal level crossings. A locomotive shed was built at Pinhill on the edge of Banbury on land purchased from Banbury Co-operative Society on 13 July 1920. Thirty-three steam locomotives worked on the system in the course of its history. Initially ore was taken from the quarries for calcining in kilns at Pinhill. They were no longer used after 1925, but calcining in open clamps continued until 1932. A crushing plant was built about 1930 five miles west of the junction with the GWR. Subsequently the lines into the quarries from which ore was delivered in tipper wagons to the crushing plant were worked by 0-4-0 saddle tank engines with female names such as *Phyllis* and *Gwen*. Trains of main line wagons were taken from Wroxton to Banbury by 0-6-0 side tanks with male names, such as the 42-ton *Sir Thomas*, delivered by Hudswell Clarke in 1918, as well as some saddle tanks. Empty wagons were usually pushed up the gradient to Wroxton.

The Oxfordshire Ironstone Co's first locomotive 'Sir Thomas', built by Hudswell Clarke & Co of Leeds, in 1918, taking water in 1919. It is preserved at the Buckinghamshire Railway Centre, Quainton Road. Historic England

The quarries ceased production several times during the uneasy economic circumstances of the 1920s and early 1930s, but by 1936 weekly output had risen to 20,000 tons. During the Second World War the quarrying area was increased, extending as far west as the *New Inn* on the road from Banbury to Stratford. Two powered shovels and two draglines were acquired, together with five locomotives, three of them new, and two second hand from the quarries at Byfield and Charwelton. The workforce was supplemented by Polish refugees, accommodated in huts near Pinhill Farm, and by Italian prisoners-of-war.

Extraction continued at a high level after the war, reaching a maximum of nearly 1.75 million tons in 1956. The railway from the crushing plant to Banbury was doubled in 1953, and a new bridge was completed the following year that allowed the extension of the track beneath the A423 Banbury–Stratford road towards Balscott. Facilities were improved at the locomotive depots. The fleet of locomotives increased, and a new 0-6-0 saddle tank *Frank* was received from the Hunslet works as late as November 1958. In the same year the company purchased an ex-GWR 'Toad' (i.e. a brake van for freight trains), which replaced an adapted van in an unofficial passenger train that conveyed Banbury residents employed at the Wroxton depot and in the quarries to and from their work.

New vacuum brake-fitted hopper wagons intended for traffic from the Oxfordshire Ironstone Co were stored at Merton Street station for several years in the late 1950s, but were finally put to use elsewhere. Continuously-braked wagons were used from 1960-61, but they were tipplers, loaded in the quarries, and employed principally for carrying uncrushed ore to the Spencer Works at Llanwern where the blast furnaces came on stream in 1962. Five of the locomotives used between Wroxton and Banbury were fitted with vacuum brakes in the autumn of 1963, and seven more 'Toads' were purchased for operation with vacuum-braked wagons. In 1960-61 experiments were made with diesel traction, and in 1964 the company acquired eight diesel shunting locomotives from the Sentinel works in Shrewsbury which replaced the 0-4-0ST engines used in the quarries. The following year more Sentinels arrived and the steam locomotives were scrapped apart from *Sir Thomas*, which was stored until 1969 when it went, at the instigation of Eric Tonks, to what is now the Buckinghamshire Railway Centre at Quainton Road.

When the diesels were delivered production was running at 40,000 tons a week, and the quarry workings extended as far as Alkerton, Balscott and Hornton, Thereafter output declined, falling to no more than 2,000 tons a week by mid-1967. The workforce, about 135 in 1963, was reduced by 1967 to 52 men working a two-day week. It was scarcely surprising that it was announced in July 1967 that the Oxfordshire Ironstone Company would cease operations from the following September.

Subsequently the quarry at Alkerton was taken over by Peter Bennie Ltd, principally for the production of road stone, but from 1969 until 1978 lorries took up to 500 tons of ironstone per day to Banbury station where it was loaded into railway wagons for Shelton and Bilston. Subsequently some loads were sent to Llanwern, and on 22 October 1978 close-coupled 100-tonne bogie wagons of the kind that supplied the plant from the import terminal at Port Talbot were being loaded at Banbury station. This proved a short-lived operation and by December 1978 the ore traffic had finally ceased.[18]

'Manor' class 4-6-0 No 7819 'Hinton Manor', an Oswestry engine which had probably come south with ballast from Llynclys, heads north up Cropredy Bank on 29 June 1961 with a train of unbraked hopper wagons loaded with iron ore for Bilston or Brymbo, 29 June 1961.

Main line working

Almost all the iron ore despatched from the Banbury area travelled north on the GWR main line towards Leamington, much of it turning towards Stratford and South Wales at Hatton. Although sidings to accommodate iron ore trains were

---

[18] *RM* vol 43 (1918), 418; *LE* No 2.4 (1945); M Leah, 'Banbury's "secret" railway', *SR* No 96 (1988), 21-25; Waters, *Oxfordshire Railways*, 154; Copsey, 'Goods Operations', 192; Tonks, *Oxfordshire Field*, 138-204.

built on the BCDR in 1906, there is little evidence of ore travelling this way to South Wales. One photograph taken on 7 June 1923 shows GWR 2-8-0 No 2872 heading westward at Charlton Kings with wagons carrying ore for Baldwins. It probably originated from the Oxfordshire Ironstone Co, but most of that company's traffic for South Wales certainly travelled via Hatton.[19]

Standard Class 4MT 2-6-4T No 80043 and a 4F class 0-6-0 double-head the daily freight for Swanbourne Sidings away from Merton Street in 1956. Double-heading was necessary because the train included about 20 wagons of iron ore from the Oxfordshire Ironstone Company bound for Corby or Wellingborough.

In 1901 there were three booked ironstone workings from the BCDR line, one to Brymbo and two to Wolverhampton, and another train took ore wagons from Banbury to Bilston. In 1914 a train was booked from Astrop Sidings to Oxley Sidings at Wolverhampton, and another from Hook Norton to Brymbo, but most ore appears to have been carried on trains that also took other traffic. In the late 1930s five daily trains took iron ore northwards from Banbury, three to Bilston, one to Oxley Sidings that probably carried traffic for Brymbo, and one to Margam near Port Talbot. There were three booked return workings of empty wagons, but photographic evidence suggests these were often conveyed south on ordinary freight trains. The standard wagons used by Stewart & Lloyds were eight-plank timber-bodied hoppers with gently tapering sides, painted light brown with the owner's name in white letters. They were often mixed in block trains with short wheelbase steel hoppers with steeply inclined sides which were used for most traffic after the Second World War. At the height of the war early in 1943 ten trains of iron ore were scheduled to

---

[19] H. Household, *Gloucestershire Railways in the Twenties* (Gloucester: Sutton, 1986).37.

head north from Banbury, six to South Wales, three to sidings in Wolverhampton area for the Bilston works, and one to Croes Newydd for Brymbo.[20]

Post-war traffic was intensive and most ore was carried in block trains of unbraked all-steel hoppers. In the early 1950s three or four weekly trainloads for the furnaces at Ilkeston and Renishaw Park probably travelled via the Great Central line. On several days a week in the mid-1950s rakes of up to twenty hopper wagons for Wellingborough or Corby were taken away on the daily pick-up freight train from Merton Street. From 1960 trains for South Wales utilised the new connections at Fenny Compton and traversed the former SMJR route to

Trains of ironstone for the new blast furnaces at Llanwern were made up of vacuum brake-fitted tippler wagons such as those ascending Cropredy Bank on 31 July 1961 behind 2-8-0 No 2849. The train was routed via the junctions at Fenny Compton and Stratford completed the previous year.

---

[20] Copsey, J, 'Goods Operations', 188. 191-92; J Copsey, 'Goods Operations at Banbury, part 2', *GWRJ* No 93 (2015), 265-66; R P & R P Hendry, *Paddington to the Mersey* (Sparkford: Oxford Publishing Co, 1992), 76, 144.

Stratford, where a new junction enabled them to head south. The new class 9F 2-10-0s that arrived at Banbury early in 1960 worked many trains of brake-fitted tipplers to Llanwern. Ore for Bilston continued to be carried in unbraked hoppers and on 2 April 1965 No 6831 *Bearley Grange* in grimy condition without name or number plates, was photographed climbing Hatton Bank with 18 wagons of that type. After the new junctions had been used for only five years the former SMJR lines were closed to through traffic in July 1965 and iron ore trains from Banbury to South Wales were worked by diesel power via Didcot. They did so for only two years until the Oxfordshire Ironstone Company ceased production in September 1967.[21]

---

[21] Riley & Simpson, *Stratford-upon-Avon & Midland Junction*, 115, 117, 123; STR 65, Sep 1985; M Smith, 'Avoiding Banbury ... and Acton', *BRI*, vol 6 (1992), 313.

15. Out of the Depths: 1968-94

The railways are, and will remain for many years, by far the best way of moving bulk loads between centres of industry or population relatively far apart, or of giving a dense passenger service along routes which thousands of people must travel every day.

Sir Arthur Elton, 1947.[1]

The years between the electrification of the West Coast Main Line in 1967 and the end of steam traction in the following year and the privatisation of the railways in the mid-1990s form a distinct phase in railway history. Initially, following a decade of ill-managed contraction and plummeting morale, the system continued to shrink. Familiar features of the railway at Banbury, the freight depot, the engine shed and the hump marshalling yard, were removed and further contraction seemed inevitable. Nevertheless Sir Arthur Elton's prediction eventually proved to be a wise one. The railways concentrated on what they could do best, and the achievements of the nationalised industry in the 1970s and '80s were not inconsiderable. Nevertheless the pessimism of the late 1960s was slow to dissipate. A writer in 1987 concluded that: 'Banbury now stands, in a railway sense, virtually as it was in the 1860s, *but we can expect no expansion this time*'. This did not seem, at that date, an unreasonable observation but it proved to be wildly wrong.[2]

The lines through Banbury had become part of the London Midland Region on 1 January 1963 and remained so until regions were abolished. 'Banbury General' station was renamed 'Banbury' in 1974, some fourteen years after the closure of Merton Street removed the necessity for a distinctive name. The small engine shed of 1889 was demolished by 1975. Loop lines were removed in stages between 1968 and 1979. On 24 March 1980 Banbury North Junction signal box, whose principal purpose had ceased with the closure of the branch from Woodford in 1966, was finally closed. Most of the ex-Great Western semaphore signals near the station were removed although a few remained into the twenty-first century.

Freight and Parcels

Banbury's goods depot around the brick shed that replaced the one destroyed by bombs in 1940 passed into the control of National Carriers in 1969. The handling of small consignments ceased in 1972 and wagon load traffic ended in 1976. The shed was demolished in 1987 to allow the expansion of the station car park.[3]

---

[1] A Elton, *British Railways* (London: Collins, 1947), 46.
[2] J Copsey, 'Banbury GWR: Pt 1: The Background', *BRJ*, No 15 (1987), 237.
[3] J Copsey, 'Goods Operations at Banbury, part 3', *GWRJ* No 94 (2015), 357; B Simpson, 'Banbury: All Changes', *Backtrack*, vol 4 (1992), 177.

The goods shed after it ceased to handle wagonload traffic in 1976. In the distance one of the depot's sidings accommodates redundant iron ore hoppers. The shed was demolished in 1987 to allow expansion of the car park. John Powell

Some freight traffics proved resilient. Coal was being unloaded in sidings near the station in April 1976, and as late as August 1983 fuels were being pumped from 100-tonne tankers in the oil company sidings. In the early 1970s the steel barriers were removed from the ex-GWR cattle docks enabling them be used for unloading road stone. As detailed in chapter 14, ironstone was carried by lorry to the station to be tipped into bogie wagons until 1978. Fertiliser was being unloaded from bogie wagons in the goods yard in August 1980, and unknown goods from air-braked vans in June 1982. There were Polybulk grain wagons in the former cattle dock in April 1984. The cement works at Harbury ceased production in 1970. Until the early 1990s its silos were part of a distribution depot for cement delivered by rail from Northfleet or Weardale, but the site closed and was offered for sale in 1994. The works at Shipton-on-Cherwell used rail transport until it closed in 1989.[4]

Some freight trains in the 1970s retained an archaic appearance. One image of the early 1970s shows a class 25 diesel heading northwards through Banbury with five vans, four open tube wagons and a brake van. Trains of this kind disappeared from 1983-84 when British Rail ceased to use unbraked wagons and

---

[4] S Leleux, *Warwickshire Lime and Cement Works Railways* (Usk: Oakwood, 2014), 31-35, 51.

eliminated the standard 12-ton goods van. In the eleven years from 1968 British Rail reduced its total of goods wagons from 400,000 to 137,000, while the tonnage carried fell only marginally from 169 million to 149 million tonnes. During the 1980s most of the classes of diesel locomotives built under the Modernisation Plan of 1955 disappeared from active service, the 2000 hp English Electric type 4s (Class 40) in February 1985, the Sulzer-engined class 25s in 1987, and the bulky 'Peaks' (classes 44, 45, 46) in 1989.

Diesel locomotives were stabled between turns at Banbury in the former cattle dock sidings east of the station. As many as five could be present there – on 30 May 1982 the line-up consisted of two class 56s, a class 25, No 33 025 *Sultan*, and No 45 045 *Coldstream Guardsman*. Several locomotives were derailed when entering or leaving the sidings. On 20 December 1977 No 33 002 from the Southern Region was resting there with one bogie off the rails, and on 3 March 1979 No 47 077 *North Star* needed the attention of a re-railing unit from Saltley. The rostering of crews at Banbury formally ceased in February 1984 after which the sidings passed out of use. After the closure of the hump yard in 1970, ten of the up sidings north of the Middleton Road bridge were used for the exchange of wagons on through freight services, but they were increasingly occupied by infrastructure vehicles. By 1975 the rails had been removed from the guards' van ramp, by then overgrown with vegetation.

Through the 1970s there were usually one or two parcels vans in the bay platforms of the station whose daily movements necessitated the provision of a pilot locomotive. For long spells this was Class 08 shunter No 08 784 which carried the unofficial name *Cherwell* painted in silver letters on its tool boxes. On other occasions the duties were carried out by main line locomotives, such as No 40 063 of Haymarket depot at Edinburgh which was present on 17 August 1983. From 15 May 1986 the Post Office ended its contract with British Rail for the conveyance of Royal Mail parcels. Many parcels trains ceased to run and redundant parcels vehicles were sent for scrapping to sidings at Hinksey amongst other places. In October the Parcels Sector created in 1982 was re-branded RES (Rail Express Systems), with hubs for its mail traffic at Shieldmuir, Low Fell, Warrington, Doncaster, Bristol Parkway, Tonbridge and Wembley. Some of its trains continued to run through Banbury.

For more than four decades coal for the power station at Didcot from collieries in Nottinghamshire and the Daw Mill mine in Warwickshire was one of the principal traffics through Banbury. The power station began generating in 1970 and from the beginning received its coal in merry-go-round (mgr) trains. The principles of merry-go-round operation were developed on the Eastern Region of British Rail in the 1960s. Slack coal for power station boilers was fed at collieries into overhead bunkers from which it was discharged into four-wheel hopper wagons with galvanised steel bodies and air brakes, each carrying up to 32 tonnes. They were permanently coupled into rakes of about 30 vehicles, that could travel on main lines at up to 60 mph. Trains were hauled by diesel locomotives with low-speed controls, which enabled them to progress slowly over hoppers at power stations into which the coal was discharged through the wagons' bottom doors. At most new power stations, including Didcot, oval layouts enabled trains to pass through, release their coal, and return for another load without reversing or shunting. The first mgr train travelled to West Burton in September 1965 and by October 1981 British Rail had more than ten thousand mgr wagons. The merry-go-round concept was jointly developed by British Rail, the National Coal Board and the Central Electricity Generating Board, nationalised concerns of a kind unknown in 2017, which were nevertheless capable of innovations. A manager who worked on the project for British Rail regarded it as 'the greatest money-saver that bulk transport has ever known'.[5]

Class 56 diesel No 56101 was one of several unusual locomotives that served as station pilot at Banbury in the 1970s and 80s. The class more usually appeared on mgr trains to Didcot power station.

---

[5] R T Munns, *Milk Churns to Merry-go-round* (Newton Abbot: David & Charles, 1986), 146-75.

Initially almost every train bound for Didcot was worked by a Brush class 47/3 diesel but from the late 1970s other classes took over some trains. The Romania-built class 56 No 56020 is believed to have been the first of its class to visit the power station on 21 November 1977, and subsequently the class worked many trains to Didcot, as did classes 58 and 60. Services to the power station ceased between March 1984 and March 1985 during the Miners' Strike but subsequently resumed.[6]

Other traffics were also carried in bulk train loads. On 27 January 1976 two class 25s took a rake of ICI chemical tanks southbound through Banbury, to be followed within a few minutes by a class 47 with a load of bogie cement hoppers, while a class 33 waited in the down loop south of the station with butane tanks. LPG tanks passed through *en route* from the oil refinery at Fawley to Longport in the Potteries, and there was a flow of fertiliser in bulk from Ince & Elton to Gillingham (Dorset). A few block trains still carried domestic coal southwards in hopper wagons, and diesel fuel for locomotives was similarly hauled northwards.

By the 1970s most motor car traffic was conveyed in block trains on sophisticated articulated wagons. Most car-carrying trains despatched from Morris Cowley in the 1970s went south to the ferry ports after reversing in Hinksey Yard, but there were also trains to Bathgate in Scotland and other destinations in the north. Banbury also saw the passage of southbound trains from the British Leyland works at Longbridge, and from the Land Rover plant at Solihull, the latter loaded at Knowle and subsequently at Bordesley. Northbound rakes of flat trucks carried to Merseyside Ford Transit vans made at Southampton, while other block trains took body parts between factories at Swindon and Longbridge.[7]

The concept of the Freightliner, a train of flat wagons carrying containers, was one of the positive developments of the Beeching era. The Freightliner system was conceived as a network of depots, with gantry cranes to transfer containers from road to rail, that would be linked by trains carrying internal traffic, but it failed to develop as planned, and some depots, including those at Dudley and Nottingham were closed, while that at Coventry (Gosford Green) lasted only from 1977 until 1981. At the same time container traffic increased between the ports of Felixstowe, Tilbury, Liverpool and Southampton, and inland distribution depots, such as those at Trafford Park, Lawley Street (Birmingham), Leeds (Midland Road) and Coatbridge and Mossend in Scotland. Most container trains passing Banbury were bound to or from Southampton, where Freightliner services began in 1972.

---

[6] *RM* vol 124 (1978), 106.
[7] R Lingard, *Princes Risborough–Thame–Oxford Railway* (Oxford: Oxford Publishing Co, 1978), 129-30.

Banbury station on 31 May 1975 showing the cattle docks cleared to enable the unloading of road stone, and a Class 25 diesel stabled in a former cattle dock siding. A Class 47 diesel enters the station from the north, and there is a parcel van in a bay platform.
John Powell

    The Speedlink wagonload freight service was introduced on 13 September 1977 when Sir Peter Parker, then chair of British Rail, commissioned an exhibition train at Marylebone which subsequently visited Oxford and Birmingham Moor Street among other places. Speedlink offered transits to a limited number of destinations on trains that ran to fixed timetables, and used the up sidings at Banbury for transferring wagons between trains. The project was initially successful, providing 150 trunk services by 1984, and in 1983 it was claimed to be profitable. Subsequently Speedlink declined. Two of its hubs, the marshalling yards at Severn Tunnel Junction and Tyne Yard in Co Durham, closed respectively in November 1987 and October 1989, and operations ceased in 1991. Some trains carried very little traffic – on 11 July1990 for example, No 47018 passed Banbury *en route* from Eastleigh to Haverton Hill (Teesside) with only one wagon.[8]

---

[8] *RM* vol 123 (1977), 523.

The view north from Banbury station on 31 May 1975 as an mgr train for Didcot power station approaches. Some of the former up sidings remain in use for sorting freight traffic, for which a Class 08 shunter is employed. The ramp formerly used for guards' vans has been disconnected and is overgrown with grass. John Powell

Re-orientation

During the 1970s services to London on the Bicester cut-off became distinct from those heading for the south coast through the Cherwell Valley. In May 1971 the service from New Street via Banbury to London was amended with two services running to Paddington via Reading. It then comprised five trains between New Street and Paddington via Bicester, two via Oxford and three semi-fasts to and from Paddington that terminated at Banbury. One observer commented that the new timetable suggested that the 'Great Way Round' route was gaining a new lease of life, partly because of increasing passenger demand at Reading.[9] In addition there were three services between New Street and the south coast, one of them running to and from York. By 1981 nine through trains ran from Birmingham to Paddington via Oxford, two originating at Liverpool and one at Manchester, and there was a night time service to Reading. There were two services between Manchester and Brighton, five trains to Poole, two coming from Liverpool, one from Manchester and two from Newcastle, one of which

---

[9] *GWE* No 35 (1971), 10.

carried a portion from Leeds, as well as an early morning train from Derby to Bournemouth. In total there were eight through services to the south coast, where there had been three in 1973. Some trains from Paddington through Oxford to Birmingham passed through New Street station and took the ex-Midland Railway route to Worcester, returning to London along the Cotswold Line and through Oxford.

In 1973 class 115 diesel multiple units began to run between Marylebone and Banbury, and in the spring of 1974, when the London Midland Region took over the whole line, it was announced that all trains between Paddington and Birmingham New Street, with one exception in each direction, would travel via Oxford. Marylebone became the London terminus for most travellers to and from Banbury, a development that was subsequently significant, but at the time it scarcely seemed an improvement. The class 115 diesel multiple units were designed for suburban traffic not for journeys of seventy miles. In 1966 a business traveller from Banbury, as his early evening train, descended from Ardley Tunnel towards the Souldern and Aynho viaducts, might have relaxed in a smooth-riding restaurant car enjoying a glass of port accompanying a cheese board ornamented with radishes, grapes and celery. The bumpy ride, cramped seating, odoriferous toilets and lack of refreshments in the class 115 units represented a vast downgrading. Nevertheless the aversion in the 1970s of the threat of closure of the line between Princes Risborough and Aynho Junction can be seen with hindsight as a significant achievement.

From the beginning of the summer timetable on 2 May 1977 most trains between Banbury and New Street travelled from Leamington through Warwick and Kenilworth to Coventry. This enabled them to call at Birmingham International station, opened on 26 January 1976, and served Birmingham Airport and the National Exhibition Centre, which staged its first event in February 1976.

Resurgent steam

When British Rail withdrew from service its last steam locomotives in 1968 it placed an embargo on steam workings over its lines, but as heritage railways flourished, there was pressure to allow preserved engines to head special trains. From 1971 steam trains returned to the main line, and on 11 July 1972 No 7029 *Clun Castle* passed through Banbury with a special chartered by the Great Western Society. Subsequently the Society, based at Didcot, established a Vintage Train of former GWR coaches. On 1 October 1972 two of the vehicles were included in the stock for an excursion headed by No 6998 *Burton Agnes Hall*, and two years later the complete train was headed by No 7808 *Cookham Manor* and No 6998. Subsequently the train went to Stratford, to the Woodhead line in the Pennines, to Shrewsbury and the Central Wales line, in each case passing through Banbury on the outward or return journeys. The train's final venture on to the main line was on 26 January 1980 when it was headed by No 5051 *Earl Bathurst*.[10]

Steam excursions multiplied in the 1980s and a Charter Train Unit, a sub-sector of InterCity, was set up in 1983. From February 1985 the unit ran a Sunday Luncheon Express from Marylebone to Stratford-upon-Avon on which during the summer season 150 of the 252 seats were taken by an American travel agency. Locomotives that worked the train during 1985 included No 35028 *Clan Line*, No 5593 *Kolhapur*, No 46229 *Duchess of Hamilton*, No 4498 *Sir Nigel Gresley* and No 4771 *Green Arrow*.[11]

The restored pacific No 71000 *Duke of Gloucester* headed a train of Pullman cars from Didcot through Banbury to Derby on 7 April 1990 and on 9 November of the following year the Great Western Society's No 5029 *Nunney Castle* became the first of its class for 25 years to haul a main line train out of Paddington when it headed the *William Shakespeare* excursion to Stratford.

Management and motorways

The most obvious changes of the early 1980s were in management. From 4 January 1982 responsibility for managing services was placed with five sectors, Freight; Parcels; InterCity; London & South East (later Network SouthEast) and Provincial. In a national context there were long-awaited changes in technology such as the elimination of vacuum-braked and unbraked freight wagons and steam-heated carriages.

There was also a rethinking of the roles of transport systems in the changing economic and social context of the 1980s. This was stimulated in part by the effects of the M4 London-South Wales motorway, the English section of which was completed with the opening of the stretch from Maidenhead to Swindon on 22 December 1971. Five years later the Western Region of British Rail introduced HST (High Speed Train) 125 sets on services between Paddington and Bristol and South Wales. It became evident that while motorways abstracted some traffics from the railways, the changes they engendered in the economy, increased activity in distribution, consultancy, information technology, media and universities, actually caused passenger numbers to grow. Increased train speeds created the possibility of commuting over greater distances, reflected in July 1985 by the re-naming of the station at Didcot as Didcot Parkway, which served as the railhead for London commuters resident in the Vale of the White Horse. From 1984 the number of commuters into London grew rapidly.

Customer involvement in railways through Banbury increased in September 1989 with the formation of the Cherwell Rail Users Group, which proved to be

---

[10] *GWE* No 41 (1972), 6; *STR* March/Apl 1980, 46.
[11] *STR* No 62, June 1985, No 63, Jly 1985.

concerned not just with short term issues such as unpunctuality and the state of the class 115 multiple units, but also with future strategy. The Group compiled a paper 'The M40 Corridor and its Rail Services' which demonstrated to government that the improvements already being undertaken by railway managers had widespread public support. Similar groups were formed at Solihull, Leamington and Haddenham & Thame Parkway.[12]

Meanwhile, long before it was completed, the M40 motorway had a direct influence on Banbury's railways. The motorway was opened from London to Great Milton near Oxford in 1974. Approval was given in 1983 to its extension to Birmingham, and, after lengthy enquiries, construction of the section around Banbury began in February 1988. It was completed between Great Milton and the M42 south of Birmingham in January 1991. A road stone terminal was established on the site of the former down sidings at Banbury and by February 1988 materials for the motorway were being unloaded there. The terminal remained in use after the motorway opened, and still operates.

The 1980s saw other changes to the physical fabric of the railway. Banbury's northern ring road, Henneff Way, was being constructed in the autumn of 1984 and the new bridge across the railway near Grimsbury Mill was almost complete by March 1986 when the earthworks that formed the junction with the Great Central Line were being obliterated. By the summer of 1991 housing stood on the site of the reception sidings of the hump yard, and an almost completed office block had replaced the former GWR stationmaster's house. Operation of signals and points at Aynho Junction was transferred to Banbury South in 1992.[13]

Marylebone reprieved

The service between Banbury and Marylebone in 1980 was one of the worst on British Rail. Stations were unpainted and uncared for. The signalling and track had not been modernised, which restricted trains to 60 mph. Spares for the engines of the class 115 diesel multiple units were in short supply and the maintenance depot at Marylebone was no longer fit for purpose. Off-peak trains to Banbury ran at roughly two-hourly frequencies, with the fastest accomplishing the journey in an hour and 40 minutes. Fares were increased as services deteriorated. The remaining return service to and from Paddington was abandoned after which the line between Old Oak Common and Northolt Junction was little used.

It seemed likely in the early 1980s that the services from Banbury to Marylebone would be withdrawn. Margaret Thatcher, then prime minister, was advised on transport matters by Sir Alfred Sherman who was committed to replacing trains with motor coaches. In 1986 it seemed possible that a scheme that

---

[12] H Jones, *The Chiltern Railways Story* (Stroud: The History Press, 2010), 20.
[13] *GWE* No 118 (1992), 3, 8-9.

he supported to convert Marylebone into a coach station, from which coaches would travel through the existing tunnels to Neasden, would be implemented. Trains from High Wycombe were to run into Paddington and those from Aylesbury on to the Metropolitan Line.

On 6 May 1984 a class 50 diesel locomotive pauses at Banbury with a Cross-Country train while a class 115 multiple unit waits in the bay platform to leave for Marylebone.
John Powell

Chris Green, who began his professional career in railway management at Banbury in 1965, revived the railway system in Scotland, after which he was appointed managing director of the London & SouthEast sector from January 1986. With other managers, he realised that Sherman's scheme would not withstand scrutiny at a public enquiry, and on 30 April 1986 he was able to announce the withdrawal of the closure notices for Marylebone. On 10 June 1986 Green launched the Network SouthEast brand, with a red, white and blue livery for locomotives and carriages, coupled with a drive to clean up the entire London commuter network. Since the lines from Marylebone were effectively self-contained it was possible to implement a programme of Total Route Modernisation, which was intended to be a showpiece for the Network. Chris Tibbits was appointed route director for the services. An early indication of an expansionist attitude was the opening of Haddenham & Thame Parkway station in October 1987. The modernisation plan was formally launched at Marylebone in 1989, when authorisation was obtained for the purchase of 77 class 165

Networker units. Painters and builders restored all fifty stations, with red lamp posts, network maps and varied special offers, while retaining and enhancing the best features of the Victorian and Edwardian buildings. A start was made in the replacement of the bull head track and the existing signalling system. In 1991 the first Chiltern turbo multiple units were delivered, enabling the retirement of the 30-year-old class 115s.[14]

There were also significant changes north of Banbury. Through services between Paddington and Snow Hill station at Birmingham ceased in March 1967, but suburban services from Leamington and Stratford continued to terminate at Snow Hill. From 2 March 1968 they were cut short at Moor Street and the tunnels into Snow Hill were no longer used. Local services from Snow Hill to Wolverhampton and Langley Green continued until March 1972, when the station was completely closed. Its buildings were demolished in 1977, but from 2 October 1987 trains run through the tunnels to a smaller station.

Total Route Modernisation on the Chiltern lines was completed in 1992 after an investment of £85 million. One objective was the restoration of services from London to Birmingham through High Wycombe and Banbury, in competition with trains from Euston to New Street, and in May 1993 trains from Marylebone began to run to Snow Hill station. Privatisation legislation passed through Parliament in 1993 and in August of that year Adrian Shooter, then director of engineering performance for British Rail, was appointed to manage Chiltern Railways, which from 31 March 1994 became a Train Operating Unit within British Rail. Hugh Jones has detailed the process by which Shooter used the autumn and winter of 1993-94 to appoint his management team. At the beginning of the summer timetable of 1994 Chiltern increased the frequency of its services to Birmingham, and took over the stations at Banbury and King's Sutton. From 1 April 1995 Chiltern Railways became a separate company. Shooter and his colleagues had to combine running the railway with preparing a bid with due financial backing that would permit them to carry forward their aspirations. It was announced by the Strategic Railway Authority on 10 June 1996 that they had been awarded the franchise. Further changes followed which are detailed below, but essentially a customer-orientated railway that was relatively simple to operate had been created before privatisation.[15]

The local trains between Oxford and Banbury through the Cherwell Valley, calling at Tackley, Heyford and King's Sutton were worked by various diesel multiple units, including class 121 single unit 'Bubble Cars'. The same units were used on the service between Oxford and Bicester, introduced in May 1987 with sponsorship from Cherwell District and Bicester town councils. This might

---

[14] Jones, *Chiltern Railways*, 110-13.
[15] Jones, *Chiltern Railways*, 31-42.

be taken as a sign of revival but it could also have been an attempt to retain services from Bicester to London in the event of the withdrawal of trains serving Bicester North from Marylebone. Thames Turbo units took over services between Oxford and Paddington from 1992, and, as their number multiplied, operated local services to Banbury.

Banbury station from the north on 4 June 1985 as a class 47 diesel locomotive leaves with a Cross-Country train mostly of Mark II stock. The former cattle sidings to the left are no longer used for stabling locomotives nor for unloading road stone, and there are no parcels vans in the bay platforms which are overgrown with grass. John Powell

Cross Country

From 1982 the services from the north through Birmingham New Street and Banbury to Paddington and the south coast became the responsibility of Cross Country, a sub-sector of Inter City, managing long-distance services not using a London terminus. Some Cross Country trains nevertheless originated and terminated at Paddington, although they were intended primarily to serve the Thames Valley, and used facilities in London for operating convenience. In 1981 there were nine trains from Birmingham to Paddington via Oxford, three originating further north, and eight trains from Birmingham and places further north through Banbury to the south coast. Most called at Birmingham International and Coventry before joining the GWR main line at Leamington. Services became increasingly diverse, and for a few years there were again through trains between Paddington and Merseyside.

From 12 May 1986 Cross Country operated seven daily trains from the north via the West London line to Dover, Newhaven and Brighton on the south coast, some taking the West Coast Main Line to Willesden, others proceeding from New Street via Banbury and Reading and then through Ealing Broadway and North Pole junction to Kensington Olympia, and thence to Clapham Junction. The Newhaven trains were soon withdrawn, but the others attracted significant patronage and trains between Folkestone and Liverpool and Portsmouth and York were added in the following years.[16] Cross Country trains in the 1980s were notoriously prone to delays at Birmingham New Street caused by changes from diesel to electric traction, but from 1989 most trains were hauled throughout by class 47/8s, variants of the Brush Type 4 fitted with additional fuel tanks.

High Speed Trains (HSTs), after proving successful on the Great Western and East Coast main lines, were introduced by Cross Country from the winter of 1981-82, initially on services from Newcastle and Leeds to Cardiff and Plymouth, and later on trains to the south coast. Cross Country requested 36 HST sets but only half that number were delivered and most trains still consisted of locomotives and Mark II coaches. Train names were revived. The *Wessex Scot* ran between Glasgow and Edinburgh and Poole, and the *Sussex Scot* between the Scottish cities and Brighton. From 1991 the name of the *Pines Express* name was revived for an HST service from Manchester to Poole. In May 1988 the Cross Country sector introduced sleeping cars between Poole and Scotland, on trains which passed non-stop through Banbury. There have been few sleeping car trains that did not serve London, and this service appears to have been poorly patronised. It finished with the change in timetables in May 1992.

In the summer of 1991 five trains from Birmingham and places north ran through Banbury to Paddington. There were eight trains to Poole, two of which ran non-stop through Banbury, originating at Stockport, Manchester (three services), Glasgow, Aberdeen, Wolverhampton and York, one to Dover from Liverpool, and one to Brighton from Manchester. There was still a demand for summer weekend trains to coastal resorts, and Saturday services in 1991 included trains from Aberdeen, Manchester and Wolverhampton to Weymouth (also serving Southampton, Bournemouth and Poole), from Manchester to Gatwick, and from Glasgow to Eastbourne.

---

[16] M Brown, ed, *Jane's Railway Year 1986* (London: Jane's Publishing Co, 1987), 111.

16. Privatisation

Banbury never fails to impress, not only with the number of workings in a short period of time but the mixture of motive power observed.
Railway Observer, vol 85 (2015), 561.

More than two decades have passed since 1994 when railways in Great Britain passed into the control of Railtrack on 1 April, and the Channel Tunnel opened on 6 May. Banbury's railways have been transformed in that time with changes in infrastructure, a proliferation of passenger services and innovations in freight traffic, There have also been increases in fares and subsidies – although Chiltern ceased to receive the latter after 2008.

Privatisation reflected changes in other European countries where monolithic state-owned railway corporations were broken up, allowing smaller private or public sector concerns to supply certain services, supposedly because they would be more responsive to markets. In the United Kingdom control of the infrastructure passed to Railtrack, after which franchises were distributed to Train Operating Companies. Most rolling stock came to be controlled by leasing companies. Chiltern Railways, previously a Train Operating Unit within British Rail, became a separate company in April 1996, and was awarded the franchise to work services out of Marylebone on 10 June of that year. Flaws in the system were highlighted by horrific accidents, at Ladbroke Grove on 5 October 1999, at Hatfield on 17 October 2000, and at Potters Bar on 10 May 2002. Railtrack was abolished with effect from 2002, the Strategic Rail Authority was established, and management of the infrastructure passed to Network Rail, a state-controlled non-profit company. Further changes came under the Railways Act of 2005 under which the Strategic Rail Authority was abolished, and its functions transferred to the Department of Transport and a new Office of Rail Regulation.[1]

Chiltern Railways has been one of the railway successes of recent decades. Adrian Shooter, its chairman, saw privatisation as an opportunity 'to make the railway something that is valuable to the community' and to take it away 'from the sterile yoke of a nationalised industry'. Nevertheless, as Hugh Jones's book on the company makes clear, government ministers and civil servants were involved, not always helpfully, at every stage of the company's development. Shooter admitted that 'there is a large number of people … whose mission seems to be to stop things getting done'. Privatisation did not bring unfettered free enterprise.[2]

---

[1] I Jack, *The Crash that Stopped Britain* (London: Granta, 2001).
[2] H Jones, *The Chiltern Railways Story* (Stroud: History Press, 2010), 186-88.

Infrastructure

The most significant change in the infrastructure of the railway network around Banbury has been the re-doubling of the 27 miles of track between Princes Risborough and Aynho Junction, carried out at the instigation of Chiltern Railways. Work on the eighteen miles between Bicester and Princes Risborough began on 27 October 1997. The line was shut down between 17 and 25 January 1998, and the track was handed over ready for use on 19 July of that year. The doubling enabled an increase in the frequency of services, but its very success increased pressure on the single track between Bicester and Aynho Junction. The doubling of this section, part of Chiltern's Project Evergreen, began on 18 February 2002, the same day that the company received a 20-year extension of its franchise. Most late evening and Saturday trains during April 2002 were replaced by buses, and some trains from Birmingham were diverted to run into Paddington. A complete closure took place between 20 April and 6 May 2002. The new signalling was commissioned and the new track brought into use during August 2002.[3]

Chiltern also made changes at Banbury itself. The completion of a programme of refurbishment at the station was marked by a party on 9 September 2000, which also commemorated the 150th anniversary of the opening of the line from Oxford. In July 2001 an integrated control centre for the Chiltern network was opened on the site of a former coal yard near Banbury station. The success of Chiltern and other companies led to pressure on the station car park which came to occupy almost all the former goods yard, as well as a factory and its yard on Tramway Road. A multi-storey car park on the site of the former Railway Mission was opened in July 2014. It has direct access to the bridge linking the booking hall on the west side of the station with the platforms.[4]

Operations at Banbury were influenced by developments elsewhere. The most significant included the refurbishment of Marylebone station and the opening of Warwick Parkway station on 8 October 2000. At an early stage in its existence Chiltern opened a maintenance depot at Aylesbury and added two bays to it in 2004, while a depot at Wembley was opened on 7 September 2005.[5]

The rebuilding of the station at Reading, begun in 2010 and completed in 2015, also influenced services through Banbury. During the reconstruction there were several blockades, one at Easter 2013, when trains from Bristol and South Wales to Paddington were diverted from Didcot to reverse at Banbury and reach Paddington over the Bicester Cut-off. The completion of five new platforms and the opening of a flyover that separates conflicting flows of traffic enabled more Cross-Country trains to progress south beyond Reading, and increased the capacity for freight trains between Southampton and the North.[6]

---

[3] Jones, *Chiltern Railways*, 65-67, 80, 84; *RO* vol 72 (2002), 213, 261, 404, 447.
[4] Jones, *Chiltern Railways*, 78-79, 84.
[5] Jones, *Chiltern Railways*, 43, 85, 112.
[6] *RO* vol 83 (2013), 371-72; vol 85 (2015), 171.

There were also significant developments north of Banbury. Network SouthEast's services between Snow Hill and Marylebone were taken over by Chiltern, from May 1993. On 24 September 1995 a new link was opened with the line to Stourbridge, Worcester and Hereford, with stations at The Hawthorns and Jewellery Quarter, and an interchange with the main line from Birmingham to Wolverhampton at Galton Bridge. From May 2001 some Chiltern services were extended by this route to Stourbridge Junction and Kidderminster. Chiltern were also involved in the transformation of Moor Street station, where the former Great Western entrance hall re-opened in June 2003.[7]

The most imaginative project carried out by Chiltern has been the inauguration of a second route between Oxford and London, part of the third phase of Project Evergreen, outlined in 2003. A chord at Bicester, two thirds of a mile long, links the line from Marylebone with the Buckinghamshire Railway route from Bletchley to Oxford. The service between Oxford and Bicester Town station, restored in 1989, was withdrawn from February 2014 to enable the creation of what is in effect a new railway.

The rails on the chord were in place by December 2014. Bicester Town station was re-named Bicester Village, acknowledging the large numbers of passengers from London, many of them visitors from overseas, attracted to the eponymous outlets centre. Islip station was rebuilt, and a park-and-ride station, Oxford Parkway, was built at Water Eaton. The first timetabled trains from Oxford Parkway to Marylebone ran on 26 Oct 2015, and services to and from Oxford's main station began on 12 December 2016.[8]

The railway landscape at Banbury was transformed within nine days in July and August 2016, as part of a project that began with weekend closures through 2015 and a closure over the Christmas holiday period of that year. Until August 2016 trains were controlled by a mixture of colour light and upper and lower quadrant semaphores signals, operated from Banbury North signal box, which dated from 1901, and Banbury South, dating from 1908. Preliminary work on the new layout began in June 2015. During a blockade from 30 July until 7 August 2016 the railway was completely re-signalled on the Siemens Trackguard Westlock computer-based interlocking system, control being transferred to a single desk at the West Midlands Signalling Centre at Saltley, Birmingham. Banbury South box was demolished during the blockade but the North box, after a period when it was open for public visits that ended in October, was not demolished until March 2017.

---

[7] *RO* vol 71 (2001), 308; RO vol 73 (2003), 408, 547.
[8] Jones, *Chiltern Railways*, 86; C Behan, 'A 100 Years – But worth the Wait', *RM* vol 161, (2015), 14-20.

Two Freightliner locomotives haul a long container train from Southampton past Banbury North signal box shortly before it was decommissioned in July 2016 during the blockade in which the layout of the tracks shown here was radically altered. John Powell

The view north from Banbury station in August 2016 a few days after the 9-day blockade. Tracks have been re-aligned but the North signal box remained since it was opened to visitors for a further two months.

Banbury station from the north immediately after the nine-day blockade for engineering work in July/August 2016. The most significant alteration was the creation of a new up platform. The multi-storey car park completed in July 2014 is also visible.

Connections were installed for the Chiltern Railways depot then under construction. The track layout was altered with 24 new sets of points, 14,000 metres of new rail, 11,200 new concrete sleepers, and 50,000 tonnes of ballast. The most significant alteration was the creation of a new up platform, something which, inexplicably, was not part of the 1958 station modernisation. The train operating companies arranged replacement buses, and there was consensus that the project was efficiently handled. It was followed, between 30 July and 14 August, by flood protection work south of Oxford, where in previous years flooding had seriously delayed trains.[9]

Trials and Tribulations

Train operating companies using the lines through Banbury have faced a succession of difficulties since the beginning of the twenty-first century. The reaction to the crash at Hatfield on 17 October 2000, caused by a broken rail, led to the imposition of speed restrictions across the whole railway system. The Chiltern lines were affected less than others, but for many weeks trains were delayed. In 2003 and again in 2007 floods at Banbury caused severe disruption.

---

[9] *Rail* No 810 (2016), 56-59; *RO* vol 85 (2015), 537.

Chiltern services were severely affected by the collapse of a tunnel being built across the tracks on the up side of the station at Gerrard's Cross to accommodate a Tesco supermarket. On 30 June 2005 the 17.30 from Stratford-upon-Avon to Marylebone was leaving Gerrard's Cross when its Banbury-based driver noticed clouds of dust ahead of him as the tunnel collapsed. Fortunately he was able to stop the train and there were no casualties, but the line was closed for seven weeks, re-opening on 20 August. Delays were compounded by the effects of the London bombings on 7 July, and by a major fire at a chemical plant near the lineside at Wembley. Work on the tunnel resumed in January 2009 and the Tesco store eventually opened in November 2010. Chiltern Railways lost traffic to other lines, but its revenue had recovered by the autumn of 2006.[10]

On 31 January 2015 there was a land slip in the deep cutting at Harbury south of Leamington, on a stretch of line for which there were no obvious alternative routes. Chiltern and Cross Country organised bus services from Warwick Parkway and Leamington stations to and from Banbury and beyond, while freight trains were diverted. Some 350,000 tons of spoil were removed before the line re-opened, ahead of schedule, on 13 March 2015.[11]

Chiltern Enterprise

Chiltern inherited a fleet of class 165 Networker Turbos, delivered in 1991 as part of the Total Route Modernisation of the lines from Marylebone. The class 168 Clubman units were ordered in 1996 from the Derby works of what was then ABB (later Adtranz, now Bombardier), and were the result of research by Chiltern management, although there were problems when they were introduced in 1998. They still form the majority of Chiltern trains through Banbury. With the cessation of Wrexham, Shropshire and Marylebone services in 2011 Chiltern took over the company's class 67 locomotives and its standard Mark III coaches, adapting the latter to modern requirements by fitting them with plug doors. From 2014 the class 67s were replaced by new class 68 diesels, the first of which was tested in August of that year. The first revenue-earning service to be worked by a class 68 was the 07.44 Banbury–Marylebone on 14 December 2014, and all locomotive-hauled trains were taken over by the class from 24 May 2015. The company now operates 8 class 68s together with 31 Mark III coaches and six DVTs.[12]

Chiltern has attracted passengers bound to and from events at Wembley Stadium. The original Wembley Stadium station on a loop line between Neasden Junction and Wembley Hill station was last used by spectators at the FA Cup Final in 1968, and was officially closed in September 1969. The station on the

---

[10] Jones, *Chiltern Railways*, 12-16.
[11] *Rail* No 768, Feb 2015; *Railnews*, 4 Mar 2015; *RO* vol 85 (2015), 228-29, 244-45, 302.
[12] Jones, *Chiltern Railways*, 112, 171-76; *RM* bol 161 (2015), 76; *RO* vol 85 (2015), 517.

Neasden–Northolt line, opened in 1906 as Wembley Hill, re-named Wembley Complex in 1978 and Wembley Stadium in 1987, is well-situated for the stadium and has been adapted to handle the large crowds leaving major events. Turnback facilities enable the operation of a shuttle service to and from Marylebone, and Chiltern also run special trains from Birmingham through Banbury.[13]

With a DVT at its head and a class 68 diesel locomotive at the rear the Chiltern Railways 11.04 Birmingham Snow Hill–Marylebone approaches Banbury on 28 April 2017, while a GBRf class 66 on the down relief line awaits the road northwards with a haul of twenty 100-ton ballast wagons.

For nearly three years trains operated by the Wrexham, Shropshire and Marylebone Railway Co called at Banbury. The company, established in 2006, resulted from frustration in Shropshire and North Wales at the withdrawal by Virgin Trains of through services to Euston. The company applied to operate trains under 'open access' conditions, but the restrictions imposed were more restrictive than those that govern Grand Central and Hull Trains on the East Coast Main Line. Trains from Wrexham stopped at Shrewsbury and Telford Central then passed through Wolverhampton to call at Tame Bridge Parkway near Walsall. They then either went to Stechford and passed Coventry non-stop *en route* to Leamington, Banbury and Marylebone, or took the route through Birmingham New Street, where they were not allowed to call, Bordesley and Solihull. Travellers from Marylebone could not alight at Banbury, but northbound trains were allowed to pick up passengers. Similarly passengers for

---

[13] Jones, *Chiltern Railways*, 92-94.

London could not join southbound WSMR trains, although these restrictions were lifted from December 2009. The service began in April 2008 with five daily trains in each direction, but there were only four from March 2009 and three from December 2010. Trains took 4¼ hours to reach Marylebone from Wrexham, but faced competition from a Virgin service introduced in April 2008 which did the journey in 2½ hours via Chester. With the benefit of hindsight it is unsurprising that such a slow service failed to attract sufficient custom to be viable, and the last trains ran on 28 January 2011. Standards of comfort were high since the service was operated with standard Mark III coaches pulled and pushed by Class 67 diesel locomotives which were acquired by Chiltern Railways when the service ceased.[14]

Chiltern recorded 7.7 million customers in 1996, a total which rose to 24.5 million in 2016, while the number of services operated per day rose from 240 to 431. The company provides Banbury with a faster and more intensive service than has ever been available in the past, 47 weekday departures to Marylebone, of which three are non-stop, and 36 to Birmingham, of which four terminate at Kidderminster and one at Stourbridge Junction, with three trains serving Leamington and Stratford-upon-Avon. The fastest service is the 16.15 ex-Marylebone which reaches Banbury in 53 minutes at 17.08. The objective of restoring services from London through Banbury to Birmingham Snow Hill was achieved before privatisation in 1993, and Chiltern realised its ambition to create a second route from the capital to Oxford in 2015-16. It has also created a significant source of revenue at Banbury where the number of passengers rose from 1,580,000 in 2008-09 to 2,055,000 in 2012-13. Those who created Chiltern displayed imagination as well as technical and managerial skills. It required creative thinking in the early 1990s to contemplate the re-generation of the line from Marylebone to Banbury – it was precisely the lack of such imagination that led to the closure of the Great Central line in 1966.

Cross-country

British Rail's Cross-country sector passed into the control of Virgin Trains on privatisation. Some services through Banbury were then worked by HSTs, but the majority by class 47/8 diesel locomotives hauling Mark II carriages. Some southbound trains terminated at Paddington, some at Reading, some at Bournemouth and Poole, some at Gatwick and Brighton, and, on Saturdays, some at Portsmouth or Weymouth. Northbound destinations included Manchester, Liverpool, Glasgow, Edinburgh, Newcastle and Blackpool. The nature of the service changed from 2002. Virgin Trains ordered 34 four-car class 220 and 44 five-car class 221 'Voyager' diesel units which were delivered from 2000.

---

[14] R Harper & G Rushton, *Wrexham & Shropshire Open Access* (Milton Keynes: Adlestrop Press, 2014); Jones, *Chiltern Railways*, 85-86.

The latter were fitted with tilting mechanisms, similar to those on Virgin's Pendolino units, enabling them to travel at high speeds round curves on lines which included that between Banbury and Oxford, but the function was disabled in 2008. The fleet is based at the purpose-built Central Rivers depot near Burton-on-Trent. From the summer of 2001 Virgin undertook public trial runs from Birmingham to Reading, Redhill and Gatwick. In September 2002 Operation Princess involved the replacement of all locomotive-hauled cross country services with Voyagers, with four- or five-coach trains operating at greater frequency to a clock face timetable. The last Virgin Cross-Country locomotive-hauled service through Banbury was the 06.00 Paddington–Manchester Piccadilly on 17 August 2002. Its red and black Mark II coaches were topped and tailed by Nos 47818 and 47843.[15]

A Voyager unit forming the 09.46 Southampton Central–Newcastle-upon-Tyne heads north from Banbury on 28 April 2017. The site of the Banbury North signal box, demolished in the previous month, is evident behind the last coach.

The new service met with problems. Punctuality fell to 54.1 per cent in the last quarter of 2002, and operations were subsequently simplified. Cross-Country trains ceased to serve Liverpool, Paddington and destinations south of Bournemouth in 2003 and those to Gatwick and Brighton were withdrawn in 2008. From November 2007 the franchise passed from Virgin to Arriva trains. The present service surpasses any in the past. In the 2016-17 timetable there are 31 departures from Birmingham through Banbury to Reading, where nine trains

---

[15] *RO* vol 71 (2001), 308, 401, Vol 72 (2002), 261.

terminate, while six proceed to Southampton, 15 to Bournemouth and one to Guildford. There are 31 northbound services from Banbury, 14 terminating at Manchester, 11 at Newcastle-upon-Tyne, and six at Birmingham.

The Cherwell Valley

Local trains from Banbury to Oxford, serving the village stations at King's Sutton, Heyford and Tackley, have been operated since privatisation by the companies holding franchises for the Great Western main line, Thames Trains until 2004, then First Great Western and, since a re-branding in 2015, the Great Western Railway. Until 2004 trains worked through Banbury to Stratford, but Stratford services were taken over by Chiltern in that year. The weekday service in 2017 consists of twelve departures, eight of which continue from Oxford to Paddington.

Freight

In 2015 some fifty freight trains a day used the line between Banbury and Leamington. It was anticipated that the Channel Tunnel, opened in May 1994, would generate new flows of rail traffic, some of which would pass through Banbury. In the late 1990s Michael Pearson described a journey on a train taking cars to Italy from Birmingham via Banbury and the West London line to Dollands Moor at the tunnel entrance, but between 2011 and 2016 no new cars were exported through the tunnel. Rail-borne freight traffic reached a peak in 1998 when it amounted to 3.14 million tonnes, but in the aftermath of closures caused by fires on road vehicles on Euroshuttle trains, and the precautions taken to prevent migrants from boarding trains at Calais, traffic has declined, totalling only 1.42 million tonnes in 2015, although that was a higher figure than in some previous years.[16]

The RES (Rail Express Systems) operation was transferred to English, Welsh & Scottish Railways in 1996, but since then parcels traffic has effectively disappeared. Mail and parcels trains were still passing through Banbury in 2002, and Christmas mail trains were operated that year between Reading and Warrington, but RES lost its contract with Royal Mail in 2003. While some services using purpose-built class 325 units have been operated from November 2004 by GB Railfreight, none of them pass through Banbury.[17]

Freight operations were transferred on privatisation to several train operating companies, foremost among them English, Welsh & Scottish Railways formed in 1995 and initially headed by Ed Burkhardt formerly of the Wisconsin Central Railroad. EWS handled trainload operations, notably coal, and took the lead amongst British companies in ordering powerful diesel locomotives, denominated

---

[16] M Pearson, *Coming up with the goods* (Tattenhill Common: Wayzgoose, 1999).145-60.
[17] *RO* vol 73 (2003), 69.

class 66, from General Motors, that were initially built at London, Ontario. They replaced an inheritance of 1,600 locomotives most of which were more than thirty years old. The first class 66 was landed at Immingham in June 1998. They were subsequently ordered by other companies and scarcely an hour at Banbury station passes without the passage of one of them. The last of the class was delivered to Newport in 2014. EWS handled coal trains from the Midlands to Didcot A power station, a high proportion of the freight traffic passing Banbury until the power station closed in 2013. Oil from the Lindsey refinery was also delivered to Didcot by rail, as was coal imported at Portbury (Bristol) that passed Banbury *en route* for Rugeley B power station in Staffordshire, which closed in June 2016. GB Railfreight (GBRf), is responsible for deliveries of London Underground stock from the manufacturers at Derby or the test track at Old Dalby near Melton Mowbray, through Banbury to the depot at West Ruislip. Other traffics have flourished and dwindled. Amongst them in the years since 1994 have been steel and steel scrap, cars and car components, china clay, military supplies to and from Burton Dassett, fertilisers, road stone, and tanks containing petroleum products, LPG and calcium carbonate.

The road stone depot on the site of the down departure sidings, established prior to the construction of the M40 motorway and still operating in 2017.

The one traffic handled at Banbury is road stone that is delivered by a self-discharging train, once or twice a week, to the terminal on the site of the down marshalling yard, travelling overnight from Mount Sorrel via Leicester, Wigston North, Nuneaton, Landor Street Junction, Bordesley Junction and Leamington.

The Freightliner company, formed in 1995, took over the container-carrying sector of British Rail and followed the example of EWS in ordering class 66 diesels from General Motors. While EWS began to carry containers, Freightliner established a heavy haul business in 1999 for bulk traffics. Freightliner's container trains, some of great length, now dominate freight traffic at Banbury. Most start or finish their journeys at Southampton, but some, when the West Coast Main Line is blocked, serve other ports. The range of destinations in the North and Midlands has been increased by the opening of terminals at Widnes, Wakefield, Hams Hall at Coleshill and Birch Coppice at Dordon.[18]

Reflections

'*Banbury, in north Oxfordshire, was the meeting place of eight railway lines*' was the sentence that began this study, and it was true between 1919 and 1951. Now there are three, all of which are busier than at any time in the past. Their nature has changed many times. It is ironic that the nine-day blockade of the station in 2016 took place at the very time of year when fifty years previously seaside holiday traffic would have been at its peak. In 2016 commuter traffic was probably at its lowest in the first weeks of the school summer holidays, but most commuters would have been using road or air transport for their holidays. The spring 2017 timetables offer nearly 50 daily departures for London via the Bicester cut-off and others via Oxford, more than 60 to Birmingham, 14 to Manchester, 11 to Newcastle-upon-Tyne and 21 to Southampton. Freight trains through Banbury are of a size and move at speeds that would have been unimaginable in the past, and, what would have been equally unimaginable, they no long fulfil the original raison d'être of the English railway by carrying coal.

It is easy to be nostalgic about past services. A 'King' class locomotive hauling 14 coaches south from Banbury on the 15.54 departure for Paddington, reached in 81 minutes in 1959, provided a magnificent spectacle for all who saw it, but the next express via the Bicester cut-off did not depart until 19.01 and did not reach Paddington until 20.35. In 2016 a passenger arriving at Banbury station at 15.54 would have to wait ten minutes for the departure of the 16.04 to Marylebone, which takes 68 minutes for the journey, and over the next three hours he or she would have the choice of a further eight departures for the capital, most of them in much faster times than the 81 minutes of 1959.

---

[18] *RO* vol 72 (2002), 261.

Traffic on other lines similar to those through Banbury linking medium-sized towns with big cities, and particularly in the south-east of England, has substantially increased, if not quite on the same scale. Nevertheless, while changes at Banbury may reflect national trends, that does not diminish the achievements of those who have brought them about. The history of railways in Banburyshire highlights the achievements of those whose managerial and technical skills have been combined with imagination, the transformation of the Great Western's northern line from the 1890s, the promotion of cross-country services by Sir Sam Fay, and the revitalisation of the Stratford-upon-Avon & Midland Junction Railway by the Willmotts.

It is difficult logically to regret the closure of four of the eight lines that focussed on Banbury. The infrequent trains on the Northampton & Banbury Junction Railway were never well-patronised, nor did the line carry significant freight traffic. The Banbury & Cheltenham Direct Railway provided a service to ironstone quarries between King's Sutton and Hook Norton, but its stations were inconveniently-situated and its stopping trains could not compete with motor buses. The Oxfordshire Ironstone Company's line to Wroxton served a useful purpose for 48 years but closed when the iron industry no longer required native ores. The line from Bletchley provided competition for the GWR for half-a-century but declined from the beginning of the twentieth century as competition reduced its business at Brackley and Buckingham. Its revival in 1956 demonstrated the transformation that energetic marketing can bring to a railway, but whether the passenger levels could have been sustained in the age of the motor car is doubtful. Unlike the Oxford line of the Buckinghamshire Railway, the Banbury branch had limited potential for inter-regional travel. It is now difficult to determine where Merton Street station once stood.

The closure of the Great Central line is a matter for more regret, the result, it would seem, of decisions by those in the late 1950s and 1960s who had pessimistic views of the future of railways. To see a lengthy container train making its way from the Leamington to the Nuneaton line at Coventry sprawling across all the routes through the station is a reminder of what was lost when the Great Central was starved and closed in the 1960s.

Optimism about the future of railways in 2017 cannot be unhampered by doubts. The raising of footbridges at the village stations between Banbury and Oxford will accommodate a catenary as well as larger containers, but the postponement of electrification from Didcot to Oxford means that there will be even more delays before electric trains reach Banbury, as surely one day they will. HS2, the high speed line from London to Birmingham, will pass through the eastern fringes of 'Banburyshire'. Its likely effects are difficult to measure but it is certain to bring more changes to Banbury's railways.

Via Banbury: a town and its railways from 1850

Bibliography:

For abbreviations see page vii.

R D Abbott, ed, *The Last Main Line* (Leicester Museum and Art Gallery, 1961).
B Adkins, 'Banbury Rest Station and Canteen 1914-19', *C&CH* vol 8 (1979), 13-16.
R Adley, *The Call of Steam* (Poole: Blandford, 1982).
Agricultural Economics Research Institute, Oxford, *Country Planning: a Study of Rural Problems* (Oxford University Press, 1944).
C J Allen, *Titled Trains of Great Britain* (3rd edn, London: Ian Allan, 1953).
  'Last Main Line into London', *Trains Annual 1955* (London: Ian Allan, 1955), 36-47, 112.
J Alves, 'Resorts for Railfans 19: Oxford', *TI*, vol 12 (1959), 596-606.
P Atkins, 'Off the Beaten Track', *RM* vol 161 (2015).
S Austin, *From the Footplate: Cambrian Coast Express* (Shepperton: Ian Allan, 1992).

C Barman, *The Great Western Railway's last look forward* (London: Allen & Unwin, 1947, as *Next Station*; rep Newton Abbott: David & Charles, 1972).
S Bartlett, 'Indian Summer of Wolverhampton (Oxley) Castles', *SD* No 308 (2015), 5-22.
K M Beck, *The Great Western north of Wolverhampton* (Shepperton: Ian Allan, 1986).
  & N Harris, *GWR Reflections: a collection of photographs from the Hulton Picture Co* (Wadenhoe: Silver Link, 1987).
A Beesley, *The History of Banbury* (London: Nichols, 1841).
C Behan, 'A 100 Years – But worth the Wait', *RM* vol 161, No 1376 (November 2015).
G Behrend, *Gone with Regret* (Sidcup: Lambarde Press, 1964).
J Betjeman, *John Betjeman's Collected Poems* (London: John Murray, 1980).
R J Blenkinsop, *Shadows of the Great Western* (Oxford: Oxford Publishing Co, 1972).
  Big Four Cameraman (Oxford: Oxford Publishing Co, 1975).
  Locomotives Illustrated: 50: GWR Double-framed 4-4-0s (Shepperton: Ian Allan 1986).
M Bonavia, *The Birth of British Rail* (London: Allen & Unwin, 1979).
  British Rail: the first 25 years (Newton Abbot: David & Charles, 1981).
  The Four Great Railways (Newton Abbot: David & Charles, 1980).
F Booker, *The Great Western Railway: A New History* (Newton Abbot: David & Charles, 1977).
S Bradley, *The Railways: Nation, Network and People* (London: Profile, 2015).
G Bradshaw, *Bradshaw's Descriptive Railway Hand-Book of Great Britain and Ireland* (1863, rep 2012, Oxford: Old House).
S Brindle, *Paddington Station: Its history and architecture* (Swindon: English Heritage, 2004).
British Railways Press Office, *British Railways in Peace and War* (London: British Railways Press Office, 1944).
P Brookfield, 'Sydenham Quarries', *C&CH* vol 17 (2009), 287-95.
B Brooksbank, *Train Watchers No 1* (Burton-on-Trent: Pearson, 1982).
M Brown, ed, *Jane's Railway Year 1985* (London: Jane's Publishing Co, 1986).
  Jane's Railway Year 1986 (London: Jane's Publishing Co, 1987).
A Buchanan, *Brunel: The Life and Times of Isambard Kingdom Brunel* (London: Hambledon, 2002).

A C Cawston, *A Railway Photographer's Diary* (Bracknell: Town & Country Press, 1972).
W G Chapman, *"Caerphilly Castle": a book of railway locomotives for boys of all ages* (London: Great Western Railway, 1924).

R Christiansen, *A Regional History of the Railways of Great Britain, vol 7, The West Midlands* (Newton Abbot: David & Charles, 1973).
D Clark, 'The Railway Mission', *Railway Magazine*, June 2013, 34-43.
R Coleman & J Rajczonek, *Railway Images around Northamptonshire* (Wellingborough: Wharton, 1992),
P Collins, *Rail Centres: Wolverhampton* (Shepperton: Ian Allan, 1990).
H Compton, *The Oxford Canal* (Newton Abbot: David & Charles, 1976).
N Cooper, *Aynho: A Northamptonshire Village* (Kineton: Leopard's Head Press / Banbury Historical Society vol 20, 1984).
J Copsey, '28XXs in the North during the Great Western era', *GWRJ* No 11 (1994), 459-69.
  Banbury GWR: Pt 1: The Background', *BRJ* No 15 (1987), 223-37.
  '"Kings" on the Northern Line', *GWRJ* No 3 (1992), 109-17.
  '78XXs in Traffic', *GWRJ* No 15 (1995), 637-48.
  'The Ports to Ports Services', *GWRJ* No 45 (2002), 274-84.
  'Goods Operations at Banbury', *GWRJ* No 92 (2014), 182-201.
  'Goods Operations at Banbury, part 2', *GWRJ* No 93 (2015), 264-91.
  'Goods Operations at Banbury, part 3', *GWRJ* No 94 (2015), 347-59.
  & M Clifton, 'Banbury – The Shed, the Engines and the Men', *GWRJ* No 3 (1992), 90-104.
M Creese, *North and South – the Signal boxes of Banbury* (London: Blurb, 2011).

B Darwin, *War on the Line* (London: Southern Railway, 1946, rep Midhurst: Middleton Press, 1984).
R Davies & M D Grant, *Forgotten Railways: Chilterns and Cotswolds* (Newton Abbot: David & Charles, 1975).
C Dodsworth, 'The Early Years of the Oxford Cement Industry', *Industrial Archaeology*, vol 9 (1972), 285-95.
G Dow, *Great Central, vol 1, The Progenitors 1813-63* (London: Locomotive Publishing Co, 1959).
  Great Central, vol 2, Dominion of Watkin, 1864-99 (London: Locomotive Publishing Co, 1962).
  Great Central, vol 3, Fay sets the pace, 1900-1922 (2nd edn., Shepperton: Ian Allan, 1971).
J Drayton, *On the Footplate: Memories of a GWR engineman* (Truro: Bradford Barton, 1976).
J Drinkwater, *Inheritance: being the first book of an autobiography* (London: Benn, 1931).
J Dummelow, 'Banbury as a Railway Centre', *RM* vol 50 (1922), 80-85.
J M Dunn, *The Stratford-upon-Avon & Midland Junction Railway* (Lingfield: Oakwood, 1952).
H J Dyos & D H Aldcroft, *British Transport: an economic survey from the seventeenth century to the twentieth* (Leicester University Press, 1971).

A Earnshaw, *Britain's Railways at War* (Penryn: Atlantic Transport, 1995).
D Edwards & R Pigram, *The Final Link* (London: Bloomsbury Books, 1988).
C H Ellis, *The Engines that Passed* (London: George Allen & Unwin, 1968).
A Elton, *British Railways* (London: Collins, 1947).
J Evans, *Last Rites: from the track to the scrapyard* (Stroud: Amberley, 2016).

M G D Farr, 'The Banbury–Buckingham railcar experiment', *TI*, vol 12 (1959), 594-95.
R B Fellows, 'Four Pioneer Services to the Seaside', *RM* vol 87 (1941), 289-92.
G F Fiennes, *I Tried to Run a Railway* (London: Ian Allan, 1967).
  Fiennes on Rails: Fifty Years of Railways (Newton Abbot: David & Charles, 1986).
D L Franks, *Great Central Remembered* (London: Ian Allan, 1985).

W K V Gale, *Iron and Steel* (London: Longman, 1969).
  The Iron & Steel Industry: A Dictionary of Terms (Newton Abbot: David & Charles, 1971).
G E Gardam, 'The Brymbo Ironworks, Hook Norton', *C&CH* vol 3 (1968), 226-27.
G E Gardam, 'The Brymbo Iron Works, Hook Norton', *C&CH*, vol 4 (1970), 138-40.

D Gerhold, *Carriers & Coachmasters: Trade and Travel before the Industrial Revolution* (Chichester: Phillimore, 2005).
J S W Gibson, 'Railway Mania', *C&CH* vol. 13 (1995), 129-33, rep *BG* 23 May 1844.
 ed, *An Alphabetical Digest of Rusher's Banbury Directory to Trades and Occupations 1832-1906* (Banbury Historical Society vol 34, 2014).
 Banbury and the Origins of the Coventry to Oxford Canal 1768-1778 (Banbury Historical Society, 2015).
R Gorton, 'The Hook Norton Ironstone Companies', *C&CH* vol 9 (1982), 14-22.
G Goslin, *Goods Traffic of the LNER* (Didcot: Wild Swan, 2002).
S Gosling, '57-239 Causeway, Banbury', in C Paine *et al*, 'Working Class Housing in Oxfordshire', *Oxoniensia*, vol 43 (1978), 201-04.
T R Gourish, *British Rail 1974-97: from integration to privatisation* (Oxford University Press, 2002).
 British Railways 1948-73: a business history (Cambridge University Press, 2011).
P Gray, *Rail Trails: South West* (Wadenhoe: Silver Link, 1992).
Great Western Railway, *Through the Window: Paddington to Birkenhead* (London: Great Western Railway, 1925).
J G Griffith & J A K Gray, 'The Oxford and Bletchley Branch of the LMSR', *Railway Magazine*, vol 69 (1931), 89-92.
S Griffiths, *Griffiths' Guide to the Iron Trade of Great Britain* (1873, ed W K V Gale, Newton Abbot: David & Charles, 1967).
R Griffiths & P Smith, *The Directory of British Engine Sheds, vol 1, Southern England, the Midlands, East Anglia and Wales* (Shepperton: Oxford Publishing Co, 1999).
A E Grigg, *Town of Trains: Bletchley and the Oxbridge line* (Buckingham: Barracuda, 1980).
 Country Railwaymen: A notebook of Engine Drivers' Tales (Buckingham: Calypus, 1982).

C Hadfield, *The Canals of the East Midlands* (Newton Abbot: David & Charles, 1966).
 The Canals of the West Midlands (Newton Abbot: David & Charles, 1966).
J A B Hamilton, *Britain's Railways in World War 1* (London: Allen & Unwin, 1967).
R H N Hardy, *Steam in the Blood* (London: Ian Allan, 1971, paperback edition, 1975).
R Harper & G Rushton, *Wrexham & Shropshire Open Access: the one that got away* (Milton Keynes: Adlestrop Press, 2014).
B Harrison, *Seeking a Role: the United Kingdom 1951-70* (Oxford: Clarendon Press, 2009).
 & B Trinder, *Drink and Sobriety in an Early Victorian Country Town: Banbury 1830-1860* (London: Longman, 1969).
G C J Hartland, 'Gas-Making in Banbury', *C&CH* vol 4 (1969), 47-54.
R Hartree, 'The Banbury Aluminium Works 1929-2009', *C&CH* vol.20 (2015), 3-30.
M Hawkins, *The Great Central Then and Now* (Newton Abbot: David & Charles, 1991).
J M C Healy, *Echoes of the Great Central* (London: Greenwich Editions, 1996).
W. Hemmings, *The Banbury & Cheltenham Railway, vol 1* (Didcot: Wild Swan, 2004).
 P Karau & C Turner, *The Banbury & Cheltenham Railway, vol 2* (Didcot: Wild Swan, 2004).
R P & R P Hendry, *Paddington to the Mersey* (Sparkford: Oxford Publishing Co, 1992).
G Herbert, *Shoemaker's Window: Recollections of Banbury before the Railway Age* (3rd edn, ed C S Cheney and B Trinder, Banbury: Gulliver Press, 1979).
W E Hipkins, *The Wire Rope and its Applications* (Birmingham: J & E Wright, 1896).
D Hodgkins, *The Second Railway King: the Life and Times of Sir Edward Watkin 1819-1901* (Cardiff: Merton Priory Press, 2002).
J R Hodgkins, *Over the Hills to Glory: Radicalism in Banburyshire 1832-1945* (Southend: Clifton Press, 1978).
P Hopkins, *Great Western Pictorial* (Didcot: Wild Swan, 1995).
H Household, *Gloucestershire Railways in the Twenties* (Gloucester: Sutton, 1986).

D Hucknall, *On Shed: A portrait of the steam locomotive depot* (London: BCA, 1993).
R Humm, 'King's Sutton Station', *C&CH*, vol 5 (1973), 96.
J F Husband, 'The Banbury and Cheltenham Railway', *RM* vol 59 (1926), 353-60.

R Irons and S C Jenkins, *Woodford Halse: A Railway Community* (Usk: Oakwood, 1999).

I Jack, *The Crash that Stopped Britain* (London: Granta, 2001).
S C Jenkins, *The Oxford, Worcester & Wolverhampton Railway* (Tarrant Hinton: Oakwood, 1977).
  The Great Western & Great Central Joint Railway (Tarrant Hinton: Oakwood, 1978).
  The Northampton & Banbury Junction Railway (Oxford: Oakwood, 1990).
W Johnson, *A History of Banbury* (Banbury: Walford, n d, *circa* 1863).
H Jones, *The Chiltern Railways Story* (Stroud: History Press, 2010).
K Jones, *Once upon a time by the Lineside* (Nottingham: Challenger, 1998).
K B Jones, *The Wenlock Branch: Wellington to Craven Arms* (Usk: Oakwood, 1998).
A & E Jordan, *Away for the Day: the Railway Excursion in Britain, 1830 to the present day* (Kettering: Silver Link, 1991).
C W Judge, *Thro' the Lens: A Pictorial Tribute to the Official Work of the GWR Photographers* (Poole: Railprint, 1985).

J R Kellett, *The Impact of Railways on Victorian Cities* (London: Routledge & Kegan Paul, 1969).
Kelly's Directories Ltd, *Kelly's Directory of Banbury and Neighbourhood 1950* (London: Kelly, 1950).
B Kirkham, *Our World Was New* (Banbury: privately published, 2012).
C F Klapper, *Sir Herbert Walker's Southern Railway* (London: Ian Allan, 1973).

J L Langley, 'Memoirs of Late Victorian Banbury', *C&CH* vol 2 (1963), 51-56.
  'Further Memoirs of Late Victorian and Early Edwardian Banbury', *C&CH* vol 3 (1966), 39-45.
M Leah, 'Banbury's "secret" railway', *STR* No 96 (April 1988), 21-25.
S A Leleux, *Warwickshire Lime and Cement Works Railways* (2014). Usk: Oakwood.
M Lester, *Memories of Banbury: an illustrated record of an Oxfordshire childhood* (Banbury: privately published, 1986).
  Those Golden Days: an illustrated record of an Oxfordshire market town from the 1930s (Banbury: privately published, 1992).
R Lingard, *Princes Risborough–Thame–Oxford Railway* (Oxford: Oxford Publishing Co, 1978).
B Little, *The Changing Faces of Grimsbury* (Witney: Robert Boyd, 1999).
  & D Shadbolt, *The History of Banbury Spencer Football Club* (Witney, Robert Boyd, 2013).
S Lloyd, *Reminiscences* (Birmingham: privately published, 1913).

E T MacDermot, *History of the Great Western Railway* (1927, rev edn ed C R Clinker, 3 vols, London: Ian Allan, 1964).
S Major, *Early Victorian Railway Excursions: 'The Million Go Forth'* (Barnsley: Pen & Sword, 2015).
B Mason, *Banbury 1853, the first detailed map of mid-nineteenth century Banbury and Neithrop* (Banbury Historical Research, 2004).
G Measom, *The Official Illustrated Guide to the Great Western Railway* (London: Measom, 1861).
T Middlemass, ed, *Railway Reflections: photographs from the '30s by F C Le Manquais* (Wellingborough: Patrick Stephens, 1989).
V Middleton & K Smith, *Princes Risborough to Banbury,* (Midhurst: Middleton, 2002).
  Didcot to Banbury: Western Main Line (Midhurst: Middleton, 2003).
  Branch Lines to Princes Risborough (Midhurst: Middleton, 2003).
  Banbury to Birmingham. (Midhurst: Middleton, 2004).
  Banbury to Cheltenham. (Midhurst: Middleton, 2005).
  Oxford to Bletchley including Verney Junction to Banbury (Midhurst: Middleton, 2005).
  Branch lines around Towcester. (Midhurst: Middleton, 2008).

J Minnis & S Hickman, *The Railway Goods Shed and Warehouse in England* (Swindon: Historic England, 2016).
P Mottershead, 'The Memoirs of Peter Mottershead, Mason City, Iowa', *Locomotive Engineers' Journal*, May 1908.
C L Mowat, *Britain between the Wars 1918-1940* (London: Methuen, 1955).
R T Munns, *Milk Churns to Merry-go-round: a Century of Train Operation* (Newton Abbot: David & Charles, 1986).

G P Neel, *Railway Reminiscences* (London: McCorquedale, 1904; rep Wakefield: EP Publishing, 1974).
K Northover, *Banbury during the Great War* (Witney: Prospero, 2003).

Oxfordshire County Council, *A Handlist of Plans, Sections and Books of Reference for the Proposed Railways in Oxfordshire 1825-1936* (Oxford: Oxfordshire County Council, 1964).

M Page, 'We're off to Leamington', *SD*, No 313, Sept 2015.
S Parissien, *The English Railway Station* (Swindon: Historic England, 2014).
R Partridge, 'Woodford Halse: a Railway Community recalled', N Harris, ed, *Railway World Annual 1987* (Shepperton: Ian Allan, 1986).
D Pearce, 'The last weekend of the Great Central's London Extension', *SD*, September 2016.
M Pearson, *Coming up with the goods: journeys through Britain by freight train* (Tattenhill Common: Wayzgoose, 1999).
H Perkin, *The Age of the Railway* (London: Routledge & Kegan Paul, 1970).
C R Potts, *An Historical Survey of Selected Great Western Stations, vol. 4* (Poole: Oxford Publishing Co, 1985).
W Potts, *Banbury through One Hundred Years* (Banbury Guardian, 1942).
W Potts, *A History of Banbury* (Banbury Guardian, 1958).
M Prior, *Fisher Row: Fishermen, Bargemen & Canal Boatman in Oxford 1500-1900* (Oxford: Clarendon Press, 1982).

M Rhodes, *From Gridiron to Grassland: the Rise and Fall of the British Railway Marshalling Yard* (Sheffield: Platform 5, 2016).
M Rhodes, 'The Rise and Fall of the British Marshalling Yard: part 1, The 19th century to 1963', *RM* No.1351 (Nov 2013), 32-40.
R C Riley, *Great Western Album* (London: Ian Allan, 1966).
R C Riley & B Simpson, *A History of the Stratford-upon-Avon & Midland Junction Railway* (Witney: Lamplight Publications, 1999).
M Robbins, 'From R B Dockray's Diary', *JTH*, vol 7 (1965-66), 1-13, 109-19.
   The Railway Age (Harmondsworth: Penguin, 1965).
K Robertson, *The Last Days of Steam in Oxfordshire* (Gloucester: Alan Sutton, 1987).
R Robotham, *Great Central Railway's London Extension* (Shepperton: Ian Allan, 1999).
   & F Stratford, *The Great Central from the Footplate* (London: Ian Allan, 1988).
L T C Rolt, *Railway Adventure* (London: Constable, 1953).
   Red for Danger: A History of Railway Accidents and Railway Safety Precautions (London: John Lane, 1955).
   Isambard Kingdom Brunel (London: Longmans Green, 1957).
   The Making of a Railway (London: Hugh Evelyn, 1971).
A Rosevear, *Turnpike Roads to Banbury* (Banbury Historical Society vol 31, 2010).
J W P Rowledge, *Heavy Goods Engines of the War Department, vol 1, ROD 2-8-0s* (Poole: Springmead, 1977).
   Austerity 2-8-0s and 2-10-0s (London: Ian Allan, 1987).
Rusher's *Banbury Lists and Directories* (*see* J S W Gibson, Banbury Historical Society, vol 34, 2014).

J H Russell, *The Banbury and Cheltenham Railway 1887-1962* (Oxford: Oxford Publishing Co, 1977).
A Pictorial Record of Great Western Coaches 1903-1948 (Sparkford: Haynes, 1990).

C I Savage, *The History of the Second World War: Inland Transport* (London: HMSO-Longman, 1957).
F Scopes, *The Development of Corby Works* (Corby: Stewart & Lloyds, 1968).
W J Scott, 'The New Competitor (the Great Central)', *RM* vol 7 (1900), 305-07.
The great Great Western 1889-1902 (London: Railway Publishing Co, 1903, rep Wakefield: EP, 1972).
P W B Semmens, *The Heyday of GWR Train Services* (Newton Abbot: David & Charles, 1990).
C E R Sherrington, 'Notes on the History of the Great Central Railway', *RM* vol 77 (1935), 313-20.
S Sidney, *Rides on Railways* (London: Orr, 1851; ed B Trinder, Chichester: Phillimore, 1973).
J Simmons, *The Railway in England and Wales 1830-1914: Vol I, The System and its Working* (Newton Abbot: David & Charles, 1978).
The Railway in Town and Country 1830-1914 (Newton Abbot: David & Charles, 1986).
The Express Train and other Railway Studies (Nairn: David St John Thomas, 1994).
The Victorian Railway (pb edn, London: Thames & Hudson, 1995).
B Simpson, *The Banbury to Verney Junction Branch* (Oxford: Oxford Publishing Co, 1978).
Oxford to Cambridge Railway, vol 1, Oxford to Bletchley (Oxford: Oxford Publishing Co, 1981).
'The Banbury Branch (LNWR)', *BT*, vol 1 (1987), 106-13.
'Banbury: All Changes', *BT*, vol 4 (1992), 173-79.
A History of the Railways of Oxfordshire, part I, The North, Banbury and Witney (Witney: Lamplight, 1997).
J N Slinn & B K Clarke, *Great Western Railway Siphons: An account of vehicles built for milk traffic on the GWR* (Penryn: Atlantic, 1986).
D J Smith, 'Water Troughs on the GWR', *GWRJ* No 48 (2003), 422-39.
M Smith, 'Avoiding Banbury … and Acton', *BRI* vol 6 (1997), 312-23.
M Stacey, *Tradition and Change: a Study of Banbury* (Oxford University Press, 1960).
M Stratton & B Trinder, *Twentieth Century Industrial Archaeology* (London: Spon, 2000).
J Stretton, *British Railways Past and Present: Oxfordshire: A second selection* (Great Addington: Past & Present Publishing, 2006).
L A Summers, ed, *The Didcot Guide* (Didcot: Great Western Society, 2016).

A J P Taylor, *English History 1914-45* (Oxford: Clarendon Press, 1965).
A M Taylor, *Gilletts: Bankers at Banbury and Oxford* (Oxford: Clarendon Press, 1964).
D St J Thomas & S Rocksborough Smith, *Summer Saturdays in the West* (3rd edn, Newton Abbot: David & Charles, 1983).
D St J Thomas & P Whitehouse, *BR in the Eighties* (Newton Abbot: David & Charles, 1990).
R E Threlfall, *The Story of 100 years of Phosphorus Making* (Oldbury: Albright & Wilson, 1951).
K Tiller & G Darkes, eds, *An Historical Atlas of Oxfordshire* (Oxfordshire Record Society, 2010).
R Tolley, *Steaming Spires: Experiences of an Oxford engineman* (Newton Abbot: David & Charles, 1987).
E Tonks, *The Ironstone Quarries of the Midlands, History Operations and Railways, Part 2, The Oxfordshire Field* (Cheltenham: Runpast, 1988).
S Townsend & J Gibson, *Banbury Past through Artists' Eyes* (Banbury Historical Society, vol 30, 2007).
N Trevenna, *Steam for Scrap: the complete story* (ed A Earnshaw, Penryn: Atlantic Transport Publishers, 1992).
B Trinder, 'Joseph Parker, Sabbatarianism and the Parson's Street Infidels', *C&CH*, vol 1 (1960), 25-30.
ed, *A Victorian MP and his Constituents: the Correspondence of H W Tancred 1841-1850* (Banbury Historical Society, vol 8, 1969).
'The Railway Marshalling Yard at Banbury', *C&CH* vol 4 (1970), 131-36.

B Trinder *ctd*, 'The Changing Seventies: Review of a Decade', *Shropshire Railway Society Newsletter*, 117 (March 1980).
   'Fifty years on – Banbury in 1931'*, C&CH* vol 8 (1981), 117-37.
   Victorian Banbury (Banbury Historical Society, vol 19; Chichester: Phillimore, 1982, pb edn 2005).
   ed, *The Blackwell Encyclopedia of Industrial Archaeology* (Oxford: Blackwell, 1992).
   'Banbury Memoirs of the Nineteenth and Twentieth Centuries', *C&CH* vol 15 (2003), 286-303.
   'Banbury's Victorian Lodging Houses'*, C&CH* vol 16 (2004), 138-57.
   'Centenary Reflections on the Bicester Cut-Off'*, C&CH* vol 18 (2010), 103-23.
   'Banbury: Metropolis of Carriers' Carts', *C&CH* vol 18 (2011), 210-43.
   Britain's Industrial Revolution: the Making of a Manufacturing People (Lancaster: Carnegie, 2013).
   ed, *Victorian Banburyshire: Three Memoirs, Sarah Beesley, Thomas Ward Boss, Thomas Butler Gunn* (Banbury Historical Society, vol 33, 2013).
   'Navvies in Banburyshire', *C&CH* vol 19 (2013), 34-52.
   The Industrial Archaeology of Shropshire (2nd edn, Logaston: Logaston Press, 2016).
C Turner, 'Banbury Merton Street', *BRJ*, No 70 (2001), 178-207.
   'Banbury Station Pilot', *GWRJ,* No 43 (2002), 122-37.
S J Tyrrell, *A Countryman's Tale* (London: Constable, 1973).

M A Vanns, *Rail Centres: Nottingham* (Shepperton: Ian Allan, 1993).
A Vaughan, 'Water Troughs on the GWR', *Railway World* vol 51 (1990), 278-80, 370-74.
   The Great Western at Work 1921-1939 (Sparkford: Patrick Stephens, 1993).
   The Heart of the Great Western (Wadenhoe, Silver Link, 1994).
   The Great Western's Last Year: Efficiency in Adversity (Stroud: The History Press, 2013).
Victoria History of the County of Oxford, vol XI, Bloxham Hundred (Oxford University Press, 1969).
Victoria History of the County of Oxford, vol X, Banbury Hundred (Oxford University Press, 1972).

A J Wallis-Taylor, *Aerial or Wire Rope Tramways: their construction and management* (London: Crosby Lockwood, 1898).
L Waters, *Last years of Steam: Paddington – Wolverhampton* (Shepperton: Ian Allan, 1988).
   Oxfordshire Railways in Old Photographs (Gloucester: Sutton, 1989).
   'Steam days at Banbury', *SD* (1998).
   Great Western Manor Class (Locomotive Portfolios) (Barnsley: Pen & Sword, 2016).
   & T Doyle, *British Railways Past and Present: Oxfordshire* (Wadenhoe: Past & Present Publishing, 1994).
H C Webster, *British Railway Rolling Stock* (Oxford University Press, nd c 1946).
S Wenham, *Pleasure Boating on the Thames: A History of Salter Bros* (Stroud: The History Press, 2014).
C Whitehall, *The Buckinghamshire Railway* (1849, rep Charleston, North Carolina: Nabu, 2011).
J S Whiteley & G W Morrison, *The Great Western Remembered* (Poole: Oxford Publishing Co, 1985).
A Williams, *Brunel and After: the romance of the Great Western Railway* (London: Great Western Railway, 1925).
M Williams, *Steaming to Victory: How Britain's Railways won the war* (London: Preface, 2013).
A Wilson, 'The GWR's RODs', *SD* No 311, July 2015, 21-32.
R Woodley, *The Day of the Holiday Express* (Shepperton: Ian Allan, 1996).
L Woolley, 'How the Railway changed Oxford', *Oxfordshire Local History*, vol 9 (2013-14), 18-43.

W B Yeadon, *London & North Eastern Railway Locomotive Allocations 1st January 1923* (Oldham: Challenger, 1996).
   Yeadon's Register of LNER Locomotives, vol 22, Class B1 (B18) to B9, The GC 4-6-0s (Nottingham: Booklaw/Railbus, 2001).
A Young, *General View of the Agriculture of Oxfordshire* (London: Sherwood, Neely & Jones, 1813).

Note

I am grateful to Tony Foster for enabling me to use a collection of cyclostyled publications from the mid-1940s. They are as follows

BLR. *British Locomotive Record*, published from Birmingham, vol 3 in May 1945; from August 1945 re-named *Railway Locomotives*.
FD. *Flying Dutchman* published by SBLC (South Birmingham Locomotive Club).
IRB. *The Iron Road* (Birmingham) published by Birmingham Railway Club. Last issue No 10, Apl 1945.
LE. *The Locomotive Enthusiast*. Published by Midland Locomotive Society. Vol 1 No 2, Aug 1944. January 1945 is numbered No 19, Vol 2.
RL. *Railway Locomotives*, from Aug 1945.
RR. *Railway Record* published by Three Spires Locomotive Club, Coventry. Vol 1, No 8. Jan 1945.
WRL. *West Riding Limited*, published by the West Riding Railway Society. Vol 2 No 22, Oct 1944.

Films

Banbury Museum: *Banbury's Explosive Role in the First World War: National Filling Factory No 9* (2015).
British Transport Films, *Lets go to Birmingham* (1962).
LMSR, *Carrying the Load* (1941).
Southern Railway, *War on the Line* (1946).
British Universities Film & Video Council, *Twenty Four Square Miles* (1944).
Wolverton Rail, Locomaster Profiles: *Banbury Boxes*.

Junctions at Banbury

Index

The dates of birth and death of individuals are shown where they are known.
Peers of the realm are indexed by family names with cross-references to titles.
The names of towns and villages in the British Isles are followed by their ancient (*i.e.* pre-1974) counties.

A

Aberdare, Glam, 51, 117
Aberdeen, 102, 108-09, 152, 155, 226
Aberystwyth, Cards, 68, 151, 167
Abingdon, Berks, 18, 179
Abthorpe, Northants, 47
Adderbury, Oxon, 37-38, 40-41, 60, 109, 126, 153, 187, 190-91, 199-201
Aird & Son, contractors, 47
Aird, John (1806-76), civil engineer 47-48
Aird, Sir John (1833-1911), civil engineer 47
Akeman Street station, Bucks, 148
Alcester, Warks, 91
Aldershot, Hants, 82, 90, 112, 124, 130
Alkerton, Oxon, 189, 208
Allan, Ian (1922-1915), railway publisher 1, 194
Allen, Cecil J (1886-1973), railway journalist 108
Allied Cement Manufacturers (Red Circle), 121
Andoversford, Gloucs, 40
Angel, John, (b 1825), quarry manager 199
Anglo-Swiss Condensed Milk Co, 28-29
Annesley, Notts, 74, 76, 125, 156, 168-69, 173, 180
Ardley, Oxon, 54, 68, 71, 178, 189-90, 220
Arkell, William, navvy 47
Ascot, Berks, 112, 114, 160
Ashchurch, Gloucs, 34
Ashendon, Bucks, 68, 148
Ash Junction, Surrey, 112
Ashford, Kent, 4, 106, 129-30, 166, 168
Ashridge, Herts, 58
Associated Portland Cement Manufacturers (Blue Circle), 121
Atherstone, Warks, 26, 55
Attlee, Clement, first Earl (1883-1967), prime minister 138
Australia, Australian people, 47, 54, 92

Automatic train control, 98
Auto-trains, 67, 70, 78, 101, 110, 127-28, 131, 153-54, 178
Avebury, Wilts, 45
Avonmouth, Som, 35, 92-93, 189
Avonside Engineering Co, locomotive builders 96
Aylesbury, Bucks, 9, 10, 50, 74, 77, 82, 181, 223, 228
Aynho, Northants, 13-14, 59, 65, 68, 70-71, 114, 135, 167, 179, 183, 187, 220, 222, 228

B

Bacon's House siding, Finmere, Oxon, 29
Baddesley Ensor, Warks, 55
Badminton, Gloucs, 42, 66
Bagnall, W G & Co, locomotive builders 144
Baker, Henry W, farmer and quarry master 204
Baker Street station, London, 28
Baldwin, Alfred (1841-1908), ironmaster 199
Baldwin, E, P & W, ironmasters 199, 205, 210
Baldwin, Stanley (1867-1947), ironmaster & politician 199
Balmoral, Aberdeenshire, 22
Balscott, Oxon, 208
Banbury:
  Aluminium factory, 4, 53, 120, 126
  Banbury Spencer Football Club, 191-92
  Banks, 31, 43
  Barrows & Stewart, mechanical engineers 57
  Bell Inn, 53
  Blacklocks' Arms, 131
  'Blockade', in July 2016, 228-231, 238
  Bombing raid, 1940, 124-25
  Boy Scouts, 92-93
  Brewing, 54, 57
  Bridge Street, 28, 52, 54
  Britannia, 51
  Britannia Works, 54, 56-58, 71, 95, 120
  Broad Street, 160

Banbury *continued*
 Bus services, 109, 127, 155
 Canal, 3, 8-9, 55
 Canal Street, 109
 Cattle trade, 63, 214-15, 218, 225
 Causeway, 53
 Cave & Son, railway agents 54
 Cheney & Son, printers & publishers 28
 Cherwell streets, 24, 50, 52-53, 55
 Coal supply, 3, 8, 22, 26, 55, 61, 214
 Congregational chapel, 56
 Conservative Club/Party, 56-57
 Co-operative Society, 56, 207
 Country carriers, 7-8, 53-54, 76
 Crouch Street, 92
 Davies, J & T, builders 54
 Duke Street, 53
 Early Closers' Association, 91
 East Street, 135
 Elephant and Castle, 53
 Elim church, 72
 Engineering industry, 3, 7, 9, 95
 Engine sheds, 6, 24-25, 53, 63, 65, 72-73, 94-96, 125, 233-38, 140, 143,153, 178, 183-186, 188-89, 196, 213,215, 217, 225
 Filling Factory No 9, 95-96
 Fish Street, 52, 71
 Flooding, 238
 Flying Horse, 8
 Food storage depot, 127
 Freehold Land Society, 26, 52
 Friendly Societies, 56
 Frost, Bernard T, & Co, coal merchants 160
 Gas works, 25, 28, 63, 71, 125, 188
 Gibbs Road, 53
 Gillett, Tawney & Gillett, bankers 25
 Goods depots & freight traffic, 28, 63, 119-20, 124-25, 191, 213-14
 Grammar School, 160
 Great Western (Bridge Street, General) station, vi, 4, 25, 63, 99,125, 137-39, 155, 172-73, 176-77, 204, 213, 218, 224-25, 229-231
 Grimsbury, 52, 113, 117, 119, 125, 222
 Hardwick, 44
 Henneff Way, 222
 High Street, 54
 Hightown Road, 91

Banbury *continued*
 Horsefair, 92
 Horton Hospital, 92
 Howard Road, 135
 Hunt Edmunds, brewers 54
 Jolly Waterman, 51
 Labour Party, 53, 138
 Liberal Party, 25,
 Lime Avenue, 138
 Lodging Houses, 43, 50,
 Market, 7-9, 32, 34, 41, 61, 71-72, 104, 117, 120, 155
 Marshalling yards, 64, 72, 88, 117-18, 125, 132-35, 137-38, 146, 157-58, 191, 196, 213, 215, 218
 Mechanics' Institute, 56-58
 Merton Street, 51, 53, 72
 Merton Street station, vi, 22, 25-30, 33, 53, 56, 60, 93, 96, 103-05, 113, 120, 124, 127, 138, 148, 153-56, 158-60, 177-78, 188, 194, 196, 208, 210-11, 213, 222, 239
 Michaelmas Fair, 53
 Middleton Road, 26, 53, 131, 135, 138, 215
 Midland Marts Ltd, auctioneers 104
 Midlands Tar Distillers, 71
 Oil companies, 71, 214
 Old George, 51
 Oxford Road, 43
 Palmer & Sons, coal merchants 160
 Parsons Street, 153
 Pilot engines, 164, 176, 185, 192, 215-16
 Pinhill, 207
 Plush manufacture, 9
 Race meetings, 43
 Rag Row, 43
 Railwaymen, 4, 50-54, 72, 117, 196
 Railway Mission, 53, 72-73, 228
 Red Cross, 91-92
 Red Lion, 9, 54, 119
 Road stone depot, 218, 222, 225, 237-38
 Robinson Bros, tar distillers 71
 Rusher's Lists, 8
 St John Ambulance Brigade, 53, 91
 Salvation Army, 72
 Shops, 3, 54, 119
 Siding connecting GWR with LNWR, 22, 63, 71, 187

Index

Banbury *continued*
  Signal boxes, signalling, 6, 77, 135-36, 206, 213, 222, 229-39, 232, 235
  Southam Road, 120, 206
  South Bar, 56
  Spital Farm, 44
  Stage coaches, 7-10
  Sunday schools, 57
  'Target' workings, 91, 142
  Temperance Society, 56
  Town Hall, 43
  Trades Unions, 53, 177
  Tramway Road, 228
  Truss, W A, fish merchant 155
  Waggon services, 8, 10
  Warwick Road, 43
  Waterloo, 43
  Welford, William & Sons, coal merchants 160
  Wesleyan churches/circuit, 77, 92-93, 131
  West Street, 51, 92-93, 119, 131
  Wheatsheaf,
  White Lion, 8, 54
  Windsor Street, 52, 71
  Woolworth, F W, 3, 119, 155
  Wykham Park, 231
  Wymans, newsagents, 99
Barby, Northants, 131
Barford St John, Oxon, 131
Barmouth, Merion, 143, 166
Barmouth Junction station, 167
Barnsley, Yorks, 80
Barry, Glam, 42, 87, 189
Baschurch, Shrop, 114
Basel, Switzerland, 136
Basingstoke, Hants, 18-19, 24, 50, 57, 66, 69, 71-72, 84, 90, 92, 94, 107, 116, 132, 147, 164, 190-91
Bath, Som, 45, 69, 82, 152, 185
Bathgate, West Lothian, 190-91, 217
Battle, Sussex, 68
Bedfordshire: *see* Bedford, Leighton Buzzard, Luton, Oakley Junction, Sandy
Bedford, 34, 79, 93
Bedlington, Northum, 11
Beeching, Richard, Baron (1913-85), manager 177-79, 217
Beer, Mrs, railway guard 135

Behrend, George (1922-2010), writer on railways 74, 123-24, 136-37
Beighton, Yorks, 74
Balper, Derbys, 43
Bennerley, Notts, 55
Bennie, Peter, & Co Ltd, quarry operators 189, 209
Berkshire: *see* Abingdon, Ascot, Didcot, Maidenhead, Milton, Newbury, Radley, Reading, Steventon, Taplow, Wallingford, Windsor
Berkswell, Warks, 187
Berlin, 49, 68
Berry Brow, Yorks, 181
Bescot yard, Staffs, 187
Betchworth, Surrey, 89
Betjeman, John (1906-84) poet
Bicester, Oxon, 7, 27, 53, 68, 71, 104, 109, 120, 130, 147, 151, 184, 195, 224-25, 228-229
Bidford-on-Avon, Warks, 36
Bilston, Staffs, 51, 189, 198, 200-01, 209-10
Binley, Warks, 55
Birch Coppice, Warks, 238
Birkenhead, Ches, 24, 62, 66, 68-69, 85-86, 99, 106, 116, 127, 132, 143, 149-50, 152-53, 160, 164-68, 185-87, 190-91, 199, 224, 233-34, 238
Birmingham: *See stations:* International, Moor Street, New Street, Snow Hill, Bordesley Junction, Bromford, Bridge, Duddeston Viaduct, Saltley, Tyseley, Washwood Heath *et passim*
Birmingham & Midland Motor Omnibus Co, 109, 155
Birmingham International Station, 220, 226
Birmingham New Street Station, 41, 152, 182, 185-87, 193-94, 219-29, 224-25, 233, 235
Birmingham Moor Street Station, 164-66, 168-169, 187, 218, 224, 229
Birmingham Railway Carriage & Wagon Co, 148 199
Birmingham Snow Hill Station, 64, 86, 106-107, 113, 147, 13-0560, 163, 165-77, 169, 182-83, 185-87, 194, 224, 229, 234
Birtley, Co Durham, 130
Bishop's Itchington, Warks, 45
Blackburn, Lancs, 192

252　　　　　　　　　　　　　　　*Index*

Black Country, 25, 32, 51, 132, 197-98, 201, 205
Blackpool, Lancs, 23, 57, 167, 234
Blackthorn, Bucks, 71 131, 154
Blenheim & Woodstock station, Oxon, 39, 84
Bletchington, Oxon, 70, 121, 179, 181,191
Bletchley, Bucks, 4, 9, 12, 19, 24-29, 93, 103-05, 126, 131, 155-56, 158-60, 178, 193-94, 229, 239
Blisworth, Northants, 8, 11, 33, 35, 41, 57, 127, 154, 197
Blockley, Gloucs, 32, 37
Bloxham, Oxon, 41, 58, 60, 131, 135, 201-02
Boat Race, Oxford & Cambridge, 57
Bodicote, Oxon, 80
Bodley, Edward, shopkeeper & country carrier 48
Bonavia, Michael Robert (1909-99), railway manager 182
Bordesley Junction, Warks, 16, 22.90, 118, 121, 130, 186-87, 217, 133, 238
Boston, Lincs, 86
Boulogne, France, 57
Bourne End, Bucks, 67, 160
Bournemouth, Hants, 69, 84-86, 91, 106-07, 112, 135, 143, 145, 147, 151-53, 160-61, 163-70, 172-73, 179-81, 185, 220, 226, 234-235
Bourton, Great & Little, Oxon, 45-47, 60
Bourton-on-the-Water, Gloucs, 37-38
Brackley, Northants, 7, 25, 28, 31, 53, 74, 76, 104, 109, 155, 158, 16, 187, 239
Bradden, Northants, 47
Bradford, Yorks, 76, 84-85, 107, 147, 152, 167, 169
Bramley, Hants, 94, 131
Braunston, Northants, 8
Brazier, Richard, coal merchant, 55
Brentford, Middsx, 51, 120
Brighton, Sussex, 57, 69, 104, 112, 155, 165-166, 168-69, 219, 226, 234-35
Brill, Bucks, 71, 131-32, 154
Bristol, 11, 18, 21, 34, 45, 50-51, 65-67, 72, 84 86-87, 89, 96, 107, 132, 152, 157-58, 190-191, 215, 228, 237
British Leyland, vehicle manufacturers 217
Brixworth, Northants, 202
Broadstairs, Kent, 49
Bromford Bridge, Warks, 187,

Bromsgrove, Worcs, 187
Broom Junction, Warks, 33, 35, 125, 158 190-191
Brora, Sutherland, 201
Brown, Henry, stationmaster 60
Brown, H R, stationmaster 54
Brunel, Isambard Kingdom (1806-59), engineer 11, 15, 21, 84, 86-87
Brymbo Steel Co, 41, 96, 198, 202-03, 205, 209-11
Buckinghamshire: *passim*
Bulleid, Oliver Vaughan Snell (1882-1970), locomotive engineer 170
Bunton, William (1823-93), news agent 57
Burford, Oxon, 109
Burke, James B, civil engineer 49
Burkhardt, Ed, railway manager 136
Burnham, Bucks, 50
Burton Dassett, Warks, 45, 49, 131, 187, 190-191, 204-05, 237
Burton-on-Trent, Staffs, 187, 235
Bushbury, Staffs, 22
Butlers Marston, Warks, 49
Butlin's holiday camps, 116
Butlin, Thomas, ironmaster 197
Byfield, Northants, 34, 80, 124, 208

C
Calais, France, 5, 7, 236
Calne, Wilts, 114
Calvert, Bucks, 125, 189, 193
Cambridgeshire: *see* Cambridge, Whitemoor
Cambridge, 27, 93, 105, 125, 155
Canada, Canadians, 120, 237;
　　and see Ontario: Hamilton;
　　Quebec: Montreal.
Canterbury, 50, 57, 106, 166, 168
Cardiff, Glam, 82, 87, 132, 136, 147, 175, 226
Carlisle, Cumb, 93, 180, 191
Cartwright, Sir Thomas (1795-1850), diplomat 59
Cartwright, William, landowner 59
Catesby tunnel, Northants, 76
Catterick, Yorks, 168
Census, vi, 4, 45-51, 79
Central Electricity Generating Board, 216
Chacombe, Northants, 27, 74, 78, 111, 154
Channel Islands, 5, 72, 106-07
Channel Tunnel, 74, 227, 236

Chapman, Edward (1839-1906), scientist, railway director, politician 77
Charlbury, Oxon, 15
Charlton Kings, Gloucs, 210
Charwelton, Northants, 65, 79, 84, 125, 208
Cheddington, Bucks, 9
Chelmsford, Essex, 45
Cheltenham, Gloucs, 9, 37-38, 40-42, 66, 28, 87, 152, 194
Chepstow, Mon, 87
Cherrington, Warks, 54
Cherwell, River, 33, 43, 62, 99
Cherwell Rail Users Group, 221-22
Cheshire: *see* Birkenhead, Chester, Crewe, Ince & Elton, Middlewich, Nantwich, Rock Ferry, Stockport, Widnes
Chester, 19, 23, 47, 57, 68, 106, 140, 151, 165, 168, 187, 191, 198, 234
Chesterfield, Derbys, 81, 198
Chichester, Sussex, 146
Chippenham, Wilts, 46m 108, 114
Chipping Campden, Gloucs, 15, 32
Chipping Norton, Oxon, 7, 18, 32, 36-38, 40-42, 53, 55, 87, 109, 111,124, 131, 200, 202
Chipping Norton Junction station, *see* Kingham
Chipping Warden, Northants, 131
Chorley, Lancs, 130
Churchill, Sir Winston (1874-1965), statesman 137
Cirencester, Gloucs, 81
Clapham Junction station, 226
Clarke, Bernard K, railway historian 1-2
Clarke, Seymour, railway shareholder 42
Clay Cross Co, ironmasters 198, 202
Claydon, Oxon, 8, 45-47, 49, 60
Claydon House, Bucks, 27
Cleethorpes, Lincs, 81
Coaching stock: See also: Auto-trains, Diesel multiple units, Diesel railcars, Pullman cars, Railmotors, Restaurant cars, Sleeping cars, Slip coaches, Tavern cars
'Barnum', 169
'Birdcage', 170
Corridor coaches, 66
Four-wheelers, 62
Mark I, 149, 177, 184
Mark II, 184, 225-26
Mark III, 232-34
Saloon, 170

Coalbrookdale, Shrop, 198
Coatbridge, North Lanark, 198, 217
Cobb, Edward, solicitor & banker 43
Cobb, Timothy Rhodes, banker 25
Cochrane & Co, ironmasters 201
Cockley Brake junction, Northants, 25, 33, 47, 60, 93
Cohen & Co, scrap merchants 96
Colchester, Essex, 25, 33, 47, 60, 93
Collingridge, John, coal merchant & publican 59
Colwick, Notts, 129, 146
Compton Verney, Warks, 36
Copperworks Junction, Glam, 132
Corby, Northants, 160, 198, 210-11
Cornwall: 5, 51, 178, 199; *see also* Helston, Padstow, Penzance, St Blazey
Cosford, Shrop, 128
Cossons, Sir Neil, museum director 1
Coventry, Warks, 7, 10, 55,107, 123, 179, 187, 191, 217, 220, 226, 233, 239
Crabtree, Joseph, railway manager 47
Crampton, John George, civil engineer 49
Crampton, Thomas Hellas, civil engineer 49
Crampton, Thomas Russell (1816-88), engineer 49
Craven Arms, Shrop, 161
Crewe, Ches, 4, 5, 23, 69, 72, 93, 132, 146-47, 181, 185, 188, 191, 194
Croes Newydd, Denbs, 140, 189, 198, 211
Cromer, Norf, 152
Cropredy, Oxon, 45-46, 49, 6, 70, 95, 121, 127, 154, 183, 209, 211
Cross country services, 66-67, 85-86, 105-09, 129-37, 151-53, 234-35
Croughton, Northants, 131
Croydon Airport, Surrey, 113
Crystal Palace, Sydenham, 47, 56-57
Cudworth, Yorks, 89
Culworth, Northants, 74, 78, 182
Cumberland: *see* Carlisle

D
Daffurn, W H, goods agent 138
Daniel, Charles Eckersley, railway contractor 38
Darby, Charles E (1822-84), ironmaster 198
Darby, William H (1819-82), ironmaster 198
Darlington, Co Durham, 144

Dartford, Kent, 191
Dassett Hills, 204-05
Daventry, Northants, 7
Daw Mill mine, Warks, 215
Dawson, George (1821-76), lecturer 58
Day, Freda, philanthropist 91
Deal, Kent, 54, 69, 86, 106, 166
Dean & Dawson, travel agents 81
Death, William, railway contractor 49
Death, William Price, station master 49
Denby Dale viaduct, Yorks, 181
Denham, Bucks, 65
Derbyshire: see Chesterfield, Clay Cross, Derby, Ilkeston, Renishaw Park, Staveley
Derby, 11-12, 220-21, 237
Devon: see Exeter, Ilfracombe, Kingswear, Newton Abbot, Paignton, Plymouth, Tavistock Junction
Didcot, Berks, 10, 12-13, 18, 20-21, 40, 42, 62, 64-66, 70, 72, 86-87, 91, 94, 106-07, 113, 125, 132, 134-35, 137, 139, 152, 163-64, 189-91, 194, 211, 215-17, 219, 137, 239
Diesel locomotives, 145, 147-48, 160, 164, 170, 180-85, 187, 208, 214, 217, 220-21, 226, 228, 236-38
Diesel multiple units, 177-78, 180-81, 187, 220, 222-23, 225, 232
Diesel railcars, 107, 111, 155, 163, 178
Dockray, Robert Benson (1811-71), civil engineer 24, 26, 43
Doncaster, Yorks, 113, 116, 162, 215
Donnington, Shrop, 131
Dorchester, Dorset, 57
Dorrington, Shrop, 115-16, 146
Dorset: see Dorchester, Gillingham, Poole, Weymouth
Dorton, Bucks, 109
Dover, Kent, 49, 57, 68-69, 82, 86, 91, 106, 166, 226
Dowdeswell, Gloucs, 38
Drayton, John (b 1907), engine driver 2, 98, 116-17, 120
Drayton Bassett, Staffs, 26
Drinkwater, John (1798-1878), stage coach operator and publican 8, 54
Droitwich, Worcs, 15
Duddeston Viaduct, 16-17
Dudley, Worcs, 15, 20, 217
Duffield Iron Corporation, 201

Dunkirk, France, 122, 131
Dunn, J M, shedmaster & railway historian 1
Dunstable, Beds, 127
Co Durham: see Birtley, Darlington, Durham, Haverton Hill, Low Fell, Sunderland, Tyne Yard
Durham, 24, 49-50, 60, 88,113, 153

E
Ealing, Ealing Broadway station, Middsx, 50, 124, 139, 226
Eastbourne, Sussex, 69, 106, 165-66, 169, 174, 115
East Leake, Notts, 121, 189-90
Eastleigh, Hants, 69, 146-47, 187, 190-191, 194, 217
Easton Neston, Northants, 34, 57
Ebbw Vale, Mon, 105, 198
Edgehill, Warks, 95, 205
Edinburgh, 109, 113, 215, 226, 134
Edmunds, Richard, ironmonger & mayor of Banbury 32
Edwinstowe, Notts, 143
Elizabeth (1900-2002), Queen, Queen Mother 158
Elliott, John, engine driver, 49
Elton, Sir Arthur (1906-73), film director 213
English Electric, locomotive builders, 164, 215
Epsom, Surrey, 38, 57
Erewash, River, 197
Essex: see Chelmsford, Colchester, Harwich, Thaxted, Tilbury, Waltham Abbey
Euston station, London, 16, 19, 24, 27, 41, 204, 131, 183, 186-87, 193, 224
Evacuees, 124
Evesham, Worcs, 15, 32, 88
Exeter, Devon, 82, 190
Express Dairies, 115
Eydon, Northants, 74-76, 78, 80,
Eydon Road halt, 111, 154

F
Farnborough, Hants, 164, 194
Farnborough, Warks, 45-46
Farndon, Northants, 76
Farthinghoe, Northants, 25, 29, 60
Fawley, Hants, 187, 190-91, 217
Fay, Sir Sam (1856-1953), railway manager 81, 84, 87, 108, 129

Felixstowe, Suffolk, 217
Felling, Co Durham, 49
Feltham, Middsx, 125
Fenny Compton, Warks, 12, 17, 21, 33, 45-47, 49-50, 70, 132, 158, 179, 187, 196, 204, 211
Festival of Britain 1951, 140
Fields, Dame Gracie (1898-1939), singer 104, 113
Finmere, Oxon, 29, 31
Fisher, John, navvy 50
Fitzgerald, John, navvy 47,
Flynn, Thomas, clerk 47
Folkestone, Kent, 69, 82, 106, 226
Ford Motor Co, 188, 217
Forest of Dean, 197, 199
Foster's Express, railway agents, 54
Fowler, Sir Henry (1870-1938), locomotive engineer 105
France, French people, 57-58, 68, 91, 97; *and see* Boulogne, Calais, Dunkirk, Le Havre, Lille, Mauberge, Mulhouse, Paris
French, Sir John (1852-1925), army officer 95
Friswell, James & Son, scrap merchants 186, 188, 201, 204-05
Fritwell & Somerton station, 70, 114, 139, 179
Frome, Som, 58
Fulwell & Westbury station, Bucks, 29

G
Gallipoli, Turkey, 92
Galton Bridge station, Staffs, 229
Gardner, James (d 1846), mechanical engineer 9
Garston, Lancs, 189
Gas turbine locomotives, 148
Gatwick Airport station, 226, 234-35
Gauge questions, 10-25, 57, 62, 66, 90
Gaydon, Warks, 49, 131
George V (1865-1936), King 5, 81, 98
George VI (1895-1952), King 158
General Motors, 236-38
Gerhold, Dorian, historian 8
Germany, German people, 68, 90, 123-24, 137, 201, 206; *and see* Berlin, Hamburg
Gerrard's Cross, Bucks, 232
Gillingham, Dorset, 217
GKN (Guest, Keen & Nettlefold), steel makers 198

Gladstone, William Ewart (1809-98), politician, 11
Glasgow, 28, 33, 105, 107, 134, 159, 226, 234
Gloucestershire: *see* Andoversford, Badminton, Blockley, Bourton-on-the-Water, Charlton Kings, Cheltenham, Chipping Campden, Dowdeswell, Forest of Dean, Gloucester, Hatherley, Leckhampton, Moreton-in-Marsh, Patchway, Wotton-under-Edge
Gloucester, 16, 32, 40, 42, 87, 93, 125, 152, 163, 185, 200
Godley Junction, Ches 112
Golby, Thomas, railway parcels agent 54
Gooch, Sir Daniel (1816-89), engineer 13, 23
Goring, Oxon, 65
Grantham, Lncs, 112
Great Exhibition 1851, 13, 32, 56, 197
Great Milton, Oxon, 222
Great Western Society, 20, 194, 220-21
Greatworth, Northants, 47-48, 131
Great Yarmouth, Norfolk, 152, 163
Greaves, Bull & Lakin, cement manufacturers 121, 189-91
Green, Chris, railway manager 233
Greenford, Middsx, 156, 193-94
Green's Norton, Northants, 33, 35, 47, 93
Greenwich, Kent, 47
Grendon Underwood, Bucks, 67, 148
Gresley, Sir Nigel (1876-1941), locomotive engineer 102-03, 107, 158, 162
Griffiths, Samuel (d 1881), writer on iron 197
Grigg, A E (Sam), engine driver & writer, 1, 2, 105
Grimsby, Lincs, 80, 88-89, 116, 140, 158, 161, 189
Guildford, Surrey, 20, 106, 124-25, 236
Gunn, Thomas Butler (1826-1904), artist & journalist 27
GUS (Great Universal Stores), mail order retailers 155

H
Haddenham, Bucks, 67, 71
Haddenham & Thame Parkway station, 222-23
Halifax, Yorks, 86
Hambridge, George, engine driver 139
Hamburg, Germany, 68
Hamilton, Ontario, 24

Hampshire: *see* Aldershot, Basingstoke, Bournemouth, Bramley, Eastleigh, Fawley, Gatwick Airport station, Lymington, Pokesdown, Southampton, Winchester, Isle of Wight
Hams Hall, Warks, 238
Harbury, Warks, 3, 21, 44-47, 189, 232
Hardy, Richard, railway manager 80, 182
Harris, C & T, bacon & sausage producers 114
Harris, George, stationmaster 51
Hartlebury, Worcs, 60
Hartshill, Warks, 8, 2
Harwich, Essex, 92-93
Hastings, Sussex, 68-69, 106, 158, 165-66, 168-69, 185
Hatfield, Herts, 227, 230
Hatherley, Gloucs, 42, 200
Hatton, Warks, 18, 88, 127, 132, 189, 210-11
Haverton Hill, Co Durham, 218
Hawkesbury, Warks, 8
Hawksmoor, Nicholas (1661-1736), architect 57
Hawksworth, Frederick William (1884-1976), locomotive engineer 143
Haydn, Franz Joseph (1732-1809), composer 57
Heathrow Airport, 165
Helmdon, Northants, 33, 36, 45, 47-48, 57, 75, 133, 154
Helston, Cornwall, 114
Hemmings, William, railway historian 1, 37
Henley-in-Arden, Warks, 91
Henley-on-Thames, Oxon, 18, 160
Hereford, 37, 116, 163, 229
Hermon, Edward S (b 1851), stationmaster 58
Hertfordshire: *see* Ashridge, Tring
Heyford, Oxon, 70, 111, 113, 131, 139, 178, 224, 236
Hickman, Sir Alfred (1830-1910), ironmaster 198
Hickman, Alfred & Sons, ironmasters 198-201, 206
High Speed Trains (HSTs), 221, 226, 234
High Wycombe, Bucks, 18, 67, 98, 134, 187, 223-24
Hinton, Northants, 76
Hodgson, Charles, inventor 204
Hollings, J S, ironworks director 205
Holyhead Road, 7

Honeybourne, Worcs, 18, 66, 93, 108, 196
Hook Norton, Oxon, 37-39, 41, 55, 60, 80, 95, 108-10, 119, 127, 132, 191, 197 200, 202-204, 210, 239
Hopcraft & Norris, brewers 28
Horn, John (b 1822), railway agent 60
Hornton, Oxon, 208
Horse racing, 43, 112-14, 160
Houlston, John (1810-75), excursion agent 56
Howe, Richard, publican & coal merchant 59
Huddersfield, Yorks, 86, 181
Hudswell Clarke, locomotive builders 96, 207
Hull, Yorks, 87, 89, 113, 116, 146-47, 158, 189
Hunslet Engine Co, locomotive builders 76, 208
Hunter, Sir John, civil servant 205
Huntley & Palmer, biscuit manufacturers 113

I
ICI (Imperial Chemical Industries), 178, 217
Ilfracombe, Devon, 86, 107
Ilkeston, Derbys, 211
Ilmer, Bucks, 109, 122
Immingham, Lincs, 81, 93, 146, 158, 161, 237
Ince & Elton, Ches, 217
Independent Milk Supplies, 115
Invergordon, Ross & Cromarty, 93
Ireland, Irish people, 11, 43, 47, 49-50; *and see* Belfast, Dublin
Irthlingborough, Northants, 105
Isle of Man, 101
Isle of Wight, 57-58, 85, 164, 169
Islip, Northants, 201
Islip, Oxon, 229
Italy, Italians, 91-92, 95, 137, 208, 236
Ivatt, Henry George (1886-1976), locomotive engineer 145, 158

J
Jakeman, Edward (1808-83), stationmaster 26
Johnson, Samuel Waite (1831-1912), locomotive engineer 105
Jones, Hugh, railway historian xi, 6, 224, 227
Jones, Kenneth (1921-2012), fireman & historian 135

K

Kenilworth, Warks, 187, 220
Kennington, Oxon, 18, 110, 125
Kensal Green, Middsx, 158
Kensington Olympia station, 69, 112, 164-66, 168, 226
Kent: *see* Ashford, Broadstairs, Canterbury, Dartford, Deal, Dover, Folkestone, Margate, Northfleet
Kettering, Northants, 197, 201
Kidderminster, Worcs, 8, 15, 229
Kidlington, Oxon, 39, 70, 84, 113, 179, 186, 234
Kineton, Warks, 33-34, 49-50, 109
Kingham, Oxon, vi, 32, 37-38, 40-42, 87, 108-109, 111, 118-19, 124, 127-28, 132, 139, 153, 195-96, 200
King's Sutton, Northants, 37-38, 40, 42, 55, 58, 70-71, 87, 95, 150, 157, 162, 187, 196-197, 199-200, 224, 236, 239
Kingswear, Devon, 86, 152, 169
Kingswinford, Worcs, 132
Kirkby Junction, Notts, 89
Kirtlington, Oxon 70
Knaresborough, Yorks, 43
Knightcote, Warks, 16-17, 45
Knowle, Warks, 65, 217

L

Lacemaking, 48
Ladbrook, Warks, 54
Laisterdyke, Yorks, 189
Lancashire: *see* Blackpool, Chorley, Garston, Liverpool, Manchester, Newton-le-Willows, Oldham, Rochdale, Trafford Park, Warrington
Land Rover, 217
Langley Green, Worcs, 183, 191, 224
Lapworth, Warks, 98, 163
Lawrence, W F, railway contractor 38
Leamington Spa, Warks, 7, 13, 16-17, 21-22, 24, 40, 44, 46, 50, 65, 70-71, 88, 93, 98-99, 107-09, 113, 121, 124, 127, 132, 137, 142, 146, 149, 153-54, 13, 167, 169, 179, 187, 189, 190-91, 220, 222, 224, 226, 232-35, 238-39
Leckhampton, Gloucs, 42
Leeds, Yorks, 10, 96, 113, 144, 179, 181, 206, 217, 220, 226
Le Havre, France, 107

Leicestershire: *see* Leicester, Lutterworth, Market Harborough, Melton Mowbray, Moira, Mountsorrel, Old Dalby
Leicester, 8, 11-12, 40, 74-77, 80, 84-86, 89, 103, 107, 109, 112, 116, 132, 136, 140, 147, 152-53, 158, 160, 163, 167-68, 181, 191, 236
Leighton Buzzard, Beds, 194
Lester, Horace Spencer, bookmaker 101
Lewis, James, bricklayer 47
Lickey Incline, Worcs, 194
Lincolnshire: *see* Cleethorpes, Immingham, Grimsby, Lincoln, Scunthorpe, Stamford.
Lincoln, 81, 89
Lille, France, 68
Lilleshall Company, ironmasters 204
Littleton, Staffs, 55
Littlewood & Co, mail order retailers 155
Liverpool, 27, 57-58, 69, 112, 155, 190, 217, 219, 226, 234-35
Liverpool Street station, London, 28
Llandudno, Caerns, 57, 167
Llangollen, Denbs, 143
Llanwern, Mon, 189, 199, 208-09, 211
Lloyd, Samuel (1827-1918), ironmaster 199
Lloyd George, David (1863-1945), politician 95
Llynclys, Monts, 209
Locke, Joseph (1805-60), civil engineer 84
London:
   Birmingham services in 1914, 60
   Competition for traffic from Banbury, 27-28, 31
   Excursions from Banbury, 56, 98
See also: Baker Street, Clapham Junction, Crystal Palace, Euston, Great Exhibition, Kensington Olympia, Liverpool Street, Old Oak Common, Paddington, Marylebone, St Pancras, Smithfield, Victoria, Waterloo
Longbridge, car factory, 217
Longhurst, Richard, railway contractor 59
Longport, Staffs, 217
Loughborough, Leics, 125
Lovatt, Henry, railway contractor 38
Low Fell, Co Durham, 215
Lucy, William, stationmaster 51
Luton, Beds, 194
Lutterworth, Leics, 74
Lye, Worcs, 51
Lymington, Hants, 85

M

Macclesfield, Ches, 1
Mackay, Alexander, mining engineer 205
Maidenhead, Berks, 18, 67, 221
Malvern, Worcs, 58
Manchester, 23, 27-28, 57, 69, 71, 76, 78, 80, 84-86, 106-07, 151, 155, 180, 182, 185-86, 191, 194, 219, 226, 234-36, 238
Manning Wardle Co, locomotive builders 49, 202, 205
Mansfield, Notts, 113
Marchant, Robert Mudge (1820-1902), railway contractor 15
Marcus, Henry (1804-75), excursion agent 56
Margam, Glam, 210
Margate, Kent, 81, 106, 165-66, 168, 185
Market Drayton, Shrop, 23, 185, 188
Market Harborough, Leics, 75
Marks & Spencer, 153
Marlborough, Dukes of, *see* Spencer-Churchill
Marlborough Farm Camp, Warks, 131, 205
Marlow, Bucks, 113
Marston St Lawrence, Northants, 47-48
Marylebone station, London, 35, 67-68, 74, 76, 82, 85-86, 89, 115-16, 147, 156, 178, 180-181, 193-94, 218, 220-23, 227-29, 231-34, 238
Mauberge, France, 90
Maunsell, Richard (1868-1944), locomotive engineer 97
Mauritius, 92
Mawle, Sidney, ironmonger 91
Maybach Motorenbau GmbH, engineers 183
Melcombe Bros, builders 79
Melton Constable, Norfolk, 152
Melton Mowbray, Leics, 237
Metropolitan Vickers, mechanical engineers 148
Mewburn, William (1817-1900), stockbroker 131
Mexborough, Yorks, 89
Michelin, tyre manufacturers, 105
Mickleton Tunnel, 15
Middlesex: *see* Brentford, Ealing Broadway, Feltham, Neasden, , Northolt Junction, Old Oak Common, Park Royal, West Ruislip depot, Southall, Wembley
Middleton Cheney, Northants, 52, 60
Middlewich, Ches, 166

Milcombe, Oxon, 40, 202
Military depots, 89, 95, 130-31
Minera, Denbs, 198
Milton, Berks, 94, 131
Milton, Oxon, 40, 201-02
Mitchell, David (b 1812), railway agent 47
Mitchell, John (1810-71), railway contractor 47
Moira, Leics, 55
Moll, A W, stationmaster 138
Mollington, Oxon, 45-46
Monmouthshire: *see* Chepstow, Ebbw Vale, Llanwern, Newport, Pontypool Road, Rogerstone
Montreal, Quebec, 80
Moreton Cutting Yard, Berks, 125
Moreton-in-Marsh, Gloucs, 15, 32
Moreton Pinkney, Northants, 35-36
Morris Cowley station, 110, 120-21, 132, 190-91, 217
Morris, John, stationmaster 60
Morris Motors, 110, 126, 132
Morris, William, first Lord Nuffield (1877-1963), motor car manufacturer 110, 120
Mossend, Lanark, 217
Motor coach services, 109
Motorways, 221-22
Mottershead, Peter (b 1815), engine driver xi, 23-24
Mountsorrel, Leics, 238
Mulhouse, France, 49
Munns, R T, railway manager 182
Murfitt, Joseph, stationmaster 80

N

Named trains:
 Aberdeen-Penzance Express, 107-09
 Banburian, 194-95
 'Banbury Motor', 78, 111, 145
 Belfast Boat Train, 101
 Birmingham Pullman, 182-83
 Cambrian Coast Express, 101, 151, 166-67, 177, 183-84
 Cheltenham Flyer, 141
 Chiltern 200, 194-96
 City of Leicester Holiday Express, 163
 Cornishman (Paddington-Penzance), 86
 Cornishman (Wolverhampton-Penzance), 152

Named trains *continued*
  Farnborough Flyer, 164
  Hampton, 116
  Inter City, 149, 166, 184
  Isle of Man Boat Train, 101
  Northern Flash, 116
  Pines Express, 69, 152, 185
  Ports-to-Ports Express, 42, 87, 108, 136, 152-53, 175
  Southern Docker, 116
  Stour, 116
  Sunny South Express, 69, 151
  Sussex Scot, 226
  Thames Avon Severn Tour, 194
  Wessex Scot, 226
  William Shakespeare, 149, 221
Nantwich, Ches, 23, 168
Napton, Warks, 8, 54
National Coal Board, 216
Navvies, vi, 44-50, 55, 75
Neasden, Middsx, 67, 144-45, 147, 223, 232-233
Neilson & Co, locomotive builders 33
Nesscliffe, Shrop, 131
Newbury, Berks, 65, 85, 107, 114, 125, 136, 160
Newcastle-upon-Tyne, Northum, 5, 42, 50, 84-85, 87, 107-08, 112, 130, 135-36, 143, 145, 147, 152-53, 162-63, 165-67, 169-70, 172, 235-36, 238
Newhaven, Sussex, 226
Newport, Mon, 42, 87, 134, 152, 158, 199, 207
Newton Abbot, Devon, 132, 165-66
Newton, Sydney Walter Alfred (1875-1960), photographer 75
Norfolk: *see* Great Yarmouth, Norwich, Reedham, South Lynn, Wells-next-the-Sea.
Northamptonshire: *passim*
Northampton, 7-9, 34, 41, 53, 59, 105, 127, 159, 166
Northamptonshire Ironstone Co, 202
North British Locomotive Co, 134, 159
North Camp station, Surrey, 130
Northern Rubber Co, 164
Northfleet, Kent, 214
Northolt Junction, Middsx, 67, 187, 233
Northover, Kevin, historian 92
Northumberland: *see* Bedlington, Newcastle-upon-Tyne

Norwich, 28, 45
Nottinghamshire: *see* Annesley, Bennerley, Colwick, East Leake, Edwinstowe, Kirkby Junction, Mansfield, Nottingham, Retford, Ruddington, Shirebrook, Toton, West Burton power station, Worksop
Nottingham, 11, 40, 74, 76, 84, 86, 89, 112-14, 129, 132, 135, 146, 153, 160-62, 164-65, 167, 180-82, 217
Nuffield, first Viscount, see Morris, William.
Nuneaton, Warks, 8, 26, 29, 144, 146, 191, 238-39

O
Oakley Junction, Beds, 93
Oil-fired steam locomotives, 143
Old Oak Common, Middsx, 61, 64, 67, 116, 132, 143, 147, 149, 186-87
Old Dalby, Leics, 237
Olney, Bucks, 34-35
Olton, Warks, 98
Oswestry, Shrop, 140, 209
Oxfordshire: *passim*
Oxford:
  GWR stations, 13
  Hinksey Yard, 125, 147, 190-91, 215, 217
  Links between GWR and LNWR, 21, 126
  Local service to Banbury, 24, 67, 110-11, 154, 178, 235
  Rewley Road station, 27, 105, 195-96
  St Giles Fair, 53, 47-58
  Second World War, 123, 126, 131
  See also: Kennington, Morris Cowley station, Morris Motors, Wolvercote, Yarnton *et passim*
Oxford & Shipton Cement Co, 121
Oxfordshire Ironstone Co, 120, 159, 189, 197, 201, 205-12, 139
Oxley, Staffs, 22, 54, 61, 118, 123, 132, 169, 181, 187, 190-91, 210

P
Padbury, Bucks, 29
Paddington station, London, 16. 18-21, 24, 27, 41, 62, 64-69, 82, 99-100, 102, 112-14, 116, 127-28, 135, 139, 141, 143, 147, 150-51, 158, 160, 163-64, 166-67, 170, 177, 182-84, 186-87, 190-91, 193-94, 199, 219, 225, 228-29, 134-35, 238

Padstow, Cornwall, 1
Paignton, Devon, 107, 165-66
Palmerston, Lady Emily (1787-1869), wife of Henry John Temple (1784-1865), third viscount 33
Parker, Revd Joseph (1830-1902), Congregationalist minister 56
Parker, Sir Peter (1924-2002), chair of British Rail 218
Parker, Revd Theodore (1810-60), theologian 56
Park Royal, Middsx, 5, 94, 116
Paris, France, 68
Paxton & Clark, auctioneers 59
Pearson, Michael, writer on railways 236
Pegler, Alan (1920-2012), entrepreneur and railway preservationist 164
Penistone, Yorks, 84, 107, 181
Penzance, Cornwall, 80, 107-09, 114, 152
Perkins, T R, (1872-1952), railway journalist 62
Perth, 155
Peterborough, 45, 80,
Pick, Frank, (1878-1941), railway manager 124
Pickfords, carriers, 54
Plester, John, shed labourer 49
Plymouth, Devon, 45, 80, 82, 84, 109, 158, 226
Pokesdown, Hants, 167
Poland, Polish people, 50, 52, 208
Pollitt, Harry (1864-1945), locomotive engineer 3
Pollitt, Sir William, (1842-1908), accountant and railway manager 74
Pontypool Road, Mon, 93
Poole, Dorset, 147, 167, 169, 185-86, 219, 226, 234
Porth Dinlleyn, Caerns, 12
Portsmouth, Hants, 5, 19, 57-58, 69, 82, 106, 151, 161-62, 164-66, 168-69, 226
Port Talbot, Glam, 113, 189, 209-10
Poundon, Bucks, 48
Pressed Steel Ltd, 120
Price, Harry, railwayman & mayor of Banbury 147
Priestfield Junction, Staffs, 21
Priestley, J B (1894-1984), dramatist 113

Princes Risborough, Bucks, 17, 67, 71, 109-11, 120, 128, 134, 147, 178-79, 187, 190-91, 196, 220, 228
Priorslee, Shrop, 204
Pullman cars, 28, 124, 170, 182-83
Pwllheli, Caerns, 68, 151, 166-67

Q
Quainton Road station, Bucks, 27, 74, 78, 196, 207-08

R
Radclive, Bucks, 155
Radley, Berks, 93, 125
Railmotors, 103
Railway companies, lines, regions and sectors:
Arriva, 235
Aylesbury & Buckingham, 27-28
Banbury & Cheltenham, 1, 37-60, 63, 87, 108, 120, 152, 177, 188, 196, 200-02, 204, 210, 139
Banbury, Moreton & Shipston, 32
Barry, 42
'Bicester cut-off', 14, 31, 67-68, 70-72, 82, 94, 100-01, 114, 128, 137, 14,164, 178, 182, 196, 219, 228, 238
Birkenhead, 19
Birmingham & Derby, 11
Birmingham & Gloucester, 11, 16, 47
Birmingham & Oxford, 12, 18, 46-47
Birmingham, Wolverhampton & Dudley, 16
Bourton-on-the-Water, 37
Bristol & Gloucester, 16
Buckinghamshire, vi, 12, 24, 16, 22, 25-31, 33, 55-57, 60, 71, 74, 93, 95, 103, 120, 126, 155, 178-79, 189, 229, 239
Caledonian, 23
Chiltern, xi, 6, 35, 224, 227-36
Chipping Norton, vi, 32, 37
CrossCountry, 231-32, 234-35
Didcot, Newbury & Southampton, 65, 85, 107, 125, 136, 179
East & West Junction, 33-36, 47, 49-50, 75, 204
East Coast Joint Stock, 112
East Coast Main Line, 178, 226, 233
Eastern Region, 138, 167, 179, 215-16

Railway companies, lines, regions and sectors *continued*
Easton Neston Mineral & Towcester, Roade & Olney Junction, 34
Edge Hill Light, 131, 205
English, Welsh & Scottish, 236
Evesham, Redditch & Stratford-upon-Avon Junction, 33
Festiniog, 193
First Great Western, 235
Freightliner, 217, 230, 238
GB Railfreight (GBRf), 233, 237
Grand Central, 233
Grand Junction, 9, 11, 22
Great Central, 3, 31, 35-36, 42, 45, 51, 53, 63, 65, 67-68, 72, 74-91, 93-97, 102-03, 107-08, 112-13, 117, 119-20, 125, 129, 136, 143-45, 156, 160, 167, 170, 177, 182, 239
Great Eastern, 35, 103, 145, 170
Great Northern, 45, 70, 74, 87, 102-03, 125, 144, 164
Great Western, 10-12, 14-22, 24-25, 27-28, 31, 37, 40-45, 47, 49-51, 54-55, 57-58, 62-72, 74-75, 77, 81-82, 85-86, 90, 93, 97-98, 105-09, 115, 117, 119, 124, 130, 163, 170, 202, 206
Great Western & Great Central Joint, 71, 187
HS2, 239
Hull & Barnsley, 88, 89
Hull Trains, 233
Isle of Wight Central, 36
Lancashire & Yorkshire, 104
Lancashire, Derbyshire & East Coast, 35, 81, 89
Liverpool & Manchester, 9-11
London & Birmingham 9-12, 25
London & North Eastern, 80, 97, 102-05, 107, 109, 124, 129-30, 156-57
London & North Western, vi, 11, 15-17, 19, 21-23, 25-28, 33, 35-36, 41, 50, 54, 55, 57, 60, 63, 68-70, 91-93, 96, 103, 105, 115 179, 187
London & South Western, 19-20, 65, 69, 72, 81, 84, 93, 106, 170
London, Brighton & South Coast, 205
London, Midland & Scottish, 41, 103-05, 113, 121, 124, 130, 133

London Midland Region, 138, 146, 149, 167, 178-79, 184, 213, 220
London Transport, 123-24, 237
Manchester, Sheffield & Lincoln, 74-75, 80
Manchester South Junction & Altrincham, 170
Mansfield, 89
Metropolitan, 28, 68, 74, 104, 223
Midland, 11, 15, 17, 22, 33, 35, 40-41, 69, 90, 93, 105, 113, 133, 160, 186, 219
Midland & South Western Junction, 40, 81-82, 152
Midland Counties, 10-11
Midland Counties & South Wales, 33
Network Rail, 227
Network SouthEast, 223, 229
Newport, Abergavenny & Hereford, 19, 62
Northampton & Banbury, 25, 33-37, 41-42, 47-50, 57, 60, 75, 111, 177, 202, 239
North British, 108
North Eastern, 42, 84, 88, 103, 108, 124, 129, 133, 135, 145
North Eastern Region, 146, 179
North Midland, 11
North Warwickshire, 66
Oxford, Fenny Compton & Rugby, 12-13, 15-16, 18
Oxford, Worcester & Wolverhampton, vi, 12, 15-16, 18-19, 22, 27, 32, 37, 40, 42, 198
Piccadilly line, 123
Railtrack, 227
RES (Rail Express Systems), 215, 236
Shrewsbury & Birmingham, 15, 19, 22
Shrewsbury & Chester, 15, 19, 23-24
Shrewsbury & Hereford, 19
Shropshire Union, 15, 19
Speedlink, 218
Somerset & Dorset Joint, 69, 82, 185
South East & Chatham, 93, 170
South Eastern, 20, 68-69, 74, 106-07
Southern, 97, 106, 112, 124, 130-32, 168
Southern Region, 107, 147, 168, 170
Stockton & Darlington, 24
Stratford & Midland Junction, 1, 4, 34-36, 41, 91, 93, 105, 125, 131, 153, 158-59, 187, 189, 194, 196, 205, 211, 239
Stratford & Moreton, 91

262   *Index*

Railway companies, lines, regions and sectors *continued*
Stratford-upon-Avon, Towcester & Midland Junction, 34
Talyllyn, 163, 193
Thames Trains, 236
Virgin Trains, 233-35
Welsh Highland, 203
West Coast Joint Stock, 155
West Coast Main Line, 182, 186, 226, 238
Western Region, 138, 155, 167, 177, 187, 221
West London, 226, 236
West Midland, 19, 27
Wisconsin Central, 236
Worcester & Hereford, 19
Wrexham, Mold & Connah's Quay, 81
Wrexham, Shropshire & Marylebone, 232-234
Wycombe, 18

Railway: Management:
Grouping 1923, 98-105
Nationalisation, 138-39
Privatisation 227
Sectors, 221
Railway Mania, 11-12
Railway Mission, 45, 53, 72-73, 225

Railway: traffics:
Ambulance trains, 91-92, 135
Bananas, 5, 35, 189
Cattle, 4, 29-30, 32, 104, 120, 132, 159-60, 186, 188
Cement, 121, 132, 189-90, 214, 217
Coal, 26-27, 76, 88, 146, 156, 191, 217, 238
Excursion trains, 19, 56-58, 111-13, 160-64, 187, 191-96, 199
Fish, 5, 88-89, 116, 140, 147, 158, 188-89
Fruit, 5, 72, 88, 146
Iron ore, 3, 32, 37, 41-42, 72, 105, 119-20, 159-60, 177, 189-212
Mail, 105. 107, 135, 143, 155, 164-66, 215, 135
Meat, 118
Milk, 29-31, 104, 114-15, 147
Motor Cars, 120-21, 217, 235
Newspaper, 113, 165, 181-82
Oil, 187, 190, 214, 217
Parcels, 4, 114, 181, 215, 236
Pigeons, 114, 172

Railway: traffics:
Prisoner-of-war trains, 135
Road stone, 8, 29, 237-38
Steel, 156
Troop trains, 128-29
Steam-hauled excursions, 220-23
Ramsgate, Kent, 106, 165-66
Ratley, Warks, 205
Ravenstone Wood Junction, Bucks, 34, 93
Reading, Berks, 5, 18-20, 24, 50-51, 66, 68-69, 82, 93, 94, 102, 106, 112-13, 124-25, 131, 134, 139-40, 151, 153, 164, 166, 168, 185, 187, 190, 219, 226, 228-29, 234-36
Redditch, Worcs, 33
Redhill, Surrey, 20, 68-69, 86, 106, 124-25, 128, 130, 165-66, 168-69, 185, 135
Reedham, Norfolk, 80
Renishaw Park, Derbys, 211
Restaurant cars, 66, 85, 91, 106-07, 109, 130, 162, 166, 168, 220
Retford, Notts, 113, 164
Reynolds, Henry, bookstall manager 51
Rhine, River, 136
Richard Thomas & Baldwin, ironmasters 198-99
Risley, Revd William Cotton (1798-1869), clergyman & landowner 59
Roade, Northants, 91
Robbins, Michael (1915-2002), railway historian 10
Robertson, Sir Henry (1816-88), ironmaster 198
Robertson, Sir Harry Beyer (1862-1948), ironmaster 198
Robert Stephenson & Hawthorn Ltd, locomotive builders 144
Robinson, John George (1856-1943), mechanical engineer 81,102-03
Rochdale, Lancs, 113
Rock Ferry, Ches, 187
Rogerstone, Mon, 126, 132
Rollright, Oxon, 40
Rolls Royce Ltd, engineers 198
Romania, 217
Rosyth, Fife, 93
Rotherham, Yorks, 88-89, 173
Round Oak steelworks, Worcs, 198, 204
Rowington, Warks, 65, 91

Index

Rowley, Arthur (1926-2002), football manager 192
Royal Agricultural Show, 57
Royal Ordnance Factories, 130-31
Royal trains, 22
Ruabon, Denbs, 143, 165-66, 193
Ruddington, Notts, 125, 130
Rugby, Warks, 10, 12, 17, 26, 53, 74, 80, 108, 125, 181
Rugby Union football, 112-13
Rugeley, Staffs, 237
'Runners', 156, 180
Russell, James H, photographer & railway historian 1
Ruyton-XI-Towns, Shrop,
Ryde, Isle of Wight, 164

S
Sabbatarianism, 56
Sacré, Charles Reboul (1831-89), locomotive engineer 78
St Blazey, Cornwall, 51
St Pancras station, London, 93
Salisbury, Wilts, 50, 124
Salter Bros, river boat operators 113, 160-61
Saltley, Warks, 62, 146, 229
Samuelson, Sir Bernhard (1820-1907), engineer, ironmaster, politician 9, 32, 58
Samuelson, Sir Henry Bernhard (1845-1937), politician 58
Sandwich, Kent, 166, 168
Sandy, Beds, 125
Saunders, Charles Alexander (1706-1864), company secretary 44
Saunderton, Bucks, 134
Scapa Flow, 93
Scarborough, Yorks, 84-85, 107, 164
Schlieffen, Alfred von (1833-1913), field marshall 90
Scotland, Scottish people, 22-23, 49, 52, 80, 113, 120, 190, 197-98, 217, 226, 233;
and see
Aberdeenshire: Aberdeen, Balmoral; Edinburgh; Glasgow; Lanark: Mossend; North Lanark: Coatbridge, Shieldmuir; West Lothian, Bathgate; Perth; Scapa Flow; Sutherland: Brora
Scott, Middleton & Co, contractors 68
Scott, Walter & Co, contractors 75, 77

Scrivenor, Harry, writer on iron 197
Scunthorpe, Lincs, 88
Seaside hoidays, 5, 164-70
Sentinel Waggon Works Co, locomotive builders 208
Severn Tunnel, 42, 66, 152, 189
Severn Tunnel Junction, 93, 132, 134, 218
Shakespeare, William (1563-1616), poet 35
Sheffield, Yorks, 40, 74, 76, 84-85, 87-88, 91, 102, 107, 112, 114, 119-20, 129-30, 132, 136, 142, 151-53, 164, 167, 169, 177, 180-181
Shelton Bar Ironworks, 189, 209
Sheringham, Norfolk, 152
Sherman, Sir Alfred (1919-2006), right wing ideologue 222-23, 233
Shieldmuir, North Lanark, 215
Shifnal, Shrop, 43
Shipton-on-Cherwell, Oxon, 3, 62, 121, 132, 189-90, 214
Shooter, Adrian, railway manager 224, 227
Shropshire: *see* Baschurch, Cosford, Donnington, Dorrington, Market Drayton, Nesscliffe, Priorslee, Ruyton-XI-Towns, Shrewsbury, Telford, Wellington
Shrewsbury, 15, 19, 23, 57, 68, 115-16, 139, 151, 163, 165-66, 185, 187, 191-93, 208, 220, 233
Sibford, Oxon, 204
Sidney, Samuel (1813-83), writer 8
Siemens Ltd, engineers 230
Silverstone, Northants, 158
Simkiss, John (b 1832), stationmaster 60
Simmons, Jack (1915-2000), railway historian 1, 68
Simpers, Thomas, navvy 47
Simpson, Alfred, engine driver 116
Siphon vans, 2, 114
Slapton, Northants, 47
Sleeping cars, 108, 112, 124, 149, 164-65, 226
Slinn, Jack N, railway historian 1-2
Slip coaches, 24, 63, 66, 68, 82, 101, 104, 151, 156, 184
Slough, Bucks, 94, 107, 190
Smith, Albert (1816-60), lecturer 58
Smithfield, London, 118
Solihull, Warks,
Somerset: *see* Avonmouth, Bath, Frome, Taunton,

Somerton, Oxon, xi, 217, 222, 233
Somme, Battle, 59, 70
Souldern, Oxon, 68, 183, 220
Souter, Joseph, stationmaster 59
Southall, Middsx, 51, 69, 156, 187, 190
Southam, Warks, 45
Southam Road & Harbury station, 70, 120-21, 179
Southampton, Hants, 5, 82, 84-85, 90-91, 105, 107, 130, 135, 146-47, 151-53, 189-90, 217, 226, 229-30, 235-36, 238
South Lynn, Norfolk, 145
Spencer-Churchill, Charles Richard John, 9th Duke of Marlborough (1871-1934), landowner 84
Spittle, Miss, porter 135
Staffordshire: *see* Bescot yard, Bilston, Burton-on-Trent, Bushbury, Drayton Bassett, Littleton, Longport, Oxley, Rugeley, Sedgley, Shelton, Smethwick, Stafford, Stoke-on-Trent, Swynnerton, Tame Bridge Parkway station, Tutbury, Walsall, Wednesbury, Wolverhampton, Woodseaves
Stafford, 15, 26, 144
Stage coaches: 7-10
  Novelty, 9
  Railway, 9
  Regulator, 8-9
  Rival, 10
  Sovereign, 10
Staines, Middsx, 20
Stairfoot, Yorks, 119, 132
Stamford, Lincs, 9
Stanier, Sir William Arthur (1876-1965), locomotive engineer 149
Staveley, Derbys, 119
Stechford, Warks, 233
Stephens, Col Holman Fred (1868-1931), railway promoter 205
Stephenson, George (1781-1848), engineer 11
Stephenson, Robert (1803-59), engineer 24
Steventon, Berks, 10, 87
Stewart & Lloyds, ironmasters 198, 206, 216
Stockport, Ches, 226
Stoke Poges, Bucks, 60
Stony Stratford, Bucks, 7
Stourbridge, Worcs, 15, 116, 147, 229, 234

Stratford-upon-Avon, Warks, 7, 18, 33, 35, 40, 49, 53, 66, 82, 88, 93, 108, 132, 149, 154, 158, 187, 189, 194, 196, 208, 211, 220-21, 224, 232-34, 235
Stroud family, farmers 92
Suffolk: *see* Felixstowe
Sulgrave, Northants, 36, 47
Sulzer Ltd, mechanical engineers 215
Sumner, Harold, railway inspector 168
Sunderland, Durham, 84
Surrey: *see* Betchworth, Croydon, Epsom, Farnborough, Guildford, North Camp station, Redhill, Waddon
Sussex: *see* Brighton, Chichester, Eastbourne, Hastings, Newhaven
Swanbourne, Bucks, 22, 105, 126, 159, 210
Swansea, Glam, 87, 91, 108, 113, 152, 167-68
Swerford, Oxon, 202
Swindon, Wilts, 4, 32, 40-42, 65, 70, 73, 87, 106-09, 114, 116, 129, 133, 137, 140-43, 147, 151-52, 158-59, 163-67, 169, 181-83, 193-94, 217, 221
Switzerland, Swiss people, 85, 136-37, 148; *and see* Basel
Swynnerton, Staffs, 130
Syresham, Northants, 48

T
Tackley, Oxon, 110, 224, 135
Tadmarton, Oxon, 202
Tame Bridge Parkway station, Staffs, 233
Tancred, Henry William (1781-1860), MP for Banbury 6
Taplow, Berks, 64, 194
Taunton, Som, 114
Tavern cars, 170
Tavistock Junction, Devon, 132, 190
Tees Yard, Co Durham, 190-91
Telford, Thomas (1757-1834), civil engineer 7
Telford, Shrop, 233
Tenterden, Kent, 1
Terry, Alfred, railway contractor 38
Thame, Oxon, 18, 111, 179
Thames, River, 113, 160-61, 163
Thatcher, Margaret Hilda (1925-2013), politician 222
Thaxted, Essex, 1
Thomas, Richard (1837-1916), ironmaster 199

Thompson, Edward (1881-1954), locomotive engineer 144, 156, 162
Thompson, George (b 1816), engine driver 24
Thompson, William (b 1817), crossing keeper 60
Thoroughfare towns, 9
Thorpe Arch, Yorks, 130
Thorpe Mandeville, Northants, 74, 77
Tibbits, Chris, railway manager 223
Tilbury, Essex, 189, 217
Times, newspaper, 155
Tipton, Staffs, 198, 204
Tonbridge, Kent, 68-69, 106, 215
Tonks, Eric, historian of quarry railways xi, 206, 208
Torbay, Devon, 152, 164
Total Route Modernisation, 223-24
Toton, Notts, 117, 187
Tove, River, 33
Towcester, Northants, 7, 9, 33-35, 47, 53, 57, 90
Trafford Park, Lancs, 148, 217
Trent, River, 84, 181
Tring, Herts, 9, 27
Trowbridge, Wilts, 106, 108
Turkey: *see* Gallipoli
Turner, John, navvy 48
Turnpike roads, 7
Tustain, William (b 1854), stationmaster 60
Tutbury, Staffs, 160
Twyford, Bucks, 48
Twyford, Oxon, 44
Tyne Yard, Co Durham, 218
Tyrrell, Sidney James (b 1889), tailor & historian 75-77, 181-82
Tyseley, Warks, 61, 64, 123, 132, 141, 166, 193
Tywyn, Merion, 163, 193

U
United Dairies, 115
United States armed forces, 24, 124, 130-31, 139

V
Verney Junction station, Bucks, 25, 27-28, 78, 104, 196
Victoria station, London, 194
Vincent, Henry (1813-78), lecturer 58
Voyager units, 234-35

W
Waddon, Surrey, 113
Wakefield, Yorks, 238
Wales: Welsh people, Welsh coast, vi, 52, 66, 68, 113, 117, 151, 164-67;
and see: Cardiganshire: Aberystwyth.
Caernarvonshire: Llandudno, Porth Dinlleyn, Pwllheli.
Denbighshire: Brymbo, Croes Newydd, Minera, Ruabon, Wrexham.
Glamorgan: Aberdare, Barry, Cardiff, Copperworks Junction, Margam, Port Talbot, Swansea.
Montgomeryshire: Welshpool.
Walker, James, navvy 50
Wallingford, Berks, 18, 179
Wallis, Edward (b 1825), stationmaster 60
Walsall, Staffs, 233
Waltham Abbey, Essex, 95
Walton, Arthur, engine driver 135
Walton, Frederick, coal merchant & publican 59
Wappenham, Northants, 47-48, 154
Ward, Thomas & Bridget, lodging house keepers 43
Ward, William (b 1840), stationmaster 60
Warkworth, Northants, 53, 95-96
Warmington, Warks, 205
Warrington, Lancs, 22, 215, 236
Warwickshire: *passim*
Warwick, 7, 10, 53, 57, 146, 160, 179, 204, 220
Warwick Parkway station, 228, 232
Washington family, landowners, 36
Washwood Heath yard, 148, 187, 191
Wassall, Alfred, quarry manager 201
Water Eaton, Oxon, 229
Waterloo station, London, 20, 194
Water Stratford, Bucks, 29
Water troughs, 65, 84, 167
Wath, Yorks, 81
Watkin, Sir Edward (1819-1901), railway entrepreneur 74
Watlington, Oxon, 179
Weardale, Co Durham, 214
Webb, Francis William, (1836-1906), locomotive engineer 30, 104
Wednesbury, Staffs, 51

Weedon, Northants, 10
Weedon Lois, Northants, 47
Wellingborough, Northants, 160, 197-98, 210-211
Wellington, Shrop, 15, 19, 23, 43, 185, 188
Wells-next-the-Sea, Norf, 45
Welshpool, Monts, 19
Wembley, Middsx, 99, 113, 192, 215, 228, 232-33
West Burton power station, Notts, 216
Westbury, Wilts, 70, 106-08, 165-66, 169
West Ruislip depot, Middsx, 237
Weymouth, Dorset, 5, 57-58, 70, 72, 81, 106-07, 147, 152, 164-66, 168-69, 173, 202, 226
Whale, George (1842-1910), locomotive engineer 104
Whitehall, Charles, poet 25
Whitemoor, Cambs, 117
Whitstable, Kent, 45
Widnes, Ches, 238
Wigginton, Oxon, 40, 127
Wilkinson, John, (1728-1808), ironmaster 198
Willingsworth Iron Co, 204
Willmott, Harry, (1851-1931), railway manager 35-36, 205, 239
Willmott, Russell, (1879-1920), railway manager 35-36, 239
Wilton, Graham, journalist 178
Wiltshire: *see* Avebury, Calne, Chippenham, Salisbury, Swindon, Trowbridge, Westbury, Wootton Bassett, Yeovil
Winchester, Hants, 65, 152
Windsor, Berks, 58, 113, 160, 163
Winslow, Bucks, 25, 27-28, 30
Wire rope tramways, 214
Witney, Oxon, 18
Wokingham, Berks, 112
Wolvercote, Oxon, vi, 16, 18-19, 123, 125
Wolverhampton, Staffs, 15, 20-22, 24, 57, 64, 68, 70-71, 90, 93, 98-99, 102, 114, 116, 130, 132, 141, 143, 147-52, 156-57, 160, 165-66, 168-70, 173, 182-85, 187, 190, 192-94, 199, 210-11, 224, 226, 229, 233
Wolverton, Bucks, 9-10, 50, 80
Women railway workers, vi, 135, 137

Woodford (near Kettering), Northants, 197
Woodford Halse, Northants, 3, 35, 51, 53, 63, 67, 72, 74-86, 88-89, 93, 97, 102, 107, 111, 115-16, 119, 125, 130-34, 138, 144-45, 147, 154, 162, 169, 180-81, 188-91, 194, 213
Woodhead Tunnel, 74, 107, 112, 220
Woolwich, Kent, 95, 97
Wootton Bassett, Wilts, 50, 115
Worcestershire: *see* Bromsgrove, Droitwich, , Dudley, Evesham, Hartlebury, Honeybourne, Kidderminster, Kingswinford, Langley Green, Lickey Incline, Lye, Malvern, Oldbury, Redditch, Round Oak, Stourbridge, Worcester
Worcester, 12, 15, 19, 25, 27, 37, 40, 132, 140, 186, 194, 220, 229
Worksop, Notts, 80
World War I, 5-6, 27, 85, 90-97, 120, 201-02, 204
World War II, 5-6, 85, 89, 103, 123-38, 145, 156, 164, 203-04, 208, 210
Worsdell, Wilson (1850-1910), locomotive engineer 133
Wotton-under-Edge, Gloucs, 51
Wrexham, Denbs, 51, 198, 233-34
Wright & Sons, carriage builders 62
Wright, Col W C, ironworks director 205
Wrighton, Henry (b 1841), brickmaker 59
Wroxton, Oxon, 95, 197, 205-12, 239

Y
Yarnton, Oxon, 16, 19, 21, 27, 105, 125, 195
Yeovil, Wilts, 70
Yorkshire: *see* Barnsley, Beighton, Bradford, Cudworth, Denby Dale viaduct, Doncaster, Halifax, Huddersfield, Hull, Laisterdyke, Leeds, Mexborough, Penistone, Rotherham, Scarborough, Sheffield, Stainforth, Stairfoot, Thorpe Arch, Wath, York
York, 10, 73, 85-86, 89, 91, 107-09, 114, 119, 129, 136-37, 152, 157, 162-65, 168, 180-81, 185-86, 191, 219, 226
Yorkshire Engine Co, locomotive builders 144
Young, Arthur (1741-1820), writer 7